Gen[illegible]
and Decolonisation in Postcolonial Ghana:
A Socio-Philosophical Engagement

Charles Prempeh

Langaa

Langaa Research & Publishing CIG
Mankon, Bamenda

Publisher:
Langaa RPCIG
Langaa Research & Publishing Common Initiative Group
P.O. Box 902 Mankon
Bamenda
North West Region
Cameroon
Langaagrp@gmail.com
www.langaa-rpcig.net

Distributed in and outside N. America by African Books Collective
orders@africanbookscollective.com
www.africanbookscollective.com

ISBN-10: 9956-552-95-x

ISBN-13: 978-9956-552-95-5

About the Author

Dr Charles Prempeh is a Research Fellow at the Centre for Cultural and African Studies, Kwame Nkrumah University of Science and Technology, Kumasi-Ghana. He holds a PhD degree in Theology and Religious Studies from the University of Cambridge (Wolfson College), United Kingdom, since 2021. Prempeh's doctoral thesis – written in the Faculty of Divinity, University of Cambridge – makes a substantial contribution to scholarship on religion and politics in West Africa. Specifically, it brings into focus three apparently divergent strands of recent Ghanaian history – the institution of the southern ethnic Akan chieftainship, the associated rites and beliefs of Akan indigenous religions, and Pentecostalism (focusing on the Church of Pentecost, or CoP). In particular, his study examined how Akan chiefs have responded to the phenomenon of Pentecostal Christianity, focusing on those chiefly figures who are installed as traditional chiefs in certain Akan areas of contemporary Ghana as well as active members of the Church of Pentecost. He also holds a certificate in Public Engagement with Research (AHRC-TORCH outline course): organised by the University of Oxford, 2021.

Before joining Cambridge for his doctoral studies in October 2017, Prempeh undertook two years of doctoral coursework in interdisciplinary Social Studies at the Makerere Institute of Social Research (MISR), Makerere University (Uganda) and taught undergraduate students for a semester.

He also holds a Master of Philosophy Degree in African Studies from the Institute of African Studies, University of Ghana, Legon. In 2010, after completing his coursework, he was awarded the prestigious Agyeman Award for academic excellence. Prempeh holds a First-Class degree in African Studies from the University of Cape Coast in 2008. At the UCC, his undergraduate long-essay was adjudged one of the best for the Department of African Studies and selected for display during the university's opening day in 2009.

When Prempeh completed his MPhil degree, he worked at the IAS as a graduate and teaching assistant from 2010 to 2013. Later in 2013, he was appointed a lecturer to teach Africana Studies at the African University College of Communications, Accra. While in Cambridge, he taught in four annual summer schools, reflecting on African philosophies of belief, uncertainty, the future, and African Christology.

As an African Studies scholar, Prempeh's research has an interdisciplinary dimension, incorporating areas such as gender, popular culture, religion, history, politics, education, philosophy, and cultural studies. He has published in these areas in prestigious journals including *African Studies Quarterly*, *Journal of Religion in Africa* and *Religion Compass*. His recent book *Nima-Maamobi in Ghana's Postcolonial Development: Migration, Islam and Social Transformation* (Bamenda/ Cameroon: Langaa, 2022).

He is a fellow of the IFE Institute of Advance Studies and a former fellow of the Social Science Research Council (SSRC – 2016). He has held several leadership positions as presidents of the Student Union at the MISR, the Cambridge University Ghana Society (CUGS), currently the founding communications director of the Vacation Initiative for Science Africa (VISA), a registered Ghanaian- based NGO, and Director of Research for another registered Ghanaian-based NGO – Centre for Sustainable Livelihood & Development (CENSLID).

He has been a resident of Maamobi since 1984 when he was 2 years old and had all his education in Accra (community-related) from Kotobabi Presbyterian Primary School (1988-1995) to Kotobabi '15' JSS (1996-1998) to West Africa Secondary School (Accra – 1999-2001). Prempeh has held several leaderships as secretary Aid Afrique and Gender Action Unit (both registered non- governmental organisations) and an elected member of the Unit Committee in 2002. He taught for a few years at the Kanda Estate '2' Primary School, as a volunteer on the National Youth and Employment Programme (2010-2013) – established by the New Patriotic Party, under the government of John Agyekum Kufuor.

Dedication

For
my mother
Agartha Adjei

My wife
Josephine Tweneboaa Afrifa

The children of Josephine and I
Kwame Nhyira Amponsah Prempeh
Adwoa Adom Mmoraa Prempeh

My mentors
Professors:
Jabal M. Buaben
Kofi Asare Opoku
nana essilfie conduah
Opoku Onyinah
Wilson Yayoh
Francis B. Nyamnjoh
Kwabena Akurang-Parry
Afe Adogame
George M. Bob-Milliar
Joel Cabrita
Jeremy Morris
Timothy Quashigah
Bishop Ben Salleh
Rev Dr Rockeybell Adatura
Stephen Owoahene-Acheampong
Godwin Kwafo Adjei
Mr Nii Addokwei Moffat

My mother's brother's daughter
Regina Gyebi
To
All my teachers and professors
Professors
Wilson Yayoh
Albert A. Awedoba
Christine Oppong
Benjamin A. Ntreh

De-Valera N Y M Botchway
Bridget M. Sackey
Drs:
Mark Sey
Mary Akosua Seiwaa Owusu
M.Q. Amlor
Rev. Abraham A. Akrong
Deborah Atobrah
A.A. Agordoh
Osman Alhassan
Florence Ebila

Messrs
Marcus Agbayome
M.Q. Alidza
Douglas Frimpong-Nnuroh

To all my classmates
Sophia Acquah
Aisha Rufai
Samuel O. Adjei
Kofi S.A. Adzei
Maxwell Amofah
Agnes D. Agbanyo
Bashiru Shehu
Lawal Dauda
Edith A. Forson
Sabatho Nyamsenda
Mahir Balunywa
Noosim Naimasiah
Dr Semeneh Ayalew Asfaw
Dr Milliam Kiconco
Michael Mutyaba

To my friends
Dr Theresa B. Dery
Naidatu Hameed
Mr Isaac Gomado
Johnson Nana Kwame Ntiamoah-Amankuo
Frimpong Boateng
Susanna Adjei Arthur
Sampson Afrifa Jnr
Dr Caleb O. Nyanni

Dzifa Hukporti
Margaret Babirye
Yaa Sarkodie-Mensah
And
In Loving memory of my father

Anthony Prempeh

Acknowledgements

I would also like to thank my wife, Josephine Tweneboaa Afrifa, who continues to sacrifice her time and comfort as I often travel to and from Ghana collecting data and also spending substantive time of our family life in my study – reading and writing. It is enough sacrifice that seamlessly implies that she, at least, takes more than half of the proceeds of this book. I wrote this book, but the energy and peace of mind to write it came from the critical and continuing role of Joe as both a mother, sister, and economist of our home.

I also thank Kwame Prempeh and Adwoa Prempeh – who have endured my incessant absence from home. Usually, they wake up to find that I am either in Ghana giving seminar presentations or giving lectures on Zoom. All this is because, even when I am in Ghana, I spend countless hours in my office from as early as 3 AM to 9 PM (with a few breaks)! These children, who deserve the attention of a father, have together with Joe, paid the price for a father who is ambitious in contributing to the frontiers of knowledge as well as consolidating the gains of the family. A father who suffers epistemic madness!

In all this Josephine, Kwame and Adwoa have been a blessing to me and I pray for nothing but God's continuous blessings for them. I share the fruit of this book and anything I do with my scholarship with them. May Kwame and Adwoa benefit from the foundation Joe and I are laying for them, especially as I indulge the "no pain, no gain" to lighten their pain in future (cf. I Timothy 5:8). I have incurred many debts in the course of writing this book. To that end, I would like to begin by extending my heartfelt thanks to Prof. Jabal M. Buaben, who has been a true father to my family and me. He has always provided for the needs for my family and encouraged me throughout my stay in Birmingham (England). He is one of the most altruistic persons, I have so far met in my life (Papa, God bless you). I want to also thank Apostle Emmanuel Agyei Kwafo of the Church of Pentecost (CoP), who, though at short notice, has agreed to write the foreword of this book. In the same spirit, I thank all those who read and wrote praise words for this book. I am also indebted to Professor Francis B. Nyamnjoh. He has been very supportive in shaping my thoughts as he generously shares his works with me.

Furthermore, I am highly grateful to Mr Mathew Quamey Alidza, my 'father' and English and language lecturer at the Department of African Studies (now Centre for African and International Studies), University of Cape Coast, who provided an extensive editing of the manuscript. I also thank Dr Philip Hayab John of the Institute for Peace and Conflict Resolution, Abuja, Nigeria, Mr Nii Addokwei Moffat, retired senior journalist, Dr Solace Yawa Asafo and Timothy Quashigah (a senior lecturer) both at the Ghana Institute of Journalism, who spent hours helping with *pro bono* editorial work and also writing a recommendation for the book. Regina Gyebi, my mother's brother's daughter, has also been very helpful in reading the manuscript several times and offering editorial service. Also, I thank Mr Isaac Gomado, my senior *brother*, counsellor, friend, and creative designer, who designed the cover page. I also thank Mr Johnson Ntiamoah-Amankuo and his wife, Mrs Joan Ntiamoah-Amankuo for their kindness. Similarly, I thank Mr Anane Adjei, my friend -- Adinkra/Akan ethno-historian, who suggested the appropriate symbols for the cover page. Also, I am very grateful to the anonymous reviewer whose comments are not just insightful, but providential. I freely borrowed from the reviewer's expertise to enhance the quality of the book. I am grateful.

I am equally grateful to my natal family – my mother, Agartha Adjei and siblings: Patrick Adjei, Eric Amponsah, Frederick Sarah Adjei, Rebecca Ama Duah, and my twin sisters Deborah Adwoa Boadua and Dorcas Adwoa Boadua – for their support since I decided to write about this highly sensitive subject. Their prayers and encouragement have always energised me to push on. I thank my parents for instilling in me a sense of diligence, perseverance, and hard work. Most specifically, they introduced me to God at a tender age. I am grateful they did. I particularly appreciate my late father, Mr Anthony Prempeh, who always reminded me to internalise the wise saying, "A wise son brings joy to his father" (Proverbs 10:1a).

I also thank my wife's family: Her parents: Mr Sampson Afrifa and Madam Comfort Peprah, who have always urged me on. Her siblings: Dr Gladys Nyarko Ansah, Mr Isaac Kwadjo Asare, Madam Shirley Afranewaa Afrifa, Dr Patricia Serwaa Afrifa, and Sampson Afrifa (Jnr) have never stopped encouraging me. I register my extraordinary appreciation to Shirley Afranewaa Afrifa and her husband, Mr Frimpong Boateng and their family – they have been exceptionally helpful.

I am deeply indebted to the administrators of the Birmingham Christian College – the Bible College of the Church of Pentecost in the United Kingdom – who have been supported of my family and me. I specifically thank Mrs Briony Seymour, Martin Ankers, Mr Godfried Asante, Dr Caleb Nyanni, and Apostle Dr Lord E. Donkor, I say God bless you. Alongside these persons, I thank my church members at the St Stephen's and St Wulstan's Church, especially Maurice W. Sinclair, for Anglican Bishop of Northern Argentina.

I also thank all my professors whose teaching have shaped and informed my understanding of gender and family studies in Africa. I particularly thank: Mrs Marie-Acquiline Barton-Odro, Drs Florence Ebila of the Makerere University, Debora Atobrah, Profs. Christine Oppong, and Bridget M. Sackey of the Institute of African Studies, University of Ghana. Similarly, I thank all key informants who shared their accumulated knowledge and wisdom about the gender and sexuality with me. I as well thank my friends: Theresa B. Dery, Susanna Adjei Arthur, Lydia Amoah, Rev. Emmanuel Badu Amoah, Aisha Rufai, Samuel Owusu, Mr Eric Aki, and those whose names do not readily come to mind for often encouraging and urging me on. I also thank the headmaster, teachers and non-teaching staff of J.A. Kufuor Senior High School, including Juliana Pokuaa and Solomon Tony Adams, who offered me accommodation while I resided in Kumasi and also revised my manuscript. *Even so, I must say that none of my mentors and those I have acknowledged necessarily share my perspective on the subject of this book. I am solely responsible for ideas on gender, sexuality and decolonisation….*

Finally, and most importantly, I thank the Triune God, by whose grace and mercy alone my family and I have come this far. Indeed, the Lord has been good and kind to us. To Him alone belong the glory and honour. We humble ourselves before him in saying with the Psalmist: "Not to us, O LORD, not to us but to your name be glory, because of your love and faithfulness" (Psalm 115:1).

Praise for This Book

"Dr Prempeh makes a thought-provoking case for Akan customs and history in *Gender, Sexuality and Decolonisation.* He reviews the Akan language, its institutions, and its norms to support his view that sociogenically Akan society was silent on LGBTQ+ practices although this did not rule out the historicity of same-sex practices by individuals within Akan society. As argued by Dr Prempeh, gender relations among the Akan revolved around procreation. The Akan never evolved punitive laws for same-sex practices. Rather, the colonial system, grounded in Euro-Christian worldviews prescribed punishment for same-sex practices, which continues to exist in the law books of postcolonial states like Ghana. *Gender, Sexuality and Decolonisation* makes conclusions and recommendations grounded in Akan culture and history and that uphold Christian values. While the recommendations are contestable, this book is a rich resource for gender and sexual beliefs and practices among the Akan of Ghana."

Dr Mary Owusu, Senior Lecturer, University of Cape Coast

"This is a well-written and thorough book on a difficult and sensitive topic. The author provides an honest reflection on recent debates about homosexuality in Ghana from both a personal and academic standpoint. One of the main arguments of the book is that matters pertaining to sexuality should be dealt with within the realm of the family (nuclear or extended) and should not be treated as a legal question. The author highlights indigenous ways of dealing with difference in pluralistic societies and argues that bringing sexuality into the public sphere is problematic and linked to Western cultural imperialism. He therefore calls for a decolonial approach to the debate and study of homosexuality in Ghana. Although, there are a number of issues that I disagree with, personally and academically, I commend the effort to lay out in detail and in depth the basis of one's standpoint, argument and convictions. Charles Prempeh's deep reflections invite us to debate, and we can appreciate that invitation – and agree or disagree – with openness and readiness to listen."

Karen Lauterbach, Associate Professor, Centre of African Studies, University of Copenhagen

"*Gender, sexuality and decolonisation in postcolonial Ghana: A socio-philosophical engagement* is a great book for students and followers of the gender and sexuality debate globally and Ghana in particular. Dr. Prempeh, a critical academic and prolific writer grounds his work in great scholarship. The writer relies on his rich knowledge of religions, philosophy and culture to unearth the philosophical and ideological agenda that underpins the arguments of most scholars of gender and sexualities studies and research in Ghana and Africa. He is forceful in his argument, and quite repetitive, that in the case of gender and sexuality, African universities must be decolonized from their epistemic reliance on the North and ground their scholarship in the existential realities of the ordinary citizens of Africa to develop home grown theories or approaches that resonate with the acceptable cultures, religions and beliefs of the continent - "the gown must go to town." The book is what I term a critical alternative viewpoint to the dominant discourses on gender and sexuality in Ghana and Africa."

Solace Yawa Asafo (PhD, APR) Lecturer, the Faculty of Journalism & Media Studies, Ghana Institute of Journalism, Accra

"Charles Prempeh (Ph.D.), is a young and promising scholar who has already begun to stir the academic world with his powerful critical writings. Born and bred within the Zongo community of Maamobi/Nima in Accra, Ghana, he has been exposed to Christianity and Islam, the two dominant religions in Ghana. He attended the University of Cape Coast in Ghana and graduated with a First Class B. A. degree in African Studies. He then proceeded to the Makerere University (Uganda) and spent three years working for his Ph.D. degree before obtaining his Doctor of Philosophy degree in 2021 from Cambridge University in the U. K. *Gender and sexuality in postcolonial Ghana: A socio-philosophical engagement* addresses the issue of gender, sexuality, and the debate surrounding the controversial subject of homosexuality especially in Ghana. The author takes advantage of his rich cultural, religious and educational exposure to arrive at the conclusion that the state must sustain the criminalisation of the public acceptance of the LGBTQ+ practice since no civilisation can survive with it. The strength of this book lies in both the in-depth as well as extensive literature review presented by the author to support his argument. Quoting extensively from both primary and secondary sources, Dr. Prempeh has not only advanced fully his points from his wild but critical readings and philosophical ideas about the subject, but has also fully engaged his readers to appreciate the misrepresentations often associated with gender and sexual-related discourses in Ghanaian cultures."

MR M.Q. Alidza, Retired African Studies Lecturer, University of Cape Coast, Ghana

"Indeed, a crucial time to merge academic development and social cultural mystery for the preserve on futuristic heritage which could ensure hope and sustainable peace for the unborn generation. The humanistic value of heritage is detailed on once ontological nobility and also improve their very existence. There had never been a time in the history of Ghana where a passionate discussion of LGBTQ+ to the level of drawing a line on social cultural, intellectual, and moral value, followed a preventive approach to social order than this particular time. The book supports the protection of the right of minority group without shutting any door for cultural relativism. It also filled the gap in 1948 Universal Declaration Policy limitation on the pursue of happiness with boundary on ontological nobility in social order fit sustainable society. It is my passionate request that all readers of this great book suspend their prejudice in more respectful manner but have a sense of ownership and love to preserve and develop their heritage for future generation."

Rev. Amoah, Emmanuel Badu, Peace Educator, Analyst and Administer
Senior Pastor, Fruitful Word Assemble International Church, Accra

"Prempeh's mastery of sexuality discourse shows in his choice of vocabulary, the energy with which he writes, the attitude and the ideas. He transcends mere dazzling display of knowledge and critically explores the relationship between the Ghanaian and this sensitive social issue. A remarkable piece."

Dr Madinatu Bello, Lecturer, Department of Theatre and Film Studies,
University of Cape Coast, Ghana

"Prempeh's book provides a refreshingly unconventional and courageous account of the complex socio-cultural evolution of the human family and sexuality; while simultaneously arguing that the ontological boundaries of the family's role as the primary agent of procreation based on female fecundity and male phallic competence remains an axiomatic social reality. Obviously, a book for students and scholars interested in Gender and Sexuality Studies, Intellectual History and anyone interested in a single text that has a peerless interdisciplinary scholarly merit."

Lydia Amoah, PhD Candidate, Institute of African Studies,
University of Ghana, Legon, Accra

"*Gender, sexuality and decolonisation in postcolonial Ghana: A socio-philosophical engagemen*t is an insightful book that engages the subject of same-sex sexuality in Ghana from a socio-philosophical perspective. Since the introduction of the highly contentious "Promotion of Proper Human

Sexual Rights and Ghanaian Family Values Bill" in Parliament, there has been diverse discussions on what are the "proper" Ghanaian family human sexual values and how the country can position itself to embrace change in the global world, while preserving its cultural heritage against western pressure. This Family Law legislative Bill, deemed by some as the worst anti-LGBTQI+ bill, seeks to de-legitimise practitioners and sympathisers from advocating for the sexual freedom while preserving the rights, religio-culturally accepted sexual orientations. This bill further divided the country into supporters (mainly religious and traditional elite) and opposers of the bill. This book goes beyond the sentimental discussions to analyse the cosmology of the Ghanaian society using the Akan concepts of gender. The book fully engages with the different epochs of the society from precolonial, colonial and postcolonial eras to flesh out Akan ethos around sex and family, the encounter between the Akan ethics and 19th Century Victorian Christian ethics, and the Akan ideas of ethical and ontological boundaries that shape sexuality. This book is essentially crucial especially considering its attempts to decolonize knowledge on the ideas of sexuality emancipation. It will be of great relevance to erase all prejudice and misinformation about family and sexuality. I recommend this book to both academics and non-academics who seek to understand the cultural ethics and ontological boundaries that have shaped sexuality in Ghana to the present."

Eugenia Anderson Ph.D., Lecturer, Department of History and Political Studies, Kwame Nkrumah University of Science and Technology (KNUST), Kumasi

"Dr. Charles Prempeh, an Akan from Southern Ghana, is an evangelical Christian academic with a natural inclination towards Calvinistic theology, who has vowed not to be compelled to disassociate himself from his religious and ethnic background in his scholarship. He is a prolific writer who is focused, fearless, and a say-it-as-it is person. He is not afraid to tread where others fear. Read his convincing perspectives from the religious, historical, and other angles on why you must support heterosexual marriage as a divine-cultural mandate for the preservation of human civilisation."

Mr Nii Addokwei Moffat, Retired senior journalist, Ghana, Old Student of West Africa Secondary School, Accra, 1976

"I especially suggest this book, *Gender, Sexuality and Decolonisation in Postcolonial Ghana: A Socio-philosophical Engagement* to everyone interested in learning more about the current debate around homosexuality and to all book lovers in general. Politicians, members of the media, clergy, non-religious people, parents, and students are encouraged to read the book. To fully grasp its scholarly tone, you might need to read it more than once, but it will be worthwhile. I wholeheartedly concur with the author that the goals of this book are 'to decolonize our universities from the plundering of western theories mediated by western trained/sponsored African compradors while also celebrating heterosexual marriage as a divine-cultural mandate to support (pro) creation.'"

Emmanuel Agyei Kwafo (Apostle), The National Coordinator, Home and Urban Missions, The Church of Pentecost General Headquarters, Accra, Ghana

"The author has creatively given the historical trajectory of the nation's stance against homosexuality as well as the stance of other African heads of state. Stance that shows the practice is not only a deviation from social order but an importation of cultural imperialism which is alien to both Ghanaian and African communities. The author has creatively given the historical trajectory of the nation's stance against homosexuality as well as the stance of other African heads of state. Stance that shows the practice is not only a deviation from social order but an importation of cultural imperialism which is alien to both Ghanaian and African communities. This book comes out at the right time to educate people especially on the country's stand on this important topic."

Rev. Stephen Azundem, Presbyterian Church of Ghana, Accra

Table of Contents

List of abbreviations **xv**

AIDS	Acquired Immune Deficiency Syndrome
ACSCUS	African Centre for the Study of the United States
CDD	Centre for Democratic Development (Ghana)
CoP	Church of Pentecost
CPP	Convention People's Party
HIV	Human Immunodeficiency Viruses
IAS	Institute of African Studies
MISR	Makerere Institute of Social Research (Makerere University, Uganda)
LGBTQ+	Lesbian, Gay, Bisexual, Transgender, Queer, and Ace
NDC	National Democratic Congress
NGOs	Non-governmental organisations
NETRIGHT	Network for Women's Rights in Ghana
NPP	New Patriotic Party
PAWA	Profane Association of West Africa
UCC	University of Cape Coast

The book opens with a contextualization of the argument for appropriate civilization. What is the source of the civilization that makes sense to you? Dr. Charles Prempeh raises an argument for the civilization that sustains a healthy society and questions the noetic experience of fleeting values. True to his argumentative person, he does a voluminous work that should scare none.

Dr Prempeh aims to serve as an alternative academic voice in the face of many liberal and non-productive voices that have saturated the academic world. Possibly and probably a lone voice in the wilderness, on a unique mission across the two worlds – African and the Diaspora, to celebrate heterosexual marriages and advocate for upholding the sustaining values that have ethical ends. Dr Prempeh's journey cuts across heritage Africa, the luring colonization, the emerging civilisation, the confused sexuality of the day and beyond.

In this book, written from the well-researched, deep-seated perspectives of a historian, societal analyst, a religious educator and more, Dr Prempeh plunges his readers into an interesting discussion of what happened to the people who said they were being freed from their colonial masters. He raises the curtains on the ravages of emerging practices of skewed sexuality and flawed gender identity on the health of society and individuals.

Dr Prempeh intimates that the fact that something exists does not mean that it is acceptable. This brings to mind the biblical teaching in I Corinthians 10: 23, "All things are lawful for me, but not all things are helpful; all things are lawful for me, but not all things edify." As the world moves towards inclusiveness, unlimited rights and learnedness, the author resonates his stand that many practices can be permissible but they are not edifying.

The intellectual stint in the author, propels him to hard work, a virtue he upholds. This radiates throughout the work. Dr Prempeh is technically deep and extensive as he treats the subject of gender and sexuality with an enviable passion. He cuts across the ancient and the modern, the typically African and the imposed and superimposed Western values that are being unduly wielded across African cultures by people whom it seeks to entangle and deceitfully lure into its detestable grips.

In the strides of Dr Prempeh, runs a linear trace of radical amputation of what is attractive but destructive, a palpable blunt and aggressive dissociation from the sinful acceptance of what has come to be, what is and what intends to be and a loud call for the scales to fall off the eyes of society and individuals. A timely and worthwhile journey.

Dr Mrs Shine Ofori
Biblical Counsellor and Educator

Foreword 2

I am privileged to write the forward of this extensive research work and sound academic dimensions of this book on LGBTQ+ and the Promotion of Proper Human Sexuality and Family Values in the Ghanaian Society. I have been an ardent advocate for the passage of the private Bill, initiated by some respected eight Members of Parliament of the Republic of Ghana in 2021.

Indeed, in November 2021, I honoured the eight MPs who initiated the Bill to disallow the activities of the LGBTQ+ in Ghana at the Atuoni Palace, Suma Ahenkro in the Jaman North District at our annual Royals Retreat in the presence of the Gyaman King HRM Nana Kwasi Adinkra Agyemang II, who is currently residing in the Republic of La Cote D'Ivoire and a host of reverend ministers including Apostle Vincent Anane Dente, the Director of Mens' Ministry of the Church of Pentecost and Apostle Nii Kotei Djani, the RCC coordinator of the Bono and the Ahafo Regions of the Republic of Ghana.

I have always believed that God is not exclusive to any religion. This is so true to the extent that anything which relates to the principles of life runs through every known faith and indicates that God is the source of this life, and He alone reserves the right to determine when it should be terminated or otherwise. No one has the right even to determine when their lives should cease. Suicide is considered a heinous crime by all the known religions, including our African traditions and Islam.

The so-called human rights issues must be discussed in the context of pro-life and not the opposite. We must remember that the right to life becomes relevant when a person is born or conceived. If people are advocating for the adoption of methods and strategies that have the potential to stop procreation, where will you have the situation to talk about the right of those, your actions will discontinue their being and existence. The argument of love for sinners is funny because any love for the sinner is to help them to come out of it, but not to enable them to stay in that sin, which has the potential to destroy them. The view that minorities in society should be protected should not come into this argument because God does not use the majority or minority to do what He says is right. We must not and should not entertain any view that advocates opinions which have the potential to reduce the quality of human life in any way.

This book has extensively dealt with almost all the questions and the misconception of those who are advocating for the legalisation of LGBTQ+ activities and will contribute significantly to the efforts being mobilised to fight the attempt to force these sacrilegious foreign cultures and activities on our society, which is an insult to the teachings of God and our society in every aspect.

Moreover, it will also serve as a colossal literature bank for those struggling to appreciate the dangers inherent in the activities of this group in our vulnerable society. I hope this book will be read avidly by all those who subscribe to the core values that run through all the notable religions, including Christianity, Islam and even the Indigenous African Religions.

The author of this book has extensively discussed the pertinent issues that have exposed all those who are ignorantly pushing for the legalisation of homosexuality and its related activities and hence have stopped being reasonable and still asking for good people to sympathise with their activities.

The critical questions the author is asking have always been begging for answers, and it is relevant now than ever. The author has raised crucial issues regarding other minority groups in our society like the armed robbers, smokers, drunkards, rapists, kidnappers, and human sacrifice ritualists if they will also be suitable to ask for their rights to be respected and legalise their activities in any society.

No matter what we do, there will be minority groups, but as long as their activities are damaging to life in general and even the very lives of those who are involved, it is the responsibility of society and established leadership to restrict their activities to preserve lives. It is the responsibility of the same society to protect the larger society by preventing activities of individuals and groups that have far-reaching consequences on the sustainability of the human race.

This book is a wealth of vital research information for all those who are against homosexuality. I highly recommend it to all Christians, the traditional African authorities and the Muslim community as a source of an academic and social knowledge bank to deal with any argument that has been raised in an attempt to force these evils on our rich culture to destroy our future.

HRM Odeneho Dr Affram Brempong III,
Omanhene Suma Traditional Area

Micro to macro contextual analysis: The Promotion of Proper Human Sexual Rights and Ghanaian Family Values Bill 2022 and Emerging issues

In this book, I argue for a need for context-specific analyses of the Lesbian, Gay, Bisexual, Transgender, Queer Plus (LGBTQ+) issue as a vortex of social, economic, political and transnational politics – all morphing into my understanding of Ghana in the modern world. While I focus on the LGBTQ as the entry point of discussing this complex cultural issue, I am really neither making a new argument nor targeting just academic audience. Instead, I am recapitulating the old clarion call for Africans to premise their development, quest for modernity on their culture (Hagan 1992).[1] In terms of audience, I target both academic and non-academics, as the subject of same-sex sexuality affects everyone, directly and/or indirectly. For this reason, I tend to be very pedantic and more detailed with issues that experts may find rather redundant. But given that I am appealing to a wider audience, I crave the patience of the academic world.

I also admit that culture is a complex term, very difficult to define. But suffice it to say that I agree with Busia that there is hardly any society of people who would not have something that they would cherish forever and would hardly allow it to change (Busia 1962). From my perspective, what will remain forever cherished among majority of Ghanaians is marriage and procreation and the broadening of kinship relations. Certainly, my position may hardly be universally shared, but it is against that perspective that I discuss every other social and political lived realities in Ghana, including decolonisation of the universities. For this reason, the main driving argument of this book is that human beings are embodied beings whose existence is intricately tied to sociogenic activities. Admitting the plurality of knowledge on the subject, I appeal to my Christian faith as the basis of contributing to the decolonisation debate.

The complexities of the same-sex sexuality debate begin with the acronym. The acronym LGBQTI+ needs to be explained. It is misleading to assume that it is known or understood. Clearly, the

---

[1] Hagan, G.P. (1992). 'African cultures and parameters in planning processes,' In Aryeetey, E. (ed.), *Planning African growth and development*, 57-72. Accra: Ghana: ISSER/UNDP.

acronym refers to a range of identities and practices that are different from heterosexuality and (maybe) challenge heteronormativity. The problem is while these identities are also termed minority sexualities, and usually work together to amplify their exclusion and marginalisation, they are also very diverse and not necessarily internally coherent. Indeed, in social media lately the "trans" identity has stoked a lot of controversy in western societies. This is because of controversial policies which allow children to transition to other genders. The problem that is increasingly debated is that in western societies adolescence is accepted as a time of emotional turbulence (the so-called storm-and-stress syndrome). As a result, many argue that the self-diagnosis of gender dysphoria is misleading. The medical fraternity stands accused of acting in haste without extending psychotherapy to these young people. They are accused of cashing in on experimental and expensive surgery. This is unethical. Furthermore, gender reassignment surgery once done is irreversible. Increasingly, many erstwhile "trans" persons choose to "de-transition" later in life. Thus, where gender reassignment surgery has taken place, the surgery itself becomes a violation of rights. Furthermore, the transition entails a life on artificial hormones whose long-term impact is not known. The medical community has not been transparent with the public about these drugs and impact of surgeries. Many discover later that their artificial genitals do not work sexually. Medical insurers are not willing to foot the bill for more surgery, drugs etc. Thus, many who transition are left to their devices with modified bodied but without due support to access requisite drugs etc. Yes, social media documentations show that these individuals do not have lives worth living as they have to contend with disability (hacked body parts, raging natural vs artificial hormones, disability, sexual dysfunction, repeated infections on/in artificial genitals etc). These problems are not visited on gay men or lesbian women per se.[2]

My point in explaining this is: the acronym does not stand for "homosexual sex" it is often admitted in the public because each of those letters represent a different practice in a long continuum of non-heterosexual sexualities. But then again, are Africans likely to take to gender reassignment surgery? Do we have the surgeons? Do we have the funding? Is this an immediate problem for Ghanaians? For this reason, my basic argument is that the LGBTQ issue should not be read as simply a legal issue and explained in isolation of local and trans-local politics. Instead, I argue that the subject is basically about social beings

[2] I am very grateful to the anonymous reviewer for bringing this insightful issue to my attention. I remain thankful and indebted.

whose entanglements involve every aspect of society. Similarly, since the continent of Africa has been in the whirlwind of decolonising the institutions of higher learning since the 1960s, I deploy the LGBTQ issue as an entry point to discuss composite issues in Ghana.

In other words, leveraging the LGBTQ issue as microscopic window into Ghana's historical and contemporary experiences, I discuss how the kinship system, morphing into socialisation and marriage, chieftaincy practices, religion, and Ghana's idea of secularism all provide multiple layers to the issues of queer sexualities – which "unveils the subjugated knowledges of those whom modernity engages through the violent silencing of their voices" (Asante and Hanchey 2021: 213).[3] This also means that, instead of just the Promotion of Proper Sexual Rights and Ghanaian Family Values Bill 2022 that seeks to advance heteronormativity, I discuss the Bill as an entry point to Ghana's political economy and decolonisation. In all this, I seek to be in the complex and uncomfortable state of "between and betwixt" to walk the complex terrain of arguing for tolerance for minority rights without tolerating the legislating queer sexualities. Perhaps, I am able to take this stance because human beings are significantly capable of cohering and embodying cognitive dissonances in psychology or possessing a hybridised culture. However, as several Ghanaians draw on religious beliefs to demarcate ethical and ontological boundaries around sexuality, it is possible (and it is the case) to have a "hybridised culture" without tolerating the legislation of queer sexualities.

The above seeming complexity has also become a reason for my own foray into the debate over LGBTQ+ as a practising evangelical Christian, Akan male, and an academic. Definitely, therefore, my views are as subjective as any other views. I only plead to be tolerated as I also acquiesce in the pleas of others to tolerate them. In the end, I take inspiration from Professor Francis Nyamnjoh, who has, since the last two decades, dedicatedhis academic career to promoting human ontological incompleteness and conviviality to curate human beings from fighting to death. I build on Nyamnjoh's insight to develop the Christian idea of human ontological dignity (expressed as "God created every human being in His image") to argue for tolerance for minority group, in this instance, queer sexualities without compromising the need for Ghana to retain its laws that protect the ethical and ontological

[3] Godfried Asante and Jenna N. Hanchey, "Decolonizing queer modernities: The case for queer (post)colonial studies in critical/cultural communication," Communication and Critical/Cultural Studies, 18,2 (2021): 212-220. I am yet to known any locally-based Ghanaian scholar who refers to himself or herself as a queer scholar.

boundaries of life as heteronormativity – against all the glocalised lobbies to legislate same-sex and queer sexualities.

At any rate, as I write below, a close reading of both the Family Bill and petition "against" it are not necessarily mortal enemies. While the two coalition groups talk about the Ghanaian family from different vantage point, they both agree that the family should not be put on the path of legal destruction. For example, the key component of the Family Bill is the protection of heteronormativity as ideal; while that of the petitions is to keep families from reporting on one another because of queer sexualities. Put together, my understanding is that both coalition groups are against treating human beings as simply legal beings. Both groups also call for the protection of the Ghanaian family against foreign intrusion – as they accuse each other of being influenced by the western world. So, if my understanding is right, while there may not be simple answers to issues of individual queer sexual rights and society's heteronormative rights, perhaps the answers lies in looking at every human being as bearing the image of God (possessing ontological dignity) – nevertheless, as I argue in this book, the image of God orbits within God's clearly defined boundaries around sexuality that, from the Christian perspective, forbids all queer sexualities. It is against the perspective of the Bible and my Christian faith that I argue against all efforts at legislating same-sex unions and queer sexualities.

It is for the above reasons, *inter alia*, that I discuss the same-sex sexuality issue, the Bill and its components broadly as part of the general daily academic and political discourses. Possibly, we could let the "lying dogs" really lie if we choose to focus on what unites as in our love for the family, instead of rendering the family as a legal entity – which regrettably put conjugal and consanguineal relationships on transactional engagement, instead of affection – a major component of the family. As humans we cannot avoid arguments about who is family and who is not. As simply and complicated that question is, it affects succession into office (re: chieftaincies), inheritance of estates etc. Concomitantly, if the two camps think allowing the west into our social space will destroy the family, possibly, we could all heed the ancestral sagacity that "When siblings fight to death, it is strangers who will take over what belongs to them." Ghanaians have, in both popular and academic discourses, compared our development with Singapore. While I am certainly not a fan of such comparisons, as it blurs contextual analysis, the fact that it is only this year (2022) that Singapore is seeking to decriminalise same-sex sexuality is enough of a message for Ghanaians.[4] We spent the whole of last year (2021) talking about same-sex sexuality, while Singapore won the heart of Germans who are building one of the largest vaccination centres in Singapore in a world of pandemics![5] Why not Ghana? Maybe, we were discussing sex amid a global pandemic, while Singaporeans were discussing how to attract international attention to a global pandemic.

The year 2021, will undoubtedly go down memory lane in Ghana's history as highly episodic in view of the fact that it marked a major shift in the Lesbian, Gay, Bisexual, Transgender, Queer Plus (LGBTQ+) debate since it became a national issue in the country's Fourth Republic in 2006. Contentions around the subject morphed into formalised and institutionalised counter-movements and ideas about the rights, cultural appropriateness or otherwise of Ghanaians who identified themselves as either lesbian, gay, bisexual, transgender or other.

Indeed, until 2021, there have been several rumours and speculations about same-sex sexual practices among students, particularly those in secondary schools. Known variably in popular language as "Supi" for women or "Azorkwaff" for men, discussions about the subject had often gone undercover or spoken in undertones in public, or sometimes summarily dismissed as student fads and crazes. But in 2006, the Ghanaian religious public, paid attention to the subject when the newspapers widely reported that a group of members of the LGBTQ+ in South Africa intended to host their international conference in Accra.

The religious community swiftly moved in, impressing upon the political elites to disallow the LGBTQ+ group from hosting their conference in the country. The President of Ghana at the time, Mr. J.A. Kufuor, responded favourably to the conservative religious community's demand and closed the borders of the country to the community. The issue appeared to have gone quiet until another related development surfaced in 2011. In that year, the former Prime Minister of the United Kingdom, David Cameroon threatened to cut aid to countries that failed to decriminalise same-sex sexual practices. Again, the religious community in Ghana were up again in arms, forcing the then President of the country, Prof, J.E.A. Mills to declare his stance

---

[4] Philip Heijmans (August 21, 2022), 'Singapore takes cautious step to abolish ban on sex between men,' https://www.bloomberg.com/news/articles/2022-08-21/singapore-says-to-abolish-law-criminalizing-sex-between-men?leadSource=uverify%20wall (Accessed: September 5, 2022).

[5] Michelle Jamrisko (May 10, 2021), 'BioNTech to build Covid-19 vaccine facility in Singapore by 2023,' https://www.bloomberg.com/news/articles/2021-05-10/biontech-to-build-covid-19-vaccine-facility-in-singapore-by-2023?leadSource=uverify%20wall (Accessed: September 4, 2022).

on the subject. Consequently, the president said he would never lead Ghana to legalise LGBTQ+.

Again, matters went quiet over the issue. But, by this time, a group of Christians and non-Christians, led by persons including Mr Moses Foh-Amoaning, a lawyer, formed a civil society group in 2013. The group, called the National Coalition for Proper Human Sexual Rights and Family Values (NCPHSR&FV), is an amalgamation of Christian and para-Christian bodies, religious bodies including the Ghana Pentecostal and Charismatic Council (GPCC), the Coalition of Muslim Organisations (CMO), Ghana, the National Chief Imam's Office, the Catholic Bishops' Conference (CBC), the Advocates for Christ, non-religious bodies, the National House of Chiefs and opinion leaders in Ghana. The Coalition started putting documents together to firm Ghana's criminalisation of LGBTQ+ issues.

While the group was now involved in secondary school campus ministry, encouraging students to desist from same-sex practices, the year 2021, was rather a different period for a test of their mettle. As the nation was reeling under the novel Coronavirus Pandemic, which had overwhelmingly disrupted both the economy and nearly all social activities, the LGBTQ+ issue came up again. This time, some members of the LGBTQ+ constituency had contributed and built a centre to solidarise with them and also reflect on how they could negotiate their lives in Ghana's religious public that they found rather hostile.

On the inaugural day of the centre, both traditional and social media widely reported the event. Unfortunately, for the members of the LGBTQ+ community, the visible presence of foreign diplomats, including delegates from the European Union (EU), the Austrian High Commissioner to Ghana and the Danish Ambassador to Ghana, rather incurred the wrath of the Ghanaian religious constituency. The presence of foreign diplomats rather ditched the already religious public hostility towards LGBTQ+ issues. More so, deploying the pervasiveness of social media, the EU, on its official Facebook, advertised its participation in the event and reiterated its support for all civil society organisations supporting the LGBTQ+ group. Appearing to have affirmed a longstanding suspicion that the international community was fostering neo-colonial tendencies in the country, Lawyer Foh-Amoaning and others quickly prepared a Bill that was submitted to the Parliament of Ghana for consideration.

The Bill, called The Promotion of Proper Human Sexual Rights and Ghanaian Family Values Bill 2022 seeks "To provide for proper human sexual rights and Ghanaian family values, proscribe LGBTQ+ and related activities; proscribe propaganda of advocacy for or promotion of LGBTTQQIAAP+[6] and related activities; provide for the protection of and support for children, persons who are victims or accused of LGBTTQQIAAP+ and related activities and other persons; and related matters".[7]

Basing the rationale of the Bill on the opening of an LGBTQ+ advocacy resource centre in Accra, the group said it enjoyed the support of the National House of Chiefs, the National Chief Imam, the Christian Council, the Catholic Bishops' Conference and the Coalition cited the position of chiefs as follows:

> The (National) House wants to state without equivocation that throughout history, nowhere does Ghanaian culture subscribe to the LGBTQ+, which is a taboo, inhuman and alien to our society… In God's wisdom, man and woman were created to fill the procreation of humans on earth to satisfy God's will … . The symbolism for sex [and] marriage was between man and woman, as such, the idea of man marrying man and woman marrying woman is an abomination to our tradition and culture as Ghanaians.[8]

From the above, the Coalition presented LGBTQ+ as a threat to the concept of family and the associated value systems that are central to the social structure of all ethnic groups in Ghana. The Coalition subsequently defined and maintained that "The concept of family for Ghanaians has always been a unit of society initiated by marriage between a man and a woman, each of whose gender is assigned at birth".[9] Partly responding to international pressure on Ghana to liberalise Ghana's stance on sexuality, the Coalition further appealed to international laws, including Article 2(4) of the United Nations Charter to argue that Ghana has the sovereignty to make laws to protect their values and identity, provided the laws do not infringe on fundamental human rights. Treating LGBTQ+ as injurious to public health and safety, the group proposed the outlawing of all advocacy activities in favour of LGBTQ+. The group also justified its Bill on their assertion

---

[6] Lesbian, Gay, Bisexual, Transgender, Transexual, Queer, Questioning, Intersex, Ally, Asexual, Pansexual.

[7] The Members of Parliament promoting the Bill as a private Bill include: Hon Samuel Narty George, MP for Ningo-Prampram; Hon Della Adjoa Sowa, MP for Kpando; Hon Emmanuel Bedzrah, MP for Ho West; Hon John Ntim Fordjour, MP for Assin South; Hon Alhassan Sayibu Suhuyini, MP for Tamale North; Hon Rita Naa Odoley Sowah, MP for La Dadekotopon; Hon Hellen Adjoa Ntoso, MP for Krachi West; Hon Rockson-Nelson Dafeamekpor, MP for South Dayi. https://cdn.modernghana.com/files/722202192224-0h830n4ayt-lgbt-bill.pdf.

[8] Ibid., p. 1

[9] Ibid, p. 1.

that the laws against "Carnal knowledge" was outdated, given the multiplicity of genders in the contemporary world.

Beyond Ghana, the Coalition cited Articles 18(1) and (2) of the African Charter on Human and Peoples Rights to affirm its definition of family:

1. The family shall be the natural unit and basis of society. It shall be protected by the state, which shall take care of its physical health and morals.
2. The State shall have the duty to assist the family, which is the custodian of morals and traditional values recognised by the community.

The Bill also claimed to provide support for those they framed as victims of LGBTQ+. It stated as follows:

> The existing legislative framework is … silent on support mechanisms for victims of LGBTQIAAP+ sexual activities and persons whose biological make-up make them prone to "questioning" their sexuality. It is clear that economic inequalities and poverty, create a fertile environment for promoters of LGBTTQQIAAP+ activities to take advantage of poor youth and lure them into these activities. Recognising these vulnerable persons as victims of the exploitation of powerful forces, there is the need to enact legislation that creates a support system for persons who are victims of lifestyle LGBTTQQIAP+ persons.[10]

The Bill also proposed to provide medical and psychological support to members of the LGBTQ+ community who are victimised, both physically and psychologically, as a result of a clash between them and Ghanaian values. In terms of the expansiveness of the Bill, it "Applies to a person who holds out as lesbian, a gay, a bisexual, a transgender, a queer, an ally, a pansexual, or a person, or a person of any other sociocultural notion of sex or sexual relationship that is contrary to the sociocultural notions of male and female or the relationship between male and female; a person who may be questioning that person's sexuality; a person who is involved in the promotion of, propagation of, advocacy for, support of or funding of LGBTTQQIAP+; a person who provides or participates in the provision of surgical services to enable gender reassignment or the creation of sexual category other than the category of a person assigned at birth, except where the surgical procedure is to correct a biological anomaly, including intersex;

[10] Ibid., p. 8.

and any other person engaged in a sexual activity prohibited under the Bill.[11]

Clause 7 of the Bill prescribes the punitive measure for violators. It states as follows:

> A person who commits an offence is liable to a summary conviction to a fine of not less than a twenty-five penalty units and not more than five hundred penalty units or be a term of imprisonment of not less than three months and not more than three years or both if the person, by threats or intimidation, procures another person to engage in sexual activity prohibited under the Bill or by false pretence or false representation, procures another person to engage in sexual activity prohibited under the Bill.

The Bill also ensured the protection of LGBTQ+:

> Bill should not be abused, assaulted or harassed whether verbally or physically. A person who abuses, assaults or harasses an accused person or a person suffering from any gender or sexual identity challenge commits an offence under the Bill and is, on summary conviction, liable to a term of imprisonment of not less than six months and not more than three years. The provision accords with the general protections provided in Chapter Five of the 1992 Constitution for persons accused of criminal offences, particularly article 15(1) which stipulates that "The dignity of all persons shall be inviolable." By prohibiting such acts, persons accused of offences under this Bill are guaranteed fair treatment and trial and will be accorded the dignity that every citizen deserves.[12]

Ghana family values include:

1. Respect for the sanctity of marriage as a lifelong relationship between a man and a woman, each of whose gender is assigned at birth;
2. The recognition
    i. of the nuclear and extended family as the basic unit for all Ghanaian ethnic communities; and
    ii. that the ultimate purpose of the role of Government is protecting and advancing the family as the basic unit of society is to safeguard and promote the best interest of children;
    iii. the obligation of parents, guardians and teachers to ensure that children and young persons receive special protection against exposure to physical, emotional and moral hazards;

---

[11] Ibid, p. 10.
[12] Ibid, p. 16.

iv. the recognition of chiefs and the chieftaincy institution, as established by customary law and the Constitution, as the ultimate source of traditional political authority and leadership and as the custodian of the customs, traditions and customary laws, rules and precepts that underpin Ghanaian ethnic groups and communities;
v. the recognition of Ghanaian ethnic group, of "gender" as a social construct to only male and female humans each of whose gender is assigned at birth; and
vi. the duty to uphold the cherished societal ideals of selflessness, communalism and good neighbourliness, hard work, discipline, truthfulness, compassion towards the weak and vulnerable, the acquisition of wealth through hard work and genuine entrepreneurship and every customary ideal that will help establish a free and just Ghanaian society and nation.[13]

LGBTTQQIAAP+ includes Lesbian, Gay, Bisexual, Transgender, Transexual, Queer, Questioning, Intersex, Ally, Asexual, Pansexual and any other sociocultural notion of sex and sexual relationship that is contrary to the sociocultural notion of male and female assigned at birth.

With these provisions, a coalition of academics and heads of civil society organisations[14] petitioned Parliament to block the Bill from being considered. The group summarised their evaluation of the Family Bill as follows:

> The LGBT+ Bill currently before Parliament is a major step backwards for democracy, inclusiveness, the protection of minorities and the vulnerable in society, and of fundamental human rights in Ghana. Under the grand sounding banner of "***proper human sexual rights and Ghanaian family values"*** the Bill seeks to send the country back centuries into the past. Its language of "recant and treatment" echoes the middle ages of Europe where the state and the Church, driven by misguided notions of heresy and witchcraft, hunted down innocents in the name of God and religious values. Blinded by religious zealotry and intolerance, the theocratic State and its Church forced innocent vulnerable persons to "recant" their religious beliefs and burnt nonconformists at the

[13] Ibid, p. 23.

[14] They included: Akoto Ampaw, Professor Emerita Takyiwaa Manuh, Professor Kwame Karikari, Professor Kofi Gyimah-Boadi, Professor Audrey Gadzekpo, Dr. Rose Kutin-Mensah, Dr. Yao Graham, Professsor Dzodzi Tsikata, Professor H. Kwasi Prempeh, Kwasi Adu-Amankwah, Dr. Kojo Asante, Kofi Ofei-Nkansah, Akunu Dake, Tetteh Homerku-Adjjei, Professor Raymond Atuguba.

stakes in the misguided belief that their gruesome murder would, somehow, purge their souls of evil.[15] In essence, when all the fanciful justifications, supposedly grounded in culture, tradition and religion, are stripped of their beguiling clothes and adornments, what is left of the high sounding "Bill for the Protection of Proper Human Sexual Rights and Family Values" is stigmatization, bigotry, intolerance, repression, authoritarianism, violation of the fundamental human rights of LGBQT+ persons, false piety, cruelty to, and lack of empathy for, them.[16]

On the question of Ghanaian cultural and traditional values, the group stated that:

> The sponsors of the Bill conveniently refuse to acknowledge that not all of our cultural and traditional "values" can stand up to the demands of inclusiveness, diversity, and fundamental rights within a democratic republic such as Ghana. For instance, traditional Ghanaian values do not fully accept persons with disability as persons having full and equal rights as those without disabilities. The custom and values of some communities, especially in the past, considered twins as an abomination, with the result that they, by custom and tradition, had to be killed as evil, just like how the Bill's sponsors consider LGBTQ++ persons inhuman and as evil. The infamous witch camps in northern Ghana where vulnerable women and old ladies are, even to date, banished for unproven allegations of witchcraft, are a product of our culture and tradition. There is also the *trokosi* cultural phenomenon, in the Volta Region, where very young girls are given away to the god or spirit represented by a priest or priestess for the "sins" of other family members, and become virtually enslaved for the rest of their lives. Even until recently, the notion of gender equality was largely alleged to be repugnant to African or Ghanaian cultural values. These are all cultural beliefs and practices based on traditional norms and values. Indeed, in parts of Eastern Africa, albinos are targeted and murdered because of their pigmentation, based on similar false cultural beliefs! But the fact that these are part of Ghanaian and African cultural and traditional norms and values do not make them acceptable in modern Ghana, in a free and democratic Republic.[17]

The group also challenged the idea that homosexuality is foreign to Africans.

---

[15] memorandum to select committee on the constitutional, legal and parliamentary affairs on the: *promotion of proper human sexual rights and Ghanaian family values bill, 2021*, p. 1.

[16] Ibid, p. 10.

[17] Ibid., pp. 7-8.

The promoters of the Bill seek to whip up their misguided version of Ghanaian cultural nationalism by raising the scare that LGBTQ+ rights are alien to Ghanaian culture and tradition, and are being promoted by a morally depraved West. In the first place, it is Ghanaian LGBTQ++ persons who are fighting for social tolerance and acceptance, having suffered in the obscurity of darkness and social exclusion for years. Secondly, it is simply not true that LGBTQ+ tendencies and inclinations are foreign to Ghanaian or African societies. Indeed, there are historical records of Ancient Egypt that suggest and indicate that homosexuality existed as early as the 5th Dynasty, that is, around 2,380 BCE/BC. Mural representations in the tomb of two male manicurists depict a relationship that may be considered the earliest historical record of a homosexual relationship between Niankhkhnum and Khnumhotep, who were chief manicurists of the Pharaoh and other royalty. Other references to homosexuality/ lesbianism in Ancient Egypt can be found in a specific text of the female author of the Egyptian" *Book of the Dead*", written in 970 BCE/BC thus: *"I never had sex with a woman in the temple"*, suggesting that she had sex with women outside the temple. While we do not use these records to suggest that homosexual and lesbian practices, to the extent that they existed in Ancient Egypt, were the same in nature and extent as they exist in modern society, these historical allusions indicate the need for anti-LGBTQ++ warriors to be more questioning of their dogma that such practices are alien to Africa and African societies, and are solely the product of decadent western imperialist cultural onslaught. Indeed, as a matter of fact, LGBQT persons have been a well-known "secret" in Ghanaian families and society for a long time, and not just the product of any external advocacy. We are all aware of the familiar references to "male" individuals who display distinct roles and habits of women, who are sometimes openly referred to as, for example, *Kodjo besia' or 'Kwesi besia"*, depending on the day on which he was born. It is also not a secret that as far back as the 1960s, if not earlier, some pairs of girls in girls-only secondary schools developed close sexual relationships known as '*supi', a practice that continues today.* These are well known homegrown facts, and not western inspired.[18]

Concerning the definition of family, the group said as follows:

> What constitutes the Ghanaian family unit is hardly uniform or static. For example, the nuclear family unit or household, comprising two married heterosexual partners and their biological children, though increasingly common among elite or middle-class urban Ghanaians can

[18] Ibid, p. 9.

hardly be said to represent the Ghanaian cultural norm. To many, particularly outside the urban elite enclaves, the family is still reckoned, for example, in "extended" family or polygamous terms, with the nuclear family of the urban elite regarded as foreign. Single parent-headed households are also quite prevalent, as are various other permutations and combinations.[19]

With respect to the idea of religion and the secular, the group said as follows:

> It is given that some Christians and Muslims may find LGBTQ+ activities offensive and may detest them. That may be well within their rights, as persons with strong religious views, though such an attitude does little in promoting a diverse, tolerant and inclusive society, in which the interests of minorities and vulnerable groups, including LGBTQ+ persons, are deserving of equal respect. But can we imagine what would happen to our democratic republic, if we started imposing as the law of the land the religious dogmas and tenets and edicts of one or the other dominant or ascendant religious community? Let it be stated without equivocation that ours is a secular democratic republic, not a theocratic Christian or Islamic Republic or an African traditional monarchy or chiefdom.[20]

The Coalition also asserts that:

> In its 2018 report to the Human Rights Council on its 37th Session, the United Nations Independent Expert against Violence and Discrimination based on Sexual Orientation and Gender Identity concluded as follows:
>
> *"...the rising number of hate crimes based on sexual orientation and gender identity correlates with a steep rise in ultraconservative political and religious groups using their platforms to promote bigotry, dehumanize persons on the basis of sexual orientation, gender identity or expression, and foster a stigma and intolerance among constituencies. Such discourse sometimes is used* **as a means to bolster popularity** *and detract attention from pressing economic and internal political problems, ...in the last Universal Review period for Ghana (AHRC/37/7, the recommendations in paragraph 146.59 (which enjoyed the support of Ghana) state that Ghana should "[take the steps necessary to protect lesbian, gay bisexual, transgender and intersex people from violence and discrimination on the basis of their sexual orientation and gender identity."*

---

[19] Ibid., p. 11.
[20] Ibid, p. 12.

On 28th July 2021, the Speaker of the ECOWAS Parliament, Sidie Mohammed, in an interview with TV3, advised that Ghana should be cautious in passing the Bill because of its implications in promoting insecurity and undemocratic principles.

The African Commission on Human and Peoples and Human Rights, in its Resolution 275 of 12th May 2014, condemns systematic attacks by State and non-state actors against persons on the basis of their imputed or real sexual orientation or gender identity, while in addition making discrimination against LGBTQ++ persons a violation of their fundamental human rights.

South Africa, Mozambique, Sao Tome and Principe (2012) and Cape Verde (2004), as well as Lesotho (2012) and Seychelles (2016) in Africa have all abolished colonial penal legislation criminalising homosexuals. The Angolan National Assembly passed a new penal code that abolished criminalising homosexual relationships, while making attacks on persons because of their sexual orientation as well as discrimination against people on the basis of their sexual orientation a crime punishable by not more than two years imprisonment. It came into effect in February 2021.

The affirmation of the rights of LGBTQ++ persons as human rights is not only by legislation. African courts have also upheld the right of LGBTQ++ persons to protection against discrimination and the enjoyment of their fundamental human right to human dignity and the right to organise and to advocate LGBTQ++ rights. Thus, in ***Eric Gitari v NGO Board & 4 others*, [2015]**, the Kenyan High Court in Nairobi upheld the rights of LGBTQ++ persons to assemble, noting at paragraph 104 of the judgment thus:

> "*As a society, once we recognise that persons who are gay, lesbian, bisexual, transgender or intersex are human beings...however reprehensible we may find their sexual orientation, we must accord them the human rights, which are guaranteed by the Constitution to all persons, by virtue of their being human, in order to protect their dignity as human...*"

Citing judicial rulings from other jurisdiction that favourably support the LGBTQ+ community, that Coalition continued:

> Again, in *Attorney General of Botswana v. Rammoge & 19 Others*, the Court of Appeal of Botswana (the highest court in Botswana) upholding the decision of the High Court affirming the right of an organisation by the name Lesbians, Gays and Bi-sexuals of Botswana ("LEGABIBO") to register an LGBTQ++ organisation stated as follows":

"Members of the gay, lesbian and transgender community, although no doubt a small minority, and unacceptable to some on religious or other grounds form part of the rich diversity of any nation and are fully entitled in Botswana, as in any other progressive state, to the constitutional protection of their dignity".

The academics and activists concluded as follows:

> As far back as November 1992, in the seminal judgment of the Supreme Court of Ghana in **NPP v. IGP,** affirming the right of the people to assemble, demonstrate and process against the repressive Pubic Order Decree 1972 (NLCD 68), Amua-Sekyi JSC, as if anticipating these dark days that our Republic is threatened with today, stated in a compelling and deeply insightful dicta at pages 470 to 471 of the Ghana Law Reports 2 [1993 – 1994] GLR, his opinion as follows:
>
> > "In countries that practice true democracy, supporters and opponents of every conceivable cause are given freedom to associate and express their views. In the end, some have succeeded, and their unpopular demands have eventually become majority wishes and have been recognized. The examples are the anti-slavery groups in eighteenth century England and nineteenth century America and the suffragettes of both countries at the beginning of this century. Today, in these countries those who favour and those who oppose abortion may assemble and hold demonstrations and processions in support of their cause, while in the less tolerant societies one may be permitted and the other banned. In this country it would be unthinkable for any police officer to grant homosexuals a permit to hold a demonstration in support of so-called gay rights, but I ask, if in nineteenth century England the supporters of child labour had been prevented from stating their case, would its evil consequences have ever been recognized? **In this day and age, it is necessary for us to see that consent not force is the basis of a just society, and that it is not for the government or our neighbor to tell us what to think or feel or do**? [Emphasis added].
>
> "Most of the restrictions on our liberties, which after years of repression we have come to accept, are inconsistent with democratic norms. Except in a time of war, when a state of emergency has been declared, **it cannot be right for any agency of the executive to suppress the free expression of any opinion, however unpopular that opinion may be**. The believer in absolutism, the anarchist, those who oppose equal rights for women – **yes lesbians and**

homosexuals too - are all entitled to the free expression of their views, and the right to assemble and demonstrate in support of those views. Once the state takes for itself the power to license association, assemblies and processions, it resorts to support of the status quo, and the only way of changing the prevailing state of affairs is by use of force." [Emphasis added].[21]

Preliminary evaluation

To say the least, the issues around LGBTQ+ are very contentious and do not yield themselves easily to a zero-sum and exclusive response without offending one party or the other. This is primarily because, after all the legal and social issues, the LGTBQ+ persons involved are human beings whose ontological worth must be protected. Nevertheless, as human beings with inherent dignity, there must be rules that must protect them as well as the interest of the general public. Perhaps, the tension, in my evaluation, lies in how Ghanaians can negotiate for a middle ground between protecting minority rights without the majority similarly feeling their cherished values submerged.

In between these two complex terrains are all manner of legal and sociocultural arguments that then almost take attention from the common concerns of Ghanaians to other polarising matters. In the end, middle grounds are blurred, as history and cultural practices are *re*-interpreted to suit opposing camps with hardly any attempts at building a consensus. In an effort at legitimising their respective positions, through a highly partisan dialogue, the two camps have appealed to the country's Parliament. But chances are that Ghana's Parliament, for pragmatic reasons would pass the Bill in favour of heterosexual marriage as the norm. Most likely, the pro-LGBTQ coalition protecting minority sexual rights would appeal to the court for redress. In this sense, social beings would be reduced to legal beings, whose relationship with their families and the larger community may suffer. This means that the individual self-awareness and self-consciousness is both individually and communally established. Owusu and Bosiwah succinctly captured the idea of human sociality as follows:

> Beings is … a statement of self. To be African is to know the self as African. It is a statement of self-knowledge. It is a cultural statement and

[21] Pp. 16-19.

a cultural affirmation. Self and world are fused in reciprocal relations (2015: 132).[22]

I maintain that as social being, we are as well dependent beings with a natural predilection towards gregariousness, the lives of individuals are intertwined with the social and reciprocal networks they establish – social networks that thrive on economy of affection that fosters what Ibn Khaldun, the Arab philosopher of the 14th Century called *Asabiyah* – altruism-based solidarity for social cohesion and foundation of civilization.[23] Reducing human beings to legal beings would result in the construing of human relations as highly transaction which may potentially result in the economic exploitation of Marx's commodity fetishism – where money is valued more than human beings (labourers to be specific).[24] Currently, the Parliament of Ghana is divided over the issue, though not equally divided. Clearly, given that the country's minority party, the National Democratic Congress (NDC) has largely taken a decision to push through the Bill, they have threatened to resist the passage of other government's bills – which will definitely stifle government business in the House.[25]

In the end, whether same-sex unions are indigenous or not, historically, families and societies have had several ways of protecting queer sexualities and identities. Indeed, African societies have been highly accommodative of difference. While this is a fact, the issue is also more about the spaces where queer sexualities were/are assimilated. Were queer sexualities in different precolonial societies in what later became known as Ghana accepted as sociogenic practices, endorsed by social norms and folklore? or were they largely identifiable with special locale, among special groups of people and treated as symbolic? I address these questions by contextually discussing the Akan ethos around sex and family, the encounter between the Akan ethics and 19th Century Victorian Christian ethics, and the Akan ideas of ethical and ontological boundaries that shape sexuality – which excludes queer sexualities from the public sphere.

---

[22] Mary A.S. Owusu and Lawrence Bosiwah, "Constructions of masculinity among the Akan people of Ghana," *Journal of Social Sciences and Humanities*, 1, 2 (2015): 131-137.

[23] Ibn Khaldun, *The Muqaddimah, An introduction to history* (trans. Franz Rosenthal) (Princeton, NJ.: Princeton University Press, 1980).

[24] Karl Marx, *Capital* (London: Penguin Classics, 1990).

[25] Ghanaweb (June 9, 2022), "WE will resist passage of other gov't bills over delay tactics on anti-gay bill – Minority," https://www.ghanaweb.com/GhanaHomePage/NewsArchive/We-will-resist-passage-of-other-gov-t-bills-over-delay-tactics-on-anti-gay-bill-Minority-1556774 (Accessed: September 3, 2022).

Beyond the assimilative nature of indigenous cultures that appreciated pluralities, the introduction of western education and Judeo-Christianity and Islam into Africa adds complexity to Africa's social texture. Since colonialism, western schools and institutions of higher learning have hardly tolerated traditions of knowledge of the colonised world. Similarly, both Islam and Christianity tend to translate their different understanding of monotheism to similarly discard differences that they consider diverge from the order of creation – in this case heterosexual normativity. Historically, therefore, the singular and uniform narratives of Christianity and Islam have regrettably resulted in religious fanaticism and intolerance of differences. Sadly, the western complex rejection of Christianity and Islam has also given way to two emerging philosophies, capitalism and socialism, as systems.

As systems, capitalism and socialism have proven unrelentingly resentful of middle ground. Capitalists and socialists, like religion, lay claim to a singular, grand theory that hardly allows room for the ideological *Other.* Just like religion, capitalism promises freedom to individuals to work and acquire worth, but does not emphasise the virtue of redistribution. In the end, a few individuals accumulate so much with the majority of people floundering in poverty. Similarly, socialism promises to break the tide of individualism by emphasising the state. But because the state is a social construct, in the end, individual revolutionaries complexly become oligarchs – repeating the capitalist cycle in a complex way. In the end, as two novels, George Orwell's *Animal Farm* and Ngũgĩ wa Thiong'o's *The devil on the cross*, demonstrated as contrary opinions, both socialism and capitalism are ultimately oppressive.

As religions and philosophical systems hardly solve the complex human challenge of accepting the "*un*like", sometimes what appears like polemics takes over. For example, were issues such as twins as an abomination, with the result that they, by custom and tradition, had to be killed as evil, cherished values? What about witchcraft accusations, usually directed at women – were they cherished values? Similarly, was the phenomenon of *trokosi* accepted as cherished value and custom? Yes, there were cultural beliefs, based on which, these practices were undertaken, but were they cherished values?

While these practices may have formed or continued part of Ghana and Africa's lived realities, I do not agree that they were cherished. These practices, similar to human sacrifices, were considered destruction for constructive purposes. Of course, the idea of destroying human lives for whatever reasons remains repugnant, but sadly, it formed part of the Ghanaian and African quest for finding meaning. It is for this reason that Evans-Pritchard considered witchcraft as carrying the function of helping pre-modern societies make sense of what was rationally inexplicable (Evans-Pritchard 1937).[26] The same explanation has been offered by G.K. Nukunya who argued that the belief in witchcraft had a social function that allowed for reordering society away from extremes. These extremes included poverty, wealth, beauty, and character. Persons, considered extremely rich or poor risked being tagged as witches or wizards. For this reason, such persons are compelled to share (Nukunya 1992).[27] Indeed, persons of extraordinary personalities and characters, such being brilliant and successful at what one does are often talked about within the rubric of witchcraft (Onyinah 2012).[28]

Rationalising the above hardly takes away the repugnance of marginalising minority groups who looked very different. Even so, what we find in the literature is that these practices were not part of the acceptable normal practices of society. They were "oddities" that were appealed to as part of making sense of life. Consequently, several of them, such as the killing of twins, have either ceased to exist or are practised in secrecy. The Asante people for example detested suicide and the practice of witchcraft. Even *trokosi*, which has hardly ended is still not accepted. At any rate, part of the colonial engagement with the people of Ghana was the abolition of some of these practices.

In all this, both the camps of those seeking to promote heteronormativity as cherished Ghana culture and those who seek to promote minority queer sexualities think education is critical in cultural change. While the two appeal to the schools as a force for change, we cannot readily assume that the two intend the classroom to be used for the same purpose. For example, the Coalition intends to use the classroom to protect traditional values and customs undergirding heteronormativity. Contrarily, the academics and civil society groups intend to use the classroom to promote major cultural and moral revolutions that allow for the acceptance of queer sexualities as normal social practice.

For the differences in which the two groups intend to use the classroom, the issue of decolonisation comes to the fore. As I indicate in the course of this book, the decolonisation agenda has largely found expression in Gender Studies in Ghana. Perhaps, provincialising Gender Studies as the domain of decolonising academia is because of

---

26 E.E. Evans-Pritchard, *Witchcraft, oracles, and magic among the Azande* (Oxford: Clarendon Press, 1937).

27 G.K. Nukunya, *Tradition and change in Ghana: An introduction to Sociology* (Accra: Ghana Universities Press, 1992).

28 Opoku Onyinah, *Pentecostal exorcism: Witchcraft and demonology in Ghana* (Blandford Forum: Deo Publishing, 2012).

the tensions around gender and family. The question, for me, is about the extent to which Ghanaian family values, which tend to structure unequal roles between males and females, will be allowed in Gender Studies.

Methodology and conceptual framework

Dealing with such a sensitive and polarising matter is, needless to say, difficult. People are not just social beings, but they also acknowledge their sexualities as part of who they are. Sexuality is therefore, part of identity. By implication, commenting or writing about such a subject can expose one to the multidimensionality of social exclusion and inclusion, depending on which side of the two camps one leans most. Even so, one can hardly assume a position of neutrality – not least in the social sciences. Thus, I agree with Berger and Berger that "The social sciences, whatever their uses, cannot produce judgements of value" (1983: viii). My own values as an Evangelical Christian, Akan male and a believer in the heterosexual family inform my analysis. Concurrently, while I remain tolerant of diversities of knowledge about the subject, I definitely have a position. Indeed, my position may not, of course, and rightly so, be shared by several people, including those within my social bracket. Nevertheless, I have a position that I must say is deeply partisan. At the same time, I strive to remain as academic as I avoid taking extreme positions.

I will soon express my philosophical position but suffice it here to mention my research approach. The data for this book is not strictly based on ethnographic research, involving intentional interviews with any of the contending parties or members of the LGBTQ+ community. Instead, it is primarily my reflection of extant materials, including online newspaper reports, on the subject. As the discussion also centres on Gender Studies, I draw from the experiences of highly accomplished Ghanaian women, who were pioneers in their respective fields of expertise, as part of making sense of the trajectories of women's experiences in the country. So, similar, but not the same as intellectual history, I discuss an extensive review of the theories underpinning Gender Studies, merging with other disciplines, in Ghana. Admittedly, this may appear boring to experts in the field, but at least, I do believe that, given that my book is meant for both academic and popular discussion, the public will benefit from such an adventure.

I must also mention that given the debates around LGBTQ+ in Ghana are discernible that the issues integrate with nearly every aspect of public life. For example, both the Coalition that drafted the Bill and those seeking to protect minority rites see LGBTQ+ as a micro-issue to discuss broader issues. Thus, both camps rope in chieftaincy, religion and politics, colonialism and culture, local and geopolitics, "tradition" and "modernity" and the role of families and educational institutions in advancing their arguments. Unmistakably, therefore, the subject is not just about LGBTQ+, but also about nearly everything that concerns Ghanaians. This is precisely because, as I have said, the LGBTQ+ community is not just asking for legal rights, they are also appealing for social rights, which would routinise their identity as a composite in the country. Since identity is, indeed, a composite that entwines with the history, social, religious, political and economic lives of a people, my book is similarly contextual in engaging the subject. More importantly, the nature of the Akan and other indigenous cultures is such that they are kin-dominated societies or multiplex societies where economics, politics and religion are all merged to define the identities and roles of an individual (Barton 1983).[29] The chief is, therefore, the principal officer, representing the ancestors, in ensuring that the custom of the Akan is kept. The interface between chiefs and the ancestors is also because the custom of the Akan is highly influenced by their morals and religious beliefs (Ocran, 2006). Any appeal to law or legal instruments would prove very difficult to overturn any particular cultural practice of the Akan. This is precisely because, as Ocran observed, "The core tenets of African customary law are its emphasis on collective responsibility, respect for the elderly, collective rights, and respect for long-established institutions" (Ocran, 2006: 468).[30] Also, the appeal to the chiefs, religious authorities is as a result of the customary law remaining one of the major sources of Ghana's democratic constitution. The current 1992 Constitution of Ghana defines customary law as "rules of law, which by custom are applicable to particular communities in Ghana."[31]

Concurrently, my book takes up the LGBTQ+ issue as an entry point to discussing how every single opposition emanating from the Ghanaian religious public is imbued with layers of complex socio-political and historical issues that complicate the debates. My analysis of the subject, therefore, involves several detours – which is also deliberate for me to bring issues together for the public who may hardly

[29] Barton, J.H; Gibbs, J.L.; Li, H.V., & Merryman, H.J. (1983). *Law in radically different cultures* (American Casebook series). St. Paul, Minneapolis: West Publishing.

[30] Ocran, J.M. (2006), 'The clash of legal cultures: The treatment of indigenous law in colonial post-colonial Africa.' Akron Law Review, 39(2): 465-481.

[31] 1992 Constitution of Ghana (Accra: Asempa Publishers, 1993), p. 10.

have the benefit of doing further research on untouched, but the cognate aspect of the subject of LGBTQ+ debate.

In all this, I centre the discussion on the need for decolonisation. I incorporate decolonisation because, as I shall indicate in the book, both camps of the debate accuse the other of imposing either western homophobic or western sexual liberation on Ghanaians. For this reason, as much as my reading allows me, more recently since the publication of Feminist Africa, the discussion on same-sex sexualities has also been about repudiating legacies of colonialism in academia. As an African Studies student or more appropriately early academic in the field, I have had the benefit of reading extensively on the issues of decolonisation of the universities in Ghana and Africa. With my background, therefore, I enter into an area that may be considered unacademic – Christocentric perspective as part of the decolonisation of higher education in Ghana. I take this position and advocate the incorporation of a Christocentric perspective into the subject because, having read the various perspectives of several African and non-African scholars on decolonising the university or institution of higher learning in Africa, my preliminary conclusion is that worldview is at the centre of it. My understanding is that everyone has a worldview that informs "why" and "how" they engage the subject. Indeed, whether we are conscious about it or not, what we *believe* complexly shapes how we *live*. Individuals may combine multiple, sometimes seemingly contradictory worldviews in making sense of life, but that in itself is deeply part of the social construction of human beings as both incomplete and in search of conviviality (see: Nyamnjoh: 2006, 2018).

Following the above, my ideas are informed by several interdisciplinary perspectives, but I privilege my Christian faith as foundational and Akan identity as secondary. Again, my ability to combine the two may be unique to me, which also means that I do not expect my approach to be accepted by all – at the risk of repetition, not even among Akan male Christians. Nevertheless, with such a stance, I maintain that the LGBTQ+ issue should be left to families; the state should not be involved through legislation to determine human beings, whose relationality is anchored more on sociality than legality. In sum, I argue that, since the family is both anterior to religion (as in institutionalised religion) and the state (as a social contract), families should be allowed to determine how they deal with queer sexualities they have. Given that marriage is prior to the state, in particular, the Ghanaians, both Muslims and Christians, have often rejected any attempt by the state to alter the indigenous understanding of marriage. For example, Ghanaians, through the Parliament, rejected the Marriage, Divorce, and Inheritance Bill of 1961 that proposed to make monogamy the only form of legal marriage (Ardayfio-Schandorf 2006: 137).[32] It was defeated in parliament even after it had gone through repeated reviews. Often Ghanaians accepted family-related laws that rather reinforced indigenous family structures. This explained why in 1963, both the Administrative of Estate Bill and in 1965 (amended in 1971 and 1977), the Maintenance of Children Act were both passed in parliament (Ardayfio-Schandorf 2006: 137). That the family comes before the state partly explained the Muslim rejection of the colonial imposition of aspect of Islamic family law, known as the Muhammadans Ordinance, 1907 on Muslims in the Northern Territories during the late colonial era was rejected (Anderson 1955: 249).[33] The public, though hardly neutral, should not be saturated with queer sexuality politics, as it may polarise society. The state should also not venture into the domain of issues that are, intensely personal to families. Instead, the state should play the role of an umpire, ensuring that the rights of minority groups are protected – they are not denied access to education, work, and movements, as rightly established, first in Ghana's constitution and second, reaffirmed in international conventions.

At the risk of repeating myself, the state will run into challenges if, for any reason and despite the activism against same-sex union, it decides to legalise queer sexualities. This is because the subject, as I have said is composite, will cascade into nearly every aspect of Ghana's public life – a situation that will split families, friends, killing conviviality and social cohesion to build a nation. Not only internally, but the tensions that will emerge from the state's efforts at legislating same-sex unions will fracture Ghana's international relations with the western world. Since the world needs cohesion to deal with globally shared challenges such as climate change, health crisis (the current pandemic) and threats of nuclear and biological wars, I think it will be prudent for the Ghanaian state and the world to resist anything that would undermine global collaboration to solve global issues.

---

32 Elizabeth Ardayfio-Schandorf, "The family in Ghana: Past and present perspectives" in Yaw Oheneba-Sakyi and Baffour K. Takyi (eds), *African families at the turn of the 21st Century*, 129-152 (Connecticut: Praeger, 2006).

33 J.N.D. Anderson, *Islamic law in Africa* (London: Routledge, 1955).

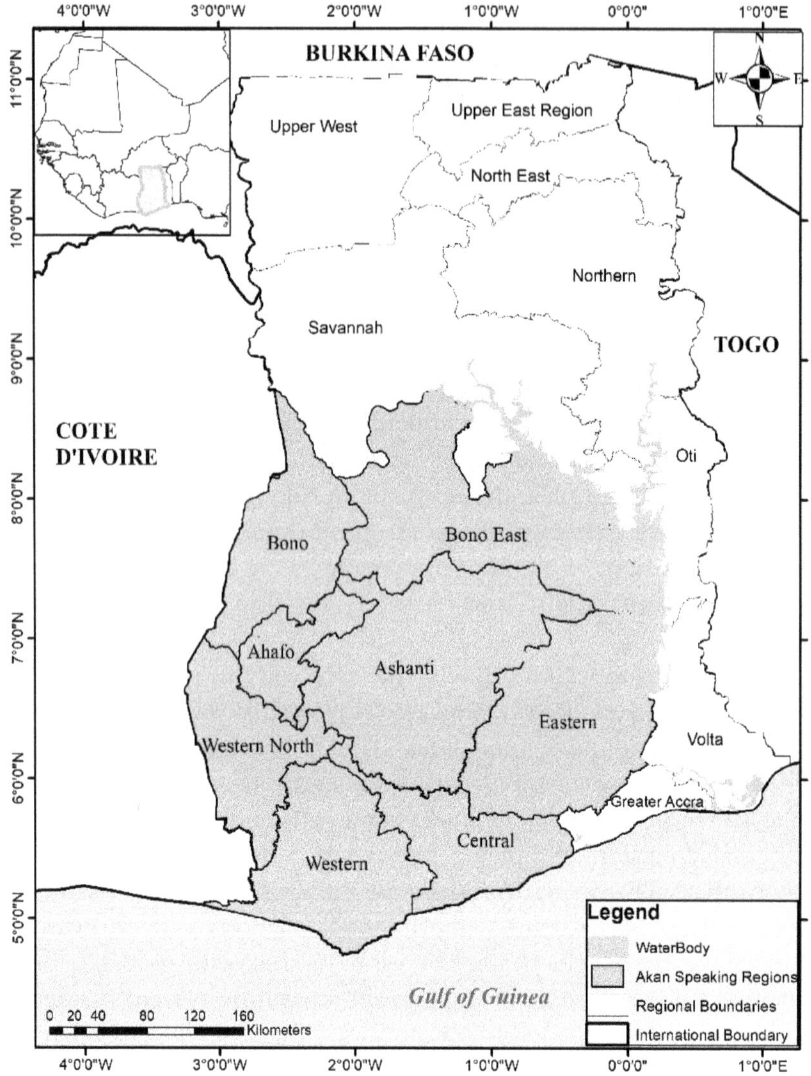

Map: Showing the major Akan-speaking Regions in Ghana (produced by Selorm Awiah Dzantor at the University of Cape Coast – UCC, Cape Coast)

Chapter 1

Personal foray into the homosexual discourse

If you kill Ananse (spider), the world will collapse (Akan idiom).

A woman does not throw away the fruit of her womb to replace it with leaves (Akan Proverb).

A child craves his or her father's womb after he or she has failed to secure the womb of his or her mother (Akan Proverb).[1]

My joy is that one day when I die; I will have someone to throw water on me before burial (My father – Anthony Prempeh)

To the woman, God said, "I will intensify your labour pains; you will bear children with pain. Your desire will be for your husband, yet he will rule over you" (Genesis 3:16).[2] Indeed. The reality is in fact that the rule of husbands are impossible in precolonial matrilineal societies. The prompted colonialists to get to work undermining matriliny and imposing patriliny. So, the domination of husbands is alien to matriliny.

Preamble

Healing a fractured world

Since the turn of the millennium, the homosexual debate has gained much more public attention than anything else in Ghana's socio-cultural history. The reasons are not far-fetched. The economic challenges of the country since the 1980s and the consequences of

[1] This proverb emphasises the centrality of matriliny, uterine connection without discounting the centrality of fathers and paternity. As I discuss later in the Chapter, among the Akan phallic culture is very important as men's fertility, phallic competence and performance of social responsibilities are the epicentres of family organisation.

[2] While colonialism is often blamed for the supposed erosion of women's autonomy, among the Akan and several Ghanaian ethnic groups, men have assumed enormous control over their household, which included his wife (wives), children, and other relations or tenants (See: Akosua Adomako Ampofo, Michael P.K. Okyerefo and Michael Pervarah, "Phallic competence: Fatherhood and the making of men in Ghana" *Culture, Society & Masculinity*, 1, 1 (2009) – 59-78, p. 64.

western imposition of neoliberal regime opened up Ghana to the international community to infiltrate the country with its sexual liberalisation ethics. The economic liberalisation had a widespread effect including media freedom. Similarly, the western sponsorship of Ghanaian/African scholars to study abroad deepened cultural imperialism as the majority of these students returned as cultural elites.

Since the beginning of the millennium, therefore, several NGOs with international connections and feminist groups registered their presence in the country. The international financial institutions' dislocation of funding from the state to the western trans-national NGOs weakened political development in the country. Given these factors, the state had become very susceptible to western cultural wars – as both reformed Islam and evangelical Christians confront the agenda of western-trained cultural elites to impose the decriminalisation of Lesbian, Gay, Bisexual, Transgender, Queer (LGBTQ+) on Ghana. Concomitantly, but also expectedly, research on the subject has increased exponentially – majority of which support the decriminalisation of the subject. That aid and research funds are largely attached to pro-LGBTQ+ scholarship, as well as subtle and sometimes open hostility against academics who write against the subject, has sustained cancel culture.

This book is, therefore, my contribution to the subject, pushing for the state (Ghana) to sustain the criminalisation of the public acceptance of the practice. I agree with Berger and Berger that "the social sciences, whatever their uses, cannot produce judgements of value" (1983: viii). My own values as an Evangelical Christian, Akan male, and a believer in the heterosexual family informs my analysis. While I remain open to other views and do not also claim my views may be shared by people who share my social attributes, this book is deeply not neutral, much as it is academic. Given this brief methodological preamble, my argument is that no civilisation can survive for long with LGBTQ+ practices. No amount of de-stigmatising of LGBTQ practices would survive a moral world that is inhabited by moral beings, under the watch of an uncreated Triune Creator who ultimately set moral standards around everything, including sexuality. In his recent publication on decolonising African studies, Toyin Falola admitted that even countries like South Africa that have decriminalised LGBTQ+ rights have not overcome the moral stigmatisation of people within that social range (Falola 2022). Similarly, the controversies and perceived marginalisation of the rights of Christians who stand against performing services for or commentating against the LGBTQ+ are treated as indication of not just digital dictatorship, but the pernicious effect of normalising individual private idiosyncrasies and universalising them as human rights.[3] Similarly, in some parts of the world, including Ghana, there are reports about flogging of persons suspected of identifying with the LGBTQ community.[4] But in all of this, I similarly hold the position that the ontological dignity of members of the LGBTQ+ community should be protected against all forms of discrimination and victimisation. If it is the practice of non-heterosexual sexual practices that are to be abhorred, the inherent worth of persons in the LGBTQ community should be protected. For this reason, I support the Promotion of Human Sexual Rights and Ghanaian Family Values Bill that is currently under consideration by Ghana's Parliament. The Bill, obviously, needs to be given thorough consideration to ensure that it essentially protects the rights of minority groups, as well as the future of the family for procreation. In other words, we cannot with certainty say that allowing men attracted to or have sex with other men to have their relationships without fear or fervour will necessarily prevent procreation. Surely, many men who have sex with men desire and do have children with women or use technology do achieve these aims! But my personal position is that the state should allow families to determine how they procreate.

To foreground my argument in both the corridors of academia and public circuits of conversation, I employ the strength of transdisciplinary constitutive analyses. Thus, as a scholar in African Studies with two years postgraduate course work in Interdisciplinary Social Studies from the Makerere Institute of Social Research (MISR), Makerere University, I migrate across disciplines, by integrating history, sociocultural studies, politics, gender, philosophy and the art of an amateur theologian, but an evangelical Christian to argue against the public acceptance of homosexual practice. In other words, I argue

---

[3] Colleen Slevin (March 24, 2021), "Christian baker sued again for refusing to bake a cake," https://www.christianitytoday.com/news/2021/march/colorado-christian-baker-jack-phillips-sued-lgbt-cake-court.html; Ken Chitwood (January 3, 2022), "Finnish Bishop and politician face trial for LGBT statements," https://www.christianitytoday.com/news/2022/january/finland-lgbt-trial-pohjola-rasanen-elmdf.html.

[4] Solace Brothers Foundation, "Human rights violations against Lesbian, Gay, Bisexual, and Transgender (LGBT) People in Ghana: A shadow report," submitted for consideration at the 117th session of the Human Rights Committee Geneva, June-July 2016, https://tbinternet.ohchr.org/Treaties/CCPR/Shared%20Documents/GHA/INT_CCPR_CSS_GHA_24149_E.pdf.

against the fact that sociogenically, homosexuality has always been foreign to Ghanaians and Africans. While I have read the biological arguments for and against the practice, I do not consider myself competent enough to cause any stir in that area – I leave that to the experts.

I hope that my modest contribution provides an alternative Ghanaian academic voice to the saturation of the public universities with liberal and counterproductive theories that undermine Nkrumah's call for the "gown to come to town" in epistemic production. I also hope to speak for my non-western trained mother and members of her constituency whose labour and sweat fund the public universities and yet do not have their views represented.

The book is therefore to both celebrate heterosexual marriage as a divine-cultural mandate and an ontological reality to support (pro) creation and also decolonise our universities from the dominance western-minted theories.[5] By so doing, I hope to contribute to recuperating and redeeming the university as a city for universal knowledge where every evidence is subject to empirical, rational and theological test to prove their cogency and profitability for human flourishing. Currently, the muting of voices that speak against LGBTQ+ practices is undemocratic and unbecoming of the modern university that prides itself as founded on *re*-research. I stand with religion and heterosexual marriages because they are anterior to the state and cannot be part of state needless control. The state does not grant people the right to marry heterosexually, the state guarantees it. Similarly, the state does not grant people the right to worship, but it guarantees it.

The existence of the two institutions is part of the ontological and aetiological existence of creation. They are never part of human cultural creations and cannot be deconstructed without the dangers of putting human civilisation on the false precipice of collapse. Likewise, because heterosexual marriage and religious affirmation of life predate the state as universal God-given human heritage, it beats any stretch of imagination to assume that Africa's discontent with homosexual practices is a foreign import. Relatedly, while it does not make sense to

[5] For the past three years, I have observed that in a postgraduate course on Theories of Social Sciences, students at the University of Ghana have reading list that privileges only western theories. There is hardly any reference to the works of formidable Gold Coasters, such ss J.M. Sarbah, J.E.A. Casely Hayford, J.B. Danquah, and K.A. Busia, who contributed significantly to the frontiers of knowledge in the social sciences.

claim that homosexuality possibility did not exist in Africa, the practice is foreign to African and all cultures as sociogenic practice. As argued out, that even in South Africa, where the cultic-induced rather a negative take practice of homosexuality is said to have been present with the *Sangoma* (divine healers), the practice as cultic was part of the African accommodation of difference. It could also be rightly argued that as a cultic practice, it helped African societies to accommodate and deal with behavioural oddities or deviance such as barrenness, effeminacy, chronic illness, chronic suffering or marginalisation etc. Once an individual says or is diagnosed as possessed by a powerful "other" being, most African societies perform rituals either to appease or somehow accommodate the being so that it does not hurt its hosts or her relatives.[6]

What is more, the popular and academic appeal to secularism/ secularisation to neutralise the public sphere of all religious values for the impossible triumphant match of homosexual practices is short-sighted. Again, as I shall demonstrate in the course of this book, there is nothing like "secular" to denote the absence of religion. The state is also not neutral; the public is not neutral either, since the idea of social contract did not mean to muffle and privatise people's worldviews and beliefs. Even so, the idea of secularism is based on two faulty assumptions. The first is that some people are religious, while others are not. The second is that the state should rid itself of religion – all morphing into the banality of the idea of a "naked" public sphere (Tweneboah 2020: 12). Indeed, as I take up in the following discussion, secularism is neither the absence of religion nor religion as something private. Instead, secularism in a pluralistic society is more about public governance of religious plurality, as religion can hardly be privatised or kept out of the public – the public is hardly culturally, politically and ideologically neutral.

The confusion around secularism and religion, as I understand is because of the misunderstanding of religion. Concurrently, I argue that religion is not just about beliefs; religion is not even about rituals or belief in God. Religion is largely about the paradigms through which people respond to the existential questions of life: i.e. Why am I here? Where do I go from here? and is there life after death? These questions are central to all human beings, because all human beings are meaning seeking creatures (Armstrong 2008: 1). To answer them, human beings appeal to everything including rationality, myths – all concretised in

[6] This insightful observation was shared with me by the anonymous reviewer, to whom I am very much grateful.

sociogenic activities. So, since everyone seeks meaning for without which life is empty, everyone is religious in one way or the other – the difference is where we strike preponderous emphasis. Aspects of religion could be broadly considered a "cult" as they enable human beings to make sense of what is considered rationally inexplicable. "Cultic" aspects of religion, such as the "mystery" of the Catholic Eucharist is not given a space as a shared public practice or even imposed on the public. Instead, through the "mystery" of the Eucharist, Catholic Christians reinforce their unity and affirm the hope of resurrection that the life and works of Jesus Christ embodies. My point is that, matters that were considered "cultic", once they are translocated from the religious space to the public would definitely divide society.

At the same, beyond the "cultic" aspect of religion, it could hardly be accepted that anyone is without a worldview that inform their understanding of the world. It is, therefore, inconceivable for anyone to think the public sphere will ever be "naked" and/or neutral of values. After all, the ultimate aim of the social contract that gave birth to the state was to manage, manageable sociogenic differences, not to marginalise. This is because the state of nature is poor, nasty, brutish and short (Hobbes 1651: 78). In biblical terms, it is a state where people do as they want, because of the absence of an authority.[7] But since the state of nature is unruly because of human ontological selfishness, rationality alone cannot unite people in the public sphere. It is for this reason that almost every state in the world would have to inscribe sacredness into material objects like flags and currency (Hastings 1997), and imbued constitutions with "sacred inspiration". It is also the reason so-called civil governments often fall back to reinvent primordial religious sources of political legitimacy (Squiers 2018; Rathbone 2000).

This logic deconstructs the idea of secularism in governance; it also betrays the simplistic binary of Donald Ray's theory of divided sovereignty where traditional authorities and civil leaders derive their authorities from different sources (Ray 1996). The same error of conflation is made by Seth Tweneboah, whose book I discuss in the next section. He wrote that, "The precolonial, ethnically homogenised societies derived political sovereignty and legal legitimacy largely from the spiritual forces of nature" (Tweneboah 2020: 11). The precolonial society was far from ethnically homogenous – made up of non-ethnic members who could be politically influential (Perbi 2004). Instead,

[7] Judges 21: 25.

taboos were imposed on a diversified group to create a sense of homogeneity (Wilks 1967). The same, as I shall argue is done in contemporary Ghana with the notion of citizenship. Ghana was never and has never been declared secular – a naked public sphere. Religion has always featured prominently in the country's postcolonial public spheres, since Nkrumah published his highest philosophic treaty of religious synthesisation for governance – *consciencism* in 1964 (Nkrumah 1964).

Engaging Seth Tweneboaha's *Religion, Law and Human Rights in Ghana*

One of the recent academic works that sought to merge politics, religion and human rights issues, including homosexual right in Ghana is Seth Tweneboah's *Religion, law, politics and the state in Africa.* As a monograph from his doctoral thesis, Tweneboah contributes to the uncomfortable entanglements among religion, politics and homosexuality. Nevertheless, the book's major deficiency is the author's failure to conceptualise secularism, religion, and human rights. These are terms that are seamlessly (not complexly) entwined and must definitely be given highfalutin and brain racking exposition to make sense of any argument about LGBTQ+ rights in Ghana (Tweneboah 2020: 10). Because Tweneboah did not explain these terms, but took them for granted, he conflated many falsities into his argument. Particularly, he created binaries between religion and politics, secularism and religion, and homosexuality and human rights (Ibid. 8-9). Regrettably, but expectedly, he concluded with a false notion of a public sphere that must accommodate homosexual practices.

As I take up the issue of secularism in the course of this book, suffice it to say that the genealogy of the word or term "secular" has never been connected to the absence of religion. As I have argued elsewhere in a forthcoming chapter of a book, historically, in western history, particularly England until the second half of the 19th century, the concept was used to designate the transfer of church property, particularly land lay ownership (McLeod 2000: 653). In the middle of the 19th century, the terms "secularism" and "secularists" were introduced into English by freethinkers to avoid the charge of their being "atheists" and "infidels" (Asad 2003: 23). Also, because Tweneboah, a scholar of religions, implicitly assumed religion has a simplistic definition and cultic-focus, he conjectured that the homosexual debate is a tension between religious and non-religious people – blaming Pentecostals for retaining the guardrails against LGBTQ+ rights in Ghana. Since I have explained this trite understanding of religion above, I will leave it here and take it up later in the book.

Otherwise, the author followed the complex argument of whether homosexual practices are foreign import or African without any nuancing. The existence of something does not make it acceptable. For example, there are several things that exist in the private sphere that people hardly care about until it comes out. If it is private then people do not know about it. But, of course, once it is out in the open then it is open to discussion and critique! The issue, then becomes a matter of how it is discussed without polarising society. It is also about how morality could be protected as part of individuals subordinating their personal interest for communal good. This is especially the case when what is "cultic" is legislated as public practice. When it is not even imposed on everyone, because of the composite nature of human beings, an aspect of life may interconnect with others. This is precisely because as social beings, any legislative instrument will similarly have a cascading effect into other social aspects of life. Nevertheless, the LGBTQ issue has become an important subject of discussion in higher institutions of learning since the 1970s. My concern is that since what hitherto was a private disposition has become part of public identity and ideology, there is a need for liberal academic institution to embrace diversity of opinions without seeking to mute other voices. Similarly, the downplaying of historical cultural condemnation of homosexual activity tends to narrow the gateways of publishing to largely liberal scholars in favour of LGBTQ – this is my personal experience. Instead of recapitulating the above tiring debate, he should have situated the discussion in the logic of sociogenic practices. As I have said, in all societies, whatever reinforces human flourishing is mainstreamed in public activities, including folklore. There is hardly any evidence that homosexual practice as a sociogenic practice ever existed in Africa. I will be returning to this, as I engage on a review of extant literature on the subject. For this reason, it is regrettable that Tweneboah repeated the idea of *ɔbaa bɛrima* (i.e., *female-male*) as representing gay. The issue is even more troubling, given that he did not engaged with Akan teknonyms.[8] Among the Akan and several ethnic groups, teknonyms are employed to describe, not to prescribe, seeming contradiction. Males are expected and encouraged to demonstrate characters such as

[8] Tweneboah, *Religion*, p. 124.

virility, strength, authority, power and leadership qualities, the ability to offer protection and sustenance, intelligence and wisdom, and the ability to bear physical and emotional pain (Boateng, Adomako-Ampofo, Flanagan and Yakah 70).[9] So, males with feminine features, are, indeed, male, but with feminine features. There are several of such people that I have interacted with, including those I have taught. In Maamobi, the Hausa call people with teknonyms like, "Maikafa" (to wit: "Seller/owner of kafa – a type of food).[10] Does that make the woman "kafa"? In my estimation, if Tweneboah had provided any shred of evidence to show that such teknonyms implied homosexual practice, at least, his work would have contributed significantly to the contentious issues between religion and human rights. Well, Tweneboah argued that he did not find any material evidence of a prosecuted homosexual (Tweneboah 2020: 122). But why would you want to "search through the eyes of the dead to find flies?"

Tweneboah also creates binaries to further confuse and conflate the purpose of his book project. First, he assumed that there is a separation between customary/religious norms and state/public laws. He, therefore writes that for customary and religious laws, "They are to apply in relation to private law, family and domestic relations. In case of conflict of law, the new nation-state allows choice of law rule to apply" (Tweneboah 2020: 8). Here, too, it is clear that because the author failed to conceptualise "secularism", the state, and religion, he created non-existing binary to make an argument. Well, I imagine he is tacitly discussing the perceived tension between law and morality. I presume for the author because, by assuming that the family laws are private and the others are public, I imagine, he is looking at the governance of the state and family as discrete realms. If my assumption is right, the author is right in making a distinction, precisely because as I have said the family is anterior to the state. Also, religion in relation to the state has an a priori existence. To explore the relationship between morality and law, I acknowledge and find useful the various definitions of marriage that Anthropologists offer – I will discuss them in the course of this book. But given my own stance on marriage,

---

[9] John K. Boateng, Akosua Adomako-Ampofo, Connie C. Flanagan and Jemima Yakah, "Gender socialization of pre-teen youths in Ghana: Alternative approaches for extension," Paper presented at 22nd Annual Conference of the Association of International Agricultural & Extension Education (AIAEE) at Clearwater Beach, Florida, 2006: 70-78.

[10] Charles Prempeh, '"Food before pressure": Food and food cultures in Muslim inner-city in Maamobi-Accra since the 1980s,' (accepted in *African Journal of Social Sciences* Education – In press).

informed by my understanding of Christianity, I will argue that the family is based on covenant, largely informed by blood and different forms of consanguineal relations with ***love*** as the guardrails of relationships. The state is rather based on social contract with law as the guardrail of interpersonal relationships. The family, like religion, seeks to unite, through the mediation of love and empathy/economic of affection. The state seeks to manage difference, through laws and contract. Relationships in the family/religion is unconditional because "blood (often social constructed among the Akan) is thicker than water". My understanding of the family as both biologically and sociologically constructed surely means that not all family relations are based on blood/biological relatedness!

But there is a direct interlocked relationship, as I discuss in the course of this chapter between the family/religion and the state. In other words, morality and law are closely connected. The family is the basic unit of society; it is there that all the cherished public virtues are practised. It is also the family that provides citizens. Certainly, I subscribe to a largely Judeo-Christian assumption that if morality collapses in the family, the public can hardly be governed with law – giving some credence to the assertion that charity begins at home (Sacks 2021). This is also because morality is hardly rational, which means people must love their own anyways, but the public is based on Max Weber's rational-legal engagement (Weber 2019). It is highly pragmatic. So, without morality, where individuals would be considerate and show affection including forgiving civil offences to non-consanguine members in the public, the public governance would collapse. So, if indeed charity begins at home, and yes, it does, then the home and the public cannot be separate into silos – they are acts in complementarity.

As I reflected elsewhere (Prempeh 2021), there is a longstanding debate over the correlation between law and morality. These debates morphed into what is known in legal studies as the Hart-Fuller debate. Hart argued that laws are no more than what societies formally promulgate. He, therefore, separated morality from law. Fuller, on the other hand, argued that laws must conform to fundamental principles embodied by natural law. Can law and morality be fused as one? Should an individual be governed by the law or morality, or both? Can one have a moral justification to disobey a law? What should govern the life of an individual - law or morality? This debate has tested the minds of legal philosophers for decades (Lacey 2008).[11]

---

[11] Robert Shour, The Hart-Fuller debate, emergence and data mining', (May 2019): 1-13, DOI: 10.13140/RG.2.2.33000.52481,

Nevertheless, the two eminent scholars made considerable statements. Hart observed that, "law may be law but too evil to be obeyed." Fuller also observed that "If law is not fused with morality it 'may become dangerous'" These two statements signify the need to have a balance between law and morality, framed around one's agency (Keown and George 2013).

In resolving the entanglement between law and morality, I summarise Harold J. Berman's conclusion on the two as follows: laws govern external behaviour, morality emphasizes intention; law establishes a correction between rights and obligations, morality prescribes duties which do not bring forth subjective right; law establishes obligations sanctioned by power, morality escapes organized sanctions (Berman 1983).

While the distinction between law and morality could be arid, I argue that the two are the same, but looked at from different perspectives. Morality is believed to hinge on God, whereas (positive) law is based on society's invention. Broadly, the debate is over God – theocentric and man – anthropocentric as the sources of morality and law, respectively. Either way, law and morals are united in the fact that they are informed by beliefs and values. Separating the two is to obfuscate the importance of beliefs and worldviews in shaping the law. In all this, I agree with Mark Greenberg that, "Legal institutions – legislatures, courts, administrative agencies – take actions that change our moral obligations. They do so by changing the morally relevant facts and circumstances" (Greenberg 2014: 1288). So, we cannot create any false and artificial binary between law and morality in the homosexual debate. We must not box the two separately because the public as the sphere of economic and political activities is a sphere of tension and conflict. When people share power and wealth, they lose, so tension is very high in the public sphere; but when people share affection, which is the base of the family, there is tenderness and compassion. So, morality is as much needed in the public sphere to bring about economy of affection, even as law is needed to checkmate the challenge of neopatrimonialism.

Taking on the work of Tweneboah, in order to transpose plurality of law – however that is defined – to imply plurality of moral values, he said: "At the moment no traditional society in Ghana can be said to be culturally and religiously monochrome" (Tweneboah 2020: 14). This statement is flawed on several grounds. First, as I have said, traditional

---

https://www.researchgate.net/publication/332868987_The_Hart-Fuller_Debate_emergence_and_data_mining;.

societies were hardly uniformed culturally and religiously (Owusu-Ansah and Akyeampong 2019). Unfortunately, Tweneboah made this sweeping statement without any example. So, instead of the simplistic statement of "there was monochrome or not", I want to rather say that, like contemporary Ghana, precolonial societies were both. People had the freedom to worship the deities of their choice and decide the type of heterosexual marriages they established – monogamy or polygyny. So, at the interpersonal level, there were several pluralities in cultural choices, which were mediated by private délit.

Between the individual/s and the ɔman/state, there were shared or uniform moral visions. There were also rules that defined ethical and ontological boundaries. This was precisely because at the communal level, the action of one affected everyone else. So, if one murdered someone; incest, cowardice in war, treason, adultery with chief's wife, words of abuse against the chief, stole from the shrine or raped someone in the bush, such actions constituted public délit that were communally denounced and punished (Busia 1962; Sarpong 1974: 53-54). We can transpose this to contemporary Ghana, where Tweneboah discusses the absence of homogeneity in the public sphere as the country witnesses inter and intra-religious conflicts, especially between Pentecostals and indigenous authorities and, let me add, among Muslims. But it is obvious that since 2014, the Pentecostals have significantly ironed out their differences with indigenous authorities. For example, the CoP has reconciled its frontiers with chiefs, such that since 2014 the church now allows its members to be elected as chiefs (Prempeh 2021). Similarly, the Muslims have made significant progress in uniting their ranks (Kobo 2015); though Yunus Dumbe thinks there are a few undercurrent tensions over orthodoxy (Dumbe 2019). But it is also true that since the outbreak of the current coronavirus pandemic in Ghana in March 2020, the Muslims have united their ranks in an unprecedented way (Prempeh 2021). Also, early in 2022, the Ga paramount chief opened up his palace for an evangelical Christian group, the Full Gospel Business Men Fellowship International that has been operating in Ghana since the 1950s to possibly establish a branch there.

There may still be some differences and low-intensity tensions as the country recently witnessed with the cases of the Rastafarian students whose admission to Achimota was withheld by the school, because of their locked hair. There was also the case of a female Muslim student at the Wesley Girls Senior High School who claimed that she was not allowed to fast in the month of Ramadan. Incidentally, while Muslims,

Rastafarians, and Christians were at each other's throat over the two issues, the three groups had to give up their ranks to speak against the rising tide in gay advocacy. So, whereas the various religious groups may always demonstrate internal fragmentation, the groups, once they stick to their shared non-created divine-cultural mandate, will constitute a formidable bulwark against homosexual practices – often considered a threat to human civilisation. Finally, Tweneboah talked about the increasing rise in child witchcraft accusations and maltreatments.[12] But again, the various religious groups unanimously condemn all forms of witchcraft accusation. Opoku Onyinah, one of the towering figures of Pentecostal Christianity, dedicated his doctoral thesis, submitted to the University of Birmingham – supervised by Allan Anderson, to deconstructing the mystification of the practice. From the basis of scholarship and practice, Onyinah has been very influential in curating the frontiers of Pentecostal pneumatological practices away from what I prefer to call "witchcraft mentality" among Pentecostals, especially the so-called "one-man churches". Within the Church of Pentecost, a church Onyinah led as its chairman, undertook revolutionary reforms in 2010, and the Christian community in general in Ghana, he has succeeded in reshaping Pentecostal theology and praxis away from the extremities of witchcraft accusations.[13]

Engaging the counterpoints of LGBTQ+ Bill in Ghana

I have been writing journalistic articles about homosexuality since I completed my Master of Philosophy in African Studies in 2011 when the issue became more topical. It was at the time when David Cameron, former Prime Minister of the United Kingdom, had had the courage and temerity to threaten Ghanaians with cultural imperialism tied to aid

[12] Charles Prempeh, The man Professor Francis Nyamnjoh: An academic mentee augmenting his mentor over witchcraft in light of incompleteness and conviviality (Accepted book Chapter in a book project in honour of Professor Francis Nyamnjoh – In press).

[13] As part of deconstructing excessive emphasis some Pentecostals place on demonological practices, which he referred as witchdemonology, Onyinah has led several transnational conferences to both create awareness among Pentecostals and Christians about the damaging effective of witchcraft mentality. On October 1, 2022, he led an online conference on, "How are we dealing with contemporary spiritual warfare within Christianity in Africa today and the West yesterday? Before then, on November 20, 2021, he led a conference discussion titled: "Are there more demons in Africa than the Euro-American West today? Pastoral responses to the widespread deliverance ministry in African Christianity – origin(s), impact, prognosis and solution".

and decriminalisation of homosexual practices. But my academic interest in the subject peaked when I arrived in Cambridge towards the end of 2017 as a doctoral student.

Just about three months after I had arrived in Cambridge in January 2018, a group of white students were engaged in a hearty discussion on homosexuality and several other cognate theories. Having been drawn to the conversation by my own curiosity, the white students were quite surprised when I motioned to make a point. All my efforts at gaining their attention yielded no results. I decided not to cave in, so I continued to listen to the conversation until one of them for whatever reasons motioned at me to contribute to the discussion. I ended up speaking for about an hour uninterrupted – straddling theories, cultures, and politics around the subject of homosexuality. Since that incident, these students often made something like an obeisance when we met.

Long before I began my doctoral studies at the University of Cambridge, I had written about the subject of homosexuality, first in the Graduate Student magazine of the University of Ghana in 2011 and later on social media news portals, including *Ghanaweb* and *Moderngħana.* But my scholarly contribution to the subject came only in March 2021, when I responded to a call for a chapter of a book project on *Africa in Fact, Issue No 58*, on the Biden Administration from African Centre for the Study of the United States (ACSUS) via the email list of the Social Science Research Council. Based at the University of Witwatersrand in Johannesburg, South Africa, ACSUS was established in March 2018 to address the imbalance in the knowledge flow between the US and Africa. Since its establishment, it has served as a hub for Africa-generated knowledge and nuanced understanding of the US as a nation and society.[14]

With my own philosophical position as an African Studies student/early academic, I seek to merge the advancement of knowledge from both Afrocentric and Christo-centric perspectives. My position is informed by the fact that issues about sexuality are not just about neutrality nor just a matter of rationality, as it is about worldview. It is certainly a clash of worldview: a worldview that believes in individual expressionism, morality as feelings and subjective, self-expression as "coming out", on the one side, and a worldview that believes in morality as absolute and sublation of personal interest to the communal good. As a Christian, Akan and an early academic, my perspective is the

[14] https://africa-usforum.africa/.

latter, informed by my Christian faith, which enjoins me to seek the good of the other more than myself. In other words, by arguing from the Afrocentric and Christocentric perspective, I look at queer sexuality as deeply personal that has hardly been accommodated in the Akan public sphere; it is also a practice that is not accepted by any Christian group in Ghana. Put together, my foray into the LGBTQ debate is informed by a need for society to separate personal sexual preferences from the public sphere. It is very unthinkable and quite inane for me to see an individual who is either "he" or "she" and imagine "he" or "she" is "they". With my philosophical positionality, I submitted a draft of my chapter, which received a few comments from the editor, which, inter alia, said:

> I enjoyed reading the well-argued historical and contemporary dynamics linking LGBT debates to democracy and human rights between the west and Africa.

After I did the minor revision, my chapter was published in December 2021. Before then, on March 19, 2021, the ACSUS invited me to participate in a conversation on the subject that was published online.[15] On the whole, my chapter has been well received in the academic circle. For example, one review commented on it as follows:

> **Charles Prempeh**'s argument for African agency and human rights is based on an uncommon but equally vital issue. Of course, homosexuality is a sensitive issue in many African nations, with many people framing it as illegal. This chapter was very intriguing to read since the thesis was based on decoupling financial aid from the promotion of the rights of lesbian, gay, bisexual, transgender, intersex, and queer (LGBTQI+) individuals in the context of establishing US-Africa relations.

Considering this, the author argued that the West must allow Africa's sexual ethics to progress, as both the West and Africans tactically disincentivize the abuse of homosexuals. Furthermore, the author dispels the Democratic Party of the US precondition of normalizing homosexuality as a criterion for aid, arguing that this will just deprive the continent of much-needed financial support. This prompts the dilemma of whether the accomplishment and or preservation of other people's human rights are much more vital than

---

[15] https://africa-usforum.africa/african-policy-towards-the-us/.

others, particularly when framing the discussion around the urgent need for African peace and security within the auspices of Afrocentric agency.[16]

The time I wrote my academic draft on the homosexual issue coincided with a crossfire engagement on the homosexual issue in Ghana. A group of foreign diplomats and Ghanaian pro-LGBTQ+ academics and civil society groups pressuring the Ghanaian government to decriminalise homosexuality and others. The action of pro-LGBTQ+ had earlier incurred the concerns of an overwhelming number of Ghanaians who, represented by the Coalition for the Proper Human Sexuality, had drafted and sponsored a private Bill to Parliament. The Bill was to ensure that the state protects persons in the LGBTQ+ community and affirm up, clarify and streamline Ghana's legal stance against LGBTQ+ practices – as, in terms of its public practice and endorsement, gay and lesbian practices were absolutely unknown to the Ghanaian public as a sociogenic practice. In a recent article, Odoi argued that Ghanaians' despicable attitude towards homosexual practices is more public than private.[17] Certainly, this confirms my point that if one keeps one's uniquely different practice to oneself, away from the public, people hardly care. The homosexual contestation in Ghana is, therefore, more about public governance and less of private sphere – even though the two are not necessarily mutually exclusive.

A few academics and leaders of foreign-oriented NGOs had written a memo to Parliament seeking to overturn or render null and void, as well as pushing for the decriminalisation of the LGBTQ+ practices in Ghana. Some of these academics had taught me, as a graduate student at the Institute of African Studies (2009-2011) while I also worked as a graduate and teaching assistant (2010 – 2013). I, therefore, felt it was time to contribute to the academic discourse on the subject. As a Christian and an early career academic, I also decided to write to Ghana's Parliament in support of the Promotion of Human Sexual Rights and Ghanaian Family Values Bill.

I submitted my Memoranda to Parliament and through the generosity of one of my former students, other media houses in Ghana, including the Multimedia published it. I personally sent a copy via

---

[16] Zimkhitha Manyana of the University of Johannesburg (March 8, 2022), Book Review: Africa's policy towards the US: The Biden era, https://allafrica.com/stories/202203080797.html (Accessed: June 29, 2022).

[17] A. Odoi, Homophobic violence in Ghana: When and where it counts', Sex Res Soc Policy (2021), https://doi.org/10.1007/s13178-021-00655-x.

WhatsApp to one of the influential journalists at Citi FM on October 6, 2021, I then followed up with a short self-introduction, highlighting the fact that I gave the Heritage Month Lecture for Citi FM in 2019.[18] The journalist responded tersely, "Thanks; 28 pages wow". I wrote a few more words to explain why I write long pieces, but no response except that later the following day, I searched and found the memo published on citinewsonline.com.[19] Upon finding my memo online, I wrote to the journalist wanting to know if he had any questions for me to answer. I asked the question because of three main reasons: First, I realised that the media had demonstrated a clear bias towards the few academics who had written against the Bill that promotes family and proper human sexuality. Certainly, the media has often been in alliance with the cultural elite to push western cultural imperialism (Wasserman 2011). Secondly, the journalist was one of the respected media men who had received extensive recognition from my church, The Church of Pentecost, to speak to its youths. Thirdly, I also thought it was fair that I was allowed to also be heard and respond publicly on air to questions the academics and civil society groups were raising on the audio-visual media.

More tellingly, just around the same time that I requested that I respond to questions related to my memo and other issues raised by the academics, the journalist rather interviewed two academics, one an associate professor of Economics, who had written a 34-page memo in support of the Bill to Parliament, and Professor Akosua Adomako Ampofo who had written a short letter condemning Christians for not reflecting and extending the love of Christ to members of the LGBTQ+ community.[20]

While I never had the chance to speak to the public about my memo, the internet programmed algorithmically to foster digital dictatorship saturated online space with my memo. My memo and the Bill held the

---

[18] Citinews (March 19, 2019), Heritage Month Series: Chieftaincy and religion in Ghana' https://soundcloud.com/citi97-3/heritage-month-series-chieftaincy-and-religion-in-ghana; https://soundcloud.com/citi97-3/heritage-month-series-chieftaincy-and-religion-in-ghana (Accessed: June 28, 2022).

[19] Delali Adogla-Bessa (October 7, 2021), 'African Studies scholar prepares memo backing anti-LGBTQ Bill', https://citinewsroom.com/2021/10/african-studies-scholar-prepares-memo-backing-anti-lgbtq-bill/ (Accessed: June 28, 2022). https://citinewsroom.com/wp-content/uploads/2021/10/MEMORANDUM-TO-PARL-OF-GHANA-OCTOBER-26-2021.pdf.

[20] CitiTube (October 12, 2021), #PointofView: A closer look at the LGBTQ bill in Prof. Adomako and Prof. Charles Ackah', https://www.youtube.com/watch?v=KMlwmhDhPE0 (Accessed: June 28, 2022).

sanctity and ontological value of gay and lesbians. To show that I was not breathing hot and cold against homosexuals and their cognates, I concluded my nearly 16000 words of the memo as follows:

> In the end, we should retain the Promotion of Proper Human Sexual Rights and Ghanaian Family Values Bill, 2021, pass it into law, as we incorporate compassion rather than condemnation, without compromising our Christian-based ontological values on heterosexual relations, in our engagement with homosexuals.

My memo has unsurprisingly received mixed responses. Mr Moses Foh-Amoaning, a prominent lawyer and a key advocate, drafter and supporter of the Bill called to congratulate me on my contribution to promoting the boundaries of sexuality and heterosexual marriage. He added that my memo was submitted as one of his group's key pieces of evidence to Parliament. Unfortunately, the day Mr Foh-Amoaning and his group were presenting their case before Parliament, I had just arrived in Ghana and was on a bus heading to Kumasi from Accra. Nevertheless, a few friends, including those in the United States of America, called to warn me about the consequences of my memo for my academic career. A few of my transnational friends who sympathise with the LGBTQ constituency, promised to read and respond to my memo. Sadly, none has so far responded.

While I have received no intellectual response to my memo, which was not even meant for an academic exercise, the global media presented the pro-heterosexual family and life-affirming Bill as haters. The eighteen academics and civil society groups also referred to the Christian community as haters; while Professor Akosua Adomako Ampofo who said she had been a Christian for about 40 years could not come to terms with Christians' lack of love for LGBTQ+ people. She said she could not see Christ in the Bill.[21] In Adomako's six-page article to the public, appealing to Christian conscience, she asked the question: "Whose morals become the benchmark, and whose becomes the judge? She proceeds to quote Matthew 7:1-3 which reads: "Do not judge, or you too will be judged. For the same way you judge others, you will be judged, and with the same measure you use, it will be measured to you."

---

[21] Akosua Adomako Ampofo (October 10, 2021), 'Why Christians should extend grace and not support anti-LGBTQ+ Bill', https://www.myjoyonline.com/akosua-adomako-ampofo-why-christians-should-extend-grace-and-not-support-anti-lgbtq-bill/ (Accessed: June 29, 2022).

I personally agree with Adomako on the issue of compassion, except that she goes on to page 3 of her article to catalogue moral issues that she finds implicating Christianity for hypocrisy. She writes:

> Over the last several years these issues of hypocrisy have loomed large: so-called Christians have been silent when Christian leaders have sexually abused young women (and men) in the church; many are silent as brazen corruption among political, civic and religious leaders takes place; and as for issues such as women dying in childbirth due to poor access to medical services; the murder of women for being alleged witches; the rape of children; the pollution of our water bodies through poor mining whether by galamsey or large mining concessions; the destruction of our forests; unemployment and frustration of the youth— the silences have been loud. And yet law makers who could have attended to these issues are so passionate about so-called LGBTQIA+ issues that they have become guardians of our morality and in record time they have whipped up a bill so that we can criminalise other human beings for their sexual and gender identities.

More compellingly, Adomako invited us to express God's love for others "in ways that they can feel" as a reason for Christians to reject life-supporting Bill in Parliament.[22] I must argue that the issue of love looms large in discussions that involve moral dilemmas. Lawyer Anthony Akoto Ampaw, leading the pro-LGBTQ+ academics and civil society group called Christians haters who have no sympathy and love for minority groups. The questions that, obviously need to occupy all of us, particularly Christians are: Why can't Christians love LGBTQ+ practices without judgement? Are Christians not violating the call of Christ against passing judgment? These questions are not difficult for liberals, including their theologians, because liberalists want a romantic God who "sees no evil; says no evil and does no evil" – in short, a God who, according to a liberalist Catherine Nixey is "becoming more liberal".[23]

---

[22] Adomako, p. 1.

[23] Catherine Nixey (November 8, 2021), 'The Church of England's God is becoming more liberal', https://www.economist.com/the-world-ahead/2021/11/08/the-church-of-englands-god-is-becoming-more-liberal?utm_source=Albert+Mohler&utm_campaign=bb2fdae09c-EMAIL_CAMPAIGN_2019_04_08_09_12_COPY_01&utm_medium=email&utm_term=0_b041ba0d12-bb2fdae09c-309913377&mc_cid=bb2fdae09c&mc_eid=e3f9b7d0a1 (June 29, 2022).

I am not a theologian, but I have a few reflections to share on love and judgement. But before then, I must say, contrary to the charge of needless hate against Christians and religious people who support the need to protect the family, the Bill does not incriminate the ontological worth of members of the LGBTQ group. The Bill rather seeks to promote Ghanaian families in public life. This is also because in Ghana, as I have said, several of the country's citizens hardly care about what people do in private as families. My observation is that the public is responding to an attempt by some academics and civil society groups to overemphasise the preponderance of same-sex sexual relations in Africa's history as part of normalising the LGBTQ issues. As I have said above, since the issue of homosexuality can hardly be discussed in isolation of culture, governance, freedom, education and even religious practices, making it into the country's enchanted religious space would definitely create tension. The Bill, therefore, seeks legislation against what the anti-LGBTQ-Coalition considers as western efforts at normalising and imposing LGBTQ practices on Ghanaians. For Adomako to have then said that the Bill is hateful and shows a lack of love, she possibly read the proposed Bill from a different perspective – which is fine. But I also think that she may not have read the Bill as highly encompassing in taking into account how the LGBTQ issue morph into every aspect of life. By the way, Adomako and majority of those who support the decriminalisation of homosexual practices have been very consistent with their downward liberal descend since the establishment of the Centre for Gender Studies and Advocacy (Ampofo, Beoku-Betts and Osirim 2008). That level of consistency in theory is similar to the Western world where women's studies have evolved in leaps and bounds to see marriage as oppressive and lesbianism as key both in feminism and homosexual studies (Diggins, 1992; Bunch, 1972). Indeed, the same was the case with the country's Finance Minister, Ken Ofori-Atta, who condemned the Bill even though he said he had not read it.[24] Much as Mr Ofori-Atta's opinion matter in the subject, some analysts assumed the ruling political elites is largely influenced by the fear of losing foreign investments and tourism (Asante and Hanchey 2021: 214).

Certainly, since I was one time a student of this professor, I have no business even daring to write to contradict her. But at the same time, since I find my understanding and memo misrepresented and

---

[24] Paul Adom-Ochere (November 19, 2021), 'LGBTQ Bill: God created us in His own image whether man or woman, so I can't judge – Ken Ofori-Atta', https://www.youtube.com/watch?v=ez76CRwlMRY (Accessed: June 29, 2022).

maligned,[25] I have just a few comments. First, if we are unable to determine whose morality to use as a canon against ethical issues, how does the professor reconcile that position with the moral issues she raised? expect us to all agree and share the issues she raised as absolute truths?

The conflation of judgement/anger and love is critical in this conversation. First, the two are not mutually exclusive to God and to those who follow Him. The Triune of God of the Bible punishes those He loves.[26] There are multiple ways of showing love, including being non-judgmental of people's moral lives. Nevertheless, from my Christian perspective, judgement/anger and love are not contradictory, but complementary precisely because if you love someone, you will be loving enough to hate anything the person does that destroys him or her. My understanding of the Christian faith is that God punishes those He loves, which gives me the impression that if one has the power of judgement, one would use the power constructively to save the person who is loved from self-destruction. Admittedly, my position is not without its challenges, as it could be profiled as narcissistic. It could also undermine the social value of live and let live. For this reason, I do not hold my understanding as axiomatic nor prescriptive. Surely, there must be many ways of experiencing and showing love out there, but my concern is how to choreograph multiple loves from colliding in the public sphere. For example, since the same-sex issue is deeply sociogenic, morphing into and forming worldviews about other aspects of love, my curiosity is also about the kind love would not lead to other colliding love with the enchanted public? Ordinarily, pluralities of love should be tolerated, but the unfortunate reality is that try as Ghanaians have, we have not loved the *un*like. If we admit that the family is built on the social covenant of love, not the social contract of law in constructing the public sphere, then the love for queer sexualities should be limited to the family, as families know how to take care of their own better than anyone else. I may be wrong, but that is what I think!

On this score, I see a sense in what the MP for Ablakuma, Sheila Bartels, said when Nana Aba Anamoah, a journalist, asked her about the nexus between open discussion of LGBTQ and the attempt at institutionalising it. The MP said, "That is why our parents and great

---

[25] https://citinewsroom.com/wp-content/uploads/2021/10/MEMORANDUM-TO-PARL-OF-GHANA-OCTOBER-26-2021.pdf.

[26] Hebrews 12: 5-6.

grandparents decided that we should not talk about it (LGBTQ) because they do not want it."[27] While this may be read as a way of silencing others, it was rather part of the Akan society sustaining commonly shared values through the sublation of individual queer sexualities. The Akan society had a form of a social contract of collective responsibility where individuals were expected to subordinate their idiosyncrasies to the good of everyone (Sarpong 2019).[28]

Again, I also agree with the Coalition to support minority right, though I think they misrepresented the Bill. Otherwise, their assertion that legislating sexuality would collapse the moral sentiment of sympathy for "difference", as it betrays the filial love in families – leading to sister's betraying brothers and vice versa is apt. It is also this reason that what is uniquely a family affair must be kept as such. That there is merit in both the Bill and the petition spring from the fact that protecting the sanctity of the family and the rights of minority group both have their historic roots in Judeo-Christian cultures. Regrettably, consensus building and the zest to keep to one's position has turned the conversation around sexuality into a battle between non-negotiable demands; making compromise nearly impossible. Based on love, it appears the challenge in the LGBTQ debate is how one can tolerate queer sexualities without one encouraging it. For me as a Christian, the issue is also about how to engage the cultural war or sexual revolution by becoming a cultural communicator without becoming a cultural militant.

Even with the push for God's romantic love that is accommodative of homosexual love, foreign observers and analysts still think Ghanaian feminists and their NGOs are not pushing the LGBTQ agenda hard enough (Tucker 2018). More to the point, when on September 2, 2016, she, along with a few other colleagues, mobilised students and academics and petitioned the Members of the University of Ghana Council to remove the statue of Mohandas Karamchand Gandhi from the campus of the University of Ghana,[29] was she demonstrating love,

---

[27] Ghanaweb (July 8, 2022), "Sam George being paid to sustain LGBT issues for eventual acceptance – Sheila Bartels," https://www.ghanaweb.com/GhanaHomePage/NewsArchive/Sam-George-being-paid-to-sustain-LGBT-issues-for-eventual-acceptance-Sheila-Bartels-1577858 (Accessed: September 3, 2022).

[28] Peter Kwasi Sarpong, *From the hut to Oxford: The autobiography of the Most Reverend Peter Kwasi Sarpong, Emeritus Archbishop of Kumasi* (Accra: Sub-Saharan Publishers, 2019).

[29] September 2, 2016, #GandhiMustComeDown Movement, 'Gandhi's statue at the University of Ghana must come down' https://www.change.org/p/the-

hate or constructive love or both? Was Gandhi incorrigibly racist or was he a historic figure who reflected his time? In concluding his question on whether Gandhi was a racist or not, Vijay Chauhan wrote as follows:

> Gandhi's political pedagogy was to show humanity that it is possible to bring people together across the differences of race, caste and creed. Such concepts like swaraj, swadeshi and satyagraha can never be attained if the society is not founded on self-respect and respect for all different communities, language groups, regions, and religions.[30]

The position of those who fought against Gandhi and also the furore of collapsing statues after Derrick grotesque murder of African-American, George Floyd pointed to people's philosophy of history. As part of the "post" theories, people treat the past as if they are removed from it. Through the kind courtesy of existentialist and post-modernist and post-structuralists, including Jean-Paul Sartre and Michel Foucault, the past is nothing, but oppressive. So, transplanting and translocating this logic to the past, it was easier for those calling Christians unforgiving to exhume the dead remains of Gandhi for eternal damnation. They had to call for the total erasure and dismantling of any traces of Gandhi, because, for being "racist", he was more a sinner than everyone else. Gandhi, though lived before the cancel culture age, he had to suffer its pernicious effect, all the same. In my own reflections on the pulling down of statues, condensed in a journalistic article, I argue that,

> We should not shy away from our problematic past by sanitizing it. We must face the past and possibly reinterpret it to make sense of the present and surge on into the future. We should also not pretend we have a different narrative to leave posterity. Obliterating the past will only blindfold us to the evil we often commit.[31]

---

members-of-the-university-of-ghana-council-gandhi-s-statue-at-the-university-of-ghana-must-come-down (Accessed: June 29, 2022).

[30] Vijay Chauhan, 'Was Mahtama Gandhi a racist?' *Purva Mimaansa*, 10, 1-2 (2019): 65-70 (p. 69).

[31] Charles Prempeh (July 30, 2020), 'What do we do with statues? Confronting our ugly past', https://citinewsroom.com/2020/07/charles-prempeh-writes-what-do-we-do-with-statues-confronting-our-ugly-past/ (Accessed: June 29, 2022).

By the way, analysing the impact of the implications of the Gandhi statue controversies for Ghana-India relationship, Jewel Okraku Mantey, whose Master of Arts thesis was supervised by Professor Appiagyei-Atua, a signatory to the anti-Gandhi statue, concluded, *inter alia*, that:

> The reality is also that Ghana-India relationship is very crucial and strategic for both countries but more crucial for Ghana. It is an undeniable fact that India's economic investment in Ghana is critical for the strength of the Ghanaian economy and so caution must be taken not to derail or jettison the harmonious relationship Ghana has forged with India over decades. The incumbent New Patriotic Party (NPP) led administration has ambitious plans of strengthening the private sector and embarking on plans of industrialization in the programme known as "one district, one factory" and in this development agenda all potential foreign investors including the significant one from India remain imperative. Therefore, in as much as this work makes the first recommendation, the government must strike a balance and not throw the baby away with the bathe water, for as the popular Akan adage goes if your child drowns in a river it does not mean you cease to drink water in your thirst (Mantey 2018: 44).

It may be complex in establishing any direct nexus between saying Gandhi was a racist and marred Ghana-Indian relations. Nevertheless, since pulling down a statue is read as potentially disruptive of international relations, the point I seek to highlight is that the peculiar love we hold dear may contradict in the public square of pluralities.

One could clearly see this mutually inclusive nexus between love and judgement (punishment) right on the first paragraph and page of the "Promotion of Proper Human Sexual Rights and Ghanaian Family Values Bill, 2021".

The object of the Bill is to provide for proper human sexual rights and Ghanaian family values; proscribe LGBTQ+ and related activities; proscribe propaganda of advocacy for or promotion of LGBTTQQIAAP+ and related activities; provide for the protection of and support for children, persons who are victims or accused of LGBTTQQIAAP+ and related activities and other persons; and related matters.

Over the last decades, several scholars have written about the utilitarian value of anger in the fight against injustice (Barnhart 2021; Banks; Stavans 2001). The Bible is similarly not against anger. Jesus was angry and Christians cannot pretend not to be angry. Anger is an emotional exertion against evil. Anger against anything that undermines human flourishing implies our intolerance and unwillingness to give in to life-destructive forces. I believe that scientific inventions are a result of human anger against the world's imperfections. The search for an Artificial Intelligence response to death is part of human anger against the brevity of life on earth and the icy hands of death which remains inevitable – anyways, until Christ returns. Certainly, without anger, we cannot excuse ourselves from being accomplices of life's negating forces.

The condition against anger is that it should be kept within control. Anger should have boundaries with the biblical caution, "Be angry but do not sin."[32] Anger should not extend beyond its limit to the point of destruction. That is why the Bible warns Christians not to sin. In a recent article, I talked about how Muslim youth in Maamobi-Nima, where I have lived since 1984, can apply the Islamic concept of *wasatiyyah*; moderation to encourage Muslim youth to use their anger constructively.[33] So, clearly, it could be seen from the preamble of the Bill that it is an expression of anger against practices that the drafters perceive could destroy the very people who practice it. It is also an attempt to keep human civilisation from collapsing, for civilization would hardly survive without procreation. The simple fact is that economics begin to take a nosedive when consumer demand falls short.

While my intentions, chiming with the Bill, reflect the love for a minority group, those who stand for their convictions tend to suffer cancel culture. The internet revolution and the explosion of social media technology since the 1970s and 1990s, respectively, have deepened cancel culture. The two technological breakthroughs in communication have not encouraged plurality of conversations, but rather sought to impose "group-think" and uniformity of opinion on everyone else. While it is true there is cancel culture; it is equally true that regardless of the rabid form of intolerance on social media, all manner of ideas and arguments co-exist. In fact, one soon realises that sexuality and sexual politics are truly complex human concerns. I may not have been personally attacked for sharing my thoughts, but the liberalists' weaponization of cancel culture against persons who hold

[32] Ephesians 4:26.

[33] Charles Prempeh, 'Re-imagining Wasatiyyah as a socio-theological mediation of youth anger in Accra', *Indonesian Journal of Interdisciplinary Islamic Studies* (IJIIS), 40, 1 (2022): 103-128.

conservative view of marriage as a union between a biological man and a biological woman is simply undeniable.[34]

As the Western world continues to gravitate towards liberalism, including the liberalisation of morality since the 1960s, the morality and sexual preferences of the minority are legislated and protected as human rights. Under this regime of human rights, there is hardly any definition of the "human" and the "right" in the human rights. I consider the direct involvement of the Western world in the homosexual debate, including their tying of aid to sexual liberation as a form of imperialism. My own position is that Ghanaians and Africans should also be allowed time and space to determine their sexual laws. Nevertheless, the rights of persons who belong to the LGBTQ community must be protected from marginalisation (Prempeh, 2021a). As I shall discuss in the course of this chapter, among persons in support of the Family Bill, the issue of rights is confused with what the persons in the community need. For example, Mr Moses Foh-Amoaning said in an interview with Accra-based Joy FM that "what homosexuals need is help, not to translate it to a human rights". Explaining his point, he argued:

> It's not part of our constitution, people were trying to push it but it's not there. In our customary law, there is no ethnic group that permits this sought (sic) of behaviour. Section 4 of our Criminal Offence At makes unnatural canal knowledge as criminal offence. In 2017, this whole issue was placed before the European Court of Human Right and it took about one and half year to investigate everything. At the end, all 47 judges concluded that they are not human right and they also said if there is any country like Ghana which does not permit any such thing, then that country is not in breach of any international law principle in respect of equality or discrimination.[35]

There is also a general fear among the Christian community that when homosexuality is decriminalised it will become a form of

---

[34] Dan Cancian (October 4, 2022), "New Essendon CEO Andrew Thorburn resigns one day after being appointed over links to controversial church that condemns homosexuality and compared abortion to the Holocaust," https://www.dailymail.co.uk/sport/afl/article-11278289/Essendon-CEO-Andrew-Thorburn-resigns-ONE-day-appointed-ties-controversial-church.html (Accessed: October 12, 2022).

[35] Evans Annang (February 22, 2021), "What homosexuals need is help, not human rights – Foh Amoaning," https://www.pulse.com.gh/news/local/what-homosexuals-need-is-help-not-human-rights-foh-amoaning/c4b4l41.

imposing minority rights on everyone, including forcing it on the education system, children's games/cartoons and threatening with imprisonment persons who keep their sanity from supporting homosexual practices.[36] The fact that the advocates of the Family Bill see sexual rights as personal and not public right is also informed by the Akan the proverb said: "If the eye does not see it, it is not repulsive." This means that what is allowed in the sphere must not be counter-cultural, counter-productive and counter-civilisational. For this reason, even rabbis who consider themselves orthodox Jews and practice homosexuality admit that the practice was not allowed in public until recently – even if these rabbis interpret the Jewish Bible to normalise their sexual desires (Greenberg 2004).

Can any civilisation survive without childbirth? Is there any society where homosexuality was celebrated as a sociogenic culture and invited the state to legislate? Even in the Greco-Roman world of cultural perversity, the practice had to be controlled. Imagine how China would have survived the post-Covid-19 world if it had legislated and imposed homosexual practices in the country. How would China have survived as it similarly removes restrictions on the one-child policy to keep its population afloat?[37] On June 20, 2022, a court in Japan which is saddled with aged population and decreased childbirth upheld the country's criminalisation of LGBTQ+ rights. The sitting judge at the Osaka District Court ruled that:

> Freedom of marriage in the 1947 constitution only means male-female unions and does not include those of the same sex … marriage for heterosexual couples is a system established by society to protect a relationship between men and women who bear and raise children.[38]

---

[36] Kaylee Mcghee white (March 20, 2022), 'Of course Disney wants to indoctrinate your children', https://www.washingtonexaminer.com/restoring-america/community-family/of-course-disney-wants-to-indoctrinate-your-children?utm_source=Albert+Mohler&utm_campaign=37724241cd-EMAIL_CAMPAIGN_2019_04_08_09_12_COPY_01&utm_medium=email&utm_term=0_b041ba0d12-37724241cd-309913381&mc_cid=37724241cd&mc_eid=90c482e36e (Accessed: June 29, 2022).

[37] Evelyn Cheng (July 21, 2021), 'China scraps fines, will let families have as many children as they'd like,' https://www.cnbc.com/2021/07/21/china-scraps-fines-for-families-violating-childbirth-limits.html (Accessed: June 29, 2022).

[38] The Associated Press (June 20, 2022), 'Japan court says ban on same-sex marriage is constitutional', https://www.npr.org/2022/06/20/1106313824/japan-court-ban-on-same-sex-marriage-constitutional?utm_source=Albert+Mohler&utm_campaign=04fe510024-EMAIL_CAMPAIGN_2019_04_08_09_12_COPY_01&utm_medium=email&utm

Beyond individuals satisfying their sexual urges and hosting orgies, what is the civilisational contribution of homosexual practices – weighed against the importance of childbirth and population growth? Without the heterosexual family, that is responsible for procreation, human civilisation is impossible (Ellwood 1910: 28-19). Indeed, it could be argued that the post-modern reproduction bypasses biology, such that anyone can rent a womb and have a baby without ever having sex. So, technically gay men and women can adopt, or have children through the use of available reproductive technologies. But this will hardly square with the Akan social system where phallic competence culture imposes on men to exercise their fertility through impregnating and having children. The idea of renting a womb, much as it may raise no qualms of conscience, scientifically, would generate moral outrage as far as my Christian faith allows me. For example, I personally find it as an issue for the capitalistic use of the word "rent" in reference to a woman's womb. That a womb could be rented comes across as an overreach of capitalism to the domain of commodifying the body a woman. This monetary valorisation of a woman's womb, in my own estimation, comes close to women, being compelled by factors, such as economic challenges, to sell their bodies in the prostitution and pornography industry (Dworkin 1981; Jeffreys 1997).[39] To think of a woman renting her womb to a couple without the consideration of the emotional wreck such a woman would suffer demonstrates, for me, is a major challenge of late capitalism. To adduce evidence to the commodification of the surrogacy industry and the reality of its morality revulsion, Isabel Coles of Wall Street Journal reported that, as a result of Russian-Ukraine crossfire, babies are stranded in a war zone.[40] How would babies be stranded in Ukraine while their parents (both parents, I mean, according to the story) are in the United States of America – one of the largest markets for surrogacy?

As a Christian, I locate the issue of IVF (scientific surrogacy) within the prisms of the biblical anthropology of marriage. I consider marriage as a composite divine-cultural mandate that God has given to humanity.

_term=0_b041ba0d12-04fe510024-309913377&mc_cid=04fe510024&mc_eid=e3f9b7d0a1&t=1656623254158.

[39] Andrea Dworkin, *Pornography: Men possessing women* (New York: A Plume Book, 1981); Sheila Jeffreys, *The idea of prostitution* (North Melbourne, Australia: Spinifex Press Pty Ltd., 1997).

[40] Isabel Coles (March 12, 2022), "Ukraine is a world leader in surrogacy, but babies are now stranded in a war zone," https://www.wsj.com/articles/ukraine-is-a-world-leader-in-surrogacy-but-babies-are-now-stranded-in-war-zone-11647081997 (Accessed: October 11, 2022).

One of the composites of marriage is the expectation of procreation or childbirth. But childbirth is not left hanging. It must be situated within the ethics of heterosexual marriage, under a marital covenant with Christ as the key witness and informed by social relationality. This means that while a Christian couple may genuinely desire a baby, they may be biologically incapable of having one. Indeed, historically, there have been different avenues for such a couple to have a baby, usually through adoption. Of course, adoption began with God, the Creator Himself, who adopted the womb of Mary to have His Son Jesus Christ, incarnated. Through adoption, the Christian couple assumes the social responsibility of nurturing a child to God's glory and to also become useful to society.

But the surrogacy industry as part of the package of the LGBTQ community is deeply troubling and violates the unity of marriage in Christianity. First, it is about a presumed male-male couple who have, in the first instance, deliberately chosen a sexual path, at least, ontologically sinful from the biblical perspective, that presents them with a biologically impossible way of fulfilling one of the reasons for marriage – procreation. Second, the surrogacy industry undermines the idea of relationality, bounded by covenant, under the supervision of God, in the procreation process. It is, indeed, *queer* to rent the womb of a woman in a façade and pretentious *relationship* that is mediated by money. Money, a human invented and socially constructed object (Zelizer 1989),[41] is ontologically valueless and inferior to human beings. Yet, as part of the ethos of late capitalism, money has been idolised and considered more important than social relationship. To exchange the womb of a woman with money is troublesome for me. Certainly, Karl Marx would hardly have agreed with this – given his theory of commodity fetishism. What does it mean for a woman to carry pregnancy, nurture the baby to a point and let the baby go in exchange for money? Well, if we think she has agency, we should ask whether her post-partum emotional and social precarity could be pacified by money.[42] I cite the perspective of Wayne Grudem, a competent

---

[41] Viviana A. Zelizer, "The social meaning of money: 'Special monies'", *AJS*, 95, 2 (1989): 342-377.

[42] Indeed, the issue of adoption would mean differently for a heterosexual couple, who have fulfilled the core composite of marriage as heterosexual and whose social relationship can support the adoption of a child and the child's mother. Even so, without the least pretension of having any expertise or even seeking to valorise the issue, a heterosexual childless couple may want to seek counselling and the Lord's guidance for them to decide on the issue of IVF.

Christian theologian on the subject of surrogate motherhood as follows:

> This arrangement (surrogate motherhood) … violates God's intention that children should be conceived by and born to a man and a woman who are married to each other. In this case the child would not be born to the woman who is part of the married couple, but to the surrogate mother. In addition, the likely emotional components of this arrangement must be given serious consideration. It is likely that the personal intimacy involved in carrying and bearing a child will be so deep that the process of surrogate motherhood runs the danger of putting a nearly intolerable strain on the marriage. The husband and wife are including a third person into their marriage relationship, at least in some senses. The husband may find himself with an increasing emotional attachment to the woman who is bearing his child. The surrogate mother will likely feel a similar emotional attachment to the man whose child she is bearing. And the deep bond that inevitably develops between a woman and a child she bears will be disrupted and broken only with much headache, and possibly even legal battles (2018: 945).[43]

While the above complicates the state-sponsorship of homosexual practices in the West, as an individual and a practising Christian, I cannot support the promotion of such practices in Ghana. While I will certainly and evidently not support any maiming and discrimination against persons who claim to have genetic anomalies towards homosexual tendencies, I will be loving enough to follow the words of Jesus and not allow the life-negating LGBTQ+ practices in Ghana. This is what I stand for and this is what I will defend without pontificating any self-righteousness. If it is true that "If we don't stand for something, we fall to anything", then I find it nothing short of imperialism and epistemic injustice for a group of academics to use their networks against me. The issue is, for a few academics with global influence, to think that I cannot express a dissenting opinion about same-sex unions shows the fostering and imposition of group-think that is becoming pervasive in academic institutions. I am not claiming victimhood culture, and may God forbid, I will never consider myself victimised. Regardless of how I am cancelled, I stand for my convictions, so long as I do not engage in any activity and/or words of violence that undermine the ontological dignity of my fellow human

[43] Wayne Grudem, *Christian ethics: An introduction to Biblical moral reasoning* (Illinois: Crossway, 2018).

being. After all, like every true Christian, "I am a beggar telling other beggars where I found the bread of life (Jesus Christ)".

Unfortunately, the world is deeply polarised to the point of incurability. That the level of polarity has been exacerbated by the explosion of the internet and social media handles is also trite. Similarly, that humanity has hardly made any progress or even retrogress in answering the question: "How do I love the unlike?" requires re-interrogation. But the danger in our division based on the "us" and "them" is the issue of people suffering cancel culture – cancel culture that reduces the humanity of the other to nothing but an object to be literally killed, destroyed and defaced. Worst of all, the complexity of the polarised world is that perceptions, imaginations and assumptions have shredded any logic that "the devil is in the details" or the "angel is in the details" or "There's nothing in the details".

We have all become so impatient with ourselves to the point that we see people not as human beings, but sometimes in our perceptions, hearsays and assumptions. Unfortunately, such an intemperance approach to life has deepened a world where none is wrong other than, "We are all right in our own eyes." We all seek to mute voices and cast a deep shadow of doubt on the *Other.* We live in a world of "if I must live, he or she must cease to exist". We live in a world of "I", "Me" and "Myself" – an ontological reality that we call the "Satanic Trinity". So, "I love you" is now dangerous as the "I" is really I in the love. "You love me" is similarly less trustworthy because the "You" could mean several things – where "you" becomes a matter of convenience. To reduce my preliminary comments to simple terms: *We live in a dangerously fractured world.*

We have nevertheless lived beyond our basic human needs for basic things such as food, clothing, shelter, and we-feeling. Concurrently, we live in a world where despite growing intensity in animosity, hatred and *othering*, none of us from either "holy camps" can claim to be complete and sufficient – certainly, God never intended any of us to covert His office by laying false claim to ontological sufficiency.

We are all, in the language of Professor Francis Nyamnjoh, incomplete in need of conviviality. But as I have written in an essay on this great scholar, how do we heal the world that is deeply polarised? In other words, how do we go beyond centring "self" to see the humanity in the other? I raise the above questions because, in the last few months, I have had to reflect on the subtle and obvious cancel culture that I personally and others suffer because of the memo I penned down to support the Family Law against LGBTQ+ practices. Suddenly, I can really feel and see that I am losing friends. I am losing friends not because any of them has communicated to me that I have offended them in one way or the other. But if indeed a breakdown in communication is a prelude to conflict, then I cannot take the silence of my friends for granted.

Certainly, in such a deeply polarised world, there is no explanation for hatred. After all, hatred, as it is said among the Akan, has no cure, because it has no cause. Hatred, therefore, insanely does not square with the basic law of causality which is so basic that to undo it we have to be inhuman. Precisely also because to hate means one risks becoming alone, which in the wisdom of Aristotle is to be either an animal, or a deity. And because we don't want to be either an animal and/or pretend to be a deity, the Triune God of the Bible said axiomatically and sociologically state that "It is not good for man to be alone". Much as most haters are supported by other haters, so they are not alone, the context of the statement and God, from whom it comes, implies unity for social cohesion and human flourishing! We can deal with loneliness, through partying and other sociogenic activities, but none can stand the troubles of being "alone".

So as part of writing this permeable, I seek to correct a misconception and misappreciation of my memo to Parliament. As I have said, the extent and force of hate and intolerance in the world are rather sickening and aporia to the ethos of the rigorous academic profession. Regrettably, perceptions in the corridors of academia, where criticality and "objectivity" in a plurality of ideas (giving the university the mantra of a "universal city") expected to be celebrated, have capitulated to a unipolar world of feasting on perception as logical and conclusive.

I restate to clear misconceptions in my memo and also to express my amazement at how an epistle, not meant for the academic world, but for the Parliament of Ghana has become a bastardisation of my scholarship. This is precisely because, as I have said above, while my academic position on the subject (see below) was equally published nearly around the same time the media-saturated the internet with my memo, the polarity of the world has rather drowned my intellectual contribution to the subject.

Consequently, while I stick to my position about a need for humanity to keep, as my ancestors have always done, the lines of ethical and ontological boundaries clean and clear from infractions, because of the widespread consequence, I want to state that my position in both my memo and an academic piece on the LGBTQI+ was never meant to be confrontational. But I remain faithful to my conviction about sexuality as a Christian, a Ghanaian and an African. My convictions, which serve as guardrails for this book are as follows:

1. There are boundaries in life: These boundaries are cultural and ontological
2. Human-made cultural boundaries are amenable and flexible, but whilst changes must be carefully done with some such as food, clothing, housing, and tools, others like *Trokosi*, must be fully abolished
3. Ontological boundaries are non-changeable, timeless because they are made by God
4. Humans and human-induced institutions like the state, civil society groups, and international communities cannot violate ontological boundaries
5. Heterosexual marriage, between a biological man and a biological woman, is an ontological boundary between God and human beings as marriage is God's creation
6. Human institutions, including the state, civil society groups, international organizations or any human logic, no matter how refined it is, cannot redefine and restructure marriage
7. Marriage is God's creation, given to human beings as a divine-cultural for the essential purposes of procreation and pleasure. This implies that as divine-cultural creation, human beings may appropriate marriage to suit to their respective situations. But the fact of marriage, a mixture of a male's sperm and a woman's ovum, as an ontological reality to procreate, it divine and cannot be short-changed.
8. Historically, heterosexual marriage is the norm
9. No nation or society ever legislated heterosexual marriage into existence
10. So, no human being or institution, including the state can legislate anything to the contrary
11. Homosexual practices, breaks ontological boundary, as it involves a non-natural use of the sexual organs and the anus. Issues can be raised about the whether the mouth is naturally for kissing and whether kissing is permissible in religion. But the issue is about procreation organs, as opposed to other parts of the body that do not play active role in the procreation process
12. Lesbianism which is more recent is also unnatural as it does not produce the desire for marriage – natural means of procreation.

This is because marriage as same-sex does not naturally procreate. This is because marriage as same-sex does not naturally procreate. This means that while, heterosexual couples who are infertile do not procreate either, they fulfil the Christian composite of marriage, relationality of a biological male and a biological female that would support their adoption of a child, who would fit well into a heterosexual family as God instituted

13. Anti-homosexual laws were primarily informed by religion (particularly Judeo-Christian values) and secondly, common sense
14. England did not introduce English culture against homosexual practices into Ghana, then the Gold Coast
15. England, under Queen Victoria in the nineteenth century, brought Judeo-Christian sex ethics to the Gold Coast
16. The English extended anti-homosexual laws into the Gold Coast colony as part of controlling European explorers from exploiting Africans sexually
17. The first anti-homosexual law was passed in India in 1860 because Hinduism endorses homosexual practices
18. Sin is not unique to any particular culture, so homosexual practices are not foreign to any culture
19. That homosexual practices aren't foreign to any culture does not necessarily mean it was endorsed by societies
20. That is why most cultures in the sixteenth century, including England, considered the practice as foreign
21. All civilisations considered homosexual practices an oddity
22. Homosexuality and homosexual activism and practices are not the same – one is a feeling without practice, the other may be feeling, but also practice. The existence of *Kojo Bɛsia* and *Kwasi Bɛsia* does not mean that homosexual practice was openly endorsed in Ghana. There is hardly any research to show that homosexual practices were accepted and publicly endorsed in the Gold Coast societies before colonialism
23. In the case of *Sangomas* which many adduce as evidence of acceptance of homosexual practices in Africa, it was more about an African cosmogony creating space for queer sexuality as opposed to legislating it as a sociogenic practice
24. The world of rituals breaks ontological boundaries, example is the grotesque rituals of *Sakawa* and *Sika duro precisely what is the ritual about*
25. Marriage is not a secret practice, but sociogenic. It is God's creation and divine cultural mandate, practised in the real social

world of law and order (the natural order of a union between a biological man and a biological woman)

26. Ghanaian rejection of homosexual practice is not about cultural or democratic backwardness
27. The western decriminalisation of homosexual practices is backward as it is a relapse to their Greco-Roman ancestral past where homosexual practices were rife and pervasive
28. Real freedom is the freedom to keep ethical and ontological boundaries, including heterosexual marriage
29. That religion (and common sense) formed the basis of resisting homosexual practices means it will take secularization to promote homosexual practice
30. The west decriminalisation of homosexual practices is partly because of the decline in the role of religion in the public sphere
31. Religion is strong in Ghana, which renders the decriminalisation of homosexuality a herculean task
32. The reasons for the push for homosexual practices by Ghanaian academics are based on unsustainable god-hating and society destroying theories of Karl Marx, Frederick Engels, Charles Darwin, John Stuart Mill, Jeremy Bentham, Jean-Paul Sartre, Simone de Beauvoir, Mary Daly etc
33. These western "thinkers" sought to deconstruct society – by deconstructing religion, family, God
34. None of the Ghanaian scholars pushing through homosexuals cite eminent Ghanaian scholars like K.A. Busia, the first West African to receive PhD in Sociology from Oxford; John Mensa Sarbah and Joseph Ephraim Casely Hayford (who as peerless legal luminarics wrote copiously to defend Ghanaian cultures and family values); Kobina Sekyi who denounced western depraved cultural values, Kwame Nkrumah, who established the Institute of African Studies, inaugurated in 1963 to research and teach African values as part of mental emancipation and resetting the world from African prisms; J.B. Danquah who supported limited liberalism that promoted divine-ontologies – that human beings do not make themselves, but are created by God
35. As part of the growing debates over homosexuality, there is the need for epistemic emancipation – our universities must incorporate the teaching of African and western intellectual histories
36. No nation is secular qua secular; Ghana is more of a religiously plural country than a secular – For example, whereas the United

Kingdom as a state church, allows for the public use of the Islamic veil, France, which does not have a state church does not allow the public use of the veil. All the countries use the secular thesis to defend their stance

37. Pre-colonial societies were never secular; the colonialists did not impose secularism on Ghana even though British had secularised its politics in the 19th Century at the height of colonialism
38. Nkrumah did not envision a secular Ghana: His philosophy of consciencism was about a fusion of Ghana's religious traditions, Christianity, Islam, and indigenous religions, in the governance of the country, instead of having an irreligious country
39. The post-Nkrumah leaders have all appropriated religions in important ways
40. Religions in Ghana have been more helpful in promoting human flourishing than any civil society organisation
41. *Please refer to my publications on this subject:*
    a. Charles Prempeh, "Religion, Social Media and the Discourse on Prisons: An Analysis of the Responses to the Church of Pentecost (CoP) Prison Project in Ghana", *Prison Service Journal* 256 (2021), pp. 38-43
    b. Charles Prempeh and Lydia Amoah, "Secular governmentality and the court of the Asante Ahemaa in 21st century: An ethnographic account of Ejisu and Juaben traditional areas". In Edmund Abaka & Kwame Osei Kwarteng (Eds.), *The Asante World.* London/New York: Routledge, 2021, pp. 281-300
    c. Charles Prempeh, "Religion and the state in an episodic movement of COVID-19 in Ghana", *Social Sciences & Humanities Open*, Vol. 4, Issue 1 (2021), pp. 1-8
42. From the genealogical histories of secularism, the concept does not mean the absence of religion in a public sphere, as it is about managing religious plurality
43. Instead of arguing vaguely about Ghana's supposed secular states, we should talk about religious plurality
44. Compassion is always stronger than condemnation

Based on my respect for everyone, I live and theorise it as well. For example, I wrote my MPhil which I submitted to the Institute of African Studies, University of Ghana, on marijuana consumption. My goal was to plead against the marginalisation of marijuana consumers in the urban slums – my own people who are also God's image-bearers.

I have spent my life defending the rights of the marginalised. I only tread cautiously when in defending the rights of others, I marginalise others – for all are in the image of God and all must be offered respect.

I concretise my philosophical position on human ontological dignity with a reflection on the history of the Israelites' enslavement in Egypt recorded in the book of Exodus. I, however, focus on Chapter 12. The Book of Exodus records a tussle between Moses, Aaron, representing the Israelites on one hand and Pharaoh and his officials representing the Egyptians on the other. For several reasons including Pharaoh's hubris, he refused to grant freedom to the Israelites to even go and worship. God, mediating through Moses, inflicted mitigated punishment on the Egyptians, for which the Egyptian magicians largely countered the infallible power with fallible power.

Finally, God decided the final blow, which was to involve death. At this point, God found the Israelites and the Egyptians culpable. When it comes to dying because of death, God made that universal declaration through Adam that we are all guilty. Both the oppressed and the oppressor are all equally guilty to be punished. And both need God's forgiveness to escape punishment. Incidentally, also, none qualifies to execute that judgement. But for the final blow, Moses mediated God's mitigated punishment, but when it came to the ultimate punishment of death, God took over Himself. Why? He is merciful. Because without God's direct intervention of mercy and substitutionary justice, not even Moses or anybody would survive.

So, God had to mitigate the universal judgement of death on all with sacrifice. It was only after the Israelites had been spared by God through God's own mercy of sacrifice did the angel of death spare them. This led to the institution of the Pass Over rituals among the Jewish people which is kept till today. Without a lamb, appointed by God Himself to die in place of the Israelites they would have similarly died.

Later, a popular non-biblical story, but similarly important, has it that when the Egyptians died *en masse* as they followed to further enslave the Israelites, there was a party in heaven. The angels and the patriarchs were excited. But God had recoiled in sadness. When the angels asked why He was not celebrating the defeat of the enemies of His chosen people, God is reported to have said, "The Egyptians are my people, too."

Ultimately, Jesus became the Pass Over lamb who sacrificed His ultimate precious blood for the elect of God. In His mercy, He is not in a hurry to carry through with judgement because He is a loving

Father. When my own father died in December 2008, the usually mystical causality idea that someone had killed my father (even though the autopsy was clear about the cause of his death), my maternal aunt, out of frustration over rumours of the cause of my father's death said:

> "Kofi (referring to me), they said when God takes His stone, he does not rush to throw it. If that is the case, why does He take the stone in the first place?"

In response, I told her God is not interested in destroying His creation. His love is redemptive from destruction and sin and has graciously deferred ultimate judgement to eternity.

With the above, if it is true that the family and faith in something (God or otherwise) are both anterior to the state and operate on love, and covenant, rather than law and social contract, how do we resolve the following issue:

> *A mother standing in the state's dock, presided over by a non-family member to appeal to the state over her own biological child*

Organisation of the book

The rest of the chapters are as follows. In Chapter Two, I discuss the context of the homosexual debate in Ghana. I bring out the nuances of the petition by a group of cultural elites to block the passage of the "Promotion of Proper Human Sexual Rights and Ghanaian Family Values Bill, 2021." My goal in the chapter is to argue that subverting the ethical and ontological boundaries of life, as the homosexual advocates seek to do will rather destroy human civilisation. In Chapter three, I discuss the intellectual histories and genealogies of some of the key figures in the formulation of homosexual arguments and theories. I discuss the progression of the sexual revolution from just women coming out of their closet to overtaking even men in women's practice of polyamory. The chapter also discusses very important and critical issues about Christianity and the LGBTQ+ community. Given the tension and the anger that have circumscribed gender relations and the LGBTQ+ debates, I argue that forgiveness is very novel to the world. Emphasising forgiveness, I put before men and women the opportunity to take the path of peace of reconciliation to mend the family and restore human relations. The Chapter Four of the book provides a socio-philosophical and theological analysis of the Bible. I take much of the Bible as historical, even as it is inspirational. This, then allows me to think through and apply the Bible to the issues under discussion. In all of this my argument is that the LGBTQ+ claim to share the public sphere could potentially imperil religious freedom.

Chapter 2

The homosexual debate in context

There has been an increasing debate over issues of homosexuality, including sea waves of pushback from some Ghanaians and foreign representatives in Ghana against the proposed "Promotion of Proper Human Sexual Rights and Ghanaian Family Values Bill, 2021"– currently under consideration in Parliament. While the phenomenon is old in Ghana, and common in senior high schools, more recently since the 1960s, the entanglement of homosexuality and human rights have complicated the subject. Moreover, the rise in humanistic groups, such as the Common Sense Family and, Humanist and Atheistic groups, and the proliferation of social media since the turn of the millennium have created an atmosphere of fawning liberalism that challenges conventional sex ethics.

The challenge to gerontocratic control over sex matters, as well as a challenge to ecclesiastical authority, have all merged in defining the contours of contemporary sex ethics. Similarly, neo-liberalization of the economy which came into prominence during the third wave of democracy in the 1990s contributed to weakening the family system when confronted with the sporadic urbanization on the continent. In all this, young men and women are forced into a world of "survival of the fittest" where they subsist on their own coping strategies and subjectivities, away from the prying eyes of gerontocratic authority figures.

I argue that homosexuality is framed around a vortex of different layers of complexities: human rights, state sovereignty, internationalism, culture, modernity, religion, sexual freedom etc. In all, through the prisms of the Bible, history, philosophy and discourse analysis, I will respond to questions that have definitely been answered from different perspectives elsewhere, *inter alia*: Is homosexuality foreign to African cultures? Where from "homophobic" laws? How free can an individual be in matters of sex? Is homosexuality genetic? Must the state legislate against people's sexual preferences? How should Africa and Africans respond to western hegemony? Why are most Africans against homosexuality? Is Africa retrogressing or progressing in matters of sexuality? Why did the west begin liberalising its stance on homosexuality since the 1960s? How should we engage with homosexuals in our communities? How now shall we live? I ask these questions that have had extensive research attention since the 1960s as part of adding my own voice to the debates. But more importantly, these questions also help me to deploy the LGBTQ debate as an entry point to discuss other cognate subjects. This means that the book takes on other subjects that may not directly relate to the Bill, but that indicates the fact that LGBTQ matters cannot be discussed in isolation of other aspects of society.

Homosexuality is a very contentious subject in many African countries. In Ghana, the practice of same-sex is tabooed, such that a mere mention of it rightly attracts reprehension from the larger Ghanaian community. Rumours of homosexuality have for a very long time circulated in social media, but the practice received widespread media attention in 2006 when a group of homosexuals attempted organising a conference on LGBT issues in Ghana. The government of Ghana was brought under intense pressure from the larger Ghanaian community to disallow the conference from taking place in the country. Eventually, the government proscribed the conference from taking place.

In 2011, homosexuality once again became a dominant issue in public discourses, following the warning by David Cameron, then Prime Minister of Britain, that nations that failed to liberalise their stance on homosexuality risked losing British aid. This time, too, the government of Ghana released an anti-homosexual statement. The discussion of homosexuality in Ghana is so much clouded by entrenched western imperialistic tendencies alongside their African compradors such that the issues that must be properly discussed to set the records straight are deeply and intentionally obscured. In this book I aim to support the anti-homosexual **"Promotion of Proper Human Sexual Rights and Ghanaian Family Values Bill, 2021"** (not anti-human) laws in Ghana and where necessary Africa.

Homosexuals across the globe, particularly in some religiously-led states, claim to suffer from attacks from mainstream religious community for not conforming to the conventional construction of heterosexual social order. Homosexuality is seen as an affront to hegemonic masculinity in Africa. Accordingly, this issue arises from the failure of conservative religious society failure to accept multiple masculinities, of which homosexuality can be included. Certainly, the issues here are that masculinity is defined as linked, attracted to but dominant and different to femininities. This is the general scheme. Homosexuality scrambles this schema. Precisely because, men who are sexually passive as receptive partners play the role of women in heterosexual relationships. This challenges heterosexual masculinities. But more specifically, it challenges both the Christian and Akan notions of masculinity, where the profiling of phallic culture is about a man's fertility and demonstration of the ability to lead, provide, and protect his family. In short, an Akan man must have a phallic attribute of birth (Owusu and Bosiwah 2015). Several people have seriously debated the subject of homosexuality (Ojeda 2004). In popular and academic discourses, entrenched positions, sometimes backed by polemical books, have clouded and confused the discussion on the subject. Christian religious leaders are rightly polarised over the subject. This is because Christians against the practice are deeply convinced that homosexuality is demonic and anti-human as in it does not, in their theology support the primary goal of marriage - procreation.[44] For several Akan people, they are protesting against same-sex unions as part of an imposition of western knowledge and values on them. These Akan also contest against homosexuality as a struggle against unbridled universalism that put the world on the verge of a one-size-fits all agenda (Owusu and Bosiwah 2015: 132). I agree with Owusu and Bosiwah that gender-blindness and presenting gender and sexuality as social construct are both alien to the Akan. Instead, among the Akan, gender is primarily biological and that people perform their social roles based on their biological make up (Owusu and Bosiwah 2015).

The idea of homophobia has received greater attention in the 21st Century because it is believed that the phobia is likely to curtail freedom of expression and threatens democracy and human right (Reddy, 2009). For this reason, given the progress Ghana has made in its re-democratic experiment since the 1990s, the drafters of the petition to support minority rights in the country said that Family Bill is a major step backwards for democracy.[45] Early this year (2022), I published a journal article on homosexuality, under the title, "When cultural values clash with human rights: The Case of the Homosexual Debate."[46] The article, which was published by several online media platforms, including *Ghanaweb*, a major electronic online media in Ghana, attracted the concerns of lots of readers. I had two professors in the United

[44] For example, in 2003, the Anglican Church of Nigeria severed relationship with the Anglican Church of England over the latter's sanction of homosexuality.

[45] Memorandum to Select Committee on the Constitutional, Legal and Parliamentary Affairs on the: *Promotion of Proper Human Sexual Rights and Ghanaian Family Values Bill, 2021*, p. 1.

[46] http://www.ghanaweb.com/GhanaHomePage/NewsArchive/When-cultural-values-clash-with-human-rights-the-case-of-the-homosexual-debate-349386.

Kingdom, who identified themselves as homosexuals, writing to contest my position on the subject. Once again, I have decided to write on the subject of homosexuality to support the Promotion of Proper Human Sexual Rights and Ghanaian Family Values Bill, 2021 which is currently being considered by Ghana's Parliament Committee on Constitutional, Legal and Parliamentary Affairs. While I partly respond to the Bill, my goal, as I have stated is to reflect on the entangled socio-political issues that the LGBTQ issues generate.[47]

Recent Issues

In 2011, when the issue of homosexuality re-emerged, the Prime Minister of Britain, David Cameron, had sent a caution to all African leaders, including Ghana, to liberalise their legal stance on homosexuality or risk losing British aid. The issue once against spurred Ghanaians on to debate homosexuality. Here, too, the president of Ghana, this time under the National Democratic Congress government, John Evans Atta Mills, became the darling boy of the conservative Ghanaian community as he stated publicly that he was not going to compromise Ghanaian culture and religious sensitivity to liberalise or legalise homosexuality in the country. In 2014, there was a renewed discussion on homosexuality following the trial of a senior medical practitioner, Dr. Sulley Ali-Gabass, who was accused of sodomising a minor. Ordinarily while this matter did not translate in debates about homosexuality where activists are referring to relations among consenting adults, it reignited the debate on homosexuality! The case dragged for a year, until he was eventually slapped with a 25-year jail term in July 2022. While this was an example of a crime of paedophilia that the perpetrator can be gay or heterosexual, the issue rather rekindled the homosexual debate.

In June 2015, the Supreme Court of the United States of America ruled that same-sex marriage is legal across the United States of America. Since it is widely said that "when the United States of America coughs, the world catches a cold," the government of Ghana, once again, came under intense pressure to make a new anti-homosexual

[47] Abednego Asiedu Asante (October 8, 2021), "African Studies scholar, Dr Charles Prempeh petitions Parliament to pass Anti LGBTQ+ Bill," https://www.myjoyonline.com/african-studies-scholar-dr-charles-prempeh-petitions-parliament-to-pass-anti-lgbtqi-bill/ (Accessed: October 11, 2022). Memo: https://drive.google.com/file/d/1jJwGVvm7ZZA9gHtdB6PEuES-uWDDiZqX/view.

pronouncement on the issue. For political reasons, the government of Ghana, headed by the former president, H.E. John Dramani Mahama, remained very silent and reticent about making a statement on the issue. The silence of the government raised concerns among Ghanaians that the president, said to be a close friend of Andrew Solomon, a known gay and LGBT+ advocate, might want to liberalise Ghana's stance on the issue. Certainly, the connection between the president and Andrew Solomon was also motivated by partisan politics. Nevertheless, it is important to differentiate between Republican and Democrats administrations in the US. It is not all US administrations that tolerate sexual rights. The Christian Far Right which supports Conservatives does not ordinarily support LBGTQI+ issues.[48] So, while I am of the view that the west should keep its sexual ideas to itself, American sexual or cultural wars tend to have a spill over effect in Ghana – which demands the attention of Ghanaians.

However, we look at the debate on homosexuality in Ghana, it is conspicuous that the two main political parties, the New Patriotic Party (NPP) and the National Democratic Congress (NDC) who have alternated in ruling Ghana since the country bounced back to democratic rule in 1992, have shown consistency in their stance against homosexuality. One thing that is also clear is that all the leaders of Ghana have resisted homosexuality on the assumption that the practice is un-African, illegal, and anti-religious. This projection of homosexuality as un-African, illegal and anti-religious is in tandem with similar concerns expressed by other leaders in Africa, including Yoweri Museveni of Uganda, Sam Nujoma of Namibia, Robert Mugabe of Zimbabwe, Olusegun Obasanjo of Nigeria, and Yayah Jammeh of Gambia. In Southern Africa, (Zimbabwe, Namibia, South Africa) there is a lot of literature which shows that homosexuality (men to men sex) predates colonialism or was recorded in the early colonial era (See: Epprecht, 2013). The argument is, therefore, put across that the position of presidents does not or should not be the position of a whole nation. Nevertheless, we will have to deal with the fact that the presidents represent their nations, and as part of the social contract, they must represent the broader views of those they represent. The reciprocal relationship between the political elites and citizens, in my reading, merge on communally shared ethical values around matters as

[48] For example, in July 2022, dozens of Republicans sided with Democrats in the US House of Representatives to pass a bill that would boost legal protections for same-sex marriages. See: "Republicans help pass House gay marriage bill" July 20, 2022), https://www.bbc.com/news/world-us-canada-62232518.

foundational to the sustenance of human civilization such as sexuality and marriage.

As governors of the public sphere, which could be very contentious, the duty of the political elites is to protect minority rights, without undermining the shared moral values that keep the public sphere running. For example, procreation is a commonly shared value – though not everyone would biologically be able to fulfil that desire. But the type of sexual life one lives is decidedly a personal choice. The duty of the political elites, therefore, is to ensure that the personal, idiosyncrasies of individuals that may potentially polarise and make the public sphere ungovernable is kept away from the public. Currently, the legislation and institutionalisation of minority sexual preference, often ontologically unsupportive of procreation, is creating troubles around the world, including countries where it has been legalised. Ghana would have to avoid the polarising effect of the sexual revolution and moral progressivism that have wrecked the western world, especially the United States of America, by ensuring that same-sex preferences is not legalised.

Calling homosexual practices as un-African is not the same as saying the practice never existed or may not have existed, as it is rather to argue that in the case of Ghana and several of these countries, it never existed as a publicly accepted and institutionalised practice. Indeed, until the economic and technological revolution of the 1970s and 1980s sustained the sexual revolution agenda, several of the modern western world treated homosexual practices as non-public practice.

Nevertheless, the projection of homosexual practice as un-African has elicited nuanced responses from scholars and advocates of homosexual activities. They have provided evidence to show that while homosexuality is African, it is homophobia, which is un-African. The attempt to romanticise African past and present its environment as anti-homosexual until the advent of colonialism is emblematic of Ellis and Symond's observation that, "The people of every country have always been eager to associate sexual perversion with some other country other than their own" (Ellis et al, 1897:58, cited in Nyanzi, 2013:1).

This book seeks to contribute to the homosexual debate by situating western epistemic assumptions against that of the African, focusing on several aspects of the subject in Ghana, including the Akan concept of personhood to illuminate our understanding of the homosexual discourse in Ghana. My goal is to indicate how the entwined intersectionality between the LGBTQ debates and socio-cultural and political realities in the country indicates the layers of complexities in the local and international quest for liberalising sexuality in the country would be. More importantly, I also argue that the homosexual debate is a worldview issues – or a clash of worldview. One worldview that supports moral progression, perception of traditions and conventions around heterosexual or state routinisation of heterosexual marriage as oppressive, individual rights as key, truth as subjective, the past as conquerable (especially in matters of morality and sexuality in the context of the LGBTQ issue) and the other worldview that sees marriage as an all-time valid composite of a heterosexual social relational (between a biological man and a biological woman – tautology for the sake of emphasis) for the purpose of procreation, offered to humanity as a divine-cultural mandate by the uncreated Creator – the Triune God. This worldview argues that human beings, as image-bearers of God, have an inherent worth that must be defined and dependent on a creator who sets the boundaries of freedom of every aspect of life, including sexuality. Concurrently, this worldview maintains that morality is timeless and absolute, not subjective and not historically fossilised; human rights must be defined against ethical and ontological boundaries for the promotion of human flourishing; queer individual sexualities that are ontologically non-procreative should be limited to the private sphere and never allowed to be legislated and institutionalised as a public practice; that the family is both anterior to religion and state – implying that that state should not determine the marital choices of families and should not seek to legalise non-conventional sexual preferences of individuals in a family; families should be allowed to attend to the sexual uniqueness of their individual members and that the state could only come in when there are clear cases of physical violation and criminality against individuals with queer sexualities.

Writing as an Akan and a practising evangelical Christian, I accept my ancestral heritage of matriliny as consistent with the Bible's requirement the family structure. This is such that while the Akan privileges the woman as the origin of the family and places more emphasis on pater (social father) more than genitor (a biological factor), Akan phallic culture is overwhelmingly rated as important in man's fertility in procreation. Similarly, the Akan matriliny did not translate into matriarchy – which implies that the Akan man is the authority figure of his family who is responsible for providing, protecting and leading his family. This is a practice that both predated and survived colonialism – albeit with a few social transformations. The transformations have, however, never undermined the fact that the

Akan man's phallic competence about fertility and childbirth is the basis of the Akan family.

As I said, all this, particularly the patriarchal social structure of the Akan family, is endorsed and reinforced by the Bible. It is also my responsibility to push back the imposition of any subversive sexual practice that is, indeed, subversive of the human family. Colonialism or the missionary intrusion did not, therefore, introduce the idea of man's headship and control of the Akan family. For this reason, while decolonisation has become something like a buzzword in academia that means different thing to different people, but more so overturning what is believed as the lingering structures of colonialism oppression, the family system is not part of the decolonisation struggle, for me. Consequently, I understand decolonisation, not as part of the usual rhetoric of some African academics who profile Christianity as oppressive, but rather contesting Western, especially America's efforts at imposing its sexual wars as a neo-colonial imperialism that needs to be decolonised. The Biden-led US government that seeks to openly and tacitly impose radical sexual revolution on the rest of the world through the global advancement of diversity, equity, inclusion, and accessibility (DEIA) is imperialistic and a threat to the sovereignty of developing nations.[49] America, under Biden, has progressively become an exporter of gender revolution – to use the title of Leor Sapir's journalistic article.[50] If the US, led by Biden, is allowed to push this agenda through using both coercive and subtle means, the US will harm its international relationships as it may also set the world on the pathways of cultural and later political wars. Ghana must not be part of the herd mentality to follow the western world to legislate same-sex unions.

Rhetoric about homosexuality

As stated in the introduction, the rhetoric on homosexuality has centred on the debate as to whether it is indigenous or foreign to Africans. The paper acknowledges the turgid tension that has enveloped the homosexual debate. All the leaders of Africa, who have bared their teeth at homosexuals, have done so with the justification that the practice is un-African and antithesis to African culture. For

---

[49] DEIA Strategic Plan 2022-2026 https://www.mcc.gov/resources/doc/report-deia-strategic-plan#page-content (Accessed: October 10, 2022).

[50] Leor Sapir (August 31, 2022), "America, exporter of the gender revolution," https://www.city-journal.org/state-dept-launches-international-gender-pressure-campaign (Accessed: October 10, 2022).

example, the president of Zambia, Frederick Chiluba, castigated homosexuality by claiming:

> Homosexuality is the deepest level of depravity... . That homosexuals are free to do as they please in the West does not mean they must be free to do the same here. There will be no end to demand for rights as soon as they are permitted. There will also be more diseases... . The things they do would multiply the rate of the spread of AIDS which was first spotted among American sodomites in the first place... . But using the discovery of HIV is in itself misguided. For a country like ours, beset by increasing problems of development, homosexuality as a constitutional right would simply bring the whole republic crashing to its back, belly up... . (Reddy, 2001:84). Furthermore, such statements are exaggerations of reality. no country has ever crashed because of sexuality!

The issue of the discovery of HIV and homosexuality and that nations may crash because of the practice remains highly contentious. But similar to President Chiluba, President Sam Nujoma of Namibia also said that,

> Most ardent supporters of these perverts are Europeans who imagine themselves to be the bulwark of civilisation and enlightenment... we made sacrifices for the liberation of this country and we are not going to allow individuals with alien practices such as homosexuality to destroy the social fabric of our society. We are convinced that homosexuality is not natural and objective from moral history but a hideous deviation of decrepit and inhuman sordid behaviour. In reality lessons learned from the morals of our Namibian culture demonstrate that our morals are far more superior and acceptable to the vast majority of our people who adhered to Christianity... . Homosexuality deserves severe contempt and disdain from the Namibian people and should be uprooted totally as a practice (Reddy, 2001:84).

Robert Mugabe of Zimbabwe also considered homosexuality to be very un-African and said that homosexuals are worse than dogs and pigs, who could differentiate between male and female. He considered the propagation of homosexuality as a new form of cultural imperialism. In 1997, he is reported to have said,

> Let the Americans keep their sodomy, bestiality, stupid and foolish ways to themselves. Let them be gays in the US and Europe. But in Zimbabwe, gays shall remain a very sad people forever (Reddy, 2001:164).

In 2009, a marriage relationship between two gays, Stephen Monjeza and Tiwonge Chimbalanga, was contracted in Malawi, but the two were immediately arrested for breaching the anti-sodomy law of the country, and sentenced to fourteen years in prison. After intense pressure from international bodies and other civil societies, the president of the country, Bingu wa Mutharika, was compelled to extend presidential pardon to the two men in May, 2010. But, because he did that under duress, he stated on the day of their release that:

> These boys committed a crime against our culture, our religion, our laws. However, as Head of State, I hereby pardon them and therefore ask for their immediate release with no conditions. I have done this on humanitarian grounds, but this does not mean that I support this (Reddy, 2001).

From the above, it is obvious that homophobia in Africa is presented as state-sponsored, while homophobic speeches were underscored by the assumption that the practice is un-African, anti-religious, and illegitimate. By claiming that homosexuality is un-African and a demonstration of cultural imperialism, which came with western hegemonic wave, these politicians are assuming, however tacitly, that homosexuality is a European invention that has been transposed to Africa to dilute African culture. Again, by arguing that the practice is un-African, it is assumed that African culture has been static or has remained the same over time and space. African culture is thus denied the benefit of dynamism. What is more, the "un-Africaness" of homosexuality homogenises African culture. Again, to argue that homosexuality is anti-religious is to speak the language of conservative Christians and not African Traditional Religions, since as I will show later, some rituals in Africa had revolved around sexuality, which in fact, paved way for homosexual relations.

Finally, to argue that homosexuality is illegal is to make reference to the colonisers, who passed several anti-sodomy laws in many colonised African countries. Here, I ask the question, why did the Europeans pass anti-sodomy laws, if homosexuality did not predate colonialism? The dearth of scholarly research on homosexuality, without a doubt, is largely responsible for the well-circulated proposition that same-sex relationships are "exotic" or "un-African" (Essien et al, 2009:124). Anti-homosexual advocates implicitly argue that Africans lived in a pristine world, uncorrupted by sexual perversion.

Even so, some scholars have challenged the premise on which homophobic speeches have been made. Pro-homosexual advocates, including Epprecht, Reddy, Nyanzi, Swidler, Dlamini, Murray and Roscoe, Mbisi, to mention but a few, have argued that it is homophobic tendencies that is foreign to Africans not homosexuality. They assemble several evidence from different countries in Africa to assert that homosexuality has always been indigenous to Africans. They asseverate that Africans had always tolerated homosexuality until the advent of European colonisers. Epprecht wrote that "African men sometimes have sex with other men or boys, today as in the past. … African women also sometimes have sex with other women or girls, today as in the past" (Epprecht 2008: 6). Dlamini argues that the colonialists did not introduce homosexuality to Africa, but rather intolerance of it and systems of surveillance and regulation for expressing it. Thabo Msibi (2011) in his article, 'The Lies We Have Been Told About (Homo) Sexuality in Africa,' argues that homophobia is used as a façade that serves to entrench patriarchy and heteronormativity as legitimate and fixed in African societies (Msibi 2011:55). He argues that 'the renewed efforts to label same-sex desire as un-African represent a façade that conceals neoconservatism and resurgence of patriarchy, coated in the constructs of religion, nationalism, and law' (Msibi 2011:55).

In his article, 'Homosexuality in the African Context', Busangokwakhe Dlamini argues that homosexuality has always been part of African culture, and that the practice has been consistent with African spirituality, cosmology, and culture. He argues with evidence to the effect that the practice of homosexuality is not an invention or introduction of the west. The practice both preceded and survived colonialism, hence it is not a colonial impart. He also affirms that the fact that we might not have indigenous words to describe homosexuality does not mean that the practice never existed in Africa prior to colonialism. He thus argues that we should distinguish between practice and precept. Much as some African societies might not have words to describe homosexuality does not in any way presuppose that the practice did not exist. Dlamini cites Swidler (1993) who argues that homosexuality was not an affront to African traditional religions. According to Swidler, ritual experts of traditional religions attached spiritual significance to sexuality. He argues that African traditional religions see spiritual power in sexuality, with different types of spirituality associated with different sexual practices. In Swidler's argument, it was the introduction of Christianity among Africans that undermined the spiritual importance attached to homosexual practice.

In the case of South Africa, Swidler argues that homosexuality intensified among Africans, following the rule that prohibited free mingle between men and women on the mining compound. Mine homosexuality thus emerged as a new type of homosexual relation following the prohibition of migrant men labourers taking their wives to the mines. Swidler maintains that senior male migrant workers on the mine took young male labourers, trained them about the nature of work on the mine, and in return got sexual favours. Some of the senior male workers pay special bridewealth to young male workers on the mine to engage them in homosexuality. In relation to the paucity of books on homosexuality in Africa, a situation that elides homosexuality to have existed in Africa, Swidler avers that, "Given the predominantly oral character of African traditional religions and the tendency to privacy in sexual matters that is characteristic of most societies, there has been very little opportunity for anthropologists or other observers to acquire a systematic understanding of African attitude about homosexuality (Swidler, 1993:19, cited in Dlamini, 2006:129).

Riddinger (1995, cited in Dlamini, 2006) argues that the condescending and disparaging views Africans have developed about homosexuality should be situated within the context of colonialism. According to him, a key feature of imperialist ideology was to condemn African cultures in order to justify their so-called civilising mission. Thus, the colonisers were poised at destroying every trace of African culture, particularly religion. And since homosexuality was deeply rooted in African spirituality, attacking African religions was a tacit attack on some cultural practices, including homosexuality. It was the colonisers who criminalised homosexuality, which had been part of African culture prior to the colonial encounter, thereby casting the practice in a very negative light. Given the assertion that homosexuality was a normative sexual practice that preceded colonialism, Kendall (1996:12) asserts that, "homophobia is far more likely to qualify as un-African" than homosexuality, and that homophobia is certainly the product of certain class of white folks, arising from a particular culture which only seems normative to us because we are blinded by it.

One of the enduring myths that Eurocentric scholars constructed about Africa, according to Murray and Roscoe (1998) is that homosexuality never existed in Africa. This idea was anchored on the assumption that Africans, before their contact with Europeans in the

15th Century, epitomised "primitive man" and as such were very close to nature. And since the primitive man was not separated from nature, because he was culturally unsophisticated, he was heterosexual in sexual orientation. There were hence no homosexual tendencies among primitive man. Their inclination to sex was essentially for procreation rather than recreation. Murray and Roscoe have argued that there has always been the tendency on the part of early anthropologists to remain silent about homosexuality in Africa. As to why some early anthropologists remained silent about homosexuality in Africa is not explained by Murray and Roscoe. For example, did they hide behind the theory of evolution to explain away the existence of homosexuality in Africa? Why did western anthropologists dismiss the existence of homosexuality in pre-colonial Africa for so long? For example, Evans Pritchard, a celebrated anthropologist on African cultures, was silent about homosexuality until 1957 when he published in an obscure article about homosexual relations among Azande men.

Murray and Roscoe make argument which somehow weakens their position on homosexuality. For example, they have maintained that 'homosexual relations occur solely due to a lack of women or as part of a short-lived adolescent phase. The possibility of homoerotic desire – that an individual may actually want and find pleasure in another of the same-sex – is effective (Murray et al, 1998: xiii). They also posit that in highly sex-segregated societies of Africa, homosexual behaviour and relationships were very common among individuals of the same age, especially before they engaged in heterosexual marriage. Whichever way we look at the argument, it is obvious that homosexuality existed in pre-colonial Africa.

Religiously, Dlamini writes that those homosexual relations were very potent for achieving:

> assimilation in the African society of multiplicities. Having studied homosexuals in South Africa, she maintains that some traditional healers and ritual experts, especially men claim that they could only be successful in their practice when they have no contact with women. Because of beliefs that women are polluted and polluting because of menstruation, post-partum changes to the body, pregnancy, breastfeeding, etc. Parrinder (1980) suggests that these men did always have sexual relation with other men (Parrinder 1980, cited in Dlamini 2006:135)

There are other cultures among African Traditional Religion where male-male intimacy also has connection to the sacred. In Cameroon,

Guinea, and Gabon, the Fang peoples engage in male-male intimacy as a way to promote prosperity. Among the Buissi people (the Congo) women encourage premarital lesbian relations in the belief that this enhances fertile heterosexual marriages. In north-central Africa the Azande women have ritual ceremonies for entering into such relationships (Siker, 2007:51-52). The fact that something is reduced to "rituals" could be read as part of Africa's assimilative practices and managing the contradictions of the practice given the premium on procreation.

Nkunzi Nkabinde and Ruth Morgan in their article, 'This has happened since ancient times…: It's something that you are born with': Ancestral wives among same-sex Sangomas in South Africa' argue that homosexuality is indigenous to Africa. The article avers that there were traditional and institutionalised ways in which African women who were *Sangomas* (traditional healers) could engage in same-sex relationship, hence challenging the notion that same-sex relationships are un-African. *Sangoma*s were not recognised during the days of apartheid in South Africa, they were despised and regarded as primitive witchdoctors. The projection of homosexuality as sin is closely linked to the influence of Christianity. For example, Nkunzi Nkabinde, a lesbian Sangoma, writes that it was as a result of Christian influence that homosexuality is considered to be evil. Even so, she admits that much as same-sex relationship has a long history in Africa, the practice was kept secret. Why was it kept secret? Was it kept secret because it was limited to the 'sacred' world? Could it be that it was limited to a particular group of people or social class, if we were to consider the centrality of social space, conversations and practices? Secret societies do not talk about what they do except in their sacred groves. Women do not talk about women's issues except among women, and in women's spaces. Hunters too talk about their issues in their spaces. So, when we talk about "secrecy" what do we mean exactly? Public interest issues were public. Everything else was discussed among stakeholders in their meeting spaces. All this raise complex issues about secret or how boundaries are drawn between what is specific to a group of people and what is commonly shared among the public. Maybe, we should also ask the counterpoint here: was heterosexual sex public because it was mainstream or accepted? How do we reconcile the Ghanaian, and to a larger extent the African's, love for children, who immortalise the dead, with homosexuality? In the Ghanaian public sphere, both the advocates of the rights of the LGBTQ community and proponent of the Family Bill see the homosexual debate as a diversionary tactics away from the state meeting the needs of Ghanaians.[51] For example, in popular discourses, many Ghanaians raise concerns about why nearly the whole of last year (2021), the nation was locked up in the homosexual debate, when there was hardly any report of persecution of members of the LGBTQ community.

At the "end" of colonialism, the concern of several the first generation of post-independent African leaders, including Kwame Nkrumah, was the possibility of neocolonialism (Nkrumah 1968). While these leaders imagined neocolonialism as a major force for Africa to contend with, the means through which the erstwhile colonial world would carry through with it was not immediately clear. In many cases, the idea was that the Euro-American world and now China would leverage Africa's human and material resources at the expense of Africans. While it is true that the human and material resources of the continent continue to remain the source of economic succour to the Euro-American and the Asiatic worlds, the neo-colonial contention Africans are dealing with appears more pernicious and herculean than just fighting to save the continent's material resources from constant external exploitation. The rhetoric of neo-colonialism features very strongly in the LGBTQ debates. Both the drafters of the Bill and the petitioners against it draw on neo-colonial arguments. They both diverge on issues of Ghana's sovereignty in deciding the contours of its legislation around sexuality. In the same sense, the general debates over the LGBTQ, as I have discussed above, have focused on whether or not same-sex intimacy is indigenous or European import. All the same, the rhetoric around neo-colonialism remains an important analytical reference for both public and academic discourses on sexuality and identity.

The above is precisely because, since the invention of printing in the western world in 16th Century (though the Chinese had already discovered it much earlier in the second century), western control of the African world has become epistemic dominance. Epistemic dominance has become very visible in the postcolonial world where African universities, usually colonial legacies, have become the mediators of western epistemic injustice. Consequently, framing the 21st Century world as an information age, seamlessly implies a world of

---

51 CDD-Ghana in the News (July 27, 2021), "LGBTQ bill only a diversionary tactic from real developmental issues – Prof. Gyimah Boadi," https://cddgh.org/lgbtq-bill-only-a-diversionary-tactic-from-real-developmental-issues-prof-gyimah-boadi/.

ideological wars – which since the end of the so-named World War II has become a world of cultural wars.

The cultural wars have involved both sexual and moral revolutions since the 1960s. Since then, western epistemic production has sought to deconstruct all social structures through the axioms of the "post" theories. The "post" theories, led by its western thinkers such as Derrida and Michel Foucault, have displaced communalism, profiling sagacious insight and social structures as social imprisonment that suffocates an individual's freedom. While there is hardly any doubt that these thinkers were responding to seismic post-World Wars socio-political changes, their theories have largely become paradigmatic in several African institutions of learning. The spread of the theories of these thinkers may have found a place in Africa because Africans were similarly grappling with similar post-World War challenges. It is still important for African institutions to encourage and centre Africa's own reflections on both local and international cultural transformations.

Individuals are to look into themselves and feelings to define themselves, while those who refuse to endorse their countercultural identities suffer cancel culture. Since Foucault placed on the frontal level of ideological battle, the postcolonial universities have reflected the cultural wars of the era. Consequently, with Man/woman as the measure of truth, knowledge is what conforms to the axioms of "post" theories – making academic institutions a zero-sum space.

Through western African universities since the 1980s and the West offering of scholarships to African students, African universities have become an extension of western universities that have discarded nearly all "conventional" knowledge as oppressive. This gives some African scholars, domiciled in the West, a glimpse of hope that these young African youth would liberalise the continent towards the path of decolonising LGBTQ practices (Falola 2022). The economic morass of the African world in the 1980s also disempowered the postcolonial states on the continent, as the Euro-American world channelled funding through both local and foreign-based NGOs – later emerging as civil society organisations. These nongovernmental organisations have become the vectors of advancing western cultural wars, especially since the turn of the millennium.

At the same time, the evangelical Christians from the American world and the Islamic reformist world have intensified their mission in Africa. Their activities have made traditional authorities, custodians of ancestral customs, in several African countries, especially Ghana, which turn more towards evangelical Christianity and/or reformist Islam. This intersection between puritanical religions and chieftaincy is also because of the cultural wars of the Euro-American world, especially as it morphs into the saturation of the world with LGBTQI+ rights. These rights are read by several Africans as breaking both ethical and ontological boundaries that could potentially put human civilisation on the false precipice of collapse. At the same time, several Africans cannot fathom the aggression with which the Euro-American world is pushing through with sexual rights when countries like Ghana hardly have any satisfying evidence of haunting and hacking homosexuals to death. My concern here is that these issues are so broad that a more nuanced synthesis of their arguments and relevance for this discussion is called for. But related to my argument, it shows the complex embodied complexities of the LGBTQ debates – repudiating simplistic counter-arguments around legislations.

Similarly, it is also a surprise to the overwhelming religious community that while the continent is still struggling with both the colonial legacies and self-inflicted challenges of underdevelopment, characterised by illiteracy, diseases, hunger, conflicts, poverty, and corruption, the Euro-American world is rather promoting sexual rights. But sexual rights could be said to be not necessarily limited to gay rights. They include youth, women and men's right to have safe, healthy, dignified and pleasurable sex that is voluntarily, free of violence, coercion or shame, manipulation, trickery etc. Nonetheless, the issue of "voluntarily, free" is more complex than it is simply stated, after all, individual agency is not as free as we are tempted to think or assume. In this sense, I reject postmodernist thinking by agreeing with Margaret Archer that human beings depend on the social interactions they have with the real world that take primacy over language in the emergence of human self-consciousness, thought, emotionality and personal identity – all of which are prior to, and more basic than, our acquisition of a social identity. The basic relationality of human beings and the real world can never be severed (Archer 2004: 3).[52] I love the way Archer engaged the issue of agency (freedom, the claim of the postmodern world in matters of sexuality), so I take the liberty to quote her directly:

> The way we are organically constituted, and the way in which the world is, together with the fact that we have to interact with the world in order to survive, let alone to flourish, means that an important part of being human is proofed against language (2004: 3).

---

[52] Margaret S. Archer, *Being human: The problem of agency* (Cambridge: Cambridge University Press, 2004). 3.

To adduce evidence to the complexity that emerges when postmodernists think language could be used to subvert reality, I share the following experience I had with a white student. In September 2022, a friend in the US asked me to help her colleague student who was visiting Ghana for a preliminary fieldwork research. My friend never told me anything about the sexual identity or so-called orientation of her colleague, student. So, when my friend's friend arrived, I was just more than glad to help the "lady" (my friend's friend as I first saw her) to preliminary test the feasibility of her research. Seeing the student, I did not need anyone to tell me she was a lady – though I also realised later that her clothes were often that of male. That nevertheless took away the fact that I saw her and was similarly seen by others as a woman/lady. But later I realised she was often moody and often complained about Ghanaian men seeking to woo her into relationship. At that point, I realised I should have oriented her about that unfortunate culture of a few Ghanaian men. So, I took the opportunity to orient her about Ghanaian culture, including the popular Akan/Twi use of *ɔbroni* to signify a "white" or usually a light-skinned person. Even with all this orientation, I still observed that my visitor was discontented. She opened up by complaining against the public, old and young people, calling "her" "her". At that point, I realised I was also "guilty" because I had been calling her "her". So, I took the trouble to ask her what pronoun she identified by. She told me "they". Since then, I started struggling and often had to remind myself to be sure that I either did not call her by any pronoun or simply avoided calling her by any feminine pronoun.

But that was not all, I had to bear the burden of both counselling her and protecting her against any young man seeking to either call her or talk with her. Overtime I became tired, as her mood swings and stress over the public non-recognition of her self-imposed "they" pronoun never abated. Indeed, I could sympathise with her plight against Ghanaian men, but I could not identify with her over a "they" pronoun that is not lived social reality both in Ghana and the US? How could anyone see a "she" and assumed the "she" is a they? Well, since there are only two existential and observable pronouns "he" and "she", the burned of explanation rested with her, not the perceiver. Also, I could not bear the cross of having to explain to everyone that the "she" they saw was/is a "they" in her thinking? I just gave up that unsolicited service and asked her to reconsider where she would like to carry her research in future. Fortunately, she only spent a week in Ghana and after enduring a week of stressfully trying to explain a word "they" against the reality of either he or she, I just hoped I don't meet her to have to keep taking a burden task. I would, however, be happy to still help her carry through with her research – if she decides to return to Ghana where there is no conflation between "he" and "she" and male and female, for that is how God made it from beginning. Any words that seek to alter existential reality must bear the burden of communicating allowed every day, for "he" and "she" need no explanation. More so, to think that language or any linguistic theory could be used to demolish reality perhaps explains the aptness of Douglas Murray's description of the extremities of the sexual revolution as the madness of identity.[53]

Worst of all with the efforts by the West to saturate Africa with the moral progressivism and sexual revolutions, the West African sub-region has become more and more unstable. Religious and politically induced conflicts continue to undermine the peace of the region, even as America's president Joe Biden's "democracy summit" seeks to impose sexual revolution as a major feature of Africa's democratic experiment.

In all this, several western trained Africans have become both cultural elite and allies of the Euro-American world in leveraging the publishing industry, including their control of the universities to advance "post" theories that sustain western cultural wars. The media in Africa which supposedly had its liberty through the cultural elites have become the channels that amplify the voice of the cultural elites. The "post" theories engage in the simplistic reductionism of either profiling human beings as simply rationally independent of society or socially constructed to be in social straitjacketing. Either way, the "post" theories do not pay attention to the human self-embodiments that interact with society in a relational manner. In several African countries, including Ghana and the western world until the beginning of the 1960s, "human beings emerged as the nexus between our embodied encounters with the world" (Archer 2004: 7). For this purpose, the Akan to be specifically, engaged human beings by setting ethical boundaries that ensured what was kept as private and what was allowed as public – especially in matters of sexuality. It also means that human beings are bearers of *continuous* sense of self, which is a mixture of three mutually constitute elements of reality, natural, practical and social (Archer 2004: 9). For queer sexuality to assume that their

---

53 Douglas Murray, *The madness of crowds: Gender, race and identity* (London: Bloomsbury Continuum, 2019).

queerness could be passed into law and recognised in Ghana would only crash society as it would run against the three continuous of being.

Simultaneously, the voices of the overwhelming public, who fund the bulk of the universities in Africa, are hardly considered by the cultural elite. In the case of Ghana, Nkrumah's counsel for the gown (the university) to come to town (the public) as part of building consensus in epistemic production has been strangled. While Nkrumah enjoined Ghanaian academics as part of his inaugural speech at the Institute of African Studies (IAS), University of Ghana, Legon in 1963, to express the attributes of the African Genius, the IAS appears not to have followed Nkrumah's prescient counsel.

At the time I both studied and worked as a post-graduate student and teaching assistant at the IAS (2009-2013), it became obvious to me that Ghanaian/African students at the IAS had/have relied on Euro-American liberal scholars on virtually all subjects, including the socio-history of the family, religion, politics, and political economy. While Ghana/Africa must not limit itself to only "African knowledge", the relative saturation of the IAS with western liberal theories undermines the incorporation and integration of the ancestral wisdom of Ghanaians/Africans in the knowledge production process. For the past three years, I have taken a close look at the course outline on the philosophy of social science for post-graduate students (PhD) at the University of Ghana. Regrettably, from my perspective, while all the sub-themes could be related reflect Africa's lived realities, nearly all the references are western-based.

Consequently, the decolonisation of the university which has gained much currency in the 21st Century, since it began in the 1960s, has not necessarily implied the de-centring of western theories with African theories. It has, in my reading of the field, become largely an issue of several Ghanaian/African scholars placing themselves in the middle as they demonstrate their own creativity in deploying western theories. Apart from a few scholars, such as Kofi Asare Opoku and Cameroonian Francis Nyamnjoh, who have convincingly argued for centring the traditions of knowledge of Africa, the decolonisation agenda is nothing short of a treadmill race where African scholars hardly push the trigger hard enough against western epistemic injustice. This for me, implies that the study and debate on homosexuality must incorporate Africa's traditions of knowledge – focusing on the continent's existential Triple Heritage. It must also consider the lived socio-economic and political contexts in order to provide point of convergence for consensus building. The rhetoric of demonisation of persons who hold contrary positions on the LGBTQ debates, in my opinion, reflects the attempts at fostering monologue on everyone.

The issue is complicated by the doctrine of "publish or perish" where African universities have imposed on themselves the "curse" of publishing with western publishers and journals. With Africa's lack of confidence in their publishing industries, the continent has often had to submit the knowledge they produce to the Euro-American world for approval. Unfortunately, African epistemes that enforce and endorse the conventional knowledge of bridging ethical and ontological boundaries that undermine the LGBTQI+ are often sabotaged. The "publish or perish" dictum has more recently been taken to another level where, "one can publish and yet perish" depending on the content of what one publishes. If an academic publishes not according to the "post" truth theories of liberal universities, such an academic is either whipped to fall in line or resign.[54]

Meanwhile, the novel coronavirus pandemic and the current Russian invasion of Ukraine have unveiled the illusions of human beings having "figured it all out" through advances in science and technology, especially research in Artificial Intelligence. The global necessity of imposition of social distancing rules to stem the tide against the pandemic, which has claimed millions of lives since the outbreak of the virus in March 2020 has brought to the fore that the idea of a radical individualism is false. That China is compelled to review its childbirth policy, allowing Chinese people to have up to 3 children implies that human beings cannot wantonly break both ethical and ontological boundaries without its attending socio-economic and political consequences.

At the same time, the current Russian invasion of Ukraine informs the western world that "wars" are hardly a thing of the past. This is critical because it was the end of the so-named World Wars in the 1940s and the collapse of the Soviet world in the 1990s that partly revolutionised the Euro-American sexual and cultural wars. Both the pandemic and the war have rendered more visible, the systemic imperfections of the world, shattering the simplicity of ideological binaries - socialism and capitalism. Consequently, anger has spiked since the outbreak of both the pandemic and the Russian war on Ukraine. The anger about the visibility of injustice has further deepened

---

[54] Callie Patter (September 8, 2021), 'Portland professor slams university as "social justice factory" in a scathing resignation letter', https://nypost.com/2021/09/08/portland-professor-slams-university-as-social-justice-factory/

and polarised Ghanaians/Africans over the homosexual debate. More specifically, given the nearly state of economic morass that the Ghana and several African countries, blurring lines a drawn in the debate. Members of both camps of the LGBTQ debates think it is a diversionary tactics, either from the government, civil society groups or religious institutions, to subvert their responsibilities toward providing social services – mitigating economic challenges.

Having spent much of my time reading and studying Africa and geopolitics, it appears to me that local challenges, either as spill over effects of capitalism or political dictatorship will continue to dim economic prosperity and justice. Putting my discussion of the LGBTQ in contest, therefore, beyond the issue of whether it is diversionary or not, the questions for my reflections in this book are: Why are we here on earth? Can science and technology answer all human questions? And can human beings live without the Triune God? What are modernity and modernisation? Why is the family the centre of all things, such that the cultural and sexual revolutions remain a major threat to human civilisation? And how should Ghanaians/Africans respond? How should Africans and their academics respond to the issues of epistemic injustice, and genuine concerns about gender imbalances? And how should the world respond to the issues of existential realities of imperfections/injustice – that are either engineered by "nature" or human beings? How should human beings use their anger productively against inequalities? My point in all this is that anger is legitimate, as it usually demonstrates human discontent with life's vicissitudes. It also implies, as far as I can appreciate, that through anger we register and communicate publicly that we refuse to be complicit in matters of injustice. But, as I have said, while anger is real, because multidimensional injustice is real, the issue is about negotiating anger and productivity to support human flourishing.

In all of my studies, I have ruminated over humanistic theories, usually in competition to undo the other, which had sought to solve human existential challenges. Needless to say, the world is a world of challenges. We solve one challenge only for the other to appear. This is to the extent that while some academics with the penchant for scientism make claims of "we have figured it all out" or "we are just about getting over all human challenges", we continue to face the reality of a world that is deeply shrouded in challenges. So, whether religious, mystic, atheist, or academic, we are all confronted with a world of imperfection – imperfections that are either humanly induced and/or naturally induced. It, therefore, appears to me that everyone is angry. But that we are angry is not new, because it appears we have always been angry. Our anger may also be because of all God's creation, human beings are "naturally" discontented beings. Animals are not worried about who they are.

In all of our anger, we see our imperfection manifesting in asymmetric relations, which bleeds into multiple binaries – male/female, ruler/ruled, tradition/modernity, professor/student, learned/unlearned, religious/non-religious, public/private, and rich/poor. These binaries have been paraded as though they are irreconcilable. And because these binaries are cast in an imagined eternal binary, human discontentment often appears too fatalistic.

All the imperfections of the world appear to have been exacerbated by the current novel coronavirus pandemic. Since the end of the so-named World War II, an idea of a new world order where human beings seemed to have chattered pathways to overcoming the challenges of war, famine, diseases, and illiteracy. Yuval Noah Harari, the Oxford-trained historian and professor of History at the Hebrew University is one scholar whose work on a world progressively getting better caught my attention. In his trilogy, Harari, concludes that human beings have progressed from being biochemicals to becoming deities through the mediation of science and technology – specifically artificial intelligence.

So, since the cultural and sexual revolution of the 1960s, induced by post-World War economic prosperity, the western world has pursued an agenda of "freedom". Freedom that appears to have no limits. Freedom that allows individuals to be their authentic self. Freedom that allows individuals to seek to look within themselves to ask for public acceptance. In all of this, freedom became and has remained so, the buzz word of the world. It is, therefore, no surprise that since the 1960s, sexual "orientations" that individuals would have shelved and kept secret all assumed public attention.

Some western writers, including Michel Foucault, provided the theoretical foundation for the moral and sexual revolution of the 1960s and 70s. Foucault recapitulated the Protagoras idea of "of all things man is the measure" to really put human beings in the centre of epistemic production. Foucault's sex repression hypothesis has become key in discussion on homosexuality in Ghana. According to Foucault, until the 17th Century, sex was freely talked about and discussed without rigid constrains. The subject of sex was also freely talked about without any let or hindrance. There was very little secrecy about the subject. The seventeenth Century marked a major shift in the discussion of sexuality. The Century was distinctively marked by the rise of the bourgeois class. The bourgeois class limited sex to only marriage. They proscribed the engagement in sex out of marriage. Sex was confined to only marriage situations, and it was also necessary for reproduction not recreation. Any use of sex for recreation, especially among the unmarried ones was strictly forbidden. The bourgeois, who became very rich through industriousness and hard work, insisted that energy should be channelled to production instead of sex for recreational purposes. The bourgeois also determined who had the right to talk about sex. Once they controlled the person who had the right to talk about sex, they controlled knowledge about the subject, and once the knowledge was controlled, it meant that power then rested in their hands. The repressive sex hypothesis could be compared to the discourse on homosexuality.

With human beings enthroned as captains of life, a development in western history begins with the secularisation of knowledge in the seventeenth century, all "conventions" had to cow to human desires. Thus, since Immanuel Kant and David Hume led the western world into its so-called enlightenment, Foucault's scholarly contributions in the area of post-structuralism provided ammunition to individuals to pursue "self" against all odds. Himself gay and in love with same-sex infatuations, post-structuralism emerged as a critical theory in challenging every obstacle in the way of "authentic" self as oppressive. Words lost their meaning, while structures were bastardised as oppressive. This implies that his theory may have synchronised with the feminist, specifically what is attributed to Carol Hanisch's as "the personal is political" – a contextually double-edged statement. Besides, this statement is double-edged in this context., just as an affected, concerned Ghanaian/African, I am offended by staging same-sex issue as public – nearly reducing individuals from being social beings to legal beings. Contextually, therefore, the challenge has been how to manage uniquely individual sexual preference in the public sphere. It has also been about how Ghanaians and Africans could liberalise individual's sex preferences without upsetting the real or imagine social order that both local and translocal political economies impose on us.

It is also not accidental that the sexual revolution world resonated with United Nation's declaration of the 1970s as Women's Decade. Since the family is fundamental in human society and marriage being fundamental for *pro*-creation (support creation), the authentic was tipped to upset marriage, as women also became interested in expressing themselves. As I discuss in Chapter Three, through the works of Simone de Beauvoir who was inspired by the existentialist theory of her sexual partner, Jean-Paul Sartre, women also treated marriage as oppressive. Beginning with her *Ethics of ambiguity* and *Second sex*, de Beauvoir theorised the transcendence and immanence as embodied in man-woman relationship. She wrote that the realm of the transcendence, discussed in *Ethics*, is the space for activities such as discovering, invention, exploring, studying, writing, creativities and ingenuity. It is within the transcendence where human beings exert themselves to materialise their potentials. Society treats the transcendence as the place of work and action that is occupied by men (de Beauvoir 1952: 183; 1948: 81). Immanence, on the contrary, is the is the place to reproduction, lacks creativity but caught in the fossilised space of repeated actions. It is the space for domestic activities, such as cooking, washing, cleaning, and watching television, and above all the biological function of giving birth (1952: 63-65; 474-478). The activities of the immanence, considered the space for women, is not valued as economically profitable. Much as activities at the immanence level could be creative, it is considered the space where reasoning is absent. Ordinary, the transcendence and immanence must cohere to advance human flourishing, the inequality embodied in the two rendered it an androcentric tool for oppressing women. Women are oppressed "into a thing" (1948: 82).

Against the above context, de Beauvoir described marriage as institutionalising women as the male Other – women become "a thing" for oppression (1952: 465). Marriage forestalls women's creativity, subjugates their intelligence and self-determination and become manages of men's homes (1952, 464, 467-469). That marriage is oppressive is that it affords men the chance to advance their transcendental roles as women are stacked in the performance of immanence roles (1952: 429-430, 447-448). With all these, while men depend on women to achieve their self-interests, they do so at the expense of women. Reducing women to the performance of domestic roles, de Beauvoir considered motherhood as important in establishing the purpose of marriage and could enrich existence, marriage is not the reason for being (1952: 483, 526, 511). Impliedly, while motherhood is per se oppressive, the burdens imposed on it as an immanence activity is oppressive. The challenge with the oppression is that the transcendence and immanence morphs into division of labour, which she wrote as part of the idea bourgeois wife (1952: 482) – a wife who is given something to in the world, as if she is not part of the world already. To be sure, de Beauvoir was not against marriage per se, but the possibilities of assigned roles grounding women to domesticity.

This is because if marriage is properly practised, by allowing men and women equal opportunity to flourish, marriage could be a force for equitable social relations (1952, 425, 479, 694). Logically, therefore, feminists have said reproductive roles (pregnancy, childbirth, carework, domestic work) should be seen as real work and paid for because women's low status emanates from a naturalistic view of women's roles. That is, the idea that women's roles as mothers are effortless, part of nature or even God ordained. Women are asking men to stop penalising them for being women by paying them less, subordinating them etc.

To be sure, the demands of women are fair and necessary to keep society afloat. The challenge, perhaps is that some scholars continue to profile marriage as the institution that determine gendered inequities in societies. Consequently, gendered inequities are treated as inherent in the marriage institution (Nock 1998: 86-87). It appears that marriage becoming an institution of oppression is incurable. It is for this reason that may have inspired de Beauvoir to have written that:

> Given that one can hardly tell women that washing up saucepans is their divine mission, they are told that bringing up children is their divine mission. But the way things are in this world, bringing up children has a great deal to do with washing saucepans. In this way, women are thrust back into the role of a relative being, as a second-class person (Schwarzer 1984: 114).

The appearance of marriage as incorrigibly incapable of reforming to reform to accommodate the equity women deserve has rather contributed to a few feminists rejecting the legal basis of marriage. Generally, the logic of lesbianism has nearly become a narrative of liberating women from the privilege societies assign to men through heterosexual normativity. For example, Card argues that marriage as a social institution is oppressive and alongside motherhood (as an institution) should be abolished in favour of alternative forms of durable partnership and child rearing (Card, 2002: 25). She also argued that the laws that establish marriage and motherhood as institutions trap victims of terrorism (referring to married women) in the home (2002: 140). As a result of the encompassed nature of institutionalised marriage and motherhood as oppressive, Card argued that marriage must be more flexible in the establishment of intimate partnership and more communal or at least distributed childbearing (p. 143). In fact, she argued marriages that has the state as the third (p. 147). To cap it all, it was in the 1970s, precisely 1973 that the Supreme Court of the United States of America established the legal right to access abortion nationwide through the landmark decision in the Roe v. Wade case (Kommers 1977). In 2022, the same Supreme Court cancelled the Roe vs Wade ruling. However, this ruling really focuses our attention on bodily integrity vis-à-vis pregnancy. Can women (and men as partners) decide whether to carry a pregnancy to term or not? Can women decide to use contraception or not? Can women decide when to have sex for pleasure when to have sex for procreation? What happens if conception happens and yet the couple is not ready for parenthood? What about quality of life for babies/children and mothers if/when all conception is carried to term?

With this revolution that challenged conventional truth and facts about marriage, several western scholars became alarmed and wrote books about the genealogies of western individualism. Robert Bellah referred to it as expressive individualism, while Charles Taylor referred to it as the age of authenticity (Bellah et al. 1985; Taylor 2007). The issue for me is not so much about atavism, as it is about negotiating the complex contradictions embedded in the freedoms and responsibilities men are expected to enjoy and perform in marriage. But it also points to the interconnectedness of human society, similar to a jigsaw puzzle, where every single part plays a teleological role. That is why, for me, Ghana and Africa, can hardly discuss the LGBTQ issue as merely a fad and craze of individuals; also, indicating the need to go beyond legislations to discuss other complex matters. The Family Bill for examples, renders it nearly impossible for the LGBTQ to have a family, not even through IVF and adoption. In such a state, one could clearly understand that the Bill did not just treat the rights of individuals as an isolation of the general Ghanaian understanding of family based on childbirth, parental responsibilities, kinship ties, and social reciprocities.

As the Euro-American world, particularly Western Europe and the United States of America leveraged economic prosperity to entrench individual rights, the so-named developing economies, including Ghana, had their economies suffering major shipwrecks. But the irony of history is that while economic prosperity enforced western secularisation of morality, Ghana and several African countries entered into revitalised religious resurgence in the 1980s. The Ghanaian religious landscape became dominated by "puritanical" religious movements, which morphed in the unification of the Ahlu Sunna (reformist Islam) and incursion of American Evangelical Christianity in Ghana (Freston 2001).

As the Ghanaian economy atrophied, religions surged alongside the retention of indigenous cultural values, around sex ethics. Similarly, since the decade coincided with the HIV/AIDS epidemic, the various religious group intensified sex ethic education, framed around sexual purity as HIV/AIDS was spiritualised and considered to spread through sexual immorality (Kwansa 2013; Frimpong-Nnuroh 2006). At the same time, the 1980s economic challenges in Ghana marked an important watershed in the western world seeking to fulfil Nkrumah's prophecy of neo-colonialism by funding NGOs through building local compradors (Hearn 2007). But again, this also brings out another layer of contextual controversy where Africans also look to the West to give aid to support human development. The issue is also about how the West would give aid to Africa without insisting on changing ways of life or modes of thinking.

With Ghana, like other developing economies going through economic hardship, the western world spread their liberalism, by disempowering the state through their imposition of neoliberal regime (Mohan 1996; Hilgers 2012). Through the mediation of western financial institutions (the Bretton Woods Institution) – the International Monetary Fund and the World Bank – the western world led the country into the hands of individuals and western capitalism – weakening the sovereignty of the state in the process (Ibid). Through the state recession from the public, as the state removed subsidies on education, health, and agriculture – the key sectors of the country's economy – the Ghanaian state began to sink into total economic insolvency.

Also, as the western leaders criminalised Ghanaian political elites as incompetent in managing the country's economy, foreign and local-foreign non-governmental organisations became the principal channels for the west to "invest" in the country (Nega and Scheider 2014). For this reason and many more, the 1990s witnessed the rise of pro-American/western NGOs, such as the Centre for Democratic Development (CDD)-Ghana and feminist group like the Network for Women's Rights in Ghana (NETRIGHT). These NGOs had and continue to have the goal of serving as active civil society that would "enable choices, scrutinise errant governments, and ultimately lead to regularised, plural democracy" (Mohan, 2002: 125). Around this same time, gender studies, I will discuss later in this chapter emerging – was leading the way towards American cultural and sexual revolution. Several NGOs also became the conveyors of western cultural values – that some analysts consider as threat to destroy the cultural and social foundation of Ghana/Africa (Tandon 2015). NGOs then derive their domestic over-lordship in reshaping the cultural and moral constitution as compradors in Ghana/Africa as part of a derivative power from the Global North (Bayart 2000). In the Northern regions of Ghana, NGO's have been accused by some of the residents as creating their own fiefdoms of clients for personal promotion and given the preponderance self-seeking factionalism among NGOs, they tend to undermine the state's efforts at decentralising development (Mohan, 2002). But all these issues are complex without an easy alternative because it appears marriage has compounded the challenge of women in Ghana. Since the last few decades, several scholars have observed the changing roles of women in the families. What has become obvious is that women, upon marriage, tend to perform both expressive and instrumental responsibilities – the two often dimension the goals that women-based NGOs often hoped to reverse.

This development creates an impression in the minds of the public that the establishers of liberal are imperialist stooges. The recent publication of the CDD that sought to disentangle chieftaincy from Ghana's liberal democracy is understood by some chiefs as part of the political regime to dispossess the institution of any power.[55] At the same time, western aid and intervention has hardly benefited Ghana/Africa (Bob-Milliar 2022; Moyo 2009; Bauer 2000). The issue became more complex as some individuals read suspicion into the western world's invested interest in sponsoring Ghanaian women and men to study in western institutions.[56] While these students are not forced to study

---

[55] Adam Smith International (Ghana Centre for Democratic Development), Understanding how dirty money fuels campaign financing in Ghana: An exploratory study (CDD Ghana, 2022) https://docs.google.com/viewerng/viewer?url=https://cddgh.org/wp-content/uploads/2022/02/Final-Report-CDD-Campaign-Financing-FCDO-11th-June-2021.pdf&hl=en, accessed: 12 March 2022.

[56] As part of Ghana's marking of 400 years of enslavement of Africans in the United States of America in 2019, the Cambridge University Ghanaian Society – a student body of Ghanaian students at Cambridge, of which I served as its president that year, organised a parallel event on campus. The event was to extend to students in England the conversations in Ghana about the government inviting Africans in the Diaspora to return home to help build Ghana/Africa. Dubbed "The Year of Return" and later "Beyond the Year of Return" in 2020. We invited an African-American civil rights advocates, Bob Brown as our guest speaker. During the event, several of the guest speakers said to the embarrassment of several of us students that Cambridge is an imperialist institution, training imperialists to go and loot the continent. Given that the event was held in my College - Wolfson, with several of the College's high-ranking administrators in attendance, the event became a major challenge to some of us who had benefitted from the College – including giving us free venue for the event.

abroad, the idea that they may nourish imperialist agenda is regrettably in the minds of some extreme Afrocentric persons – including a few who continue to call Oxbridge imperialist institutions.[57] The issue is even that the economic situation which is trapped in Africa's own culture of corruption and western's pursuit of neo-colonial control renders the idea of freewill for African students a major challenge. This means that by the time Ghana entered the millennium, the assumption was that these women and men who have sojourned to the west to study had returned with a deliberate effort at introducing some form of liberal democracy that empowered individuals other than the state (Arthur 2014).

As the state continued to lose grounds in holding the public sphere and cultural elitists supposedly becoming a conveyor belt for America's sexual and Cultural Revolution, the development of the country was framed around the old narrative of western modernity. Possibly, the rate at which the so-called developing countries were becoming westernised, but with no particular indicators in terms of social services may have resulted in the United Nations' promotion of the cultures of the world's indigenous people. This initiative known in the UN's project as cultural rights was relevant in responding to the excesses of "modernisation" which tend to marginalise indigenous cultures (Oomen 2005: 3-4).

For this reason of eroding indigenous cultures, chieftaincy became the focus of Ghana's (and of course, several African countries') democratic experiment – leading to a resurgence in chieftaincy.[58] Chieftaincy, considered the vanguard of Ghana's cultural aspirations, thus became the focus of research attention (Odotei and Awedoba 2006). This was also because the political elite, headed by Jerry John Rawlings, who initially read chieftaincy as anti-revolutionary, appealed to chiefs to support the nation (Nugent 1996; Boafo-Arthur 2003). It was during this period that the Asantehene, Otumfuo Opoku Ware II instituted the idea of development chiefs, where non-royal stools were created for influential individuals to support human flourishing (Bob-Miilliar 2009). This Asante innovation spread to other areas in Ghana (Steegstra 2008). For several of these scholars, chieftaincy was presented as the viable and credible alternative to rescue the partisanship and deep-seated and threatening polarisation that was

[57] Ibid.

[58] Smith, International.

sinking the nation.[59] Others like the Ghanaian philosopher, Kwasi Wiredu, even proposed a type of consensual democracy patterned according to the deliberative and consensual nature of indigenous political systems (Wiredu 1995; Bamfo 2000).

Chiefs in Ghana are constitutionally mandated as the custodian of the various customs of Ghana. It is for this reason that in the Family Bill the drafters appealed to chiefs as the legitimate agents to determine the boundaries of marriage as heterosexual. Also, as the drafters of the Bill appealed to the chiefs, they were similarly curating their legitimacy against the petitioners. More so, with several Ghanaian Pentecostals taking up chiefly titles (Prempeh 2021), the institution has become one of the fortresses against the local and international call for Ghana to decriminalise homosexuality. With recent publication by the CDD on the impact chiefs' meddle in politics could undermine the country's democracy, the involvement of chiefs in the LGBTQ debates is partly partisan. It is one of the ways chiefs are re-stepping into the domain of partisan politics, a controversial attempt that the Constitution disallows them. Nevertheless, any altercation between the CDD and chieftaincy could frustrate the possibility of dialogue for cultural regime change; it may also make chiefs more resolute in resisting the LGBTQ community, as several of these have registered the protest against the LGBTQ community. But this vortex of tension also points to the integration of the LGBTQ debates into the larger political regime in Ghana. It could be argued that if the chiefs are democratic and can handle debate then they should convince their challengers (the people opposed to the Bill) on matters at hand. But that in itself as part of the misconstruing of the idea of democracy as "freedom" from ethical and ontological boundaries. The point is simply that the Akan or Ghanaian notion of self is not constituted in the delusion of an individual who is ontologically free from society's interactions and lived realities. For this reason, in Ghana, homosexuality and its ensuing sub-levels are not issues that one would want to entertain in public discussion. That idea of a man having sex with a man and a woman having sex with a woman is considered *musuo* – a non-negotiable abomination – in the Akan or Ghanaian enchanted public sphere.

---

[59] The major scholarly works on chieftaincy, which my colleagues and I at the IAS, Legon called Chieftaincy Bible, has been the huge, edited volume of Irene K. Odotei and Albert K. Awedoba, Chieftaincy in Ghana: Culture, development, and governance (Accra: Sub-Saharan Publishers, 2006).

It was during the challenges of the 1980s that the Ghanaian government began the devolution of power to ensure nationwide development. Already the selectivity in colonial "development" agenda where the colonialists impoverished the Northern Regions of Ghana as labour pool that resulted in a gapping disproportionate national development (Songsore and Denkabe 1995). The situation worsened under the various postcolonial governments whose efforts did not bring the Northern Regions closer to the Southern Regions. The plight of the Northern Region in particular and the nation in general in terms of poor development was exacerbated by the structural adjustment of the 1980s. But recent scholarship has sought to deconstruct this "blame-game" narrative as attention is rather focused on the economic potentials of the region (Nyaaba and Bob-Milliar 2019).

As Ghanaians considered the issue of LGBTQ despicable, the nation protested against the against LGBTQ community's proposed use of the city of Accra to host a conference of gays and lesbians in 2006. Based on his own beliefs and responsibility to protect the constitution and heterosexual custom (not culture) of Ghanaians, the then president of Ghana, John Agyekum Kufuor vowed not to both allow the conference nor decriminalise the practice (Prempeh 2021a). Until 2006, there were rather rumours about the practice. But in 2011, while I was completing my MPhil studies, the former British Prime Minister David Cameron, had the temerity to caution countries that "depended" on the UK to either decriminalise LGBTQ+ or risk being starved of aid.[60] Given the threats of Cameron, I respond with an article that was published in the graduate student journal of the University of Ghana. I sincerely think that Cameron failed to realise that his country sat on wealth, obtained through wits and daily criminality, looting, and raping of the wealth of other nations. He also did not realise that the aid he was talking about was not what Africans needed to develop and that using aid to promote LGBTQ rights was of concern to Ghanaians. So, Ghana's former president, John Evans Atta Mills who vowed never to bow to the imperialist![61]

---

[60] Press Association (30 October 2011), 'Countries that ban homosexuality risk losing aid, warns David Cameron,' https://www.theguardian.com/politics/2011/oct/30/ban-homosexuality-lose-aid-cameron, accessed: 10 March 2022.

[61] Ghanaweb (29 August 2011), 'Government will not legalise homosexuality and lesbianism', https://www.ghanaweb.com/GhanaHomePage/NewsArchive/Government-will-not-legalize-homosexuality-and-lesbianism-217399, 10 March 2022.

Since 2011, the issue of the LGBTQ+ has taken both a low and high pitch, based on how the west thinks they can push their agenda of cultural imperialism through. During the time of a "no nonsense" American leader, Donald Trump, America went relatively quiet on superimposing its cultural and sexual revolution on other nations. But with the exit of Trump and the entry of a deeply leftist American leader Joe, who would have been booed away not to contest an election in Ghana, Americans are up in leading the neocolonial agenda in the 21st Century world.

When Joseph Robinette Biden Jr, became the 46th president of the US in 2020, his first foreign speech in February 2021 included an order to all US government agencies active abroad to *promote* the rights of lesbian, gay, bisexual, transgender, intersex and queer (LGBTQI+) people and come up with plans within 180 days.[62] As part of the US government promoting the practice of LGBTQI+ globally, the policy that, the US will be pushing are:

- Building coalitions of Like-Minded Nations and Engaging Organizations in the Fight Against LGBTQI+ Discrimination.
- Bilateral relationships with allies and partners, as well as multilateral for a and international organizations, are key vehicles to promote respect for and protection of the human rights of LGBTQI+ persons and to bring global attention to these goals.
- Agencies engaged abroad should be strengthen the work they have done and initiate additional efforts with other nations, bilaterally and within multinational for a and international organizations, to: counter discrimination on the basis of LGBTQI+ status or conduct; broaden the number of countries willing to support and defend the rights of LGBTQI+ persons; strengthen their role, including multilateral fora, of civil society advocates on behalf of the human rights of LGBTQI+ persons; and strengthen the policies and programming of multilateral institutions,

[62] Joseph R. Biden Jr., (4 February 2021), Memorandum on advancing the human rights of lesbians, gay, bisexual, transgender, queer, and intersex persons around the world – Presidential action https://www.whitehouse.gov/briefing-room/presidential-actions/2021/02/04/memorandum-advancing-the-human-rights-of-lesbian-gay-bisexual-transgender-queer-and-intersex-persons-around-the-world/, accessed 10 March 2022, emphasis mine.

> including with respect to protecting vulnerable LGBTQI+ refugees and asylum seekers.[63]

The US's pro-LGBTQI+ policy further stated:

> For the purposes of this memorandum, agencies engaged abroad include the Departments of State, the Treasury, Defense, Justice, Agriculture, Commerce, Labor, Health and Human Services, and Homeland Security, the United States Agency for International Development (USAID), the United States International Development Finance Corporation (DFC), the Millennium Challenge Corporation, the Export-Import Bank of the United States, the Office of the United States Trade Representative, and such other agencies as the President may designate.[64]

I do not have to provide any surgical analysis of Biden's intention of recolonising Ghana and Africa through the extension of America's cultural and sexual revolution around the world. Biden has, therefore, become the epitome of western liberalism as he fulfils the ambitions of other European leaders, including David Cameron and Theresa May. Certainly, Biden's inspiration emboldened yet another western diplomat, the Austrian diplomat Gregory Andrews to commission the opening of a community centre set up by the LGBTQ+ Rights Ghana in the city of Accra.[65] It was partly this misjudgement of a western diplomat that resulted in a coalition of Christians, Muslims, and chiefs (representing indigenous wisdom) framing a Bill to promote proper human family – according to Ghanaian cultural values and the Judeo-Christian-Islam aspirations for heterosexual relations. The Bill that was sponsored privately in Parliament by the coalition led by Sam George, a Member of Parliament, representing the people of Ningo, Prampram, was rightly titled, "Promotion of proper human sexual rights and Ghanaian family values, 2021." The object of the Bill is stated as follows:

---

[63] Ibid.

[64] Ibid.

[65] Ghanaweb (11 December 2021), 'Australian diplomat who helped commission LGBTQ+ office to leave Ghana', https://www.ghanaweb.com/GhanaHomePage/NewsArchive/Australian-diplomat-who-helped-commission-LGBTQ-office-to-leave-Ghana-1421593, accessed 10 March 2022.

To provide proper sexual rights and Ghanaian family values; proscribe LGBTQ+ and related activities; proscribe propaganda of advocacy for or promotion of LGBTTQQIAAP+[66] and related activities; provide for the protection of and support for children, persons who are victims or accused of LGBTTQQIAAPP+ and related activities and other persons; and related matters.[67]

In response, a group of academics and heads of civil society groups wrote a counter memorandum challenging the constitutionality of the Bill. In their memo, they claimed that:

> The LGBT Bill currently before Parliament is a major step backwards for democracy, inclusiveness, the protection of minorities and the vulnerable in society, and of fundamental human rights in Ghana. Under the grand sounding banner of '*proper human sexual rights and Ghanaian family values*' the Bill seeks to send the country back centuries into the past. Its language of 'recant and treatment' echoes the Middle Ages of Europe where the state and the Church, driven by misguided notions of heresy and witchcraft, hunted down innocents in the name of God and religious values. Blinded by religious zealotry and intolerance, the theocratic State and its Church forced innocent vulnerable persons to 'recant' their religious beliefs and burnt nonconformists at the stakes in the misguided belief that their gruesome murder would, somehow, purge their souls of evil.[68]

After highlighting what they considered as the sociological and legal contradictions in the Bill, the group of academics summed their argument for the rejection of the Bill that promotes human family and acceptable sexual values as follows:

> There can be no doubt, as we have demonstrated, that the Bill constitutes an impermissible invasion of the inviolability and human

[66] The acronym stands for: Lesbian, Gay, Bisexual, Transgender, Transsexual, Queer, Questioning, Intersex, Ally, Asexaul, Pansexual and any other sociocultural notion of sex and sexual relationship that is contrary to the sociocultural notion of male and female assigned at birth, Bill, p. 23.

[67] Promotion of Proper Human Sexual Rights and Ghanaian Family Values Bill, 2021, https://cdn.modernghana.com/files/722202192224-0h830n4ayt-lgbt-bill.pdf, accessed 12 March 2022, p. 1.

[68] Memorandum to Select Committee on the Constitutional, Legal and Parliamentary Affairs on the: Promotion of Proper Human Sexual Rights and Ghanaian Family Values Bill, 2021, p. 1.

> dignity of the person and, freedom of expression and thought, freedom of assembly, including the right to organise and take part in processions and demonstrations and the right to protection against discrimination on grounds of gender, race, ethnic origin, religion, creed or social and economic status.[69]

Clearly, one could see that, the academics and professionals, led by their lawyer, Mr Akoto Ampaw have discussed the issue as they understand it best. Nevertheless, much as I have mentioned the insights their petition shed on the subject, they also dabbled in issues that complicate the conversation. There is hardly any record that the church and/or any religious entity have launched a physically violent crusade against any minority group in Ghana As academics, it would have been refreshing for them to provide evidence of persecution of members of the LGBTQ community for the state or the international community to address. It is worthy to note that the issue of LGBTQ+ peaked in Ghana in 2021 to coincide with the date of January 2021 that Biden gave for reassessment of his achievement to promote and support homosexual and transgender imaginary rights in Ghana and elsewhere around the world. But more importantly, these academics could not find in any legal instrument in Ghana where rights are accorded to sexuality. With such a difficulty in finding a logical reason to promote queer sexualities that are irreconcilable with the Ghanaian lived socio-public reality, the academics and professionals had appealed to international laws. Regrettably, their appeal to international laws further shrouded the whole debate in the murky subject of the LGBTQ constituting western agenda – blurring the nexus between local and transnational in shaping global politics and individual identities.

Beyond citing international laws, which as I have said gave put the petitioners in the bad light, they also appealed to what I rather think was equally a complex issue – their argument that advocacy should be allowed, because slavery ended because of advocacy. That advocacy led to the "end" of slavery is rather a little bit of a simplistic reading of the history of abolition of slavery. Yes, definitely, advocacy played a role. If the advocacy argument were true, and certainly it is not, why did slavery "end" in the middle of the 19th Century when advocacy against the practice began in the 16th Century with groups such as the Quakers – though the anti-slavery stance of the groups was far from uniform? (Davis 1999; Carey and Plank 2014). Why did the British who sent naval

[69] Ibid., p. 14.

ships "fighting" slavery continue to use enslaved Africans as police officers in the late nineteenth century Gold Coast? (Balakrishnan 2020). That slavery continued into the late 19th Century even after post-proclamation of the mid-19th Century disputes the assumption that advocacy ended enslavement (Akurang-Parry 2002). After an extensive fieldwork, archival research and extensive review of literature, Akurang-Parry concluded in his doctoral thesis that:

> The efforts of the colonial state in the late nineteenth century to abolish slavery/pawnship, recruit labor, and harness the transition from unfree to wage labor were dismal failures. The colonial state was hampered by a paucity of officials and by African resistance. Moreover, the indigenous rulers, the agents of colonial labor recruitment, failed in their task to recruiting labor and managing the transition to free labor. ... During the nineteenth century the colonial state failed to inaugurate a workable policy to assist free slaves in the transition from bondage to freedom. Thus, the colonial state unequivocally allied with the slave-holding class (Akurang-Parry 1999: vi).

As part of exposing people who are proud to admit that they don't know everything and also challenging "common knowledge", John Lloyd and John Mitchinson concluded on whether the British Parliament and by extension the western world, ever made slavery illegal as follows:

> There is a difference between 'abolishing' something and making it a criminal offence. Although slavery was *abolished* all over the world many years ago, in many countries the *reality* only changed when laws were introduced to punish slave owners. You might think slavery is a thing of the past and isn't relevant to modern Britain, but there are more slaves in the world now – 27 million of them – than were ever seized from Africa in the 400 years of the transatlantic slave trade (emphasis in original text) (Lloyd and Mitchinson 2010: 122).

By the way, another modern form of slavery that the Ghanaian historian, Kwabena Akurang-Parry said reflects all the vagaries of pre-modern and serves as subtle postabolition expansion of the domestic enslavement of women is called *abaawa*. *Abaawa*, alongside female porters/bearers (known as *kayayei*, who carry heavy loads as though they were beast of burden, for me is a form of forced labour – predominant in the cities of Accra and Kumasi) remains fresh in contemporary Ghana. Meanwhile, this common phenomenon in the homes of elitist women and men has not received extensive research – though feminist activists would promote everything from the camp of the leftist Western world, including breaking ethical and ontological boundaries. Akurang-Parry explained the paucity of research on issue of *abaawa* that he called "a sacred" cow in feminist activism and scholarship. More recently, however, a lot has been published and said about unpaid child domestic workers, child fosterage, child apprenticeships in west Africa across several sectors (agriculture, fishing, domestic service and the informal sector). I therefore do not see why and how feminists writing about it would make a difference. The practice is resisted on cultural grounds, poverty alleviation, kinship etc. Similarly, CNN has done documentaries on the enslavement of children in cocoa production etc.

> Due to uncomfortable fact that those engaged in activism that seeks to liberate and empower women are themselves beneficiaries of *abaawa* labor: Most upper- and middle-class Ghanaian women use the services of *abaawa* in their homes (Akurang-Parry 2010: 29).

In terms what they *abaawa* do, they serve as head porters and peddlers, truck pushers, and ice water sellers. Some of the girls work in smoke-filled and overheated workshops for roasting groundnuts on commercial scale (Akurang-Parry 2010: 36). Akurang-Parry wrote about their condition of life as follows:

> The *abaawa* institution retains the vestiges of precolonial and colonial servile institutions. What the various periods have in common regarding *abaawa* institution is that they are fraught with abuse, exploitation, harshness, and above all, underscore a social formation entailing structures of gender inequality and the feminisation of poverty and marginality (p. 41).

Instead of advocacy argument – based on morality and economic progress – which the Quakers were complexly involved in, I argue that it is functional differential that usually brings about revolutionary change. For example, given that slavery "ended" in the middle of the 19th Century (including the British who abolished it in 1834), about two centuries after the industrial revolution, it is safe to conclude, siding with Eric Williams re-evaluation of the abolition of enslavement, that the industrial revolution was key in the "abolition" of enslavement

(Holsey 2008; Williams 2014). The invention of machines and new approaches to production that relieved significantly and proved to be cost effective in production was one of the major reasons for the "end" of the slave trade. At any rate, while there is hardly any dispute that slaves were not generally treated well, the success of a slave owner relied on the welfare of his slave. The earliest enslaved Africans (20 in all) to arrive in Jamestown (British North America) in 1619 were incorporated into white families and hardly reduced to chattel slaves until 1641 when Massachusetts became the first English colony to legalise slavery (Byrd and Lori 2014).

Theorising Culture and Identity

As part of the heated arguments over gay rights in Ghana and Africa, issues about culture have been drawn in. Culture remains complex and is perhaps deliberately framed as nebulous in discourses around sexuality. In her editorial piece to Feminism Africa, Desire argued that the impact of sexuality in configuring a host of cultural practices such as heterosexuality, social identities and deep-seated cultural discourses have gone largely unacknowledged. She therefore concluded on the impediment of naturalised cultural discourses on sexual freedom as follows:

> These naturalised discourses of "culture" in Africa have functioned coercively. Fictions of authenticity, custom, and the "past" bolster patriarchal goals and desires, while perpetuating the servitude of women, and demonising both the men and women who choose to reject heterosexist norm. Such fictions carry a charged emotional force because they are linked to a sense of loyalty among those with shared history of misrepresentation and cultural marginalisation. But their claims to inclusiveness are belied by their projection of culture as an edifice of unchanging institutions, traditions and identities. Arguments about the timelessness of the latter have a particular valence in the context of colonial and neo-colonial ills. Ironically, then, the sense of "culture" fixed in dominant discourses echoes colonial projections of a static and primordial African culture is diametrically opposed to western modernity (Lewis 2003: 1).

She continued:

> Fictions of an undiluted African culture have been weapons for enforcing women's obedience, with the charge of "Westernisation" being used against women in public realms dominated by men. Women so castigated are pressurised to modify their "untraditional" behaviour or relinquish an identity that appears to bequeath communal dignity (Ibid. 2).

Similarly, contributing to an editorial comment on sexual cultures, Professor Takyiwaa Manuh, one of the eighteen academics and civil society leaders protesting against the Proper Family and Sexuality Bill in Parliament consented that US President Bush's "sexual conservatism is a threat to sexual democracy" (Mama, Pereira and Manuh 2005: 2). They also charged the schools of retaining conservative sexual culture that stifles research on sexuality (Ibid. 3). Again, as I will discuss later in Chapter Three, nearly all the major disciplines on gender and sexuality at the University of Ghana focus on western liberal sexual theories at the expense of the cultural position of the overwhelming Ghanaian funders of the university on the subject. This is precisely the group that leaned on "culture" and materialism to restudy gender and what they refer to as "ongoing dynamics of sexuality in Africa" (Ibid. 4). They also argued that "The empowerment of sexualities … might be a more effective and radical way of challenging patriarchies" (Ibid. 6). The entire Issue 5 of the journal *Feminist Africa* in 2005 was dedicated to overturning heteronormativity as part of their fight for sexual liberation for women to indulge themselves in, including lesbianism. Again, we are confronted with the tension that marriage poses. The alternative is not easy to provide, except that legislating lesbianism is similarly considered not ideal for women's liberation. This is especially the case when it is both patterned according to heterosexual marital unions with the state serving as the third party (Chad 2002: 139).

Two years before the publication of the *Feminist Africa*, Professor Manuh had published a chapter of a book on diaspora and gender in which she argued that Ghanaian patriarchal culture and women's quest for freedom was the reason Ghanaian women in Canada resent the notion of "home" in Ghana as ideal for their flourishing as agentic beings. On the contrary, men cherish and desire home because it gives them cultural locational advantage to lord it over women (Manuh 2003). Manuh's insights also raise contentions about the position of Akan women and how they should negotiate their agency. It could be surmised that Manuh is arguing that western sexual liberalism is better than African cultures that ensure gender hierarchies. Of course, in the 1980s, in her article on the Asante queen mother's court, she (Manuh

1988) argued that the Akan woman was culturally not as empowered to participate in indigenous governance of adjudication as it had been suggested by anthropologists such as R.S. Rattray. More recently, a Ghanaian Queen mother had written her doctoral dissertation in which she dismisses the idea that Akan women had no power.[70] Whatever the direction of the argument, the sexuality and gender issues are very complex and would need a sober reflection to dialogue opposing views.

Looking at all this, we would not fail to discern a few things that need discussing. But suffice it to say that the academics and civil society group leaders see themselves as cultural elite who must pursue a moral revolution agenda to decriminalise homosexuality. Second, contrary to the charge against religion as imperialistic, these cultural elite also have a religion – that is either materialistic or liberal theology. This betrays Seth Tweneboah's simplistic conflation of a binary between secular and religion in the homosexual discourse, and shames all those who rather see Christianity as major stumbling block to sexuality rights (Tweneboah 2020). After all, these materialists and liberal Christians, like conservative Evangelical Christians, have a worldview, that allows them to answer the existential questions: Who am I? Why am I here? And where do I go from here? These questions, as I will discuss in Chapter Three, forms the fulcrum of the homosexual and sexual revolution discourse.

More importantly, the discussion so far also points to the contention over what culture is and what it is not. There are counter-accusations over who is being a cultural imperialist in terms of whether homosexuality is foreign or not; and whether homophobic or homoerotic is foreign or not to Africans. I discuss this within the broader context of the dialectic nature of culture in serving human quest for meaning. Since human beings are equally in search of meaning by asking and responding to life's existential questions, every human being has a worldview/religion as a prism to make sense of the world. On the human journey for meaning, it has become obvious that humans are simply selective in their search for resources to satisfy their quest for meaning. This human quest for pluralism informs Peter Burke's idea of cultural hybridisation.

Co-writing a cultural project with Professor Akurang-Parry, we acknowledged the complexity of human cultures. We admitted that culture is a product of human beings. It is dynamic and osmotic. Throughout the ages, human beings have used language, ritual

---

[70] Because the author of the thesis is yet to defend it, I prefer to keep it anonymous.

performance, and aesthetic symbolism to archive and transmit culture from one generation to another. The challenge is how to negotiate cultural hybridity in a highly sensitive issue in the Ghanaian community such as homosexuality. Impliedly, while there is certainly nothing wrong with Ghanaian feminist borrowing from (and loaning ideas to) the West on sexuality and identity politics, the issue is more about negotiation and incorporation of multiplicity of ideas, as opposed any issue of zero-sum dismissal from the camp of those proposing the Family Bill and advocates of freedom for the LGBTQ community. Given that orality precedes literature, the myriad forms of cognitive arts contribute to (re)inventing culture. The dynamism embedded in culture is not the same across time and space. Thus, with its expanse definitions, culture is not fossilised; neither is it an ossified entity. This is emblematic of the fact that no society is impervious to 'modernity': culture has verticality of change and horizontal restitution. Ghana has transitioned from the precolonial period, the colonial epoch, to a contemporaneous post-colony of Globalisation and Glocalisation shaped by acculturation and enculturation within and without. It centralises Ghana in the Internet Age, showing the ways that the local and the foreign have paired up to shape Ghanaian culture and heritage. Underpinning this proposed anthology is how the concept of Social Change is historicised to measure the indicators of economic, political, technological, environmental, social, etc. alteration and renewal in Ghana.

Just like the *Sankofa* epistemological symbol, a metaphor of fusing the past and the future, contextualised in the present as an agency, Ghanaian societies have recorded marked transitions in the postcolonial era.

Thus, in our proposed collection of essays, our foci are to do critical pan-Africanising analyses of current cultural waves in Ghana, including what was, what has changed, and the holistic factors of change within specific seams of our culture and heritage. The proposed project aims to argue that Ghanaian cultures have demonstrated both resilience and adaptability in the face of 'modernisation,' Globalisation, Afropolitanism, cosmopolitanism, transnationalism, and the idea of the *cyborg* yet in many respects there are difficulties in invoking what may be called Ghanaian normativising.[71]

---

[71] Kwabena O Akurang-Parry, "Call for book chapters: Ghanaian culture and heritage: Contemporaneous change and continuity'. From: Kwabena Opare Akurang-Parry <kakurang-parry@ug.edu.gh>To: Kwabena Opare Akurang-Parry

In this section, therefore, I engage the discourse on culture and identity, bringing out a few nuances for public and academic considerations. Culture is a concept that has been studied by people from different disciplines. This is because it is fundamental to defining a human being. Without culture, there will be no human being. It is through a culture that one is able to delineate one person from another. It is also through culture that we can peep into the cultural nuances of a people and live with them peacefully. Culture is also the product of human beings as part of their efforts at finding meaning and satisfying their needs. Basically, culture is the totality of how a group of people live. This includes their beliefs, values, norms, language, and material culture.

Culture is very important in human society. It is the possession of culture that distinguishes human beings from non-human entities. Similarly, it is culture that sets one group as unique and distinct from the other. This is precisely because human beings are the product of their culture. The centrality of culture in defining humanity notwithstanding, the concept has not escaped the challenge of finding a common universally accepted definition. There are thus several definitions of culture, as there are different scholars about the concept, and each definition has been subjected to acute criticisms. However, in this book, I would use the definition as given by E.B. Tylor. According to E.B. Tylor, "Culture of civilization in its wisest ethnographic sense, is that complex whole which includes knowledge, beliefs, art, morals, law, customs and practices and any other capabilities of Man as a member of society" (Tylor 1871/1958: 1). I firmly stick with E.B. Tylor's definition of culture because it chimes with my refutation of moral progressivism. Also, I do not want to be comfortably part of the majority cultural elites who are redefining morality to accommodate same-sex union. As an Akan and evangelical Christian, I want to be seen to be backward to God's view of marriage as heterosexual at creation and affirmed by Christ in His redemption of the elect of the Father. At any rate, the core of Akan/African marriages, as heterosexual with men exercising phallic competence and control over their families have not had any seismic change. In the 1970s, Meyer Fortes made a similar observation about the social stability of African marriage when he said that:

<kakurang-parry@ug.edu.gh>Sent: Monday, November 8, 2021 at 04:44:09 PM GMTSubject: Fw: CFP on Ghana.

> So much is now known about the customs and institutions of marriage in all human societies that it might seem doubtful if anything new can be added. Nor are there conspicuous lacunae in the theoretical study of the subject. It so happens that Malinowski, Lowie and Radcliffe-Brown, surely the three foremost authorities of their time on the comparative sociology of marriage, all left comprehensive statements of their conclusions (Malinowski 1929; Lowie 1933; Radcliffe-Brown 1950); and the general principles they set forth do not seem to me to be invalidated by later researcher. … there would seem to be little an ethnographer can now contribute save further illustrations of well-known *facts* and *principles* (Forte 1974: 1 – emphasis mine).[72]

This leads me to similarly identify with Burke who defined culture reasonably and broadly to include attitudes, mentalities and values and their expressions embodiments or symbolisation in artefacts, practices and representations (Burke 2005: 5).

From Tylor's definition of culture, culture is all inclusive as it encompasses and embodies every facet of human life – it is not limited to drumming and dancing as it is erroneously assumed. We could also glean from Tylor's definition that humans are humanised because of culture. It is the possession of culture by human beings that sets human society as unique and distinct from non-human kingdoms. Culture is also the total way of life of a group of people.

It is very conspicuous that culture is the totality of all human activities. It is pervasive and as a result encompasses every life of humans. Because of the centrality of culture to the definition of the human person, it is instructive to note that culture did not emerge out of a vacuum; it is the product of human's careful observation and interactions with the environment. Culture is about human beings bargaining with his environment, and the by-product of that bargaining is culture. Gyekye provides a detailed account of the evolution of culture. He posits that:

> Culture, thus, comes into being as a result of a people looking for ways of dealing with the various problems that arises out of human beings living together in a society. The problem of how to survive collectively, relate to and help one another leads to the formation of a communal way of life. The problem of regulating the behavior of the members of society and bring order, social harmony, stability and peace to the society leads to the

[72] Meyer Fortes, "Introduction" in Meyer Fortes, *Marriage in tribal societies*, 1-13 (Cambridge: Cambridge University Press, 1972).

> establishment of legal and moral codes. The desire to express their creative talents and communicate their feelings leads to the creation of such artistic forms as music and dance forms. The way the people look at the universe may lead to questions about its origin and beliefs in some ultimate being (or beings) beyond the universe as worthy of reverence and worship: herein lies the beginning of religion, or religious practice. The ideas or beliefs of the people with regard to death and the hereafter lead to the kind of ceremonial practices or funerals that are instituted for the dead (Gyekye 2013:141).

Gyekye's observation is not universally shared. For example, among the San the group is an impediment to personal interests. There is a reason why the San behave like this. If/when you leave it out then the idea of the individual-group dynamics is lost. Thus, the individual can leave and join the group as and when he wants. Even so, because human beings everywhere have common basic needs – food, clothing, security, shelter and health – it is understandable that human beings will tend to have some degree of cultural practice and beliefs that are very similar. This gives rise to the idea of cultural hybridity/sization – the combination of new ideas or forms with traditional assumptions produced (Burke 2016: 4). Beyond shared human needs, cultural hybridity is also possible because of the technological mediation that results in people experiencing the cultural *Other* without migrating – leading to James Clifford's idea of "traveling cultures" about human diverse interconnectedness of travel and displacement (Clifford 1992). On the other hand, the differences in geographical locations and differences in availability of resources will result in some groups developing cultural practices that are entirely different from that of other groups. It is these differences that may occasionally give rise to cultural shock when different groups from different cultural backgrounds and orientation come into contact with other groups. Since individual groups are exposed to different environments, individual groups develop cultural beliefs and practices that are different from each other. It is thus true that no one particular culture can claim to have the mandate to determine which culture is 'civilised' and which one is 'barbaric.' It is also important to note that no particular society has the monopoly over perceived 'civilised' culture.

The encounter between Africans and Europeans in the 15th Century was unique in the sense that the Europeans did not see Africans as equal partners. Initially, they engaged Africans as traders, but later they developed the penchant for seeing Africans and African culture from a different perspective, and have begun to arrogate to themselves the duty of 'civilising' Africans. They saw themselves as torch bearers of a new civilisation. Thus, as a result of their cultural imperialistic tendencies, the Europeans had to attack the foundation of the African society: the culture of African society.

It is usually asserted that to 'civilise' Africans, as was captured in the civilising mission, the fundamental basis of Africans had to be attacked and destroyed. African culture was branded as unproductive, primitive, archaic, barbaric, pagan, and fetish. Indeed, before the advent of Europeans on the African continent, Africans had evolved home-grown cultural principles that regulated social, political, economic, and religious ways of living. Every attempt was made to undermine the viability and relevance of African culture. The colonisers treated African culture with disdain and contempt. The condescending views the colonisers had about African culture was well rehearsed to justify and rationalise the subjugation of African people and the pillaging of African resource: human and material, and to also justify the slave trade and colonialism. It is thus no wonder that slavery and colonialism became the linchpin on which the so-called European 'civilising mission' was based. The two evils of colonialism and slavery had devastating and detrimental effects on African society.

With the change in traditional culture, Fanon contended, created an inferiority complex within the soul of every colonised people. The colonial system worked to tear the colonised away from his cultural identity. Fanon writes:

> The colonized is elevated above the jungle status in proportion to his adoption of the mother country's cultural standards. He becomes white as he renounces his blackness, his jungle (Fanon, 1967:18).

Decades of European colonialism and imperialism robbed Africans of the benefit of progressive development. This cultural change was brought about through education and colonial aspects of colonial legal institutions that proscribed some indigenous practices, such as the Dipo of the Krobo of southern Ghana (Quashigah 1999). Thus, instead of civilisation and progress, Africa experienced cultural change that significantly affected indigenous social and political systems. The scourge of colonialism was so severe and sharp that Africans lost the initiative to pursue cultural changes that centre its cultural ambitions as well as accommodating hybridity. resources. Thus, slavery and colonialism suffocated and truncated progress in Africa. The colonial enterprise hugely affected African culture. Through the schools established by the colonisers, Africans were taught to perceive themselves as inferior to Europeans. The effect of western colonisation also affected the psychological framework of Africans. Gyekye (2004) also asserts that an important feature of the African colonial and post-colonial experience that has had enduring effect is the mentality acquired by the African people regarding their perceptions of the 'African way of life' compared with the 'European way of life.' That mentality, he continues, has led many Africans to prefer European 'thing' even if the African equivalent of the 'thing' is of similar worth. Thus, that mentality – colonial mentality – engenders apism and so subverts originality and creativity, because it makes people look outside rather than inside for standards of judgment. It seems that the most enduring effect of the colonial experience on the African people relates to their self-perceptions, to skewed perceptions of their own values some of which can, on normative grounds, be said to be appropriate for life in the modern world. There is, therefore, some justification for asserting that much of our contemporary African life is an unexamined life, badly in need of serious fundamental examination. Recurrent problems in our political, ideological and educational systems; our irrational rudiments to debase or denigrate our values and to apotheosise those of others; our irrational readiness to gleefully borrow institutional and ideological systems from outside, oblivious of the fact that such alien systems were hammered out on the anvil of the cultural and historical experiences of other people's; our unconscionable readiness to tinker at complex and ramifying problems by applying simple therapies to our personal, social or national problems, coupled with flirtations with, or love for, the superficial. These features of our political, mental and aesthetic life have undoubtedly resulted from the lack of serious and profound examination of African cultural life and experience, particularly since the early euphoric days of our political independence. It is a spillover effect of colonialism (Gyekye 2004: 71).

Okot p'Bitek (1973) has also observed that apemanship is one of the major detrimental effects of colonialism. He argues that apemanship kills creativity and initiative to develop. According to him the attempts by Africans to be the shadows of Euro-Americans constitute the major challenge facing the African continent. Considering the fact that African culture lost its vigour in the encounter with European culture, several attempts were made by Africans to resist European pillaging of the African continent. There were armed struggles like the Mau Mau of Kenya and the like. Other Africans who were forced to accept the

Christian faith established what became known in the study of religions in Africa as African Independent Churches that challenged the demeaning of African culture by the Europeans.

It is within these ideas about the damaging effect of European introduction into Africa that culturally identifiable movements like the Negritude emerged. Intellectually, negritude emerged as a movement to recover the lost glory of African culture. It was also a movement against European domination of the African continent and their disdain for African culture. Negritude was also about the restoration of African identity that was lost as a result of slavery, colonialism, and European racism. The assigning of negative attributes to the physiology and culture of Africa assisted the exploitation of Africans by denying their rights and way of life (Green 2000: 423). One of the pernicious ideological features of colonialism was to render African history, culture, and physiology as negative and uncivilised. And one institution that sustained and gave life to the colonial enterprise was the colonial education system. The schools built by the Christian missionaries were used not only to proselytise, but to attack the credibility of African culture. The schools became the outlet through which the Europeans launched their attack against the core values of Africa. Africans who had western education were taught to treat with contempt their cultural values and principles. For instance, Hymans (1971) writes about Senghor's particular situation:

> The missionaries taught Senghor and his friends to abandon and scorn the culture of their ancestors, ... exposing them to culture and the modern way of life, but the effect was a complete destruction of the primary equilibrium of the child (Hymans 1971, cited in Green 2000:428).

In French colonies in Africa, Africans were indoctrinated to see themselves as Frenchmen with black skin. This was effected through the policy of assimilation. The French policy of assimilation was designed purposely to render French colonies in Africa an extension of France. Under this policy, Africans were compelled to swallow hook-line-and-sinker, language, religion, the logic, dress code, eating habit, and customs of the coloniser. But as pointed out by Peter Worsley, the driving force behind the French policy of assimilation was racism. Worsley asseverates that:

> The policy reposed, as the word evolue indicates, on the simple evolutionist-racist assumption that the indigenous cultures were primitive

and backward, and that progress consisted in becoming more and more like the white man, whose culture was the highest pinnacle of human evolution (Worsley 1969:31, cited in Tomich 1979:355).

The idea that France had a superior culture that legitimised her supposed mission to civilise Africans was one of the motivating factors of French colonisation of Africa. In consequence, with the advent of colonialism, Africans suffered from a psychological dilemma as they found themselves torn between embracing European cultural values or African values. But the relationship between Africans, who had received colonial education and expected to be incorporated into the European world, was conflictual. So, out of frustration, most of these Africans turned their back on their own traditional values. This was captured by Malinowski as follows:

> Since Africans cannot share the ideals, interests and full benefits of co-operative activities with the Whites, they naturally fall back to their own system of belief, value and sentiment. To be a mere carbon copy is not satisfactory as a substitute for all the African had initially to give up ... The African thus is forced at least spiritually to recross the first line and to re-affirm many of the tribal values abandoned at the first crossing (Malinowski 196:158, cited in Irele 1965:324).

While a few feminist scholars, including Sylvia Bawa (2019), Sylvia Tamale have harped the damaging impact of colonialism on African cultures, they have hardly engaged the idea of Christian civilisation to demonstrate how it negatively affected women in the case of Ghana. Also, the idea of Christianity impoverishing the rights of women, leading to women's progressive degradation is highly speculative and not historically accurate (Boni 2001). There is no doubt that the missionaries were sometimes hasty in condemning African cultures that they hardly understood. But it is also true that nearly all the cultural practices the missionaries discouraged, such as human sacrifice, murders, panyarring[73] (Danquah 1957), and extreme forms of widowhood (Danquah writes have hardly been accepted in the postcolony). For example, extreme widowhood rites, human sacrifices, and killing of twins. Indeed, the point as I have said above is that these practices were not treated as cherished practices of the Akan or even several African societies – explaining why they are hardly accepted in

[73] Panyarring was the practice of seizing and holding a person until the repayment of debt or resolution settled.

contemporary Akan societies. While several African nationalists and Afrocentric scholars relish the recuperation of some indigenous cultures, it is chieftaincy which has surged back strongly since the late 1980s. It is also true that even when some members of the revitalised neo-indigenous religions like the Afrikania, founded by Vincent Damuah, attempted retaining *Trokosi*, they received extensive backlash from the public. This has not translated into the complete abolition of *trokosi* as several girls are believed to be given to shrines and shrine priests. But again, it shows the systemic grounding of the kinship nature of Ghanaian societies.

Christian missionaries and the idea of civilising mission

The idea of the Christian civilising mission has hardly been defined by several Africanists, except the tabling of cultural practices that the missionaries were said to have destroyed. Nevertheless, it has been expressed in novels, such as Joseph Ephraim Casely Hayford's (1911), *Ethiopia Unbound*, Kobina Sekyi's (1997) *Blinkards*, Chinua Achebe's (1959), *Things fall apart*; Ngũgĩ wa Thiong'o's (1964), *Weep not child*, and Okot p'bitek's (1966) *Song of Lawino*. Other novelists/poets have expressed their criticism of colonialism in poems. For the sake of space, I will share two of such poems I read at the university by two Ghanaian literary critics, Kofi Awoonor and Kofi Anyidoho (Anyidoho 2014).[74] Any anthropological sources by any chance?

In his poem, The Cathedral, Kofi Awoonor critiqued Christianity as follows:

On this dirty patch
a tree once stood
shedding incense on the infant corn:
its boughs stretched across a heaven
brightened by the last fires of a tribe.
They sent surveyors and builders
who cut that tree
planting in its place
A huge senseless cathedral of doom.

[74] Anyidoho, K. (2014), *The promise of hope: New and selected poems, 1964-2013*. Lincoln: University of Nebraska Press.

In his poem, Go Tell Jesus, Anyidoho (2011) sharply criticised the missionaries.[75] I will only read the third stanza of this poem to illustrate my point of his criticism:

Go
Go ask Jesus
why He did not tour the world
to spread the word of death
but gave it to a chosen few
and in parables they can't explain
Tell Him
Tell Jesus
that that little peace I enjoyed
before His messengers arrived
has been disturbed
and I cannot sleep and dream
until it is restored
Tell Him
Tell Jesus
there is chaos in my house
My sons have left their heads and hearts
My daughters their hearts and heads
They are screaming shrieking
burning each other's Souls
all because
His messengers have come
but have forgotten His words
May it please Him come again
That we may see the truth
That the truth may make us see
That peace is not a piece of bread in wine

As the idea of civilising mission remains central to the LGBTQ+ debate, I had always relished the opportunity to explore what the European missionaries of the 18th Century meant by civilising mission. So, when in March 2021, Mr Benedict Rattigan, the Director of Schweitzer Institute-Cambridge, invited me for a conference in Cambridge, I leveraged the opportunity to read more about Albert Schweitzer. It was for this reason that I read Schweitzer's own

[75] Anyidoho, K. (2011). *The pace we call home and other poems*. Oxfordshire: Ayebia Clarke Publishing Limited.

autobiography about his notion of civilising. While I do not assume that his view could harmonise with some of contemporaries, I want to reflect on civilising mission from his perspective. Albert Schweitzer was a medical missionary, Bach scholar, Christian theologian and philosopher, who decided to extend his service to Gabon as a medical missionary. So, in 1913, he arrived in Lambarene to begin mission work. He struggled throughout, including the Gabonese distrusting him initially, because of the wind of conflict that was blowing across Europe. But while as a missionary in Gabon, he reflected on the issue of Christian civilising mission.

Like several of his contemporary missionaries, he was convinced that the Christian civilisation was necessary for the Gabonese. But following the outbreak of World War I, he became disillusioned about the whole idea of civilising mission – as he painfully mused over the west losing its historic Christian values. This led him to write his book, *The philosophy of civilisation.* He defined the essential elements of civilisation as:

> The ethical perfecting of the individual as well as society. At the same time, every spiritual and every material step forward has significance for civilisation. The will to civilisation is, then, the universal will to progress that is conscious of the ethical as the highest value. In spite of the great importance, we attach to the achievements of science and human prowess, it is obvious that only humanity that is striving for ethical ends can benefit in full measure from material progress and can overcome the dangers that accompany it (1998: 148).

Clearly, Schweitzer's deployment of ethics as the primary boundary of civilisation would rule out the devastating impact of King Leopold II of Belgium in Congo as irreconcilable with Christian virtues (Hochschild 1998). It also implicates Germans and other Europeans for the atrocities they committed in and on Africa (Gewald 2004). He however did not denounce interest in the material world, because as he said, "The religions that expressly reject the world and life (Brahminism and Buddhism) show no interest in civilisation" (Schweitzer 1998: 183). Schweitzer critiqued his own faith by saying, "Christianity has a negative attitude toward civilisation because in the beginning it expected the world to end. For that reason, it shows no interest in improving conditions in the natural world (Ibid. 184). This attitude of the missionaries was demonstrable before the Reformation when Christianity was almost nothing short of a "castle religion" in West

Africa. Reflecting on the impact of the Reformation on Christianity, he said that:

> Christianity changed its negative attitude toward the world. With the affirmation of life, Christianity could work for, even create civilisation. As such a religion it joined in the struggle against ignorance, want of purpose, cruelty, and injustice, out of which the modern times a new world emerged (Ibid. 185).

Following the Reformation, the missionaries refilled their zest to embark on a holistic mission. In the Gold Coast, they built schools and other agricultural experiments. The Basel missionaries in Akropong, reinforced a similarly known Protestant ethic of hard work, frugality, and investment on the Akuapim (Sackey 2008; Miller 2003). As the logic of making the Bible available to everyone who became a Christian, the 19th Century missionaries developed the literary aspect of some Ghanaian languages. For this, one of the renowned Akan historians, J.B. Danquah, credited the translation work of the missionaries for helping keep the Akan culture afloat (Danquah 1944). Given the imperil and exploitative nature of colonialism, Schweitzer argued that colonialism and civilisation were incompatible (Schweitzer 1998: 192).

Culture and identity

Since culture is a human creation, it is dynamic. Through internal and external influences, a society's culture is changed. The dynamism of culture springs from the ability of human beings to imagine and create immaterial realities – making culture as an important index in identity construction and notions of belonging. Identity is an important index of group living. Since human beings are gregarious, belonging to a group implies sharing some key identity landmarks of the group. These identity landmarks are not natural. They are created to enforce mutual co-existence. Identity marks are meant to provide a 'naked' public sphere where people can go about their activities without any interference. Among the Yoruba of Nigeria, for example, tribal marks are commonly used for identification, beautification and even inoculation against childhood diseases (Alo & Olasode 2018). Among the Asante, Rattray, reported that some Asante would scar themselves as part separating their manifest identity from those off slaves (Rattray, 1932). And if people have no identity marks they have no means of being united? Why use the examples of marks here? It is the same identity marks that introduce the 'us' and 'them' binary which in most cases creates tension. The 'us' sees themselves as different and unique from the 'them'. Right at birth, individuals go through a systematic procedure that accords them the right to claim belonging and legitimacy – morphing into expected behaviours (Mensah and Mekamgoum 2017). Among the Munyoro of Western Uganda, for example, the processes include naming and as part of identifying them with values and character of clan ancestors (Weichs 2019). While identity is assigned at childhood, it does not negate the fact that individuals negotiate their identities at a later state in life. This is because identity is not fixed, immutable. Individual's identities change over time informed by new experiences, interactions, and new personal convictions (McMullen 2000; Haddad 1994).

Scholars have identified two main theories, underpinning identity (Burke and Stets 2009). The first is the primordial identity. Primordial identity, also known as ascribed identity, is given to an individual without any contribution from the individual. This category of identity could include ethnicity, religion, sex, race, family, and language. At the primordial level, one does not choose where one is born, who becomes the genitor, the pigment of one's skin, and the language one socialises in. Different cultures have different ways of according primordial identity. Among the Akan, the primary way of ascribing primordial identity is through naming. From the perspective of Akan ethno-philosophy, one is not yet a humanised or socialised person, fit for culturally acceptable group living, until one is named on the seventh day after birth. This is because the Akan ethno-philosophy and numerology assume that seven is a mark of a human being.[76] And so, when a child is born, the child must prove his having arrived to stay to participate in social activities by surviving through the first seven days of his life. It is after the cycle of seven days that a child is given a name. Until then, the child is simply considered a visitor (Sarpong 1974). We could read into this practice as part of the issues of high infant mortality that the Akan faced in the pre-industrial era (Gyasi 1998). But also true among the Akan is the fact that a name has power. To name and be named are all imbued in either vertical or horizontal circuits of power. As part of the psychology of names, if one names or calls a person by that person's name, one has command over the person's name. So, when a family is convinced that a child has come to stay, the child is given a name. Thus, when in Shakespeare's *Romeo and Juliet*, Juliet asked

[76] Interviewed with Prof. Kofi Asare Opoku in February 2019.

Romeo, what is in a name? The question was neither redundant, trite nor simplistic (Shakespeare 2003: 29).

The name a child is given establishes the child as a legal and social being. As a legal being a child is entitled to care and protection. He expects to receive nourishment, protection, accommodation, and love from the parents. They can also sue and be sued when they commit any blunder when they become mature and conscious adults. In terms of being a social being, the individual becomes a member of the family. They also become a member of the entire society. From the day they are named, they become the 'property' of the entire society. It is based on this that most African societies assume that it takes an entire village to raise a child (Nkosi 2010; Opuni-Frimpong 2012). The child is also initiated into the social space according to the Ubuntu philosophy of 'I am because we are and since we are, therefore I am.' Among the Akan and the Ga, through the ritual of dropping water and alcohol on the child's tongue as part of the naming ceremony, the child is introduced to the necessity of truth and honesty – this is precisely because truth and lies could sometimes be so close and difficult for one to distinguish between the two (Yankah 1995). The Akan word for truth is "anokware" which is a contraction of "ano koro" (speaking one with one mouth on the same issue) – which implies "consistency and without contradiction in the description of the same reality" (Dzobo 1992: 82).

To deepen primordial identity, the older generation makes conscientious efforts to transfer the values of society to the child. Socialisation – the conversion of a biological being to a social being– is very crucial in ascribing a primordial identity to the child (Assimeng 2006). Through socialisation, a child is prepared to be fit for group living – for this reasons people are not just people and orientations cannot just be accepted as claimed by some African scholars, domiciled in the western world. Similarly, Africa's contestation against the liberalisation is not an imposition of the morality or religious sentiment on African people as claimed by Falola (2022). As part of the socialisation, language is considered key. Given the centrality of language as the storehouse and vehicle for the transmission of culture (Holmes 2001), the child is taught the language of society. The child's acquisition of language helps them to identify with the values, norms, and beliefs of society. It is to help the child to identify appropriate and acceptable values in the society (Gyekye 1996). At this level, the child is carefully guided to internalise (imbibe) the values of society. When they go wrong, they are punished and when they do the right thing, they are commended and /or rewarded. Through extrinsic motivation, the child is trained to act in ways that conform to the shared values of the society.

As part of the imposition of group identity through naming, the child hardly has a say in terms of the values that they are given. They are compelled to conform to values that they may not necessarily share. But since they are socialised to internalise society's values, the boundaries of acceptable conduct are set. The child must, therefore, fit within those boundaries to make any claim to rights that are accorded members of the society. But since primordial identity was accorded when the child was young and unable to make personal choices, when the child grows up, they make a concession and reengage their primordial identity to determine how they meet their idiosyncrasies. This leads to another type of identity called constructionist identity (Linton 1936). This refers to an identity that individuals create for themselves. It is also called achieved identity. It includes everything the individual achieves as a member of the society. This includes a profession, marriage, and religious position. But the attainment of constructionist achievement should fit within the broader framework of what are the acceptable norms of society. This implies that sometimes there are tensions between the individual and society.

Recently, some scholars have identified shortcomings with the construction of identity along primordial and constructionist lines (Gosine 2002; McMullen 2000; Dillon 1999). They argue that these binaries are narrow and do not capture the complexities of a person's position in society. In view of that, the new term that is advocated is belonging. Belonging explores the place of an individual in society. It shows how the agency and subjectivity of individuals constitute important indices in belonging to a society. Given this, it is possible for an individual to belong and not to belong simultaneously. For example, one can call oneself a Christian without submitting to all the teachings of Jesus Christ. One can be a Muslim and also choose and pick from Islam to shape their identity. As indicated above, identity assumes that the individual must operate within a very rigid binary – primordial and constructionist – but belonging looks at how individuals (re)shape their belonging to a society. It brings out clearly how individuals borrow from a pool of norms and values to determine which ones meet their idiosyncrasies. Belonging also implies that the individual does not feel compelled to identify with the values of society.

Belonging amplifies the fluidity and malleability in identity. It shows how identities change across time and space. But in pre-industrial societies, such as the Bette-Obudu of Cross River State, Nigeria, identity as belonging, where the individual could redefine his or her identity is deliberately made complex through naming. Among the Bette-Obudu, girls are given names that locates them an exclusive domain of maternal roles with limited imperative for multiple identity formation needed to cope with modernity's pluralities. Example of such a name is Á-nyọ̀ng'bí (whomukiémá), which means "she values her husband's clothes' (Betiang 2019: 367). Many proverbs speak to the essence of collective identity. For example, the Akan have a proverb that, 'If one person carries the world, he develops a hunchback.' This proverb demonstrates the essence of cooperation in pre-industrial societies to solve common problems. Based on this collective identity, values and norms are shared. Religion is one of the ways of achieving a collective identity. In many pre-industrial cultures, one is born into the religion of the society of their birth. There is no attempt at conversion. This explains why most so-called pre-literate cultures did not have a mission-oriented religion.[77] All this implies that the views of minority groups were accepted based on two main conditions: First, did the view sharply contract society's shared ethical and ontological boundaries? For example, minority views that endorsed the public practice of same-sex sexualities was not accepted. Second, did the religious accommodativeness of a queer sexuality ever spill over into public sphere? Again, in the Akan cosmogony, queer identities were often limited to the cultic realm, not treated as socially realistic and acceptable practice. The malleability of the spiritual map of the Akan did not translate seamlessly into acceptable social practice in the public – no wonder the Akan chiefs have argued that homosexuality as a public practice is foreign to their cultures.

All this means that among the Akan and several African groups, people see themselves as a means to the family, not the inverse. Such naming practices and its sociological implication renders the family as strong resistance to any efforts at using law to redefine an individual's identity for easy acceptability. Thus, through the practice of anthroponomastics, the acceptance of a homosexual identity that runs roughshod against androcentric cultural aspiration of childbirth may lead to tension in a family. The naming practices of the Akan adds another layer to the constitutive nature of a person, such that any law

[77] The Akan religion was mutually inclusive and did not seek to convert. Also, there was fluidity in religious affiliation and offering of cultic attention not clear. An Akan could worship the Tigare cult from Wa in the North without any negative repercussion.

that seeks to breakdown kinship ties tends to suffer major backlash. This is because, for the Akan, the individual is a means to the family, not the inverse. Indeed, as I have said, the kinship system of the Akan, where nearly eery acceptable social practice is family-shared, renders the cyberworld's liberalised selfie of "I", "Me" and "Myself" self-centredness difficult to express. The constitutive nature of the Akan world is mainstreamed into different areas of social life, such that some roles are largely accorded according to marital status. At one of the public universities in Ghana, where I had my undergraduate education, it was rumoured that a woman Vice-Chancellor during the nomination and election had to reconcile with her belligerent husband for her to appeal to the electoral College of the university. It is common for people to question women who desire a higher public office whether they are married. These practices are read as oppressive to women and one of the enduring residues of indigenous kin-based system that survived colonialism – as they conflate a woman's marital status and professional performance.

Because I have responded to the petitioners in my own memorandum on the subject to parliament, it is important to say that this book is contributing to the ideals of the subject of decolonising the academia in Ghana.[78] This means that I take up the issue of decolonisation is a part of understanding the extent to which the Ghanaian kinship system tend to shape the "gown" and "town" relationship. Significantly, the decolonisation issue in Ghana, for me, must be considered from the perspective of the dominant social and political paradigms of the enchanted the country's enchanted public. The issue is even more complex when gauged from the perspective that the systemic social regime in Ghana tends to mainstream individuals into living in a state of between and betwixt – but often pandering toward the aspirations of society.

The above situation may be read as unjust, especially when we read from the angle that the Family Bill proscribes all advocacy geared at supporting queer sexualities. But it feeds into the strongly-held kinship system in the country. So, while I appreciate Mohammed Wunpini's (2021) critique of Ghanaian feminist scholars for not being radical enough, the fact remains that the university is a particular space in Ghana's public sphere that must interact with the general public. if the university for any reason decides to exclude teaching the cherished family system in its curriculum, both students and academics, as well as

---

[78] https://www.myjoyonline.com/african-studies-scholar-dr-charles-prempeh-petitions-parliament-to-pass-anti-lgbtqi-bill/.

activists, struggle to convince the public to accept any kind of cultural regime change – especially those that border on gender and the family system. I, therefore, consider the task as highly overwhelming, but African scholars need the courage to decentre western epistemology without denying themselves the fact that they could benefit from other cultures. This is because, more recently, the academic environment has become very hostile to dissenting views. The dominance of the "post" theories in the universities remains a paradigm that needs to accommodate other voices. The homosexual discourse largely constitutes the valve around which the politics of inclusion and exclusion is practiced. It has become the zero-sum game of epistemic production.

Civil society groups

Civil society organisations (CBOs) are expected to be autonomous, democratic establishment who operate within the public sphere to advance civil engagement, civil rights, mobilising grassroots activities and lobbing both local and international agents for democratic consolidation (Nugroho 2011).[79] The role of civil society groups in Africa/Ghana forms part of the political tapestries of the continent – that have orbited around civil rule, dictatorship, authoritarian regime since the late 1950s and restoration of democratic rule in the 1990s (Haynes 2003; Bratton 1994; Nyong'o 1995).[80] As part of routinising human rights and democratic consolidation, part of the western aid to Africa's decline economy in the 1980s was the re-democratisation of the continent (Abdulai 2009; Gyimah-Boadi 2004; Mamdani 1990; Nyong'o 1995).[81] Nevertheless, the democratic experiment in

[79] Nugroho, Y. (2011). Citizens in action: Collaboration, participatory democracy and freedom of information – Mapping contemporary civic activism and the use of social media in Indonesia. Report. Manchester and Jakarta: MIOIR and HIVOS.

[80] Haynes, J. (2003). 'Democratic consolidation in Africa: The problematic case of Ghana.' Commonwealth & Comparative Politics, 4(1): 48-76; Bratton, M. (1994). Civil society and political transition in Africa. Boston, Mass.: Institute for Development Research; Nyong'o, A.P. (1995). *Discourses on democracy in Africa: Democratisation processes in Africa: Problems and prospects* (Dakar: CODESRIA Book Series).

[81] Abdulai, A.G. (2009), 'Political will in combating corruption in development and transition economies: A comparative study of Singapore, Hong Kong and Ghana.' *Journal of Financial Crime*, 16(4): 387-417); Gyimah-Boadi, E. (2004), 'Civil society and democratic development.' Democratic Reform in Africa: The quality of progress, 99-120; Mamdani, M. (1990). 'The social basis of constitutionalism in Africa.' *The Journal of Modern Africa*, 28(3): 359-374.

Ghana/Africa and much of the world (possibly including the recent altercation in the US's election in 2020), is still weak – showing signs of human rights abuse, unequal distribution of development project and services etc (Opoku-Mensah 2007).[82]

In Ghana's political history, civil society groups, as non-governmental establishment emerged in the 1990s as part of consolidating Ghana's democracy (Boafo-Arthur 2006). While civil society organisations operate in Ghana's kinship-based public sphere, their activities that border on sensitive issues such as family, gender, and sexuality tend to generate controversies. This implies that while society organisations have played key roles in shaping the contours of Ghana's democracy and developmental agenda, several of the founders of CBOs have expressed frustrations in the line of duty. They accuse the political regime of not cooperating enough; and also complain about public perception that they are compradors of erstwhile colonial imperialists (Quashigah 2019).[83]

One CBO that has become representative of minority rights in the LGBTQ controversy is the Centre for Democratic Development (CDD). The CDD has become one of the allies of the LGBTQ community. Led by H. Kwasi Prempeh, the CDD has been highly involved in consolidating democracy in Ghana. The CDD recently reported that Ghana is likely to be turned away from international donors if the country passed the Family Bill.[84] While some people may read the CDD reports as part of tacitly coercing the political regime to suspend the Family Bill or part of western imperialism,[85] the CDD's report cannot readily be dismissed. This is because, as I will discuss very soon, the US government said it will consider not giving aid to countries that retain inconsiderate laws against members of the LGBTQ

---

[82] Opoku-Mensah, P.Y. (2008). 'The state of civil society in Sub-Saharan Africa.' In Heinrich, V.F. & Fioramonti, L. (eds), Civicus global survey of the state of civil society, vol. 2: 75-90. Bloomfield, CT: Kumarian Press.

[83] Quashigah, T. (2019). Civil society and democratic consolidation in Ghana. PhD thesis submitted to the University of Ghana.

[84] Ghanaweb (February 9, 2022), 'Passing anti-LGBTQ+ Bill would cost Ghana 6% budget revenue – CDD,' https://www.ghanaweb.com/GhanaHomePage/NewsArchive/Passing-Anti-LGBTQI-Bill-would-cost-Ghana-6-budget-revenue-CDD-1464943 (Accessed: September 4, 2022).

[85] Ghanaweb (February 9, 2022), 'CDD's anti-LGBTQ+ survey influenced by international donors -Sam George,' https://www.ghanaweb.com/GhanaHomePage/NewsArchive/CDD-s-anti-LGBTQ-survey-influenced-by-international-donors-Sam-George-1464763(Accessed: September 4, 2022).

community. For this reason, the LGBTQ debates should also be read as part of geopolitics. Indeed, we have seen evidence of that, as both the drafters of the Bill and the CBOs appeal to international laws to adduce evidence to their respective positions. While Ghana's overwhelming religious community seek to promote only heterosexual norms as the publicly acceptable, the Western media continuous labelling of the current Family Bill as "Anti-LGBTQ Bill"[86]

Consequently, that Ghana's same-sex debates has taken a trans-national dimension raises several issues for consideration. It shows the divisive partisanship interest that western media has taken on the subject. While the western media may have some consider their position legitimacy, their forays into Ghana's local matters further polarise the front of Ghanaians. Just like the controversies that foreign diplomats' direct involvement in a sensitive issue of helping with the commissioning of a recreation centre for the LGBTQ generated, western media are harping local tension. It could be argued that the stance liberalised western media has taken to blackmail Ghana, as part of the colonial policy of "define and rule" policy (Mamdani 2012)[87] is potentially dangerous to Ghana's peace. It needs to be discussed away from further polarising Ghanaians. My stance is also because, the advocates of the Bill claim their demands are conditioned on the country's postcolonial existential reality of a mutually inclusive Triple heritage. This Triple Heritage is framed around Judeo-Christian-Muslim heterosexual family values.

Labelling Ghana's quest for its family values as "Anti-homosexual", Western media, including the BBC and CNN, have become, in the minds of public discourse, the pipelines for hegemonising and homogenising western sexual revolution that has been brewing since the 1970s. It further complicates the issue about the LGBTQ. Dialogue and tactic is needed to for the country to secure the human dignity without also incurring the displeasure of the overwhelming religious constituency. For negotiation to be established, the Western world should allow Ghana some liberty to determine the patterns of their laws, as they grapple with the public expression of different sexualities. Obviously, this is not to argue against any form of engagement of the

---

86 Yinka Ibukun (December 2, 2021), "Ghana's anti-LGBTQ Bill risks hurting its democratic credentials," https://www.bloomberg.com/news/articles/2021-12-02/ghana-s-anti-lgbtq-bill-risks-hurting-its-democratic-credentials, Accessed: September 1, 2022.

87 Mamdani, M. (2012), *Define and rule: Native as political identity* (Cambridge, Mass.: Harvard University Press).

Western world in the discussion, but too much of it will create an impression that the West is seeking to impose Western sexual identity politics on them.

At any rate, what is happening with the division over the LGBTQ is not new with other such sensitive subjects in Ghana's colonial history with the British. In the late 19th Century, rumours spread about Mensa Bonsu, the Asantehene, murdering 200 girls. The rumours were filtered through British media, including the *Standard*, the *Times*, and the *African Times* – dividing the intelligentsia into two camps: Pro-Asante and pro-colonialism. the pro-Asante group, including King Ghartey, Rev. Hayfron, Mr. Edmund Bannerman, and Prince Owusu Ansah discounted the rumour as false. On the contrary, the pro-colonialism, led by Laing, supported the claim (Akurang-Parry 2022: 59-92).[88]

The discussion has so far highlighted the role of CBOs and the media. But in all the discussions religion and chiefs feature strongly. This is because, chiefs, who are the custodians of indigenous cherished values legitimise their authority to function from religion (Akrong 2006).[89] These two institutions are all capable of malleability to accommodate modernity, if they are engaged on a civil basis over the LGBTQ issue. So, I argue that alongside religion, chieftaincy, another important institution that predates colonialism with some flexibility, has become an important force for political mobilisation, ethnic and cultural recuperation, and socio-economic development, in reflecting the aspirations of the country's religious constituency. Since the turn of the millennium, therefore, several chiefs in both the Northern and Southern parts of Ghana have identified with evangelical Christianity and reformist Islam in promoting heterosexual family values.

The above means that, much as Muslims and Christians tend to fragment over major doctrinal differences, since the 2000s, the two religions and chiefs have united in shaping the moral landscape of the country. The two religions, sharing the Judeo-Christian virtues on sexuality – focusing on the normativity of heterosexual relationships – have been highly enthusiastic in protecting Ghana's moral frontiers against the west.

This enthusiastic, morally-informed development has brought enormous pressure on the political elite, as Ghana's *de-facto* civic religion

---

[88] Akurang-Parry, O.K. (2022). *African heritage in the whirlpool of colonial rule: African resistance in Ghana.* Tema/Ghana: Digibooks Ghana Limited.

[89] Akrong, Abraham. 'Religion and Traditional Leadership in Ghana'. In Odotei K. Irene and Albert K. Awedoba (eds.), *Chieftaincy in Ghana: Culture, Governance and Development* ,213-230. Accra: Sub-Saharan Publishers, 2006.

remains unyielding to the pressures of the western sexual revolution ethics which emerged since the 1970s. Meanwhile, as I have said above, western leaders, more recently fronted by Joe Biden, continue to extend western cultural wars to Ghana through the academics and western media as alibis.

Consequently, since 2019, the debate over decriminalising homosexuality in Ghana has become more intense, following a move by some foreign diplomats to mobilise a few Ghanaian homosexuals in Accra for advocacy. In 2021, this development, read in the Ghanaian religious public as a form of cultural imperialism, contributed to the rise of a mixture of religious groups, made up of Christians and Muslims, including Chiefs, who drafted the heterosexual-affirming Private Bill which forms the subject of the discussion in this book. In terms of the postcolonial reality of multiple cultural values in Ghana which Nkrumah referred to as *consciencism* and Ali Mazrui, framed as Ghana's Triple Heritage – Islam, Christianity and indigenous traditions – heterosexual family values have always been the norm. Again, the presence of Ghana's Triple Heritage, particularity, the translocation of the sexual ethics of Christianity and Islam into the country's public sphere needs soberness and consideration to avoid a collision. This is because it shows the multidimensionality of the LGBTQ debates as more embedded in totalising lived reality that simply passing a Bill into law to criminalise or liberalise queer sexualities.

The need for a dialogical approach to deal with the debate is because of the current local and global economic crisis. Ghana's economy has suffered a serious setback, accentuating unemployment among the urban youthful constituency. Concurrently, in 2021, young men and women leveraged social media and later street demonstrations to ask the political elites to fix the country's challenges – succinctly embodied in their label, #FixTheCountry. Given the economic challenges, Ghana cannot afford to polarise its fronts to further deepen the economic crisis of the country over sexuality issues. In other words, while the country cannot dismiss the demands of the members of the LGBTQ constituency as a fuss and a craze, the country should also concentrate on mobilising its human and material resources to support human flourishing.

Similarly, the West African sub-region has increasingly become volatile. Countries such as Burkina Faso and Mali have had *coups d'états*, read as a drawback on the region's re-democratisation since the 1990s. Alongside coups d'états is the surge in jihadist activities in the sub-region, since September 11 (9/11) – expressed in the activities of Boko

Haram and ISIS. All these have morphed with revitalised nationalistic sentiment in Francophone West Africa with countries such as Cote D'Ivoire, Burkina Faso, and Mali seeking to disengage from France's control of their central banks. As the sub-continent becomes more precarious, Ghana needs to unite its ranks without attend to more pressing issue of securing the security of the sub-region. Again, while this is not to overrule the concerns of the opposing groups on the Family Bill, the insecurity threatening the country is hardly discriminatory over issues of sexuality. So, the state and the international community can hardly afford to treat the LGBTQ debate as an isolated issue, independent of the current local and trans-local tensions in the West African sub-region.

My appeal to the Ghanaian state to secure the peace of the sub-region is borne out of the possibility of a spill over of tensions in the neighbouring countries into the country. While Ghana has had none of the politico-religious tensions, the fact that the country's immediate neighbours continue to struggle, put Ghana on a "red alert". Nevertheless, there have been media reports of a few Ghanaian men joining international religiously-inspired militant groups like the ISIS.

Given the transnational activities of jihadist movements and the transnational efforts on the part of the west to use financial aid and grants to compel Ghana to decriminalise homosexual practices, the local debate over homosexuality has, as usual, reverberated in the corridors of western media.

While several religious Ghanaian academics do not subscribe to the decriminalisation of homosexuality, this constituency has not formed any known collective public opinion to defend the proposed Family Value Bill in the country's Parliament. Instead, as I have said, a few academics, lawyers, and heads of civil society groups have put themselves out as defenders of homosexuals. Given that some of these academics, including those who write on gender and who once headed or currently head the Institute of African Studies (IAS, Legon), the debate over homosexuality has rather become more worrying and contentious for the religious constituency.

The IAS was primarily established and inaugurated by Nkrumah in the 1960s to promote African cultural studies, as part of his vision of African personality. In his *African Genius* speech at the opening of the Institute, Nkrumah insisted that Research Fellows at IAS should work closely with the public in the country's cultural revitalisation agenda. He framed this mutual inclusivity between academics and the public as "the gown must come to town".

Putting the issue of religion, chieftaincy together, I argue that ideologically the tagging of the Bill as "Anti-LGBTQ" unmistakably puts Ghana in a bad light as violators of the rights of homosexuals that must be shamed. While there is certainly no doubt that several Ghanaians are uncompromising about the western push for the country's acceptance of homosexual practices, it is very problematic to call the Bill "Anti-LGBTQ". This is because, all the various religions in Ghana, and chiefs have openly argued against punishing, maiming and discriminating against homosexuals in the country. Several of these religious people do not support any acts of discrimination against homosexuals. As the proponents of the Bill have made clear in the Bill and public engagements, their goal is to support homosexuals who are willing to embrace Ghanaian family values. The issue of criminalisation in the Bill is rather connected to advocacy and decriminalisation. Also, it must be stated that there are hardly any reports of government institutions marginalising persons because of these persons' visible physical appearance.

So, western media's framing of the Bill as "Anti-homosexual" is the Bill pro-LGBTQ as if the religious constituency is on a slaughtering mission against gays imperils Ghana's reputation in the western world. The western world could weaponised such media misrepresentation of Ghana to imperial the country's chances of securing support from its "development" partners.

As I have discussed above, the academics and heads of civil society consider themselves the initiators and vanguards of human rights in Ghana. More importantly, the force of global American and western cultural imperialism informed my interest in analysing how all the politics around homosexuality crystalise into issues of cultural imperialism and bastardising of religion. This is particularly so as Ghanaian overwhelming religious community continues to suffer some form of social exclusion. Most western analysts and their Ghanaian cultural collaborators consider them as arrogant and bigots, because Ghanaians will not cow to the banality of sexual rights. I also extracted intelligence from my observations of the evolution of the homosexual debate and issues of human flourishing in Ghana, given that I had lived in the country all my life. I have, therefore, benefitted from my immersion as a resident of this community for nearly four decades – leading to my building of contextually-embedded knowledge from my experiences – to appreciate an understanding of the western cultural imperialism.

Historically, when men married women, men gained two things. Men had right over the womb of women – called right in *uxorem* (Fortes 1977). This was such that in most cultures, particularly among the Akan, when an Akan man married an Akan woman, all the children born to the woman regardless of their biological fathers became the children of the man, of course not leaving out the woman. As I have discussed above, this means that whereas the Akan is matrilineally structured, male phallic culture is expressed in men's fertility competence and the exercise of leadership and control over his household. So, whatever the circumstance, a man upon marrying a woman became both the genitor (biological) and pater (social) father (Sarpong 1974). He totally claimed the womb of the woman, indeed, in the Akan matrilineal society.

Men have, for a very long time, put strategic measures in place to resist being controlled by women, but more importantly, men have scrambled over one another to control the womb of women. It can safely be inferred that practices such as widowhood rites, Female Genital Cutting (FGC) (circumcision), *Trokosi*, and incessant profiling of women as witches and burning them in the process are all part of man's efforts at controlling the reproductive capacity of women. As practices that oppress women, they should be banned through both legislation and dialogue.

Through the practice of widowhood rites, men (less among Asante men who rather suspected their nephews because of the tensions within Akan matrilineal social system, Akan men sought and their matriclan sought to control their wives (see: Adae 2003: 127). But women have hardly acquiesced in these practices. In several societies, including the Akan and Ewe, women were those responsible for calling the bluff of men who refused to fight. Yaa Asantewaa derided men with the expression that men considered disdained:

> How can proud and brave people like the Asante sit back and look while the whiteman took away their king and chiefs, and humiliated them with a demand for the Golden Stool. The Golden Stool only means money to the whitemen; they have searched and dug everywhere for it. I shall not pay one predawn (£8.2s) to the governor. If you chiefs of Asante, are going to behave like cowards and not fight, you should exchange your loincloths for my undergarments (*Montu mod anta mma me na monnye me tam*) (Aidoo 1977: 12).

Available literature has confirmed that gender studies in the English-speaking sub-Saharan Africa, especially towards the end of the 1980s began as an activist study on the part of women to challenge what they considered as the marginalization of women (Ampofo, Beoku-Betts and Osirim 2004). The beginning of gender studies was also to address male biases in health, gender-based violence, issues of sexuality, same-sex relationships, access to education, work and globalization, politics, the state, and nongovernmental organizations (Ibid). Since then, gender studies spread to several institutions, including the University of Cape Coast, where the Centre for Gender Research, Advocacy and Documentation (CEGRAD) in 2013 was established to provide the university with a tool to address gender-based disparities (Britwum et al. 2004). Elsewhere in Makerere University, Gender Studies similarly began in the 1990s.

It must also be noted in all this that Gender Studies in Ghana is entwined with global histories. It was, therefore, part of the United Nations' Mexico Declaration of the International Decade for Women in 1975.[90]. The prosperity of the western world, especially the United States of America in the post-World War II world affected the cultural landscape of the west (Bellah et al. 1985). As part of the economic prosperity of the 1960s, the western world entered into the secularisation of its morality. This development rendered it possible for individuals to determine their own moral choices. Subsequently, morality literally became a matter of individual preference. Since that time, the world had begun to witness the full-blown expression of Adam and his wife seeking to be a law unto themselves, as they desired to be God.

By the 1970s, several factors, including the pornographic movies contributed to the "sexual revolution" (Bronstein and Strub 2016), which was marked by new forms of sexual expressions, ethics, and sexual liberalisation. The 1970s marked an important watershed in several activist groups that sought to liberate marginalised sexual individuals, including men and women (Allyn 2016). One of the leading thinkers, also grappling with the sexual revolution, was Michel Foucault. Unlike his contemporaries who assumed that sexual liberation could come about by speaking about it, Foucault had a different understanding. In Foucault's, History of Sexuality Vol. 1, he argued that the argument that conversations about sex were hardly held in secret until the Victorians was historically accurate. He, therefore,

[90] United Nations, Report of the world conference of the international women's year – Mexico City, 19 June – 2 July 1975 (New York: United Nation, 1976).

argued against the "repressive hypothesis" as ahistorical and simplistic. Foucault was not in doubt about the ethical rigidity of the Victorian age in fostering covering of bosoms, censuring of literature and intensification of campaign against masturbation, he argued that the 17th Century was remarkable in the priest and religious regime forcing openness in sexual matters. These priest compelled people to confess their sexual lives as part of determining the extent of guilt in order to provide the appropriate penance and corresponding moral advice. But more importantly, the forced confession rather reconfigured power and control, "making it possible for new series of interventions, tactical and positive interventions of surveillance, circulation, control, and so forth, which seem to have been intimately linked with techniques that give the appearance of repression, or at least liable to be interpreted as such" (Rabinow 1984: 62). Contesting the idea of sexual repression, Foucault argued that "The central issue, then … at least is not to determine whether one says yes or no to sex, whether one formulates prohibitions or permissions, whether one asserts its importance or denies its effect, or whether one refines the words one uses to designate it, but to account the fact that it is spoken about, to discover who does the speaking, the positions and viewpoints from which they speak, the institutions which prompt people to speak about it and which store and distribute the things that are said" (1984: 299). Truth and knowledge are not just grand abstract, but they are informed by history and social realities. Foucault's position, "does not entail any preconceived reduction of knowledge to social realities. Rather, there is a consistent imperative, played out with varying emphases, which runs through Foucault's historical studies: to cover the relations of specific scientific disciplines and particular social practices" (Rabinow 1984: 5). Concurrently, Foucault's most general aim was to "discover the point at which these practices became coherent reflective techniques with definite goals, the point at which a particular discourse emerged from these techniques and came to be seen as true, the point at which they are linked with the obligation of search for the truth and telling the truth" (1984: 7).

For the above reason, Foucault's idea of repression was not about just people talking about sex, but the rules governing the statements around sex. In other words, Foucault went beyond just mere speech to entwine language and power. His use of discourse, therefore, diverged from the use of the term to describe any kind of speaking, talk or conversation in the 16th Century (Ashcroft, Griffiths and Tiffin 2007: 62). Foucault argued that knowledge is hardly free and that discourse about a particular subject, which his extensive discussion sexuality, was strongly bounded with social knowledge. Instead of assuming knowledge is just "there", Foucault argued that knowledge is constructed to serve both political and social needs – control and marginalise. Framing language as the domain of power, "sex was taken charge of, tracked down as it were, by discourse that aimed to allow it no obscurity, no respite" (Foucault 1978: 20). Through Foucault's articulation of discourse, he expressed the relationship "the historically specific relations between disciplines (defined as bodies of knowledge) and disciplinary practices (forms of social control and social possibility) (McHoul and Grace 1993: 26). Given that Foucault viewed knowledge, not just as a matter of what is known, but the social, historical and political condition under which a statement is count as true or not.

From Foucault, it became quite obvious that language, as well as institutions, could not be granted – as they constituted the domain of power and control. The nexus between knowledge and power convinced some of the leaders of the sexual liberation movement of the 1970s believed that institutions of higher learning needed reforms. Students had to be introduced to knowledge about sex that repudiated the simplistic passing of "conventional" knowledge as neutral and authentic. Through activism and the gradual push of liberalism into an institution of higher learning, the gay and lesbian communities made progress in de-stigmatising homosexual practices. The absence of an objective truth implies concurrently the absence of moral objective. To put it bluntly in a popular Ghanaian axiom, "One man's meat is another's poison." In terms of how this benefits radical feminists, Sylvia Tamale wrote that:

> Poststructural theory questions that which is assumed to be normal or common sense. It challenges the idea that individuals exist as essential beings and argues that our "being" is socially constructed (Tamale 2016: 13).

That knowledge is part of the socio-historical evolution of society and its engagement and exercise with power is important for the religious discussion of human rights. For example, how should the idea of identity and human rights be constructed – is human rights discursive? How can we generate rights about human identity that is highly flexible, discursive and osmotic? Who determines human rights and who determines the human in the human rights? Could this difficulty explain the inability of Joe Biden's Supreme Court nominee,

Judge Ketanji Brown Jackson, whom the president has admitted was nominated because she is a woman to give a definition of what a woman is?[91] This was after Republic Senator, Marsha Blackburn asked her to provide a definition of the word "woman". The question was not asked within the context of a "trans" and intersex issue – it was about whether she admitted that woman was biologically woman.[92] The irony is that she had referenced women 14 times in her first two days of hearing, but failed to define what she meant by her use of the word "woman".[93] But is that elite mass delusion the reason Ghanaian LGBTQI+ advocates could not separate between differences in dynamism embedded in family units as cultural and biological transmogrification, as biological re-engineering?[94] Incidentally, in the preamble to the United Nations Charter is stated as follows:

> We the people of the United Nations determined … reaffirm faith in fundamental human rights, in the dignity and worth of human person, in the equal rights of men and women and of nations large and small.[95]

With the words, *women*, *men*, *human person*, large and small, was the United Nations appealing to absolute concepts or fluid concepts? Did the UN have any clearly defined understanding of what it meant to be a woman and man? Did the UN leave these concepts opened to individual whims and caprices and subjectivities? From the perspective of the entanglement between knowledge and power, I surmise that these questions cannot just be dismissed – as such an action may further polarise the discussion on the LGBTQ issue. Instead, it is important for the Ghanaian society to open up to possibilities of understanding

---

[91] Elle Reynolds (23 March 2022), "If Ketanji Brown Jackson doesn't know what a 'woma' is, why does she use the word so much? https://thefederalist.com/2022/03/23/if-ketanji-brown-jackson-doesnt-know-what-a-woman-is-why-does-she-use-the-word-so-much/?utm_source=Albert+Mohler&utm_campaign=edde9aef11-EMAIL_CAMPAIGN_2019_04_08_09_12_COPY_01&utm_medium=email&utm_term=0_b041ba0d12-edde9aef11-309913381&mc_cid=edde9aef11&mc_eid=90c482e36e, accessed 29 March 29 2022.

[92] Ibid.

[93] Ibid.

[94] Memorandum to Select Committee on the Constitutional, Legal and Parliamentary Affairs on the: Promotion of Proper Human Sexual Rights and Ghanaian Family Values Bill, 2021, p. 11.

[95] United Nations, *Basic facts about the United Nations* (New York: United Nations Department of Public Information, 2017/1947), p. 4.

that broadens the frontiers of knowledge, as well as the possibility of conviviality. This sense of epistemic conviviality is not to argue that the Ghanaian public should admit queer sexualities as part of the country's public lived experiences. Instead, it is important for the citizens to be aware of the seismic cultural shift that have sought to turn upside down language and words to admit imagined reality – as in the case of my visitor from the US, whom I wrote above.

For the so-called developing economies, by the 1970s, gender studies were hardly known, even though scholarship on women and families were already taking shape. At the Institute of African Studies, University of Ghana, Legon, Professor Christine Oppong and a few other scholars had advanced the study of the African family as they anticipated the impact of "modernity" birthed by political independence on the family. As part of her pioneering research on the nexus between modernisation, globalisation and the issues of dislocation that are caused, Oppong eloquently explained how the Akan kinship systems of matriliny clearly defined gendered roles for men as providers and women as nurturers. She equally demonstrated how the matrilineal system has been buffeted by urbanisation, the rapidly escalating numbers of insecure, landless people, rapidly rising numbers of unemployed; wage work among women, dwindling value of income, decline in the extended family system and the scattering of kin far and wide and frequent separation of spouses and their children and escalating family deprivations and tensions, even conflict (Oppong 2006: 50).[96] The impact of this on marriage and family are many, but related to my subject is that there has been rebellion from "would-be feminist, who may shave her head, deplore marriage and postpone or minimize or completely avoid parenthood" (Oppong 2006: 53).

The deliberate economic policy of the western financial institutions weakened the state's ability to totally manage the public sphere, including the universities. Similarly, the economic hardship that the imposition of the neoliberal economy caused exacerbated conflicts in several countries in Africa. With this development, public conversations about difficult subject tends to raise issues about who is sponsoring who, as we have already mentioned.

All these developments eventually led Africa into liberal democracies. With the introduction of liberal democracies, African

---

[96] Christine Oppong, "Demographic innovation and nutritional catastrophe: Change, lack of change and difference in Ghanaian family systems," in Goran Therborn (ed), *African families in a global context*, 49-78 (Uppsala: Nordiska Afrikainstitutet, 2006).

countries opened up to more nongovernmental organisations, the majority of whom were western in origin. These NGOs who had more funding from western nations embarked on liberalising the African cultural space. Some of them, including the CDD-Ghana, took up the task of deepening "democracy" in Ghana. Others such as the Network for Women's Rights in Ghana (NETRIGHT), established in late 1999 embarked on promoting women's rights and access to land rights (Yeboah, Ampofo and Brobbey 2014: 293). While the proliferation of female-oriented NGOs are necessary to advancing the challenges, facing women, the charge against them as western compradors tends to further undermine their activities.

The unfolding in Ghana on gender studies were occurring elsewhere in Africa. But the initiative to promote gender studies did not seamlessly sail through without some opposition. At Makerere University, Dr Florence Ebila, who taught the Gender in History Course said several men were not happy with the intention of the course and rather suggested that Gender must include men. While the inclusion of men may not change the problematique, possibly it may allay some fears men hold that gender studies is about undermining what they consider as the roles of men and women in society. A few African men wrote to express their concerns about the narrowness of gender studies, and rather proposed that,

> Instead of focusing on the … struggle between the African man and woman, Gender Studies, should during the new millennium, address the problems of famine, poverty, disease, poor education, poor communication, conflict – in word, underdevelopment. He concluded that these problems are, it is important to note, trans-gender. But more than anything else, Gender Studies should also highlight the crucial achievements Africa has so far made in science, politics, economics, medicine, technology, art, music and education. On funding, … Africans intellectuals and governments (should) look for alternative sources of funding for Gender research. This is the only way Africa can effectively dismantle forms of knowledge authored and authorized by the West (Kisiang'ani 2004: 24).[97]

Kisiang'ani's recommendation is not without its own difficulties, as it tends to overlook challenges such as donating girls to *trokosi* shrines, child trafficking hidden as fosterage, accusing elderly women of

[97] Since the 1990s men's studies have also increased.

witchcraft and banishing them to witches' camp without contact from their children and family. these are all meaningful matters to men and women. Certainly, to assume these issues are less important is to undermine the importance of compassion and empathy in inter-human relations. In all of this, gender scholars have gone the tangent of disentangling the complexities of the position of women in Ghana, Africa and the world. These scholars have been highly selective, and sometimes seen by male academics as silencing dissenting and moderate voices, such as Florence Abena Dolpyyne, now 84 years. She became the first female vice-chancellor of a public university, the University of Ghana and after she had represented the country in several of the international conferences on women's welfare concluded that she was/is not a feminist! Her book, *The emancipation of women: An African perspective* was telling enough in terms of her decision to disassociate with radical western feminists (Dolphyne 1991). She rather took the path of discussing how the social systems of Africa could be curated enough to support women and the family.

Incidentally, but expectedly, radical feminist scholars have operated the cancel culture in such a way that women scholars who are either moderate, sympathetic to the Christian faith or cherish the centrality of the family and would not go the tangent of demonstrable epistemic injustice to God and humanity are damned. Such women have hardly been cited, their works, given no consideration, hardly get invited to feminist conferences, and when their works are mentioned, it is done as a footnote to scholarship. For example, I am yet to read any Ghanaian and/or West African feminist scholar who cites the works of Dolphyne. Meanwhile, having read the background of these feminist scholars, I know that none of them took a specific course in Gender or feminist studies. Indeed, as they admit, while they have since the 1990s pushed the study of gender, there is still no degree programme in Gender (Yeboah, Ampofo and Brobbey 2014).

These women either read courses such as sociology, law, and linguistics (the field of Dolphyne) and yet, upon their return from the US and/or engagement with the western world, they are popularly alleged to have transported the "vagina war" in America, which, as I have said, have been brewing since the 1970s, to Ghana and Africa. But all these could mean that: First, knowledge production is certainly a political project and second, women tend to share a common predicament of androcentric traditions. So, regardless of whom they reference and what they train, feminist scholars are also creatively involved in finding an answer the society's imperfections or gender imbalances. The point is how to also create a balance without throwing society off the orbit.

With all these, the 1990s were critical in these feminists pursuing a manhunt for any piece of evidence that showed that colonialism, based on a false understanding of the Victorian concept of womanhood, undermined African women (Oyěwùmí 1997). So, in the last decade, several scholarships from these women and their western allies who are also blowing hot and cold against Christianity and their own Judeo-Christian sex ethics, have laid the blame for the perceived domestication of African women to colonialism; prostitution to have been accentuated and commodified by the western intrusion (Rattray 1923). They will also selectively use historical documents, including the works of Rattray a "recanted" colonial anthropologist and apologist, to argue that Akan women were very instrumental, with a stool that was ranked higher than the male stool (Odotei 2006). Moderate voices, who are historians, will also appeal to ancient history, including Egypt, to prove that women in Africa were highly visible in politics, including taking up leadership roles. But the title of such publications, including, the voice of moderate Professor Irene Odotei, "Women in the male corridors of power" implies that indeed, the corridors of power were occupied by males – *simplicita*s. That the militaristic history of the Akan was generally the preserve of men is reinforced by Pashington Obeng who argued that Yaa Asantewaa's success in the male-dominated military arena was by virtue of her senior age, royal lineage, and religion.

A few of these scholars, including occasional male historians, such as Professor Kwame Arhin, will argue that women played a role in the Akan military (Arhin 1983). Arhin provides important insight into the military role of women among the Akan, except that he tends to overstate the assumed power women had. But while titling his chapter as "The political and military roles of Akan women" in the edited volume by Christine Oppong, *Female and Male in West Africa*, Kwame Arhin could only give an example of Yaa Asantewaa, an Asante woman, not Akan woman, as women in "Akan" military.

Given the difficulty, Kwame Arhin, one of Ghana's celebrated scholars found in providing any visible and clear evidence of Akan women in the military as his title sought to prove, he rather talked about women not directly involved in the military. So, he rather focused his attention on women performing auxiliary roles such as singing songs of insinuation to urge men to fight. Indeed, this is not new in many cultures, including the Ewe of Ghana and Ancient Israel, where women's hailing of David, a military hero rather surged a fit of destructive jealousy and anger in Saul – leading Saul to the destruction of a young man whose military excellence had saved Saul and the entire Kingdom of Israel.[98] But more importantly, Arhin did what every scholar does in contributing the discussion on gender and women's role in Africa's socio-political history. Instead of discussing the military subject, he rather goes the tangent of a fallacy of *ignoratio elenchi* – woefully failing to discuss the issue embedded in the title of his chapter. In the end, he repeats the known issue of Akan women as having a superior stool. But did a superior stool hardly translated into women exercising political power? And if it did, how did power operate between men and women political elites among the Akan? Was the power dynamics among men and women complementary or competitive?

As I respond to the above questions in the course of this book, suffice to say that, as Goldberg has observed that men's dominance tendency is primarily a result of hormonal development and not primarily of anatomy. Concurrently:

> There have been "Queen Mothers" in a few African societies, but while such "Queen Mothers" did have a measure of autonomy denied other women in their societies and some authority in secondary areas, in every case they were subordinate to male king or chief in whom the society vested highest authority.[99]

While there has hardly been any society that men did not dominate the governance of the public sphere and fact that feminist scholars can hardly deny, the works Ghana and Africa's feminist scholars have been important watershed in curating cultures away from oppressing women. Gender Studies have also provided important insights for policies that have benefited women, men and children. Through the scholarship and activism of African feminist scholars, several women and children have moved away from the poverty zone, predatory cultural practices, such as FGC, *Trokosi*, and child prostitutes, challenged. To be sure, therefore, regardless of how one feels or thinks about the works of feminist scholarship and activism, their roles have contributed to human flourishing. Away from Akan women, one of the formidable scholars of a US-based African academic who has provided

[98] I Samuel 18:7.

[99] Steven Goldberg, *The inevitability of patriarchy: Why the biological difference between men and women always produces male domination* (New York: William Morrow & Company, Inc., 1973), 32.

an important intervention is Nwando Achebe (2020). In Achebe's work, *Female monarchs and merchant queens in Africa*, she carefully pieces together the words and experiences of African females from African-derived sources to demonstrate the history of remarkable African women who significantly impact the continent.

Nevertheless, focusing on the matrilineal Akan of Ghana, in all the efforts at centring women in the Akan political system, one objective scholar who pointed out the fallacy in all such attempts was Lynne Brydon. In her article on 'Women chiefs and power in the Volta Region of Ghana', she rightly observed:

> Asante provides both a good baseline and comparison when looking at women's roles and empowerment. Asante society has a matrilineal focus, that is, entitlement to inherit wealth and key positions passes through women. In spite of this pivotal genealogical role for women, however, women were historically only the conduits as sisters and mothers of brothers and sons through which entitlement of office holding and property passed. Men held the offices and managed the property, whether the land or other forms of wealth (Brydon 1996: 228).

Brydon also added that,

> Women have authority and power only in closely circumscribed areas: within the household and family, within some areas of local markets and with respect to certain aspects of family and lineage life (Ibid. 229).

Scholars have tried to even claim, even though with a single major evidence from Yaa Asantewaa's episode that women were even militarily involved. After discussing the gender composition of the Asantemaa's court, which was female-dominated, Takyiwaa Manuh concluded that, "However, from observation, those who actually conduct the proceedings are male, and although it has not been possible so far to date their participation and indeed dominance in the court, they seem to be well aware that matters and decisions might well be different if women were the judges (Manuh 1988).

While historically, the political role of women was not romantically powerfully as evidenced by Lynne Brydon and Takyiwaa Manuh, there are other scholars whose writing suggest that colonialism ditched the influence of women. J.B. Danquah referring to evidence provided by K.A. Busia pointed out how colonialism eroded the rights of the Akan queen-mother as follows:

> Her position, always regarded with deep affection by the Akan, had remained mysterious and almost completely unknown to European administrators, who never claimed to have understood her place in the Akan political system … At all times, under the ancient Akan regime, the queen-mother was a member of the king's council, sitting on his left, as sits the sub-conscious in the mind (Danquah 1960).

The debate over whether colonialism eroded the role of queen mothers or not, what several analysts conclude is that, while the queen mother was such an important political stakeholder among the Akan, and much as the Akan political system featured gender parallelism, the role of the queen mother was largely about domestic affairs, while it was rare for a woman to be a chief (Stoeltje 1997). But as I have said, Gender Studies have unveiled important aspect of gender segmentation that have continued in subjugating women in several societies. Under colonialism, the colonial regime did not pay attention to Akan precolonial customs of bilocal residence and gave men in wage work houses. This left women in a tight spot in some marriages. This colonial dismissal of precolonial bilocal residential practices became a major challenge for traditional authorities who had to compel women of over 15 years in the 1930s, as these women challenged male-control. Framing women's search for economic freedom as a result of the cocoa boom in the 1930s as challenging of patriarchal authority, the chiefs forced these women to marry (Allman, 1996). But it is not also entirely accurate from the historical perspective that women's autonomy in marriage deteriorated as a result of colonialism. There is ample evidence that among the Akan people of Sefwi, women deliberately refused the bridewealth/monetary transaction that transferred a set of legal, sexual, and parental rights that husband acquired after marriage (Boni 2001). While some the Akan may have practised some form of bilocal residence, it hardly undermined the rights husbands had over their wives. As I have said rights men exercised phallic control over women which was expressed in the instrumental roles they performed as heads and providers of their families. Men also determined the reproductive role of their wives. But women still retained some control over their reproductive rights, which included deliberately not taking the bridewealth, as I have said above. It appears the freedom Akan women enjoyed in marriage was hardly eroded by colonialism. Talking about African marriages, in general, though his article was on Ghana, … averred that African marriages was freely entered into by persons subject to customary law with the colonial governor literally imposing limited or no restriction (Allot 1958: 174).

Since the 1990s, the debate over gender has swung in all directions. Some believe indigenous cultures were both oppressive and liberating, and there are those who think colonialism provided some of the liberations for women (Doyle 2007; Sudarkasa 1986). Even concerning the state of women in the same ethnic group, two formidable feminist scholars have bitterly disagreed (Oyěwùmí 2016; 1997; Bakare-Yusuf 2004). There are anthropological novels that bring to the fore a practice among pre-colonial !Kung married women who could have multiple lovers (Shostak 1990). Others also think the confusion over gender is because of males dominating the printing culture (Zeleza 2005; Mama 1996). There are cultures in Africa where women married, or others can have lovers. In fact, in matrilineal societies, where children's affiliation is through the mother, paternity is not important so yes women can take lovers. The children belong to the woman anyway. There are examples from Northern Zambia and Malawi. But the same could hardly be said about the Akan social system that defines the role of women and men in the family. In fact, in Ghanaian families, both in traditional and modern times, control of economic power and other power relations favour males who are usually the heads of both the nuclear and extended families (Ardayfio-Schandorf 2006: 133).

In terms of Akan male reproductivity, the Akan share with several other Ghanaian ethnic groups, including the Ga. With nearly all the various cultures, whether matrilineal or patrilineal essentially sharing the same patriarchal attitudes across age, sex and lineage (Ampofo,), the Akan shares the same phallic culture with the Ga, which Atobrah and Awedoba have discussed which are expressed in "men's fertility, phallic competence and performance of social responsibilities". Indeed, among the Akan men and other males in other ethnic groups in Ghana, men's associations between biological fatherhood and manhood imbued in phallic competence which serves as an important indicator for marital stability, re-marriage and extra-marital relationships.[100] The importance of male biological fatherhood is "not only because of the authority and control fatherhood portends, but also because of the symbolic significance of a competent, heterosexual, performative phallus. The absence of evidence of the competence of the phallus, in cases of infertility, can lead to a questioning, or anticipatory

[100] Akosua Adomako Ampofo, Michael P.K. Okyerefo and Michael Pervarah, "Phallic competence: Fatherhood and the making of men in Ghana," Culture, *Society & Masculinity*, 1, 1 (2009): 59-78.

questioning, of a man's masculinity."[101] For the Akan, the matrilineal settings may raise question about how male procreation is valued, recognised and how men are valued as fathers and how permitting the rights of other sexualities may undermine male procreation or social fatherhood. With this genuine concern, I find the response of Adomako et al., very insightful and will cite them in full. They argued that:

> Among the Akan, it is the woman who is obligated to produce descendants for her lineage, however, her family will publicly acknowledge her husband for giving them children since he makes the fulfilment of this obligation possible. If there is a suspicion, for whatever reasons, that the husband is incapable of having children (say, it is known or rumored that he is impotent) a woman's (maternal) family is likely to suggest that she divorce him.[102]

The above means that, while the Akan takes interest in pater (a social father), fecundity, paternity and biological fatherhood seem almost inseparable, and form a core feature in the construction of manhood.[103] Adomako et al., are right in their observation that,

> Formal adoption has not formed an important part of discourses of parenthood in Ghana and even today is frequently discouraged if it is perceived by others that one is considering this as an alternative to biological parenting.[104]

The centrality of entwining biological procreativity and masculinity among the Akan was so strong that among the Asante, a sub-section of the Akan group, a man who failed to make her wife pregnant within two or three years was subjected to the fecundity ritual called Krawa-goro – a male-sterility-dispelling rite.[105]

The meaning of proverbs is determined by their socio-historical context. For this reason, Pashington Obeng has observed that gendered values and ideas appearing to be systematic may contain contradictions

---

[101] Ibid., 60.

[102] Ibid., 63.

[103] Ibid., 67.

[104] Ibid., 66.

[105] T.E. Kyei, *Marriage and divorce among the Asante: A study undertaken in the course of Ashanti social survey (1945)* (Cambridge: Cambridge African Monographs-14, 1992), p. 141.

and notions of gender roles in Asante society, as did Akyaawa Yikwan, who was involved in the Asante war against the British in 1824. He concluded that "Akan proverbial lore related to masculinity and femininity thus must be understood in a larger historical and sociocultural context (Obeng 2003: 195).[106] Kwasi Yankah has also argued that while proverbs embellish language, they do not necessarily guide the speaker's judgement; neither do they take over his reasoning (Yankah 1989b: 338).

As the above, partly indicated the fluidity and accommodative nature of African cultures, Christianity is put on defence as the missionaries are also accused of domesticating women with an education that oriented women to domestic chores (Hansen 1992). Indeed, the idea of women performing domestic roles was not limited to the missionaries. It was part of the 19th Century's revitalisation of historic Christian family ethics. One of the founders of the Seventh-day Adventist Church, E.G. White counselled women on family life as follows:

> Study how to perform with alacrity the plain, uninteresting, homely but, but needful duties which relate to domestic life… Try to make a success of your domestic life. You need the culture and experience of domestic life. You need the variety, the stir, the earnest effort, the cultivation of the willpower, that this life brings (White 1885/2002: 74).

Some historians and mission anthropologists have also tried to exonerate colonialism and Christian mission as liberational rather than oppressive (Ayesu, Gbormittah and Adum-Kyeremeh 2016; der Geest 1990). Similarly, while being critical of colonialism, Akurang-Parry admitted that by the 19th C, western education has become an important agency of social mobility and advancement. Certainly, unlike Walter Rodney who blamed nearly everything about Africa's underdevelopment on Europeans (Rodney 1973), Abosede Ipadeola argued that it is not entirely accurate to externalise foreigners for the marginalisation of the continent (Ipadeola 2023; Igwe 2010). Thus, corroborating the need for Africans to discard the simplicity of "blame culture' Akurang-Parry added that "some women who acquired education used it to transcend the bounded political spaces controlled by the patriarchal structures of both indigenous and colonial states" (Akurang-Pary 2004: 469-470). I surmise from Akurang-Parry that

---

106 Pashington Obeng, "Nationalism: Forms of masculinity in modern Asante of Ghana," in Lisa A. Lindsay and Stephan F. Miescher (eds), *Men and masculinities in modern Africa*, 192-208 (Portsmouth: Heinemann, 2003), 195.

education had both benefit to women and also served as an aporia to colonialism and indigenous androcentric tendencies. For this reason, it will be simplistic to just blame missionary education for the oppression of African women. My point is supported by Florence Ebila, who wrote that androcentric marginalization and mugging of women's freedom of expression is "not only a creation of colonialism, it had also been institutionalised within the masculinist state after independence by virtue of their patriarchal inheritance from African traditions" (Ebila 2015: 147). It is important to mention that several Ghanaian academics that the domestication of women predated colonialism. Mercy Oduyoye, one of the earliest female Ghanaian theologians observed as follows:

> In Africa, the very idea of a 'free woman' conjures up negative images. We have been brought up to believe that a woman should always have a suzerain, that she should be 'owned' by a man, be he father, uncle, or husband. A 'free woman' spells disaster. An adult woman, if unmarried, is immediately reckoned to be available for the pleasure of all males and is treated as such. The single woman who manages her affairs successfully without a man, is an affront to patriarchy and a direct challenge to the so-called masculinity of men who want to 'possess' her. Some women are struggling to be free from this compulsory attachment to the male. Women want the right to be fully human, whether or not they choose to be attached to men (Oduyoye 2004/2002: 69).

Indeed, some progress had been made in pushing back the cultural challenges of women, but while the efforts of these feminist scholars toward unsettling the challenges burdening women attracted the sympathy of several men, the issue of homosexuality becomes the point of divergence within the feminist group and with the general African populace. With this, I agree with Tandon that these western agents have become agents of "western parameters, to divert attention from the root causes of African poverty, to pacify and to peddle Western values and civilisation."[107] But it is also true that same-sex discourse has become an important part of Gender Studies because heterosexual marriage has been identified as partly incorrigibly incapable in advancing the interest of women (Card 2002). As part of walking the middle ground, without pretending to be neutral, my book also builds

[107] Yash Tandon, "An African perspective," Amsterdam: Transnational Institution, https://www.tni.org/en/article/an-africa-perspective, accessed: 12 March 2022, p. 3.

on the work of Obianuju Ekeocha (2018), *Target Africa*, which casts a new insight on neocolonialism is western cultural imperialism – framed around homosexual rights and abortions.

The abortion issue is quite complex, as it brings out a section of society's efforts at dealing with what is usually referred to as unplanned pregnancies. There are moves, therefore, to ensure encourage the use of contraceptives as well as ensure that abortions are performed under hygienic conditions. These are all important issues that must be considered. Except that in the Ghanaian content, sanitising the abortion space would hardly take away the stigma that several of the citizens attached to it. More importantly, the issue of abortion, as I have observed, are entangled in both local and translocal factors. The local factors, which involves economic morass of the country and the decline in the role of the extended family system and women being compelled to take up dual responsibilities as mothers and providers. But there is also the transnational factor, largely the cascading effect of global neo-liberalism. The globalisation of neo-liberal economic ethos commodifies caregiving practices (Pocock 2005),[108] such that parents, particularly single mothers, have to pay for the care they receive for their children. With the care industry focusing more on profit, as opposed to the pre-capitalist affective-oriented care practices, the pressure on young women to abort is high, while several young men continue to remain irresponsible. So, whereas sanitising the abortion space may appear to offer some remedy, it will in the long run not solve anything. The solution to the abortion issue and women, as a result of economic hardship, refusing to even marry (as identified by Oppong) is for society to institute affective measures that would restore the duality of gendered roles performed by men and women. In the extreme, and in the case of Ghana, the state could, in addition to the Social Security and National Insurance and Trust (SSNIT), establish a body that similarly receives compulsory monthly contribution from men as security for women.

This means that while the modern Ghanaian state struggles to overcome the spill over effects of both local economic hardship and the cascading effect of global neoliberalism on women, Akan women have traditionally been creative in coping with gendered based inequalities. Boni masterfully demonstrates how African nations' dependence on western funds continue to tie the continent firmly to western ideological solutions that are opposed to the morals and the

[108] Barbara Pocock, "Work/care regimes: Institutions, culture and behaviour and the Australian case," *Gender, Work and Organizations*, 12, 1 (2005): 32-49.

cultural values of their people. The both pro-LGBTQ and anti-LGBQT coalitions involved in the same-sex debacle hardly provide any evidence that the western world of either Evangelical Christians or leftist politicians provide financial support for their respective activities. But at least these "rumours" of external funding and ideological influence may signal the fact that they both detest the idea of the west infiltration in Africa's internal matters.

In the next section, I will discuss the current LGBTQ+ rights in Ghana and the tensions it has generated. But suffice it to say that the issue with the efforts by a few feminist scholars to promote the rights of homosexuals in Ghana is precisely because sexual rights are not rights in the Ghanaian context. The fact is that, in the Ghanaian context, sex is a private issue (Bediako Akoto 2017: 16). So, how and when one decides to have sex is one's own business. Hardly is the issue of how and when one practices sex becomes part of general public conversation, except among a private group of friends. Otherwise, who would discuss the issue of how and when they have sex in a professional space? So, obviously if a group of individuals had not chosen to make a public show of their sexual preferences, Ghana would have desisted from talking about other people's sexualities. For this reason, it is unthinkable that a person would be victimised because of a private issue such as having sex. In fact, it is unthinkable that just how one looks, whether a man being too feminine or a woman being too masculine, will be any good ground for such a person to be victimised. Nevertheless, the issue is also more than these questions, as it involves the entanglement between identity and sexuality; sovereignty and transnational politics, individual freedom and communal rights. It is, therefore, what I have been saying, the fact that the same-sex conversation is about broader discussions on every aspect of Ghanaian life.

The sexual identity politics cannot be taken lightly and in isolation of the larger society. It calls for a merging of ideas to dialogue and reconsideration of the status of the family as a precursor to the state and institutionalised religion. Even so, without disregarding the multiple shades of marriage and what it must perform, I subscribe to the biblical understanding of the marriage institution. I reason that when God instructed Adam and Eve to fill the earth, the word *pro-*create aptly express that divine-cultural mandate. The prefix "pro" means to support, while creation is to bring to pass what God alone allows. So, human beings were to "pro" (support) "creation" through heterosexual marriage between a biological man and a biological woman. The naturalness of this is that in virtually all civilised societies, same-sex marriages had hardly been encouraged. It was even considered alien in countries like England that is today acting as mercenaries and missionaries for the spread of the LGBTQ+ agenda. Admittedly, however, in a postmodern world, yes, the world of "posts", people can reproduce by using surrogate mothers or using donated sperm or ovum. Anyone can use these technologies if they can afford them, married heterosexuals who are childless, single women who desire children. But as I have said, I personally lean towards heterosexual procreation as ideal – notwithstanding other possibilities.

My concern is also about the creeping commodification of the IVF technology – a development that also complicates the entanglement between technology and morality. For example, in an article in the New Times about two heterosexual couple, Elaine Meyer and Barry Prizant who had deployed the service of IVF at the Women & Infants Hospital in Providence, Rhode Island, to have son. But it turned out after they had a son in the 1990s, they also recorded three cases of miscarriage. As if that was the end of the story, while they were told about their failure to secure more children ad that the embryos were all unsuccessful, in 2017, they received a bill of $500 for the continued preservation of their human embryos. Meanwhile, they were told they had lost those embryos several years ago. But it turned out that the issue was just more than that. It involved the commercialisation of the whole processes of IVF. Dr Jeffrey Khan, the director of the Berman Institute of Bioethics at John Hopkins University, cited in the article, said "There is little regulation and no accounting of how many embryos there are in storage." The story further reported that the fertility industry "is a lucrative business, but operates largely unchecked by regulators."[109]

In concluding this section, for the religious community in Ghana, anything that does not support creation undermines belief in the sovereignty of God. It implies subversion of God's divine-cultural command of "fill the earth" with humanity. While this should not imply that that all humans live for this ultimate purpose regardless of circumstances, it partly accounts for the multiple social issues that inform the complex attitudes some Ghanaians have shown toward the LGBTQ+ community. It is also for this reason that chiefs (representing custom) and Christianity and Islam, the two main religions in the

---

[109] Katherine Rosman (April 16, 2021), 'The lost embryos' https://www.ncbi.nlm.nih.gov/search/research-news/13277/?utm_source=gquery&utm_medium=referral&utm_campaign=gquery-home (Accessed: September 5, 2022).

country have overlooked their doctrinal differences to "pro" create – support creation.

Concluding remarks

In the above chapter, I have argued against the narrow construction of the LGBTQ issue as simply a matter of legislation. I have demonstrated that, as one looks at the controversial issue over the Family Bill and its counter arguments, one is looking at a human being who is social and whose existence is not just about sexuality, but about relating with others to find meaning. Consequently, the LGBTQ issue is more than just passing a law to allow to criminalise, but about the human being as an embodied creature whose existence is dependent on the existence of both other human beings and other institutions in society. With this understanding, my point is that if the state is called upon by both sides of the Coalition to interfere in the issue of the LGBTQ with laws, the state is invited to supplant the love and affection that informs the constitution of the family. The state by definition, at least from the perspective of Max Weber, is largely about the management of the public sphere with a coercive instrument of force. The state is what it is, inter alia, because of its monopolisation and legitimate use of force (Weber 2019: 75),[110] not love – love which governs the family. The point is precisely because the public sphere is a space for political and economic activities. Since in politics, if one gives power, one loses power and in economics, if one gives money, one loses money, the public sphere is always contentious. A contention that needs the rod to whip people in order (At least the Bible – Romans 13:4 – supports Max Weber in this). Given the nature of the state and its primary function of ensuring law and order with coercive force, subjecting the family to the regulation of the state would, at least as admitted by both members of the two Coalitions, would destroy the family. If human beings are social beings who find meaning in life through their sense of gregariousness and association, then the LGBTQ issue cannot be treated as simply a matter of sexuality and its attending politics. Instead, the issues should be treated as forming the core of human beings whose have legitimate right to freedom and yet whose sense of being is based on social connection. Since I consider human ontological gregariousness as given, the next chapter discuss the philosophy behind the LGBTQ issue.

---

110 Weber, M. (2019). *Economy and society: A new translation* (trans. Keith Tribe). Cambridge, Mass.: Harvard University Press.

Chapter 3

Philosophical foundation of gender and sexuality studies

The fool who does not know how to use proverbs appropriately often uses the one which is a direct attack on himself or herself, but a sagacious not only knows and understands proverbs but he also knows that some proverbs bring quarrel and others stop quarrel (Igbo Proverb).

If you grow and you don't see, when you sin, you know it (Akan proverb).

The European who brought the pencil also brought the eraser (Just because something is written in a book does not mean it is always true and right) (Yoruba proverb).

A proverb is a horse which carry one swiftly to the discovery of ideas (Yoruba proverb).

Introduction

The above proverbs point to the importance of oral culture as necessary resource in the construction of traditions of knowledge of non-written cultures. Certainly, while proverbs hardly have any one meaning, a contextual hermeneutical approach toward them give us an important window into the cumulative wisdom of African ancestors. On Thursday, July 26, 2018, Ghana was thrown into affective laughter that also served as a vortex of many things. As part of the parliamentary proceeding, John Frimpong Osei, the New Patriotic Party (NPP) Member of Parliament for Abirem Constituency in the Eastern Region of Ghana asked the Minister of Energy, Mr Boakye Agyarko a question about communities in Mr Osei's constituency that are yet to be connected to the national grid. In response, the Minister mentioned the names of the communities, which were: "Kote Yɛ Aboa" (The penis is a fool), "Hwoa Yɛ Mmobo" (The testicle is pitiful and vulnerable),

"Etwɛ Nim Nyansa" (The vagina is wise).[111] Given the excitement that these suggestive names elicited, the Minister jokingly added that, "Providing them with electricity may interfere with nocturnal activities". Indeed, oral histories of the people indicated that the woman, represented by her genitals is more powerful politically and socially than man, represented by his genitals.[112] These were circulated on social media!

More specifically, it pointed to the extent to which at the basal level of heterosexual sex, a man becomes truly vulnerable to a woman. Beyond the jokes and jest that these suggestive names elicited, there was also the question of the assumed woman's ontological inferiority to men. As I shall discuss in the course of this chapter, through the inversion and de-contextual analysis of gender-related Akan proverbs, several Ghanaian feminist scholars and feminist philosophers, including Ipadeola, have arrived at a rather hasty conclusion that the Akan was androcentric and patriarchal, even though the Akan is matrilineal (but of course, not matriarchal) (Ipadeola 2023). Before I proceed any further, I need to say that the definition of African feminism and who African feminists are, are not neatly demarcated from the global aspiration of feminists – destabilising patriarchy. Sylvia Bawa, whose research includes structural inequality depends on a definition borrowed from Davies and Graves who argued that *genuine African feminism* can be summarised as follows:

> Firstly, it recognizes a common struggle with African men for the removal of the yoke of foreign domination and European American exploitation. It is not antagonistic to African men but challenges them to be aware of certain salient aspects of women's subjugation which differ from the generalized oppression of all African peoples. Secondly, an African feminist consciousness recognizes that certain inequities and limitations existed/exist in traditional societies and that colonialism reinforced them and introduced others. As such, it acknowledges its

[111] Ghanaweb (30 July 2018), '100-year-old woman gives history behind sexually suggestive community names', https://www.ghanaweb.com/GhanaHomePage/NewsArchive/100-year-old-woman-gives-history-behind-sexually-suggestive-community-names-673118, accessed 18 October 2021.

[112] Adom TV (2 August 2018), "History Behind Shuwa Ye Mmobo, Koti Ye Aboa and Etwe Nim Nyansa", https://www.youtube.com/watch?v=nwIQvgUidVc; GH Africa TV, The history of the (town) etwe nim nyansa and koti ye aboa – Take a look". July 30, 2018, https://www.youtube.com/watch?v=0xck46TFKeg, accessed 18 October 2021.

> affinities with international feminism, but delineates specific certain needs and goals arising out of the concrete realities of women's lives in African societies. Thirdly, it recognizes that African societies are ancient societies. So, logically, African women must have addressed the problems of women's position in society historically. In this regard, there already exist, in some societies, structures which are given to equality... Fourthly, African feminism examines African social institutions which are of value to women and rejects those which work to their detriment and does not simply import Western women's agenda. Thus, it respects African woman's status as mother but questions obligatory motherhood and the traditional favoring of sons. It sees utility in the positive aspects of the extended family and polygamy with respect to child care and the sharing of household responsibility... Fifthly, it respects African women's self-reliance and the penchant to cooperate work and social organization. .... Sixthly, an Africanist approach has to look objectively at women's situation in societies which have undergone a war of national liberation socialist reconstruction... . Finally, African feminism looks at traditional and contemporary avenues of choice for women (Davies and Graves, 1986: 8-11).

Certainly, these points need to be critiqued. They are problematic and presumptuous. It is important to mention that Davies and Graves ended what they considered as genuine African feminism, focusing on women's request to liberate fellow women from androcentric oppression, which, according to the others makes African women more favourably disposed to International Feminism, which incorporates differentiation in women's activism. As the authors indicated, this stands in contrast with the European/American model, which as they said, "fails to deal with issues that directly affect Black women" (Ibid., 10). But for her own academic interest, Sylvia Bawa quickly inserts in "it is ... [it] understands the interconnected of race, class and sex oppress (Bawa 2018: 2-3, emphasis hers)", as part of the definition. This is against the fact that Davies and Graves had stated that the insertion by Bawa (which is on page 11) of the authors' book is a theoretical African feminism understanding of "the interconnectedness of race, class and sex oppression" (Davies and Graves 1986:11).

The above definition, which Bawa endorses is clear in terms of how African feminists in the 1980s framed their activism, which was largely about supporting the socio-economic wellbeing of women, especially as the decade marked the economic morass of the continent (refer to Morgan's publication African feminists readily identified with, 1986).

But the definition in Bawa's article, because of what she inserted added her own agenda to it. So, from her article she complicates the definition of Africanism, which several African women activists do not support – I mean the rights of women to be anything, liberated from marriage, free to practice lesbianism etc.

It is for this reason that her article was clear that Ghanaian women refer to themselves as feminists. They direct their activism directly towards defending the rights of women, as women of her respondents said, "women are women" without any illusions of trans-women. She is equally right in observing that, the term feminism invokes some apprehension among Ghanaians, as the term is considered subversive to Ghanaian cultural and religious idioms about family. For this reason, feminism in academia is fronted as Gender Studies. This betrays the whole agenda of Gender Studies and other foreign-sponsored women's rights groups, which while appearing to be championing the cause of women, have upgraded their activism to include supporting people of the LGBTQ+ constituency. This reaffirms the concerns of Ghanaians over the whole objectives of feminism as a movement.

So, Bawa should have clarified the older women she is talking about in her article, because older women of the decolonisation era are clear about what they mean by feminism – fighting for the rights of women as women. This is in contrast with contemporary Ghanaian feminists trained in the post-sexual revolution Euro-American world who tend to import western radicalism into the country and continent. As these women teach in the universities, as gender scholars, they were accused of promoting radical feminism.

Just like most radical feminist scholars occupying the various departments at the University of Ghana in their attempts to mute other scholars, Bawa was deliberately silent about the work of Florence Abena Dolphyne who represented Ghana in several of the Women's Conferences, organised as part of the United Nation's Decade for Women since 1975. Dolphyne became the Chairman of the Ghana National Council on Women and Development and the first pro-vice chancellor of the University of Ghana, Legon.

Reflecting on the difficulties women from Africa had with their western counterparts, which possibly explain why most of these African women disliked the Euro-American model of feminism, Dolphyne wrote that while most of the women agreed that some social practices such as polygamy, bride-wealth and female circumcision were to be stopped, they did not agree on the measures to be taken to eradicate them and the timing of such measures. But more importantly, she observed that after the Conference, she became more and more conscious of the difference in approach to women's issues between Western women, especially "feminists", and emancipation. Consequently, she rejected the label then and now (at the time she was writing), based on experiences of the decade, not those Bawa interviewed, because as she said,

> I have never considered and still do not consider myself a 'feminist', for the term evokes for me the image of an aggressive woman who, in the same breath, speaks of a woman's rights to education and professional training, her right to equal pay for work of equal value, her right to vote and to be voted for in elections at all levels, etc. as well as a woman's right to practice prostitution and lesbianism (Dolphyne 1991: xiii).

It could be argued that prostitution is practised by women who are excluded from work, are poor and desperate to make ends mee and usually not a freely made choice. What feminists are considered to do and say is that once a woman resorts to prostitution because of despair, the public should not make her situation worse by stigmatising and discriminating against her.

Indeed, the issue of women and prostitution is quite complex, so that while others may be induced may poverty and deprivation to go into it, it is also true that not everyone would see the practice as a source of relieve from poverty. Nevertheless, Dolphyne concluded, "It is this image of the feminist, which made African men, some in highly-placed positions in government, and some women as well, rather uncomfortable about the idea of an international year for women" (Ibid., xiii). Indeed, in an interview I had with Mr Godfried Asante, a member of the Pentecost Students and Associates, the tertiary youth wing of the Church of Pentecost at the University of Ghana (formed in 1976), at the time when Professor Dolphyne led at a seminar for PENSA members in the 1990s, he said the woman told them that,

> As for me, I am a woman and a mother. When I go home from here, and I step on my doormat, I leave my professorship outside the classroom and step in the home to work as a wife and a mother and submit myself to my husband."[113]

[113] Interview with Mr Godfried Asante on Saturday, October 16, 2021, at the Birmingham Christian College (the Bible College of the Church of Pentecost in the UK where he works as the Director of Finance, Business and Operations).

Regrettably, while's Bawa's work provide some insight into the interface between religion and women's oppression, she did not provide adequate historical basis for concluding that religion oppresses women. She did not incorporate rigorous historiographical knowledge of Christianity in the many fallacies she committed. She claims, for example, that "Christianity played a crucial role in entrenching women's subordination in SSA" (Bawa 2019: 55). She hardly provided any evidence to prove that Christianity indeed suppressed women in the colonial era. Meanwhile, as Boni observed, the idea that Christianity eroded women's right and autonomy is on a shaky grounds. This is because, among the Akan of Sefwi for example, women's low status predated Christianity which only gained influence among the Sefwi people in the 1910s (Boni 2001: 21). Instead of providing any historical evidence for her degradation of women theory, Bawa cited Mbembe's work on Christianity and imperialism in Africa to support her assertion. Indeed, if Bawa had incorporated extensive reading on Christianity and colonialism in Africa, she may have toned down her ideologically-inspired invectives against Christianity. With this, I think that Bawa, like several of literature on the subject, simplistically conflated Christianity and colonialism:

> [A]nticolonial animus among African intellectuals leads to a plague-on-all-your-houses attitude under which it must almost de rigueur for African scholars to criticise anything colonial and, by association, anything Western. One unfortunate effect of this attitude is that it does not differentiate between what Christianity did and what colonialism wrought, and as a result give short shrift to the ideas of strivings of Africans who accepted Christianity but not colonialism and celebrated what it brought them in terms of social living, being human, and such like" (Táíwò 2010: 52).

He continues with a verdict,

> I would like to argue that the straight identification of Christianity with colonialism is at best mistaken and at worst just wrong. More often than not, those who base their analysis on such identification manage to conflate many issues that are not only separable but ought to be separated for purposes of clear analysis (Ibid., 52-53).

Instead of just dismissing the colonial enterprise under the façade of postcolonialism, Bawa could have reflected on the fact that "The colonial enterprise involved social, economic, and cultural transformation, not necessarily exploitation of resources and oppression" (Ayesu, Gbormittah, and Adum-Kyeremeh 2016: 3). As historians, these authors concluded their article that, "colonial agents' policies significantly influenced the provision of social amenities for women and children" (Ibid., 28).

About the role women play in the Pentecostal-charismatic churches, eminent researchers, including Brigid Sackey, who once acted as the Director of the Institute of African Studies, University of Ghana, have documented the role the churches have contributed to empowering women's leadership since the 1980s (Sackey, 2006). Indeed, it is what is perceived as a dismissive posture of western-trained African feminists who impose radical feminist theory on African scholarship that some Muslim scholars, including Lena, have rejected the colonial feminism paradigm as obstructive of the status of women in Islam (Salaymeh 2021). In the same sense, Lila Abu-Lughod has rightly rejected the western claim of an oppressive Muslim woman who needs redemption from the west (Abu-Lughod 2013).

All this brings me back to the suggestive names I mentioned above, which as I said unsettled the false assumption that Akan people had seen women as ontologically inferior to men. While there is enough evidence to show that (Akan) women were hardly suppressed, but rather followed a structured pattern that ensured ethical and ontological boundaries, the suggestive names fed into a complex narrative about gender. The pervasive, but complex status of women in Akan societies broadened the discussion on gender to include women theologians. Historically, women's experience under patriarchy has largely been characterised by experiences of oppression, objectification, subjugation, and alienation, which John Stuart Mill characterised as the subjection of the will of women to men in a marital condition, as he referred to marriage as a form of enslavement (Mill 1989: 147).[114] This is believed to have been structured along the lines of society's stratification of human beings, crystalising in marriage where men are considered to have a natural right to rule over women (Mill 1989). Similarly, a man is expected to perform instrumental roles – through his engagement in public service, while a woman is expected to perform expressive roles in the private sphere. As observed by John Stuart Mill, "The general opinion of men is supposed to be that the natural vocation of a woman is that of a wife and mother" (Mill 1989: 144). Mill's

114 Mill, J.S. (1989). *The subjection of women in On liberty and other writings* (ed. Stefan Collini). Cambridge: Cambridge University Press.

observation resonates with de Beauvoir's that the gender division of labour kept women in a cycle of patriarchal dominance.

Beyond gendered division of labour, male-dominance over women were structured in gendered cultural beliefs and practices, even, as I have said, in the Akan matrilineal society. One of such commonest held belief which largely resulted in the suppression of women was/is witchcraft accusation. Historically, several cultures around the world have sustained the practice of witchcraft accusations and burning on the stake with women being the majority victims. The male subjugation of women was articulated through men accusing women of witchcraft (Blécourt 2000).[115] Elsewhere in African cultures, including the Akan and Ga, women have been subjected to extreme forms of rituals and practices that violated their rights. These included widowhood rites. In the Northern part of the country, women are subjected to circumcision among some cultures. Among the Ewe of Southern Ghana, girl children are enslaved to a religious cult in a practice called *Trokosi*, to allegedly atone for the sins committed by their relatives. Given that these cultural practices that have been interpreted as oppressive to women, Oduyoye did not fail to see a nexus between religion and the subjugation of women. Considering how men intersect religion and patriarchy, she said "African men have no problem with religion. Men put on the masks to play God's and, loving their own individual lives more than the cohesion of the traditional community, they survive on women's selflessness" (Oduyoye 2019: 171).[116] Indeed, these cultural issues did not necessarily translate into the fact that women were held as ontologically inferior to men.

In a newspaper article, a Ghanaian female journalist, Vicky Wireko said that since the Bible declared that Eve led the world into sin, women have never had their peace of mind and never been freed from androcentric oppression. In pre-Islamic Arabia, at least the first hundred years before the advent of Islam – usually known as Jahiliyya – it is said that female infanticide was high, while women were generally considered receptacles for the man's sperm. Among the Akan, while the Akan is structured along matrilineal lines, political power was vested in male uterine kin. This is against the fact that many anthropologists who studied the Akan have concluded that the female stool is higher in authority than her male's counterpart's. But while the Akan was

---

115 Blécourt, D. W. (2000). 'The making of the female witch: Reflections on witchcraft and gender in the early modern period,' *Gender & History*, 12(2): 287-309.

116 Oduyoye, M.A. (2019). *Re-membering me: Memoirs of Mercy Amba Oduyoye.* Ibadan: Sefer Books Ltd.

matrilineal in terms of social structures, it was not matriarchal in terms of the location of power and use in governance. The reason for men's subjugation over women historically has been explained by French as emerging from men's belief that "women are not human beings, but animals designed to serve men and men's end, with no purpose in life" (French 2008: 4).[117] Oduyoye argued that, historically, the Akan (referring specifically to the Asante) political disequilibrium that favoured men over women was a result of the myth of the Golden Stool in the earliest 18th Century. As part of the formation of Asante, two men, Osei Tutu and Komfo Anokye routinised Asante politics along patriarchal lines. With their invention of the Golden Stool, power was vested in the male ruler and his male priest. This development overturned the pre-Asante Confederacy l twin-political system of that ensured the equal distribution of power between male and female political actors (see: Oduyoye 2019: 169-199). For Oduyoye, therefore, the oppression of women among the Asante, predated colonialism.

The idea of the systemic degrading status of women has been contested as untrue, as there is hardly any evidence for complementarity in matrilineal Akan society (Boni 2001).[118] Nevertheless, the subjugation of women is often structured in socialisation. As part of socialisation, boys are trained differently from girls, along with different levels of power relations. John Stuart Mill, whose philosophy on gender equality serves a purpose here, observed, for example, that, "All women are brought up from their earliest years in the belief that their ideal of character is the very opposite of that of men; not self-willed, and governed by self-control, but submissive, and yielding to the control of others" (Mill 2009: 28). This is certainly applicable to Akan cultures, where boys and girls are socialised differently to perform different roles. Among the Akan, women are expected to embodied characteristics such as modesty, dignity, perseverance, obedience, submissiveness and conformity; being caring, kind and generous; being dependent and needing protection, being weak and emotional; greedy and envious and quarrelsome (Adomako 2001: 199).[119]

117 French, M. (2008). *From Eve to dawn: A history of women Vol 1: Origins*. New York: The Feminist Press.

118 Boni, S. (2001). 'Twentieth-Century transformations in notions of gender, parenthood, and marriage in southern Ghana: A critique of the hypothesis of "retrogrades steps" for Akan women,' *History in Africa*, 28: 15-41.

119 Adomako, A.A. (2001), '"When men speak women listen": Gender socialisation and young adolescents': Attitudes to sexual and reproductive issues,' *African Journal of Reproductive Health*, 5(3): 196-211.

Since the 1950s, women have expressed the need to free themselves from the throes of patriarchy to attain authentic humanity. This has led feminist scholars and activists on different paths, usually incorporating a variety of philosophies from liberalism, radicalism, Marxism, and socialism. But underlying all this is the base philosophy of existentialism – the power of women to recreate themselves, as they reject all biological straitjacketing.

That women have suffered under patriarchy has been one of the reasons for human efforts at uncovering the root cause of this suffering. It is usually argued that men have tended to identify their own limited perspective with universal truth. In other words, the human experience has been viewed from the male standpoint (Goldstein 1960: 100; 101). Given the conflagration that has characterised gender studies in several African universities, including the University of Ghana and the Makerere University, where I studied "Gender in History" as part of my two-year doctoral course in inter-disciplinary Social Studies, I use this chapter to provide my reflections of on the theories undergirding Gender Studies.

My premise is that several western theorists never shy away from writing themselves into theories without suffering a pushback as being unscientific. For example, Michel Foucault who was gay did not shy away from using his two important works, *History of Sexuality* and *Discipline and Punish: The Birth of the Prison* to destabilise social order to normalise homosexual acts which under the inspiration of Judeo-Christian sex ethics had been criminalised in the Euro-American world until the beginning of the 1960s. Much as it could be said that Foucault tracked social change and noted that meanings and practices of the state changed as knowledge and needs changed, and that his observations may have nothing to do with being gay, it cannot be simply concluded that his theory did not chime with his own sexual preference of same-sex attraction. Similarly, Frederick Engels whose work on *The Origin of the Family*, used as the foundation text in Gender Studies, did not mince words in terms of his hatred for religion and all social structures. But aren't these texts used to give foundation theory to students on how families emerged? Similarly, Jean-Paul Sartre, who popularised existentialism, was also clear about his intention to construct ontological and social order. These theorists have influenced in no small measure the works of feminist scholars, including Simone de Beauvoir, Mary Daly and bell hooks to mention just a few whose works are influential in feminist discourses. While these theories expose academics to a pool of resources to construct knowledge, my point is for the universities to incorporate the traditions of knowledge of Africans. But more specifically, I argue that we cannot isolate individual academics from their experiences and worldview that inform the theories they develop.

If these scholars never integrated themselves into theories that got universalised in universities around the world, including Ghana, I also do not shy away from presenting my views primarily from the Judeo-Christian perspective, as I have done above in Chapter One. As I will soon discuss the contributions of the above scholars in helping us refine our understanding of the complex issues of gender and society, I also argue that the decolonisation agenda should incorporate other views. Unfortunately, while humanistic scholarship is presented as "scientific", evangelical Christian scholarship is hardly allowed as a reading list in the study of Gender in Ghanaian universities. Much as Christian and Islamic theology on women may be taught in theological institutions, I consider it appropriate for the incorporation of these religious worldviews in the teaching of gender and family in the Ghanaian context. If for nothing at all, it will be an important step to building consensus over gender and family matters. For me, studying religious notions of gender in Ghanaian public universities will help the religious constituency (particularly students to incorporate additional criticality in their hermeneutics). Certainly, this is against the background that knowledge production is a political and ideological project that is never neutral – making the classroom equally non-neutral. As I have already stated, as an Akan from southern Ghana and evangelical Christian academic, with proclivities towards Calvinistic theology, I cannot be compelled to dissociate myself from my religious and ethnic backgrounds in my scholarship. To put this study into a broader perspective, I provide an analysis of the impact of humanistic theories brewed in a "secular" west on Gender Studies in Africa.

I maintain that given the fact that the post-colonial university education in Ghana, since the end of World War II in the 1940s, seeks to be recognised in the globe, several Ghanaian university feminist scholars tend to fit Akan reality into western feminist theories. In the process, these Ghanaian scholars provide nuanced analysis that some may consider as potentially incongruous with the sagacity of Akan ancestor/ancestress on gender-related subjects. This may lead to the self-debasement of Ghanaian scholars, even as they could be accused of retaining traditions of knowledge of the Ghanaian people on the epistemic yoke and injustice of the Euro-American West. The challenge is as real as more Ghanaian females continue to study abroad in a post-

World War self-expressive world where sex has been demystified as necessary for procreation, but rather as identity construction. Several of these scholars regardless of their field of study tend to take up activism that seeks to contribute to promoting the rights of Ghanaian women. Much as we may want to critique to critique Ghanaian feminist scholars, it is also important to appreciate the fact that they are writing their experiences, observations and visions for structuring society away from the intrusive androcentrism.

Nevertheless, even as I appreciate the insights feminist scholars bring into helping me appreciate the complexity of gendered issues, I write my critique of feminism and Gender Studies from the perspective of an Akan Christian, with my epicentre of thinking is deeply Christian and Akan. This means that I have a different line of argument, based on my understanding of my ethic and Christian identity. Also, as a man, my understanding sexuality cannot be treated as representative of all men, not to even talk about women. As I do not seek to engage in a zero-sum epistemic production that excludes other traditions of knowledge, I follow the wisdom of Francis Nyamnjoh that, "any attempts at making African universities uncompromisingly inclusive institutions through embracing African traditions of knowing and knowledge production would require looking beyond the academy its current configuration for inspiration" (Nyamnjoh 2019: 1).

Historicising radical feminism

As my book is meant for the public and academics, including students who may not read Gender Studies in institutions of higher learning in Ghana, I situate my discussion in the form of an intellectual history, stringing together the key thinkers those philosophies have significantly shaped Gender Studies globally. I take this epistemic route to indicate that the feminist movement is not a reactionary, but a response to what these writers consider as consistent male-centric oppression of women. While western women intellectuals were geographically removed from Ghana, I surmise that their social-cultural experiences were not culturally removed. For this reason, the Ghanaian and western women had trans-cultural experiences of male-centric oppression that sustained the exchange of theories across continents. Dolphyne partly agrees to this, and worked toward to alleviate challenges facing women. For example, upon her return to the staff of the University of Ghana in 1965, after her education in London, she joined the women's group at the Volta Hall, the only female hall at the university. Called the Voltarian Association, together with other women, including Mrs Gloria Aryee, former Headmistress of the Accra Girls' Secondary School, she supported women financially and socially to receive education. she also joined the Ghana Association of University Women (GAWU) and International Federation of University Women (IFUW) which supported women. Later when the GAWU collapsed, she joined the Zonta Club of Accra to promoted the welfare and education of professional women and men (2021: 91-108).[120]

The point of diversion between Dolphyne and other feminist scholars is that that she thinks that the appropriation of western theories and its translocation to Africa should be firmly anchored on the existential worldview and aspiration of African women, which she said included solving problems of poverty and enjoying marriage and childbirth (Dolphyne 1991). As a result of a relatively shared cultural experiences with androcentrism, several Ghanaian and African writers have incorporated their theories of these wester women in articulating the plight of women on the continent. It is partly for this reason that Oduyoye discredited and repudiated any imagined dilemma that African women face – either going the west or African cultures to deconstruct the patriarchisation of African societies (2019: 170).

Admittedly, the liberty I have taken to provide an intellectual history of Gender Studies may sound quite odious, pedantic and repetitive for several Gender scholars/students, but I only crave their indigence as I target a much larger audience – given the importance of Gender issues to Ghana and Africa's development. Hopefully, with this intellectual genealogical background, the Ghanaian public may appreciate the need to avoid simplistic binaries between foreign and local; men and women; elites and non-elites; bourgeois and proletariat when discussing gendered issues. While these binaries cannot be easily dismissed in rigorous analysis of gendered issues, over-elaborating them would blur the purpose of Gender Studies – which will be akin to the Akan proverb, "hurting your sour because of a hasty rash to kill the housefly." We may have issues with Gender Studies, but summarily ruling out its importance of it in shedding important perspectives on society will collapse dialogue in building a convivial society.

Having laid the above introductory comments, I argue that historically, women have been presented as the human *Other* of men. Consequently, various reasons, political, economic, and religious, have

---

[120] Dolphyne, F.A. (2021). *From Achinakrom to Pro-Vice Chancellor.* Accra: Black Mask Limited.

cohered to reduce women to the role of subservient. Until the beginning of the industrial revolution in Europe in the eighteenth century, beginning in England in the 1730s, most societies around the world had socially imprisoned women to the performance of expressive responsibilities – procreation and childcare, as men perform an instrumental role – working publicly to provide for the family. A dualism on the private and public, where women occupy the former while men occupy the latter emerged as part of the ordering of nature. The industrial revolution rather unsettled the role of women, impacting them negatively as they had to deal with the challenges of taking care of the home, some women writers began advocating the need for women's liberation.

Women performing dual roles contributed to the emerging debate in the 19th Century among women scholars about how to disentangle women from social imprisonment, focusing on understanding the nature (women)/nurture (men) divide used in pushing women to the fringes of society. The preoccupation of these scholars was to ascertain whether the oppression of women was natural or a cultural invention. Different theories that were framed to explain the subjugation of women converged on the idea of biological attributes of women. But this was not convincing, as nature was given, while culture – used to divide men and women were created and could be recreated to ensure a just and equal society for both men and women.

It was this whirlwind of a search for an answer to gender segregation that contributed to the publication of Lewis Morgan's book, *Ancient Society* in 1877. Focusing on the Iroquois Indians in America and using the materialist analytical category, placing the human condition in socio-economic history, Morgan concluded that the subjugation of women was part of the rise of civil society – which shattered pre-industrial complementarity between men and women. As societies transitioned from hunting and gathering and entered into the era of cultivating the land, men assumed important roles as public workers in tilling the land, as women had to procreate to produce labour.

Inspired by Marx's idea of class conflict, Engels's work, *Origin of the Family*, which was published in 1883, concluded his analysis that the rise of class consciousness or class society was the basic reason for gender inequality. According to Engels, class consciousness which was a result of the agricultural revolution destroyed wife sharing and free-range sex practices, leading to the imposition of monogamy on women. The institution of monogamy simultaneously gave men a monopoly over women, while women were constrained in terms of whom they could have sex with. More so, the agricultural revolution resulted in the creation of surplus which was important for the accumulation of wealth – giving rise to the private ownership of property. Women were, therefore, needed for procreation to supply labour for men. In the narrative of Friedrich Engels, this was the beginning of gender inequality in society. He referred to the overthrow of the mother's right as "the world historical defeat of the female sex" (Engels 1972: 120). Ultimately, Engel's inspiration comes from his alignment with the Communist Manifesto, which sought to "abolish all religion and morality, instead of constituting them on a new basis; it therefore, acts in contradiction to all past historical experience" (Marx and Engels 1970: 56). In relation to sex and family life, the goal of the Communist Manifesto is to engage in "uninterrupted disturbance of all social conditions" (Ibid., 35). It is to bracket the family from all objective truths, values, order – in short, Engels sought to deregulate the family – by undermining family structures that clearly defines gender roles.

Engels's description of the primitive society is similar to Marjorie Shostack's anthropological novel about !Kung women of South Africa, in which she wrote that a !Kung woman could have multiple partners even when she was married to another man. Engels concluded that the evolution of agriculture revolutionised the human family. Engels speculated about preindustrial societies. He has been heavily criticised because patriarchy predates capitalism! His suggestions that societies were matriarchal at first has been dismissed as speculative and lacks empirical support! It contributed to the institution of monogamy, as the free sex range dissolved. As I have mentioned the goal of Engels, included by his atheistic Communist Manifesto, was to deconstruct all social order – including ontological ones such as blurring the gaps between men and women. Engels sought to construct all forms of social norms, including supporting women to act like men – having uninhibited sexual partners.

As the agricultural revolution created a surplus, the condition was set for the industrial revolution that began in the 18th Century. As nations industrialised, the relationship between men and women further atrophied, with women suffering domestication and marginalisation. This prompted the rise of a feminist group in the west in the 19th Century, which sought to correct the social disparity that the industrial revolution had created. One such author was Mary Wollstonecraft. She published an influential book, *Vindication of the Rights of Women* in 1792 in which she argued for the need for women to receive an education. As a liberal feminist, Wollstonecraft argued that the subjugation of women was not a result of nature or any biological idiosyncrasies of women, but rather the outcome of the industrial revolution. Since the industrial revolution had favoured men's education over women, leading to women becoming less productive in public life, she advocated the need for women to be educated to redeem the gender disparity in the industrialised world. She argued for an equal society that would help women to develop their intellectual capacity. Following through with the tradition of the 17th-Century enlightenment that "idolised" reason, Wollstonecraft argued that what separated human beings – men and women – from nature is not biological determinants, but reason. She concluded that men and women should be granted equal opportunity to be educated.

All this intellectual history shaped the 19th-Century affirmative action movement in the United States of America, which included the call for slavery to be abolished. The momentum of these liberation movements entered into the 20th Century with some radical feminists including Simone de Beauvoir and Mary Daly. These feminists also interrogated the men's use of women anatomical features to deny them (women) equal rights in the public sphere. For example, de Beauvoir brilliantly discussed the antinomies between men's performance of transcendental and immanence roles between men and women, respectively, in the perpetual subjugation of women in marriage and in public. The same argument, firming the transcultural heritage of women, in the Ghanaian context. Oduyoye observed that men have leveraged the belief in the duality of the spirit and material world to coerce women into submission. As women were/are the main means of procreation to retain the idea of ancestorship, merging the two worlds, marriage and childbirth have become manipulative tools in the hands of men (2019: 172-188).

Moving beyond the enlightenment's romanticising of reason, which men and women equally possess, feminist scholars deployed existential philosophy to deconstruct androcentrism. Shortly after the end of World War II, which brought about the liberation of France, scholars began thinking about liberating individuals as well. This contributed to Jean-Paul Sartre's philosophy of existentialism. Existential philosophy is about human's authentic self, which is not given by nature or attributed to biological traits but created. It repudiates essence as a determinate of human beings, but rather supports individuals to become existential (create themselves) by accepting responsibility for their actions (Sartre 2007).

de Beauvoir, a contemporary and lover of Jean-Paul Sartre was heavily influenced by the latter's existential philosophy. The basic tenet of existentialism is that existence precedes essence. Nothing can be assumed as natural about the human persons; there is no ontological essence against which existence could be made. Human beings are who they make themselves to be. They are not bounded by anything in the natural world – biological or not. Human beings are the only ones who are consciously in existence and must control everything else around them. No god who created human beings – human beings created themselves and define their boundaries. Existentialism breaks all ontologies, including social ontologies. James W. Sire has summarised existentialisms as follows: The cosmos is composed solely of matter, but to human beings reality appears in two forms – subjective and objective: We are the only beings in the material world who are self-conscious and self-determinate; science and logic do not penetrate the subjective realm because science does not determine values; For human beings alone existence precedes essence; people make themselves who they are; Each person is totally free as regards to his or her nature and destiny; The objective world is absurd, intruder etc it is orderly – determinate, science and law; We must rebel against any imposition of the objective world; and Ethics – the good is what we choose (Sire 2004: 114-121).

From the perspective of existentialism, de Beauvoir, challenging male dominance, argued as a woman "she is defined and differentiated with reference to man and not with reference to her; she is the incidental, the inessential as opposed to the essential. He is the Subject, he is the Absolute – she is the Other (de Beauvoir, 1953: 16). Similarly, she also said that "The division of the sexes is a biological fact, not an event in history. Male and female stand opposed within a primordial Mitsein, and woman has not broken it. The couple is a fundamental unity with its two halves riveted together, and the cleavage of society along the line of sex is impossible. He found the basic trait of woman: she is the Other in a totality of which two components are necessary to one another" (de Beauvoir 1953: 19). With this biological straitjacketing, "There is no justification for present existence other than its expansion into an indefinite future. Every time transcendence falls back into immanence, stagnation, there is a degradation of existence into the *'en-soi'* – the brutish life of subjection to given conditions – and the liberty into constraint of contingence" (de Beauvoir 1953: 27). As she writes, a woman "finds herself living in a world where men compel her to assume the status of the Other" (de Beauvoir 1953: 27).

About pregnancy and how it imprisons women, de Beauvoir wrote that, "First violated, the female is then alienated – she becomes, in part, another than herself. She carries the foetus inside her abdomen until it reaches a stage of development that varies according to the species – the guinea-pig is born almost adult, the kangaroo still almost an embryo. Tenanted by another, who battens upon her substance throughout the period of pregnancy, the female is at once herself and other than herself; and after the birth she feeds the newborn upon the milk of her breast" (de Beauvoir, 1953: 50). Despite all this, patriarchal institution presents motherhood as desirable and an important gratification for women. This is also true of many African societies where the expected destination of every female is to become a mother (Dipio 2019: 9). With all this, Adrienne Rich has concluded that the universalisation of motherhood is oppressive to women (Rich 1971: 128). As de Beauvoir observed, whereas marriage is not inherently wrong, there is every wrong with intertwining motherhood and marriage – a complex conflation that makes marriage ultimately oppressive and inspires agitation against its institutionalisation (Card 2002).

The imposition of motherhood on women as androcentric has been extended to the vexatious debate on abortion. In the contestation over women's right to abortion, the basic argument that liberal scholars have put forward is women's autonomy over their bodies. For example, in an opinion article to the "Washington Post" titled, "Leaving abortion to the states makes them agents of oppression", Ruth Marcus based her argument on the woman's absolute autonomy over her body. She said that the woman has absolute authority over her body and she can decide what she does with it, including aborting a yet to be born baby who is considered to be dependent and lacks autonomy.[121] de Beauvoir however concludes that the biological accidents are "insufficient for setting up a hierarchy of the sexes; they fail to explain why women are the Other; they do not condemn her to remain in this subordinate role for ever" (de Beauvoir 1953: 60). She, therefore, argues that "If the original relation between a man and his fellows was exclusively a relation of friendship, we could not account for any type of

---

[121] Ruth Marchs (June 4, 2021), "Opinion: Leaving abortion to the states makes them agents of oppression", https://www.washingtonpost.com/opinions/2021/06/04/leaving-abortion-states-makes-them-agents-oppression/ (Accessed: September 25, 2021).

enslavement; but no, this phenomenon is a result of the imperialism of the human consciousness, seeking always to exercise its sovereignty in an objective fashion. If the human consciousness had not included the original category of the Other and an original aspiration to dominate the Other, the invention of the bronze tool could not have caused the oppression of women" (de Beauvoir 1953: 83). This is because as she argued, "For it is not in giving life but in risking life that man is raised above the animal; that is why superiority has been accorded humanity not to the sex that brings forth but to that which kills" (de Beauvoir 1953: 89). As she said, "It is only since women have begun to feel themselves at home on earth that we have seen a Rosa Luxemburg, a Mme Curie appear. They brilliantly demonstrate that it is not the inferiority of women that has caused their historical insignificance: it is rather their historical insignificance that has doomed them to inferiority" (de Beauvoir 1953: 152).

de Beauvoir's fume against gender structuring of society has been brilliantly captured by Margaret Mead, who wrote that, "In every known human society, the male's need for achievement can be recognised. Men may cook or weave or dress dolls or hunt humming-birds, but if such activities are appropriate occupations of men, then the whole society, men and women alike, vote them as important. When the same occupations are performed by women, they are regarded as less important. In a great number of human societies men's sureness of their sex roles is tied up with their right, or ability, to practice some activity that women are not allowed to practice. Their maleness, in fact, has to be underwritten by preventing women from entering some field of performing some feat" (Mead 1950: 157-158). Again, the exclusion of women from performing creative performances in the public stifles their intelligence. When marriage is introduced as a reason to hedge women in the performance of domestic roles, then it gives credence to the revulsion some feminists have for marriage.

de Beauvoir's incorporation of existentialism to challenge male superiority is because of what she considers as men's identification of women with nature. Given this, she said, "Thus woman is related to nature, she incarnates it: vale of blood, open rose, siren, the curve of a hill, she represents to man the fertile soil, the sap, the material beauty and the soul of the world. She can hold keys to poetry; she can be mediatrix between this world and the beyond: grace or oracle, star or sorceress, she opens the door to the supernatural, the surreal. She is doomed to immanence; and through her passivity she bestows peace and harmony – but if she declines this role, she is seen forthwith as a praying mantis, an ogress. In any case she appears as the privileged Other, through whom the subject fulfils himself: one of the measures of man, his counterbalance, his salvation, his adventure, his happiness" (de Beauvoir 1953: 256).

Pushing the existential philosophy that there is nothing like essence, but everything is made, to women's liberation, de Beauvoir concluded that "One is not born, but rather becomes, a woman. No biological, psychological, or economic fate determines the figure that the human female represents in society; it is civilisation as a whole that produces this creature, intermediate between male and eunuch, which is described as feminine" (de Beauvoir 1953: 273). By this statement, de Beauvoir argued that no one is a product of nature, but culture. And since culture is made, it could be deconstructed. de Beauvoir then concluded that "To emancipate the woman is to refuse to confine her to the relations she bears to man, not to deny them to her; let her have her independent existence and she will continue nonetheless to exist for him *also*: mutually recognising each other as subject, each will yet remain for the *other*" (de Beauvoir 1953: 686). Consequently, the patriarchal culture that instituted the oppression of women could be overthrown in favour of cultural practices that support the flourishing of women. Existential feminism is thus a system of thought that provides an aetiological reason for social inequality as a reality that is not caused by biological differences between men and women, but rather by the value that society assigns to biological differences. Since existential philosophy argues that existence precedes essence – and that individuals have no essential nature, self-identity other than what they choose for themselves.

In furtherance to existential feminism, Wittig, argued that "Masculine/feminine, male/female are the categories which serve to conceal the fact that social differences always belong to economic, political, and ideological order. Every system of domination establishes divisions at the material and economic levels. Furthermore, the divisions are abstracted and turned into concepts by the masters, and later by the slaves when they rebel and start to struggle. The masters explain and justify the established divisions as a result of natural differences. The slaves, when they rebel and start to struggle, read social oppositions into the so-called natural differences, for there is no sex. There is, but sex that is oppressed and sex that oppresses. It is oppression that creates sex not the contrary. The contrary would be to say that sex creates oppression, or to say that the cause (origin) of oppression is to be found in sex itself, in a natural division of the sexes pre-existing (or outside of) society (Wittig 1992: 2). This leads to her conclusion that, "What makes a woman is a specific social relation to a man, a relation that we have previously called servitude" (Wittig 1992: 20). This kind of social relations fosters heterosexual relations as normative sex practice between man and woman – usually referred to as the obligatory social relationship between "man" and "woman" (Wittig 1992: 27). This is universalised into law, leading to "The consequence of this tendency toward universality is that the straight mind cannot conceive of a culture, a society where heterosexuality would not order not only human relationships but also its very production of concepts and all the processes, which escape consciousness, as well" (Wittig 1992: 28). In articulating the damage heterosexual society does to lesbians and gays, Wittig wrote as follows:

> For heterosexual society is a society, which not only oppress lesbians and gay men, it oppresses many different/others, it oppresses all women and many categories of women, all those who are in the position of the dominated. To constitute a difference and to control it is an "act of power, since it is essentially a normative act. Everybody tries to show the other as different. But not everybody succeeds in doing so. One has to be socially dominant to succeed in it (Wittig 1992: 29).

de Beauvoir's radical feminism paved the way for another radical feminist like Mary Daly to deconstruct the architecture of womanhood and manhood. In *Gynecology*, Mary Daly argued that language was violently used to socially imprison women. She wrote that "the all-pervasive language of myth, conveyed overtly and subliminally through religion, "great art," literature, the dogmas of professionalism, the media, grammar" (Daly 1978: 3). Daly, therefore, argued that women should break free from the boundaries of "nature" and human constituted social imprisonment – through the use of language. She framed heterosexual marriage as a form of male-centric institution that perpetuated patriarchal oppression. In place of heterosexual marriage, Mary Daly advocated lesbianism. Thus, Mary Daly, like other radical feminists, want a revolution in gender relations, not integration – framed around gynocritic writing, resistance, renaming and spinning the wheel. Radical western feminists promote lesbianism, claiming that the "lesbian society destroys the artificial (social) fact constituting women as a "natural group" (Wittig 1992: 9). Similarly, lesbianism cannot be considered unnatural in a "natural society" because there is no nature in society (Wittig 1992: 13).

To firm the lesbian movement, Judith Butler had to deconstruct gender binaries. Similar to deconstructing biological and ontological boundaries, Butler wrote her book *Gender Trouble: Feminism and Subversion of Identity*, which became revolutionary for gender studies. As a humanistic philosophical twin of existentialism, Butler used post-structural theory to deconstruct gender structuring. As part of challenging essence, she re-stated her 1990 introductory remarks in the 1999 edition of her book as, "The task of this inquiry is to center on and decentre – such defining institutions: phallogocentrism and compulsory heterosexuality". Precisely because "female" no longer appears to be a stable notion its meaning is troubled and unfixed as "woman," and because both terms gain their troubled significations only as relational term, this inquiry takes as its focus gender and the relational analysis it suggests (Butler 1999: xxxi). Challenging gender ontological differences as oppressive to identity, she said: "the 'coherence' and 'continuity' of 'the person' are not logical or analytic features of personhood, but, rather, socially instituted and maintained norms of intelligibility. Inasmuch as 'identity' is assured through stabilizing concepts of sex, gender, and sexuality, the very notion of 'the person' is called into question by the cultural emergence of those 'incoherent' or 'discontinuous' gendered beings who appear to be persons but who fail to conform to the gendered norms of cultural intelligibility by which persons are defined" (Butler 1999: 23).

Extending the breaking of boundaries and denouncing all forms of social order as oppressive, Mimi Schippers is pushing for polyamory – a practice of engaging in multiple romantic and amorous relationships with the consent of the persons involved. In her book, *Beyond Monogamy: Polyamory and the future of polyqueer sexualities*, she challenges heterosexual monogamous culture as oppressive and othering of non-heterosexual couples. Schippers, therefore, sees mononormativity as inconsistent with human autonomy and argues for the need to deconstruct monogamy – usually privileged and premised on dominant masculine subordination of women. Through the promotion of polyamory, Schippers hopes to reorient readers away from monogamy to disrupt sexual, gender and racial inequality. Her vision is to push for possible polyqueer intimacies. Even so, we could hardly argue that she making a policy recommendation, but rather a conceptual/analytic recommendation. The former suggests telling people what to do, the latter suggests a way of understanding or looking at reality through a particular lens.

Beyond lesbianism and polyamory, some women also exercise autonomy over their bodies to engage in practices such as prostitution. For example, in a study on prostitution in Accra by Ghanaian academic, Professor Akosua Adomako Ampofo, cited one of her respondents as saying that, "You know God has given me cocoa which is between my legs, so if I go into prostitution, it is my own body" (Adomako 2007: 194). The paradox in this assertion is that while this young woman admits that God is the source of her body, she paradoxically admits that she can use her body as she pleases. The tension over women's body, inscribed on them by society's socialisation is, indeed, complex – bringing into focus, again, my argument that gendered/same-sex issue cannot hardly be discussed as a fad and craze of the modern world. In all the discussion, I have shown that the complexity partly stems from defining women's ability, including intellectual creations, from their biological profile. Without dismissing the legitimate concerns of feminist scholars and most women in general over how the woman's body has been entwined with domesticity, I make reference Charles Ellwood to attempt a distinction between men and women:

> Fundamental differences between the sexes express themselves in many ways in social life. The differences between man and woman, therefore, are not to be thought of as due to social customs and usages, the different social environment of the two sexes, but are even more due to a radical and fundamental difference in their whole nature. The belief that the two sexes would be like each other in character if given the same environment is, therefore, erroneous. That these differences are original, or inborn, and not acquired, may be readily seen by observing children of different sex. Even from their early years boys are more active, restless, energetic, destructive, untidy, and disobedient, while little girls are quieter, less restless, less destructive, neater, more orderly, and more obedient. These different innate qualities fit the sexes naturally for different functions in human society, and there is, therefore, a natural division of labour between them from the beginning. Indeed, the division of labour between the two sexes may be said to be fundamental division of labour in human society (Ellwood 1910: 31).

Black feminism

Western feminism is said to be biased towards black women. Usually, white women experience is provincialised at the expense of the experiences of black women. White feminists choreograph their narratives of women oppression away from the experiences of black women. These white feminists deliberately blur the differences between the experiences of black and white women in the United States of America. This was expressed by Audre Lorde when in a discussion between her and Mary Daly, she made the following observation:

> Institutionalised rejection of difference is an absolute necessity in a profit economy that needs outsiders as surplus people. As members of such an economy, we have all been programmed to respond to the human difference between us with fear and loathing and to handle that difference in one of three ways: ignore it, and if that is not possible, copy it if we think it is dominant, or destroy it if we think it is subordinate. But we have no patterns for relating across human differences as equals. As a result, those differences have been misnamed and misused in the service of separation and confusion (Lord, 1984: 115).

bell hooks argued that black women suffer double jeopardy – racism from Eurocentric imperialism and patriarchy from black men (hooks 1982: 15). hooks wrote that black women have suffered since the trans-Atlantic slave trade era. Black women were usually beaten to submission – "They were stripped of their clothing and beaten on all parts of their body" (hooks 1982: 18). Similarly, she wrote that, "The negro woman is unprotected either by law or public opinion (1982: 43). She is beaten into submission. hooks writes, "Sometimes when the poor thing cried too loud from the pain Farrarby would kick her in the mouth. After he exhausted himself whipping her, he sent to her house for sealing wax and a lighted candle and, melting the wax, dropped it upon the woman's lacerated back. He then got a riding whip and, standing over the woman, picked off the hardened wax by switching at it" (hooks 1982: 60). Women were also profiled for their reproductive capacities, "Advertisement announcing the sale of black female slaves used the terms 'breed slaves,' 'child-bearing woman,' 'breeding period,' 'too old to breed,' to describe individual women" (hooks, 1982: 39-40). Black women were also raped as a method of torture to cow them into submission, leading to some of them arriving upon the new world already impregnated (hooks, 1982: 18). In addition to all this, they performed both expressive and instrumental responsibilities – forcing them to assume "masculine" roles, in addition to performing domestic chores (1982: 22-23). In all, as she argued, that black women were socialised out of existence (hooks, 1982).

Radical feminism: An introduction

Under this section, I have provided a brief intellectual history of radical feminism. The chapter has argued that radical feminism follows a sequence of breaking social ontologies which were set and popularised by Frederick Engels. As part of his atheistic worldview, Engels determined to deconstruct the world of order. He sought to create a deregulated world. This was done by relegating all sociological religious ontologies that structured sexual morality on a monogamous basis. From the framework of material dialectics, Engels argued that the agricultural revolution was responsible for the dissolution of the gender blindness and neutrality of the pre-agricultural, pre-industrial world. No social boundaries were limiting the sexual partnership a man or woman could establish. According to Engels's, as a result of the agricultural revolution – giving rise to the industrial revolution – men decided to control the productive and reproductive capacity of women. This gave rise to androcentrism or male chauvinism. So, to restore society to the primal vision of men and women having unlimited access to sex, human beings need to deconstruct all social, ethical, and ontological boundaries that did not exist prior to the agricultural and industrial revolution.

Engels's aetiological analysis of men's superiority over women was an important watershed for the feminist movement that became more pronounced in the 1950s. In the aftermath of World War II, Jean-Paul Sartre developed the modern idea of existentialism, as part of his vision to understand the *Being*. Moving away from the Christian dogma of creationism, which Sartre had been introduced to as a young Christian, he argued that essence is subordinate to existence. In other words, existence is anterior to essence. The world of essence is blind, irrational, orderly, and natural. It is an objective world. Everything in nature belongs to the objective world, apart from human beings. Human beings are in the subjective world – with the full conscious capacity to decide and determine their lives. In simple terms, humans have self-determining power. They decide what becomes of them. Human beings are not, they become. They determine what they choose to be. As conscious beings, human beings must not allow the intrusion of the natural world to shape their lives. Humans must control the objective world – by rebelling against all forms of natural straitjacketing imposed by the objective world.

The objective and subjective binary influenced Simone de Beauvoir, who had an amorous relationship with Jean-Paul Sartre. Frustrated by the worsening condition of women and perhaps the fact that she had to compete for the attention of Sartre with other women, de Beauvoir embarked on a journey of deconstructing masculinity. While she sexually distanced herself from Sartre, she was intellectually indebted to him. She, therefore, deployed the existential philosophy in framing feminism. So, she concluded that there is no woman, a woman becomes. Turning human beings, particularly women into creators of themselves, there appears to be no limit to pushing all forms of sexual boundaries – including human beings marrying animals, trees, and other objects. Concerning the Judeo-Christian foundation of the western world, radical feminism is a direct affront to Christian historic opposition to the opprobrium sex of the pagan Roman world.

It is clear in all this that the vision of radical feminism has significantly become a paradigm of gender studies in many African universities, including public universities in Ghana. This, as I have said, may be informed by the commonly shared cultural realities of women globally – though there may be culturally-conditioned differences. The historical context of Gender history has also implied that African scholars have formed a critical engagement with traditions of indigenous knowledge about gender relations.

As part of demonstrating how Ghanaian cultures have also structured women's bodily subjugation to men, I now refer to the social construction of menstruation. In feminist discourses, menstruation is treated as an avenue for men's exercise of androcentric power over women. This is because menstrual blood is one of the natural flows of women that in early modern texts, symbolises corruption and defilement and was subject to different kinds of censure: that is silence (Dawson 2005: 464). In the caste system in India, given that menstruation was treated as impure, women never attain the purity of men within their own caste because of their bodily flow during menstruation (Verma 2008: 290). Menstruation is also used to reinforce gender stratification and hierarchies that sustain the marginalisation of women and their exclusion from public life and participation in governance. In misogynistic discourses, because men do not menstruate, the period flow of blood among women is used as a sign of man's physical superiority (Dawson 2005: 470). In all this, however, menstruation symbolises the power and life-giving potential of women (Hogan 1995: 48).

As I said at the state of this chapter, the historical context of Gender Studies reflects the globally shared experiences of women – albeit with different conditions. For this reason, women of all scholarly background have reflected on the enigma of marriage and the culture of men's dominance over women. In autobiography, one of the foremost Ghanaian theologians, Mercy Oduyoye (2021), discussed the various male-centrism in Akan cultures that informed her interest in understanding the nexus between the Bible and women.

Printing: A case of epistemic injustice to non-western cultures: Prelude to western radical feminism in Africa

How did western experiences of patriarchy become part of Africa's Gender Studies? This question helps me to reflect on the role of printing technology and the dispersion of western epistemes to Africa. So, having appreciate the importance of global human experiences in casting nuanced understanding of Gender Studies, in this section, I consider this western epistemic injustice done to the traditions of knowledge of the Akan about gender relations as part of the enduring legacies of western mistreatment of traditions of other knowledge. This challenge has been identified by Valentine Mudimbe who bemoaned the restrain of the "colonial library" that negates the possibility of plural rationality and history – limiting any space for African scholarship (Mudimbe 1988: 208). Similarly, Francis Nyamnjoh talks about how the illusion of western epistemic completeness leads them to treat other traditions of knowledge (including those of the Akan) with contempt. In response to this epistemic challenge, Osmane Kane is inviting African scholars to consider the Arabic source (Kane 2016).[122] But, while the Arab source appears alternative to the colonial library, we must equally treat the Arabic source with concern and caution (Azuma 2001).[123] After all the Arabs, who were the first to introduce the worse form of chattel slavery in Africa – including forced castration of enslaved African men – cannot be trusted to give any better account of Africans.

The penchant on the part of African scholars to appeal to either the Arabic or Euro-American sources of episteme to legitimise their African ancestral knowledge is part of the historical episodes in human

[122] Kane, O.O. (2016). *Beyond Timbuktu: An intellectual history of Muslim West Africa.* Cambridge, Mass.: Harvard University Press.

[123] Azumah, J.A. (2001). *The legacy of Arab-Islam in Africa: A quest for inter-religious dialogue.* Oxford: Oneworld.

history. In this section, I appeal to historians to indicate the complexities of "tradition" and "modernity" in human history – highlighting the problems of a single meta-narrative and the reality of shared human history. My argument here is to disrupt the simplistic rendition of the histories of non-European cultures as uniquely inferior to foster social equality education. It is also to avoid the efforts at both romanticising and denigrating both tradition and modernity -- "colonial mentality" (Akurang-Parry 2016).

In 16th-Century Europe, the invention of printing became the entry point of Europe into the "modern" world. While printing had been invented in China in the Second Century, it did not yield the revolutionary impact it made in Europe, when the technology was reinvented and improvised in the European world. The invention of printing made the Christian reformation possible. Before Martin Luther, some reformers challenged the papal excesses. But none of them had the kind of impact Martin Luther recorded, because of the absence of printing before 16th-Century Europe.

Printing marked an imagined Europe's rupture with its "past" as it launched into the modern world. This was marked by advances in science and technology, nationalism, freedom of religious conscience, human rights – which crystalised in the post-World War II world. It also informed the idea of progress as conquering nature and the extending of European territorial control beyond Europe – leading to European imperialism and colonisation of the non-European world. All this points to antimony in Europe's "modern" – epitomised by the Christian reformation. As modern science liberated Europeans from the clutches of religious "superstition", it rationalised their persecution of dissenters, enhanced the idea of progress as an individual and rationalistic vision of social justice, and flattered the exaggerated ego of Europeans to "civilise" and universalise its version of social justice across the non-European world.

In terms of epistemic production, the monopolisation of power runs concurrently with the monopolisation of knowledge. This was because knowledge was drawn mainly from the spirit world. Since access to the spirit world was limited to the chiefs and the priestly class and sometimes to the elders, as such knowledge was based on experience, the approach to teaching was based on "sage on stage" philosophy. This "sage on stage" methodological approach to teaching potentially stifled creative thinking from the youth constituency of the Akan society. It sometimes created needless tension when individuals unreasonably challenged the religious knowledge of the Akan, as I have demonstrated with the case of the appropriate use of the name "Nyame" in early Asante religious history. All this contributed to some forms of human violation such as human sacrifices, social ostracisation of dissidents, and imposition of austere practices like witchcraft accusations and extreme forms of widowhood rites on women. All these signalled different levels of social injustice in Akan history.

As a reflection of antimony, the European "civilisation" of other non-European cultures was based on a premodern European type of violence, where non-Europeans were brutalised (Gordon 2020; Walter 2016). Limiting this to Africa, African societies that resisted European interlopers were murdered *en masse*, leading to genocide in some areas in Africa (Hull, 2008; Hochschild, 2006). Similarly, the arrogance of European scientific superiority made them dismiss the knowledge traditions of Africans (Ndlovu-Gatsheni 2013). European epistemic hegemony was concretised in their use of theories such as the Hamitic hypothesis – which Edith Sanders said thrives on the notion that everything of value ever found in Africa was brought there by the Hamites, allegedly a branch of Caucasian race – was used to summarily discredit Africans (Sanders 1969). European indifference to the cultural *Other* privileged European discourses on social justice. Francis Nyamnjoh, has strongly argued that European intolerance towards other cultures built in them an elusive sense of completeness – lacking nothing that other cultures could provide.

The European idea of scientific superiority embedded in their technological advancement led to their portrayal of Africans as weak and incapable of advancing their own narratives and choreographing their visions of civilisation. This was demonstrably seen when the Europeans built European-type of universities in Africa. These universities disregarded the African tradition of knowledge. Theocentric epistemes of Africans were silenced as pagan and fetish. This European sense of superiority also shaped Christian mission approaches in Africa in the 19th Century. For example, in that century, the European missionaries in Africa made little attempts at incorporating the cosmological worldview of Africans into Christianity (Dickson, 1965). Armed with the rationalistic logic of an enlightened Europe, the cosmological worldview of Africa was treated as childish, infantile and downright superstitious (Omenyo 2002).

This was against the background that Europeans had to depend on African languages to advance the superiority of the Christian worldview (Meyer 1999). It was also part of the reformation spirit of translating the Bible into different languages for Christians and potential Christian converts (Sanneh 2009). But unlike the European world where such works of translation contributed to a cultural and scientific renaissance of European countries, in Africa, there was hardly any translation of the Bible translation into cultural and scientific recuperation of the African "past". This inertia was relegated from mission education because, African cultures were considered incapable of capturing the pristine of science. In the end, Christianity remained a thin veneer on the continent (Busia 1961).

With all this profiling of Africans and their cultures as incongruent for civilisation, Africans suffered extreme social injustice as the cultural roots upon which they could have built their renaissance were wantonly demolished by the Europeans. This sense of culturicide remains a challenge to Africa's quest for social justice in the contemporary world. To date, Africa's cultural impotence imposes timidity in Africans. It predisposes the people of the continent to all forms of social injustice. This situation of centuries of violence has made Africans anti-self. In other words, not only do Africans lack confidence in themselves, but turn against themselves through acts of corruption to undermine their rising to the global frontier as equals.

Clearly, printing fundamentally changed the technological backwardness of Europe since the 16th Century, as it marked its imagined rupture with its past history of social injustice. Similarly, the premodern of the Ashante (Akan), as an example, did not yield sufficient social justice. But the birth of printing and its attendant crystallising of European modernity did not reverse the "ghost" of Europe pre-modern past from haunting the European *Other*. The liberation of Europe from its bleak past of social injustice produced a counter-effect on Africa, based on European rhetoric of "civilising" Africans. This implies that the idea of social justice is not necessarily rooted in scientific or technological advances. It is also not rooted in either romanticising or darkening both the past and present. In other words, rewriting history through pulling down statues is a potential danger to social justice education, for the world needs an example of both the good and bad to learn from.[124] In the following section, I will discuss the impact of western epistemic hegemony on African feminist

[124] I am aware of the argument for statues to be kept in the museum. My point is that the visibility of some statues helps to reshape the human conscience about our past and the need to forge a better future. This implies that the indiscriminate desecration of statues across the world, including that of Gandhi in Ghana, was not in the interest of social justice education.

scholars, highlighting the condescending views these feminists' profile African/Akan traditions of knowledge about gender.

Cultural revivalism as a response to Western epistemic injustice

As part of my discussion of epistemic injustice that 200 years of western dominance of "global" history did to Africans including the critical consumption of western theories by African scholars, I want to discuss how Ghanaian feminist scholars misconstrue Akan traditions of knowledge. Consistent with my critique of existentialism as the epistemic base of radical feminism – seeking to undo social structures – I will highlight instances where Ghanaian feminist scholars read into Ghanaian cultures from a Eurocentric radical feminist perspective. While there are many feminist scholars in the Ghanaian academia, creating the impression that it is highly impossible for a female scholar in Ghana to emerge as a non-feminist scholar (however it is defined), I will focus on such scholars who argue specifically from Akan cultural prisms – especially their use of proverbs.[125] In this section, therefore, I will analyse and critique two articles of Ghanaian women that deploy proverbs to indicate the oppressiveness of the Akan patriarchy. At the risk of repeating myself, I must say that these feminist scholars (consciously or unconsciously) misconstrue Akan/Ghanaian cultures to advance their radical feminist stance. In many instances, they are involved in interpreting Akan proverbs in a teleological fashion – interpreting the past from the standpoint of the present (Goody 2006: 6). But it is also consistent with their "uncritical" aping, unapt and unimpressive appropriation of existential feminist theory – that seeks to subvert social structures, including those that bind families.

The reference to proverbs tradition: This uncritical use of the term, renders them liable to the charge that they failed "to separate Africans who were desirous of being modern and lump them all together with colonialists who had other fish to fry, the outcome of the false tradition-versus-modern dichotomy whereby all Africans were traditionalists and all modernisers were colonialists (Olúfémi Táíwò 2010: 12).

I have already mentioned how 200 years of western dominance has affected the cultural and intellectual climate of other cultures. As part of the secularisation thesis, which has been in force since the

---

125 On April 18, 2021, in an informal conversation with one of my professors at the Institute of African Studies, Dr Deborah Atobrah, who taught me African Family System, she admitted that radical feminism is a challenge to the family, but added that "it is also because many have taken women for granted and exploited their altruism".

seventeenth century when knowledge was secularised, the west had arrogantly convinced itself that the modernisation of the world must seamlessly imply westernisation. This impunity of the west substantially materialized when they heartlessly enslaved Africans and colonised Africans and other non-Europeans. Since the 1960s when most of the colonised world had their independence, with Ghana emerging as the pioneer in re-asserting its independence, many scholars have examined the devastating impact of European enslavement of Africans and colonisation of the continent. At the risk of exaggerating, I could say that it is perhaps, Walter Rodney, the prominent Guyanese historian, an academic and political activist who best captured the European factor in the African predicament. With his publication of *How Europe underdeveloped Africa*, he aptly observed that colonialism created a structural dependency that has come to characterise the socio-economic and political relationship between Africa and Europe. This resulted in neo-colonialism – a new form of colonialism where Europeans deploy new, diplomatic, subtle ways of continually exploiting the continent. While I, to a lesser extent, share Rodney's assessment of the European underdevelopment of Africa, I will provide a critical review of his assessment of Christianity in the course of this book.[126]

But moving beyond the physical condition of the residue of European intrusion in Africa, it is the intellectual/psychological impact of the colonial enterprise that would occupy my attention for now. Colonialism as a socio-political and economic project had a totalising effect on Africans. This is not to say that Africans passively consumed the commodities of colonialism or did not have agency, as it were to say that the psychological impact of colonialism has had a lasting, lingering effect on Africans. This was important because colonialism was not just about Europeans using sophisticated weapons to conquer the physical spaces of Africa and Africans, but it was also an epistemic injustice – based on the works of colonial anthropologists – whose mission was to provide an intellectual rationale for the caging of the African mind. Through the enslavement of African minds, Africans

[126] One scholar whose work seeks to challenge Rodney's thesis as I have mentioned above is the Nigerian Stanley C. Igwe who published a book: *How Africa underdeveloped Africa*. Port Harcourt: Professional and Publishers, 2010. Others like Frantz Fanon (The wretched of the earth), Kofi A. Tetteh (The elites and underdevelopment in Africa: The case of Ghana) and Peter Ekeh (Colonialism and the two republics in Africa) etc., have, in addition to appreciating the devastating impact of European intrusion in Africa have highlighted the role African nationalists and intellectuals plunged the continent further into the abyss of underdevelopment.

were compelled to develop a deep sense of self-debasement – they had to consequently look to the west for epistemic redemption. African scholars who even attempt to write their own worldviews had to do so with western epistemes – as a form of saying what my friends and I as children used to say to our competitors "We also have some". So, some of the nationalists, including J.B. Danquah who wrote such an important work on the Akan doctrine of God had to situate his theo-philosophy from the perspective of Euro-theology of God. Even the churches have not been spared this. A millennialist church that abhors ecumenical tendencies like the Seventh-day Adventist Church in Ghana have to depend on and Akan cosmogony to defend their Sabbath sui generis.

All this justifies Steve Biko's observation that: "The greatest weapon in the hands of the oppressor is the mind of the oppressed" (Biko 1978: 92). He continues, "If one is free at heart, no man-made chains can bind one to servitude, but if one's mind is so manipulated and controlled by the oppressor as to making the oppressed believe that he is a liability to the white man, then there will be nothing the oppressed can do to scare his powerful masters" (Biko 1978: 92). As the President of Ghana, Kwame Nkrumah was acutely aware of the colonial mentality that had shaped the conscience of the people of Ghana (then the Gold Coast). So, in his independence inaugural speech, he called on Ghanaians to have a change of mind, since they were no longer under bondage to Europeans. Similarly, Busia made a similar observation when in defence of cultural emancipation as true freedom, he stated as follows: "Physical enslavement is tragic enough; but the mental and spiritual bondage that makes people despise their own culture is much worse, for it makes them lose their self-respect and, with it, faith in themselves" (Busia 1962: 7).

As a solution to the epistemic injustice the European disillusioned intellectual and cultural superiority did to Africans, cultural freedom has been considered very important. I have already hinted above that Busia saw cultural emancipation as real freedom. Indeed, the early Gold Coast nationalists, including John Mensah Sarbah, S.R.B. Attoh Ahuma, Kobina Sekyi, and Joseph Ephraim Casely Hayford prioritised cultural redemption over economic or political redemption. As these early nationalists set the pace for political nationalism and the Gold Coasters re-asserted their independence, the quest for self-determination in the Gold Coast was constructed along the lines of what was known as Africanisation. Nkrumah's Africanisation was embodied in his quest to challenge the legacy of colonialism and to ensure the total control of the machinery of governance by the people of the Gold Coast (Botwe-Asamoah 2005: 83). It could also be read as part of his agenda to enforce his so-named African personality idea, which articulated the ability of Africans to advance their own growth and development through a hybridised culture (compromising indigenous cultures, Christianity, and Islam) (Poe 2003: 10).

Consequently, the Africanisation of the civil service, security, judiciary, and control of Ghana's internal and external affairs should be read as part of Nkrumah's commitment to the notion that Africans were inherently able to rise beyond the legacies of colonialism. It was also part of Nkrumah's pro-nationalist attempt to rehabilitate the romanticised medieval history of Africa, by focusing on the Western Sudanese Empires (Owusu-Ansah 1997: 389).[127] Broadly, Africanising the Ghanaian socio-political and economic landscape was constructed as part of the attempts at deconstructing western epistemology that had inscribed ineptitude on the psyche of Africans. Given the rhetoric that developed around the Africanisation agenda, Ghana's nationalism, particularly in the post-World War II era, was essentially about Africanisation (Moham 1967: 218). Furthermore, Nkrumah's Africanisation agenda was part of his own egoistic and centrifugal tendencies to register his fame in Ghana's political history. It was essentially part of constructing a personality cult around him. He embossed his image on Ghana's national coinage, commemorative coin, and postage stamp. The inscription on his image read, 'Founder of the State of Ghana.' (Fuller 2014). The construction of a personality cult around Kwame Nkrumah and the merging of Ghana and Nkrumah as coterminous (Pobee 1991: 116) had a spillover in the national ambitions of Ghanaians.

The nationalist agenda left its imprint upon the religious landscape of the Gold Coast. The quest for political independence resonated with religious independence. This is to the extent that the rise of the independent church movement in Ghana has been seen as the religious counterpart of political nationalism (Beckman 1975: 123). Religious nationalism existed alongside political nationalism in the Gold Coast. It was part of the courage that Gold Coast religious leaders expressed in challenging the hegemony of European missionaries that provided the antecedent for the political nationalists (Kimble 1963: 161). This is because, before the political independence of the Gold Coast, some Gold Coasters had challenged the hegemony of European missionaries

[127] Danquah Funeral Committee (1968). *Danquah: An Immortal of Ghana.* Accra: George Boakie Publishing Company, p. 11.

in church administration. They were dissatisfied with the dominance of western culture and some of the liturgical practices of the European-mission churches. They also contested European paternalism in the running of the mission churches. There was also the political aspiration wrapped in the protest against European mission churches. Some of the founders of the African Independent Churches (AICs) did not see any significant difference between missionaries, merchants, and European political administrators. Gold Coasters viewed missionary and European administrators as coterminous since they patronised the same church, part of the edifice of European cultural imposition and political imperialism (Oduro 2007: 18).

While the nationalists were clear about deconstructing the cultural imperialist tendencies of the west, it is important to state that they were not necessarily contesting the moral legacies of the Christian faith. Nkrumah and most of the nationalists admitted the role Christian missionaries played in advancing human flourishing in the Gold Coast. So, as I return to this topic as part of my response to the critique of radical feminists under the gambit of post-colonial theory level against Christianity, I argue that most feminist writers in Ghana undo the legacies of the country's nationalists – which by the way be seen as male-centric. At any rate, the nationalist hardly incorporated the voices of women (Falola and Amponsah 2012; Zeleza 2005).[128] As I shall indicate in the section below, these feminist scholars' incorporation of the humanistic, cold individualistic theory of existentialism, brewed in the chests western thinkers could be problematic – if not contextualised. As a preliminary conclusion to this section and in terms of epistemic freedom, I reiterate the definition of freedom Biko provided: "Freedom is the ability to define oneself with one's possibilities held back not by the power of other people over one but only by one's relationship to God and the natural surroundings" (Ibid., 92). But before I delude myself into thinking it is an easy task, adapting to Biko's words on the psychological impact of western education, I ask, "Who can resist losing respect for his tradition when in school his whole cultural background is summed up in one word – barbarism? "(Ibid, 94). And heathen, indeed.

[128] Zeleza, P.T. (2005). 'Gender biases in African historiography'. In O. Oyeˇwùmí (ed.), *African gender studies: A reader*, 207-232. New York: Palgrave Macmillan.

This section also brings out the purpose of my book as both academic and popular. As an academic, the detailed account of some of the issues I discuss may, admittedly come across to academics as rather extensive. But, given that the current Family Bill and its attending complications are matters of public interest, I deem it necessary to provide great details enough to help in nurturing the culture of consensus. For this reason, I have paid a particular attention to Akan proverbs, as an entry to discussing the popular notions, held among some feminist scholars that Akan cultures are patriarchal and oppressive. Again, I must restate that my goal is not rubbish or simply discount the credibility in association some degree of patriarchalism with Akan cultures. My goal is rather to contextualise the discussion, bringing out the nuances of culture and gender. My contextual analysis further reinforces my argument that the LGBTQ issue is structured into nearly every facet of society in Ghana. The details with which I have taken this section on proverbs is also because as Oduyoye highlighted culture and custom are men's tools to trap women in patriarchalism. While my goal, therefore, is not to repudiate the views of these women scholars it is rather to nuance the discussion – arguing that it is very complex and not an easy task to just draw a black and white line between proverbs/cultures and women's oppression. For me, culture is deeply engrained that it forms a systemic system that when one side is touched, the other follows. It is this same structured social system that I deem it necessary to engage the same-sex discourse as wider and more expansive than the public readily assumes.

So far, I have discussed the extent to which radical feminists have sought to exert bodily autonomy away from the control of men and society. These radical feminists have argued that women should control their bodies and do with their bodies as they please. And since marriage, as an institution with statal support, and biological reproduction (childbirth) are supposedly used by patriarchal societies to oppress women, radical feminists have argued against the structures and normativity of heterosexual marriages (Card, 2002). Similarly, they have maintained that abortion should be determined by women and women alone, and not the state or men. As part of readers and scholars curating themselves from simplistically dismissing Gender Studies, this demand is not unfounded as men routinely decide on abortion. Also, abortion starts with refutation of responsibility by men.

Instead of the moral panic, plus and/or minus, people tend to identify with Gender Studies, the feminist demand is also because the patterns of marriage that are being protested in the Western world are considered similar to those in Africa. I have already mentioned Oduyoye's understanding of marriage as potentially oppressive to women. In several societies in Africa, marriage has seen seismic cultural changes. Kevane has observed that "more men and women are delaying marriage, or not getting married, or are simply cohabiting; age differences have been shrinking; men and women have been increasingly choosing to marry for love, eschewing lineage pressures to enter into alliances preferred by lineage elders; widows have been more resistant levirate remarriage; and polygyny has become less common in urban areas" (Kevane 2014: 147). But as Kevane observed, marriage is not just a private, it involves both the family and the state. With the direct involvement of the state and the family, marriage is not official and every entitlement of marriage, especially rights over children, are similarly not allowed. As Kevane rightly observed, "Without being married, men typically cannot have enforceable parental rights to children, no matter how much they might be willing to pay" (2014: 148).

It is important to state that these may be read as seismic change to Akan, specifically Fante indigenous marriage types – though the logic is still the same. For example, one of the earliest writers on Akan marital practices, J.M. Sarbah (1968),[129] observed that among the Fante, a marriage did necessarily go through the rituals of searching, exchange before consummation. A man and a woman who lived together, holding themselves together as husband and a wife, but have not gone through the "performative rituals" of establishment of the marriage, are recognised and treated as such by the family and society. The Asante also did not have many religious or social taboos regarding sexuality with the exception of incest – which often involved sex between people of the same clan or extended matrilineal family. Otherwise, among the Akan cohabiting adults were regarded as married couple (*mpena awadeɛ*). This arrangement, as equally observed by Boni also helped women to negotiate their autonomy. The reason was that the husband in such marriages could not claim damages in the case of adultery (Adei 2003: 108-109). The implication was/is that so long as they two were/are seen together, undertaking social activities associated with marriage, the man undertaking his responsibilities as dictated by custom, the two were

[129] Sarbah, J.M. (1904), *Fanti customary laws. A brief introduction to the principles of the native laws and customs of the Fanti and Akan districts of the Gold Coast / with a report of some cases thereon decided in the law courts.* London: W. Clowes and Sons.

recognised. This implies that while the modern state has significantly eroded the power of the family/jural group in determining the formality or otherwise of marriage, the state performs the role, nevertheless through the incorporation of the family.

But the role of men as provided has remained literally the same in Akan families. Kevane is right and Sarbah is right. While the idea of wedding may have been introduced by Christian missionaries and sustained as postcolonial Christian social practice, Sarbah's work showed that men have always been providers for their families. Consequently, I agree with Boni's perceptive observation about the continuity of the structure of the Akan family that:

> Throughout the twentieth century, the nuclear family has acted as a locus of hierarchical relations. fathers and husbands exercise their role of household heads, while wives and children were required to occupy subordinate positions. As roles were not dramatically altered, household dynamics show some degree of continuity. Changes have certainly occurred, but to focus this subject on gender relations alone produces a misapprehension of the continuity of the ideology of relations within the household (Boni 2001:36).

Boni makes an equally important observation between family and subordination in her assertion that "Subordinates have room to shape their dependency, and to demand the respect of their rights. In some instances, they may even refuse to enter in relations that imply inferiority" (2002: 36). Thus, Akan marriages may not be as oppressive and prone to seismic shift to fundamentally change the pre-marital status of Akan women. Akan women, even after marriage tend to enjoy help from their matriclan members, with entitlements that included valued resources, such as land. If for any reason, the marriage collapses, women may easily integrate back into their matrilineage. Akan women were also not obliged to hold joint account with their husbands (Takyi 2007).[130] To firm all this, among the Akan, the extended family ensures mutual helpfulness, conformity to social norms and protection (Adei 2003 89).[131] Personally, growing up in Accra in the 1980s, I observed that several Akan women, including my mother, would hardly establish

---

[130] Takyi, B.K. (2007). 'Matrilineal family ties and marital dissolution in Ghana,' *Journal of Families Issues*, 28(5): 682-705.

[131] Adae, S. (2003). African traditional marriage and biblical patterns: The case of the Ashanti of Ghana. Master of Theology thesis submitted to the University of South Africa.

permanent stores for business. While some may have been pressed by finances, others simply preferred hawking of household commodities. This allowed them easy migration back to their matrilineal families, when divorce happened. Divorce is said to be, after all, very high among the matrilineal Akan, as men and women have the same rights to leave the marriage (Adei 2003: 124; Rattray 1927: 97).[132] The easiest reason for an Akan woman to leave a marriage is to charge her husband of failing to provide for her and her children; and the process of divorce was simple and carried no stigma (Adae 2003: 126; Rattray 1927) and still is very simple, apart from formalisation of the process by the modern state.

In the end, Boni arrived at the same contextual argument that I am advancing when she asseverated that "The struggle towards equality cannot be solely centered on land access, development projects and legal rights; among the Akan, as elsewhere in Africa, it needs to address the crucial issue of the ideology of the gendered attribution of value" (Ibid., 337).

As far as my understanding allows me, the attribution of value in gendered relation is also anchored on religious beliefs. Religion is an important determinant of people's marital choices. Similarly, compared with indigenous cultures, Christianity encourages more women to receive higher education, even after marriage. As identified by Takyi, this may be as a result of two reasons: First, Christianity tends to be associated with western literate societies and has a long history of promoting education in the country; second, majority of the religious followers are urban dwellers, where formal education is quite ubiquitous (Takyi 2002: 190).[133] But even as Christianity encourages women's education, the religion hardly allows for western liberal marital norms to shape marriages, as has been identified by Diabah and Afoh (2015).

The above means that beyond the state and families, institutionalised religions, particularly Islam and Christianity also determine the rules governing marriage. In Islam, marriage is not just about individuals and families; it is also an act of worship (*Ibadah*).[134] A particular text in

[132] Rattray, R.S. (1927). *Religion and art in Ashanti.* London: Oxford University Press.

[133] Takyi, B.K. (2002). 'Religious affiliation, marital processes and women's educational attainment in development societies," *Sociology of Religion*, 63(2): 177-193.

[134] A form of worship, based on the Hadith, "Whoever has married has completed half of his faith" (Baihaqi). Qur'anic text that supports marriage as imperative is Qur'an 30:21.

Islamic tradition says that "He/she who marries fulfils half of the requirements of the family." In Christianity, marriage is treated as a covenant involving a man and a woman with Christ as the ultimate witness. While the Islamic and Christian understanding of marriage may be universally shared, the application of the principles may differ marginally across cultures and even denominations. But generally, for Ghanaian Christian and Muslim constituencies, marriage is integrated into the religious retinue of the people. This means that while the state of Ghana has the ultimate to endorse the validity of what constitutes civil marriage, the religious groups tend to exert enormous influence of how and why individuals establish marriage. The extent to which Pentecostal Christians, for example exert influence over marriage has been critiqued as an infringement of family rights (Dijk 2004).[135] But for Pentecostals, the fact that the church is a voluntary association, both socially and constitutionally, implies that persons are free to join and leave and once they join, they are bound by the boundaries the church set around the institution. Given all the transitions that marriages in Africa have gone through, Kevane defined marriage as "an occasion where rights, services, status, and prestige are transacted between bride and groom and their respective families" (Kevane 2014: 153-154). Falola and Amponsah also defined marriage as a practice that, "was, and continues to be, a transaction between two lineages that allow the lineage of a man to secure the productive and reproductive capabilities of a woman from her lineage group" (2012: 12).

While it cannot be readily accepted that marriage is oppressive to women in supposedly imprisoning women to the performance of domestic (immanence) roles, institutions of higher learning have rather proven complex for them. When I was at the Makerere Institute of Social Research (MISR), Makerere University – Uganda, where I began my doctoral studies, the oppressive regime of the Director of MISR compelled a fellow researcher to strip as part of protesting against the director on April 18, 2016. This was after students and the female researcher had explored all possible legitimate avenues, without success, to resist the oppressive regime of the Director. As the student leader of MISR students at the time, the female researcher's incident happened right in front of me and other students. Expectedly, the "nude" protest of the researcher received international attention with the BBC joining other media houses to present it in the public domain.

---

[135] Dijk, R.A. van (2004), 'Negotiating marriage: Questions of morality and legitimacy in the Ghanaian Pentecostal diaspora,' *Journal of Religion in Africa*, 34(4): 438-467.

Sadly, the underlying cause of her behaviour -the role of the male professor – hardly gained such a global attention. Obviously, this renders it reason for women talk about male bias and the patriarchal dividend through which men's excesses are not discussed while women's reactions are discussed.

Given the religious conservativeness of Uganda, the female researcher's action attracted denunciation from the public, diverting attention from Director's oppressive regime. In all the responses and all the ridicules against the female researcher, it was Professor Sylvia Tamale, who decided to provide an intellectual defence to researcher's metaphorical and literal undressing, a practice that is quite not alien to Africans – especially when we read about the protests of the Anlu and Takumbeng women of Cameroon (Kah 2011).[136] In her inaugural lecture, therefore, Professor Sylvia Tamale focused on the relationship between nudity and social protest. While she admitted that she was initially horrified and embarrassed by the researcher's nude protest, she later felt she was succumbing to male oppression and sexualisation for the woman's body. So, deploying post-structuralism – which isn't very far removed from essentialism as a humanistic philosophy – she argued that the female body is also constructed as a sexual body, much more than that of the male.

The institutional oppression of women is associated with women's bodies. Historically, the female body has been an object of attention, desire, and lust" (Tamale 2016: 12). As part of the politics of words, which is not different to the contestation surrounding the meaning of Akan proverbs, she contended that "a naked body is not the same as a nude one" (Tamale 2016:12). She explained that when women bare their nakedness to the public they are not engaging in sexual provocation, but using that as a powerful resource to challenge patriarchal oppression (ibid, 12). They concluded that the woman's body is not natural *per se*, but is read through meanings, cultural codes and symbols created by society's inscription based on culture, and religion (Tamale 2016:13). So, through post-structural theory, she challenges society's construction of nakedness as an imposition of religious normativity or common-sense logic.

In line with existential philosophy, she concluded that, post-structuralism allows her to challenge, "the idea that individuals exist as essential beings and argues that our "being" is socially constructed"

---

[136] Henry Kam Kah, "Women's resistance in Cameroon's Western Grassfields: The power of symbols, organization, and leadership, 1957-1961," *African Studies Quarterly*, 12, 3 (2011): 67-91.

(Ibid, 13). She also said that "it is necessary to understand that the body should not be simply viewed through the lens of biology. Rather, the body needs to be understood as both a material and a political entity" (Ibid, 14). Just like Fredrich Engels, Tamale's blamed the church for institutionalising the sexualisation of a woman's body. Blaming the church is because Christianity (and Abrahamic religions in general) is said to be founded on somatophobia (fear, distrust of and cautionary tales about the bodily urges such as hunger, sexual urges, anger etc). so, Christians are cautioned not to respond to the bodily urges such as hunger and especially urges of a sexual nature! Tamale, therefore, said that in the church's efforts to "purify" "the church reinforced the "puritan ethic" of covering up and associating sex and sexuality with shame and embarrassment" (Tamale 2016: 6). As I have said, women's shared heritage of patriarchal biases tends to serve a thread for women to share knowledge about their realities. In the debate over the Family Bill, several of the activists in support of minority sexual rights have critiqued the religious groups of fanatically imposing their puritan ethics on the Ghanaian public. Similar to Tamale's observation, the supporters of LGBTQ rights in Ghana have considered the churches and the various religious groups as impediment to sexual freedom. But the issue is not also so much about the church suppressing and disallowing individuals to "freely" express their bodily, sexual urges. At any rate, as I discussed above, the idea of human beings having free agency to do as they please with their body is nothing short of a convenient myth. This is precisely because as I have discussed in Chapter Two, human beings are organically structured to be relational and social – rendering the idea of freely using one's body as one pleases impossible. Our biological and social conditions are seamlessly linked in shaping our behaviours and what is allowed and what is not allowed. To think that one can use one's body as one pleases is itself a problem of the nexus between psychological "self" and lived social and natural realities. As I have already discussed above, it is not only the so-named Abrahamic religions that seek to control human bodies, the Akan considers self and the world as fused in a web of reciprocal relations. For this reason, Owusu and Bosiwah have concluded, based on the Akan worldview, that:

> How we react to the world of nature and the worlds of culture other than our own depends on the assumptions which make sense to us in terms of our worldview which necessarily consists of what we know (2015: 132).

The above discussion has laid the transnational context for the discourse around gender and sexuality. I will look at the works of selected Ghanaian feminist scholars. As part of critiquing all social structures, including what is considered "tradition" these authors deploy methodological approaches that cascade into their analysis of Akan proverbs. So, while I do not intend to necessarily dismiss the hermeneutical approach these scholars use to study Akan proverbs, I will provide my own understanding of their methods. Methodologically, these women use Ghanaian/African proverbs as a part of presenting indigenous wisdom as patriarchal, androcentric and oppressive to women. Their insights into the proverbs highlight the various ways patriarchal cultures are said to be routinised through language – reaffirming Foucault's discourse as a nexus between language and power. I appreciate the interpretations female (and some male) academics give to Akan proverbs and cultures, generally, since Akan culture is open to multiple interpretations – bringing the interpretative nature of oral tradition. I will attempt to provide a contextual interpretation of the Akan proverbs that some female academics have tagged as signifiers of women's oppression.

As part of women exercising autonomy over their bodies, two Ghanaian academics examined the representation of women espoused in Akan proverbs to demonstrate how Akan men stigmatised women. Exploring the interrelation between language, gender and culture, using a feminist critical discourse approach, these academics concluded that the female's body is a source of pleasure for men and objectification of women …. representation of women vulnerability (Diabah and Amfo 2015: 18). As part of deconstructing social structures, several Ghanaian feminist-linguist scholars are bent on redefining gendered roles by assuming that the roles men and women are simply culturally and socially constructed. I have already pointed out that the idea of gendered roles as simply culturally determined is simplistic. Nevertheless, the goal of these feminist is to reshape not just what they consider masculine's perception of women but to overturn the expected social disposition of women. For example, Diabah and Amfo bemoaned the fact that while education, finance, exposure to cosmopolitan lifestyles and globalisation have contributed to advancing the social status of women, "…these have not eroded perceptions and expectations of what it means to be an ideal Akan or Ghanaian woman – submissiveness, respectful, hard-working, dutiful, etc" (Ibid, 6). This is a highly controversial observation. These women authors write as if these attributes are necessarily oppressive. Is it not the case that these are virtues that men and women must incorporate to sustain all forms of conjugal relationships? What should the invert of these virtues and how would such inversions build the human family? In what ways would disrespectfulness and arrogance sustain a family life? Submissiveness is the issue, I think.

The challenge with the methodological use to which feminist scholars put Akan proverbs is that they usually do not acknowledge the ontological knowledge and appreciation of the Akan understanding of the woman's body or the body of human beings in general. This gap in epistemological appreciation of Akan human cosmogony, similar to what I have said above, is because these writers tend to understand the Akan wisdom from the prisms that are also part of the of modern radical feminists from the west. Similarly, they to not incorporate a socio-cultural historical appreciation of the sagacity of the Akan. While they sample several proverbs to supposedly demonstrate how proverbs reinforce hegemonic masculinity and femininity, I will give analyses of a few examples of them to show how these scholars have not provided contextual discussion of Akan – which, sadly, results in epistemic injustice to the Akan.

The first example is their interpretation of the proverb, "If a woman is sick, her vagina is not sick too" and "The woman Yaa Ataa says she is wild (lit. her eyes are hard), but we use the hair of her vagina to mark the boundary". In interpretation, these scholars write that, "These proverbs objectify the female body in ways that not only serve as a source of pleasure for men but also as a representation of their vulnerability and weakness. For example, *they* represent women as passive objects for sex (with no agency), in that even when she is sick, it does not mean the vagina is also sick; so, the man can have sex whenever he wants. This references the subordination of the woman, being at the beck-and-call of the man. In the proverb, Yaa Ataa is representative of women who are resolute and determined and dare to go against socio-cultural norms and expectations. This is based on the understanding that among the people of Ghana, twins (Ataa) are often perceived to be troublesome (especially younger ones), daring and difficult to overcome. In other words, no matter how strong a woman may consider herself to be, she is not strong enough to withstand the powers of men" (18).

To make sense of this proverb in its socio-historical context, the authors could have contextually broadened the hermeneutics of Akan philosophy by appreciating the corpus of cultural knowledge about the vagina. Similarly, they should have provided evidence to support their argument that these proverbs oriented Akan men towards androcentric tendencies. To deconstruct this kind of epistemic injustice to the Akan, I will discuss the vagina among the Akan. Among the Akan of southern Ghana, the vagina is an important part of the woman's body, even as the penis is important to the man. The cardinal value of the vagina was not for its recreational value, but procreative value. So, unlike the post-modern and late-capitalist world where the vagina has been objectified in advertisements (ads), prostitution and pornographic films, the Akan did not see the vagina in that light. Among the Akan, the vagina was adored because, through it, human beings perpetuated themselves – through the agency of the vagina, human beings fulfilled the divine-cultural mandate of procreation. It is for this reason that contemporary commodification of the vagina as an object for recreation – giving rise to licking (cunnilingus) as both commodification and recreational use of the vagina– was hardly known to my mother's generation (of the 1930s and 1940s). While this may surely appear a detour, my goal is to just take one example of how the Akan viewed the female's body. In the next section, I attend to a more culture sensitive interpretation of proverbs.

That the vagina was cherished more for its procreative value than the recreational banality and oppression to which it is put in pornographic industries is captured in the Akan proverb, "If a woman is in debt, she uses her vagina to get rid of it". This proverb is important for analysis because Diabah and Amfo used it without explaining it except highlighting the ahistorical narrative of its oppressive signalling. For this purpose, when the Akan says that the sick woman does not necessarily imply a sick vagina, we must not take it simply as literal, as the Akan culture did not institutionalise violence against women.

As I mentioned earlier, practices such as extreme widowhood rites and witchcraft accusations, much as they are condemnable today, served a functional purpose in mending some of internal contradictions in the Akan matrilineal system – the major one of which is a man giving birth and yet paying his attention more towards his sister's children than his own children – in the area of succession. With this brief detour, I want to argue that it is important for us to also look at the metaphorical representation of the vagina. Among older Akan people, the vagina is called "ahenfie" (lit: "the home of the chief or ruler" – simply state: the palace). In Akan societies, the palace is both the religious and socio-economic power block. It is the centre where power is centred and communicated to ensure both social and cosmic order. The palace is also the domain of the cherished values of the Akan – it is the home of the ancestors who serve as the moral guardians of society. The palace is also the palace where disputes are resolved; it is also the fortress against both physical and spiritual attacks from internal and external enemies of the Akan society. In sum, the palace is the is the source of life to the Akan.

Framing the vagina as the "ahenfie" has deep-seated implication for the Akan matrilineal system. This is precisely because, among the Akan, the woman is the giver of life. Every person enters into the world through the life channel – the vagina – of a woman. Just like the palace as fortress, the Akan woman is the fortress against any rapid and belligerent attacks on her children. The vagina as the symbol of life is the reason the Akan say that "if one mother's die, one family simultaneously dies." For this reason, a woman may be ill, but so long as she is not dead, her "vagina" – the source of life and power (Hagan 2000)[137] – remains a guardrail for her children. Also, as a symbol of power, the Akan say that "Oba ana owoo barima" (to wit: "It is the woman who gave birth to the man"). As I have said, the masculinity among the Akan is about power and bravery. So, if it is a woman who gives birth a man, it could as well be said, however arguably, that a man's power and authority is derivative from a woman. Obeng explained this proverb as indicating that success or strength may emanate from a place that appears not to hold any promise (Obeng 2003: 195). The Akan also have a proverb that even indicates the strength of the vagina to give life to a dead penis. The proverb is, "Ɛtwɛ foforɔ ɛnyane kote ɛwu". It is this reason, *inter alia*, that when one uses the feminine sexual organ as an insult, one is treated to have offended the one who is being referred to. Because to say to a person, "Your mother's vagina" (or your mother's cunt") in treated as undeniably painful with sadistic implications, as it reduces the one being insulted to a position of a nonentity status (Fordjour 2016: 27).[138] When a child uses the raw name of the vagina (*ɛtwe*) in communication, without any slightest to being offensive, the child is sharply rebuked or punished by any elderly person around of indecency; while his or her parents are implicated for poorly socialising the child (2016: 27).

---

[137] George P. Hagan, "Modern technology, traditional mysticism and ethics in Akan culture," Helen Lauer (ed), *Ghana: Changing values/changing technologies*, 31-52 (Washington: The Council for Research in Values and Philosophy, 2000).

[138] Emmanuel Antwi Fordjour, "Foul language in the Ghanaian electronic media: A case of some selected radio stations in Kumasi, Ghana," International Conference on Management, Communication and Technology (ICMCT), IV, 1 (2016): 26-32.

The above is my alternative interpretation of the proverb on the vagina. So, given the openness of Akan proverbs, which also reflects the logicality of orature, to multiple interpretations, we cannot accept one interpretation of a proverb as ultimate. For this reason, these authors' construction of proverbs as unamenable to innovation and individuality (Ibid, 6) is highly problematic. This is not just an *a*contextual and ahistorical but contributes to profiling African cultures as static and impervious to change. It also casts a scene of determinism on African cultures. Regrettably, these scholars did not consider the fact that cultures, including linguistic articulations such as proverbs, are highly dynamic and subject to constant change to accommodate changing trends in society. Indeed, several Ghanaian cultural anthropologists have written about the dynamism and flexibility invested in Ghanaian/Akan cultures. For examples, in the 1960s, Busia observed that, "There is no society so custom-bound that its culture does not change, and there is none so changeful as to have no cake of custom" (Busia 1962: 38).

As I said, not contextualising Akan may result in a very skewed conclusion. For example, as part of arguing that proverbs are collectively owned and shared, Diabah and Amfo said that such a cultural heritage "is reflective of the communal thought regarding an issue at stake" (Dabiah and Amfo 2015: 6). The author's use of communal thought indicates the complex roles of socialisation in structuring gendered relations among the Akan – which, as I have said, helps me to take the discussion beyond just proverbs to include the Akan notions of individualism and communalism. Even so, from the context of the author's argument, their use of "communal thought" is not just about profiling of African philosophy as incapable of producing individual thinkers, but it assumes that individuals do not have agency and cannot be creative in innovating ideas to support human flourishing. But this kind of argument is consistent with the authors' goal of deconstructing social norms that govern the male-female relationship. It is part of the existential philosophy of deconstructing the subjective world of human beings – making that world as fluid and amenable as possible without succumbing to any restraints from the so-called "objective" world – which for the Akan would include what Busia described as "cake of custom". For the Akan, this "cake of custom" that sustains female and male relationships are the very virtues these women are repudiating – respectfulness, submissiveness, and hard work.

All this description of Akan customs that relate to the general topic of sexuality, marriage or gender. My only concern is that they did not offer an insight into the Akan creative use of proverbs to routinise the legitimacy of their claims. For example, the seeming appeal to collective ownership of proverbs is not the same as saying that the Akan view proverbs as emerging from "group thought". The Akan user of proverbs would always preface his proverb with "The elders say". This opening statement of a proverb does not necessarily imply that the elders (collectively) indeed said the proverb that would be cited. It is rather creatively done to adduce legitimacy to the wisdom and social significance of the proverb. The appeal to the elders (*Nananom*) as the imagined source of a proverb is precisely because of the prominent place the elders – as first-time settlers (autochthons) and progenitors – occupy in the Akan cosmogony. All elders include those first-time settlers, autochthons and those that are socially constructed. As ancestors, Nana is considered as the embodiment of human-divine wisdom as their earthly lived experiences and their interactions with the spirit world – *Asamando* (an unending world which the home renders them sages whose words must not be contradicted).[139] They become the focus of Akan cultic practices. So, it only makes sense for persons who improvise their own proverbs to appeal to their ancestors for legitimacy. This is similar to the creative ways chiefs appeal to their ancestors to derive their authority.

It is also similar to how modern political leaders appeal to national symbols and constitutions to routinise their authority. It is also similar to how religious people appeal to their scripture to legitimise their assertions. And about these scholars, it is similar to how they cite other scholars, even when they are advancing new ideas to support their argument. With all this, as the authors did not contextualise Akan proverbs, they assumed that proverbs are group thought, unamenable to changes etc. This creates the impression that African proverbs are a form of ontological straitjacket and highly monolithic. Proverbs are figurative language and like all such linguistic genres, what we say as proverbs can be taken and reinterpreted in a new context; the same proverb, precisely because its message is not fixed, can be used again and again (Appiah 2005: 54). An example, is how in the foregoing, I have explained the Akan proverb on a sick woman and a healthy vagina.

---

[139] Kwaku Aku (February 9, 2022), 'Akan concept of God,' https://www.youtube.com/watch?v=cLQdSwKh_DI (Accessed: September 4, 2022). Also, my under graduate lecture note at the University of Cape Coast – taught by *Mrs* Marie-Acquiline *Barton-Odro (2006).*

This is precisely because these proverbs are identifiable with the cultural, historical and existential experiences of Africans, based on reflection. As has been observed, "African proverbs, for instance, (many of which bear some philosophical content), addressed or resulted from reflections on specific situations, events, or experiences in the lives of people, and that even such metaphysical concept as destiny (or fate) was reached inductively, experience being the basis of the reasoning that led to its observation and experience constituted a great part of the sources of knowledge in African tradition (Gyekye 1997: 26). For this reason, "instead of being an old-fashioned way of communication, proverbs lead us to conceive and understand the essence of human relationships, events, life's situations and the behaviour patterns of people" (Dzobo 1992: 95). They are also living expressions (Grace Ogot 1968: 35). These women scholars are not satisfied with their position in western institutions, they seek to distort, caricaturise and treat with contempt the ancestral knowledge of their ancestors. Consequently, it could be concluded that these women incorporate their use of proverbs to govern their sexual norms and behaviours and their own movement towards creating a contemporary ethos for themselves (Ansah and Dzregah 2020).

Communalism and proverbs

In the contemporary discourse on proverbs, it is assumed as collectively owned, and so, cannot constitute a philosophical source of knowledge (Hountondji 1983).[140] To make sense of the communalistic nature of African proverbs, I will discuss the philosophical axioms on which Africans socially constructed human beings. Indeed, until the reinvention of printing in the western world and its consequent enlightenment revolution, the west equally had a communalistic predisposition to life. So, to put this argument of communalism of African proverbs into perspective, I relate John Stuart Mill's doctrine of individuality to the African concept of personhood, with particular emphasis on the Akan's notion of personhood. I provide a contextual analysis between Mill and the Akan concepts because, as I have already said above, Mill was of the revolutionary thinkers whose essay seems to have found support for suffrage rights for at least women in the 19th

[140] Hountondji, P. J. (1982). *African philosophy: Myth and reality*. Bloomington: Indiana: Indiana University Press.

Century (Smith 2001).[141] Given that Mill was one of the advocates of liberalism. Our understanding of the notion of personhood is, therefore, necessary for the discourse on homosexuality. I use John Stuart Mill because, even though he did not directly talk about proverbs, his notion of individuality has been deployed by anti-African proverb campaigners to agitate for the legitimisation of western epistemic tradition in Ghanaian universities, especially gender studies. It also needs to be pointed out that Mill was very critical about what he describes as the 'tyranny of the majority', which can also be said by those who do not wish to respect the rights of sexual minorities such as the LGBTQI+. The epistemic gender discourse in Ghana is seen as a contest between the majority (who advocate traditions of knowledge of the Akan) and a minority (who advocate radical western feminist discourse). This is highly problematic as the university has become a domain for a systemic exclusion of the traditions of knowledge on deeply sensitive subject like sexuality – failure of the university, especially the Institute of African Studies (IAS) in implementing Nkrumah's admonition for the "gown" coming to "town" – signalling a need for conviviality between the university and the town for epistemic production.

The heart of John Stuart Mill's argument on individuality is that freedom of choice provides a kind of elevated or worthy human character upon which happiness ultimately depends. Hence society must be prevented from imposing any conventional or customary morality, which would restrict individual autonomy (Clor 1985: 3). John Stuart Mill argues that liberty meant protection against the tyranny of the political rulers. He also contends that the fact that we are shaped by a community's customs is dangerous, because it prevents us from being ourselves; it destroys individuality. He writes:

> Protection, therefore, against the tyranny of the magistrate is not enough: there needs protection also against the tyranny of the prevailing opinion and feeling; against the tendency of society to impose, by other means than civil penalties, its own ideas and practices as rules of conduct on those who dissent from them; to fetter the development, and, if possible, prevent the formation, of any individuality not in harmony with its ways, and compels all characters of fashioning themselves upon the model of its own (Mill 2001: 9).

---

141 Smith, S.E. (2001). 'John Stuart Mill's "The subjection of women": A re-examination,' *Polity*, 34(2): 181-203.

From the above quote, it is conspicuously clear that the debate about Akan epistemic idiom about gender is peddled from the opinion of the majority – given that the Akan is also the majority in Ghana whose cultural ethos, among others, understanding of things influence policy and public opinion – who consider their position as a defence against the eroding of tradition and custom. Mill argues that usually, where there is an ascendant class, a large portion of the morality of the country emanate from its class interest, and its feelings of class superiority. In the homosexual discourse in Ghana, the pro-LGBTQ Coalition striving for the rights of minority queer sexual group have argued that the religious community is imposing their religious sexual ethics on everyone. Similarly, as feminist authors have often described, the use of Akan proverbs tends to privilege men's sense of superiority over women. The issue, then, becomes a complex nexus between proverbs, as communal philosophy and individual agency in negotiating their freedom – this leads to my appropriation of Mill's notion of individualism.

Mill's notion of individuality is inextricably connected to the notion of freedom, and the extent to which individuals could be free from the dictates of society, based on the logic that individuals cannot be individuals until they have the freedom to act contrary to the 'tyranny of the majority'. Mill avers that individuals are to have freedom against all forms of interference, and the only purpose for which power can be rightfully exercised over any member of a civilised community, against his will, is to prevent harm to others. His own good, either physical or moral, is not a sufficient warrant. He cannot be rightfully compelled to do or forbear because it will be better for him to do so, because it will make him happier, because, in the opinions of others, to do so would be wise, or even right (Mill 2001: 13). The extent of an individual's liberty is expressed in Mill's audacious claim concerning the sovereignty of the individual from the dictates of the society, 'Over himself, over his own body and mind, the individual is sovereign' (Mill 2001: 13).

For the benefits of individualism, Mill asseverates that, 'Mankind are greater gainers by suffering each other to live as seems good to themselves, than by compelling each to live as seems good to the rest' (Mill 2001: 16). Even so, it must be pointed out that Mill does not support unrestrained freedom: he avers that:

> Acts, of whatever kind, which, without justifiable cause, do harm to others, may be, and, in more important cases, absolutely require to be, controlled by unfavourable sentiments, and, when needful, be the active

> interference of mankind. The liberty of the individual must be thus far limited; he must not make himself a nuisance to other people. But if he refrains from molesting others in what concerns them and merely acts according to his own inclination and judgment in things which concern himself, the same reasons which show that opinion should be free, prove also that he should be allowed, without molestation, to carry his opinions into practice at his own cost (Mill 2001: 52-53).

In extolling the importance of freedom, Mill argues that 'He who does anything because it is custom makes no choice' (Mill 2001: 55). This is particularly important because custom, as it comes out in the LGBTQ Bill has been read by the petitioners as stifling the freedom of queer sexuality. He also maintains that "Human nature is not a machine to be built after a model, and set to do exactly the work prescribed for it, but a tree, which requires to growing and developing itself on all sides, according to the tendency of the inward forces which make it a living thing" (Mill, 2001:55). It will probably be conceded that it is desirable people who should exercise their understandings, and that an intelligent following of custom, or even occasionally an intelligent deviation from custom, is better than a blind and simply mechanical adhesion to it (Mill 2001: 56). The despotism of custom everywhere is the standing hindrance to human development, being an unceasing antagonism to that disposition to aim at something better than customary, which is called, according to circumstances, the spirit of liberty, or that of progress or improvement (Mill 2001: 65).

A close reading of Mill's notion of liberty has it that the individual may not be subjected to coercion for his own good – physical or moral – and he may not be subjected to coercion because others disapprove of his conduct (Clor 1985: 4). Clor (1985), summarises Mill's liberty principle as follows: "there must be complete freedom to do and live as one pleases – up to the point where one's conduct directly and palpably harms identifiable and nonconsenting persons (Clor 1985: 5). The pro-homosexual debate feeds into this notion of freedom.

Mill also mentions that it is impermissible for society to repress some actions simply because society considers itself to be protecting tradition. The doctrine of liberty proscribes society from limiting the rights and freedom of individuals because of what society considers as conventional and customary. Reading this in the light of homosexuality, homosexual advocates have argued that it is impermissible for the Ghanaian society to impose the ethos of heterosexuality on homosexuality, simply because they think they are preserving traditions of society.

Having explicate the Mill's philosophy of individualism, which was also important for his support for women's liberation, it becomes discernible that the issue of individualism and communalism will feature in the LGBTQ debate in Ghana. As I said in the introductory chapter, the issue of the LGBTQ and Family Bill is also about the place of individual sexual freedom in the society. Individuality is necessary as it brings out the distinctiveness and uniqueness within the human race. The importance of individuality is to set individuals free from the grips of mediocre customs. Mill envisioned a deep-seated tension between custom and choice. He argues that 'The human faculties of perception, judgment, discriminative feeling, mental activity, even moral preference are exercised only in making a choice' (Mill 2001). From Mill's perspective any individual, who follows custom is no different from a machine. Mill was not necessarily against custom: he was rather against aping and slavishly following customs. Mill was of the view that freedom not restraint produces good character. Pro-homosexual advocates maintain that homosexuals should not be compelled to follow the heterosexual customs of society. In their argument, homosexuality should be accepted as yet another sexual disposition and expression within the human race.

Without a doubt, the discussion complicates, again, the issue of just looking at the freedom and rights of sexuality rights as simply given. The complexity of the issue is such that the Akan sense of communalism retains control over the lives of individuals. Channelled through proverbs, the Akan notion of a person becomes yet another structured way of socialising individuals into heteronormativity. For the sake of non-Akan readers, the following discussion is dedicated to explicating the Akan notions of a person, focusing on how the whole issue of individual sexual rights pales in the face of the Akan/Ghanaian society.

The notion of a person among the Akan: an analysis of proverbs

Isaiah Berlin provides a critique of freedom as espoused by John Stuart Mill. His main critique is that 'Men are largely interdependent, and no man's activity is so completely private as never to obstruct the lives of others in any way' (Berlin 1969: 124). Berlin's position dovetails into the Akan notion of a person: here, the main questions that would engage this section are: Who is a person: is a person individual qua individual or a social being? To what extent is the individual free to 'deviate' from mainstream society? How do we assess the homosexual debate given the Akan notion of a person?

As observed by Lutz (2009), one of the most striking features of the cultures of Sub-Saharan Africa is their non-individualistic character. The sociality of the African is captured in the Ubuntu philosophy: "I am because we are; and since we are, therefore, I am" (Mbiti 1969: 108-109). Yusuf Turaki reflects the African sense of community as follows: "People are not individuals, living in a state of independence, but part of a community, living in relationship and interdependence (Turaki 2006: 36).

According to Senghor, "Negro-African society puts more stress on the group than on the individuals, more on solidarity than on the activity and needs of the individual, more on the communion of persons than on their autonomy. Ours is a community society".

On communalism, Steve Biko said:

> We regard our living together not as an unfortunate mishap warranting endless competition among us but as a deliberate act of God to make us a community of brothers and sisters jointly involved in the quest for a composite answer to the varied problems of life. Hence, in all we do we always place [wo]man first and hence all our action is usually joint community-oriented action rather than the individualism (Biko 1978: 42).

Concerning the sociality of the individual, Mbiti (1969) writes that,

> In traditional life, the individual does not and cannot exist alone, except corporately. He owes his existence to other people, including those of the past generations and his contemporaries. He is simply part of the whole. The community must therefore make, create, or produce the individual; for the individual depends on the corporate group... . Whatever happens to the individual happens to the whole group, and whatever happens to the whole group, happens to the individual. The individual can only say: "I am because we are; and since we are, therefore, I am." This is the cardinal point in the understanding of the African view of man (Mbiti 1969: 108-109).

According to Gyekye "Communitarianism immediately sees the human as inherently (intrinsically) a communal being, embedded in a context of social relationships and interdependence, never as an isolated, atomic individual" (Gyekye 1992: 104). The Akan notion of the sociality of the individual is captured in the Akan proverb: "When a person descends from heaven, he descends into a human society." According to Gyekye, the conceptualisation of the human person as a communal being has some implications: (i) that the human person does not voluntarily choose to enter into human community, that is community life is not optional for any individual person; (ii) that the human person is at once a cultural being (iii) that the human person cannot – perhaps must not – live in isolation from other persons (iv) that the human person is naturally oriented toward other persons and must have relationships with them; (v) that social relationships are not a contingent but necessary (Gyekye 1992: 105).

Notwithstanding the force of communitarianism refracted through matriliny, among the Akan, Gyekye argues that the individual can deviate from the norms of society, particularly if the individual finds an aspect of the norms of society to be inelegant and archaic. His reason is that 'individual persons, as participants in the shared values and practices, and enmeshed in the web of communal relationships, may find that aspect of those of cultural givens as inelegant, undignifying or unenlightening and can thoughtfully be questioned and reevaluated. The evaluation may result in the individual's affirming or amending or refining existing communal goals, values and practices; but it may or could also result in the individual's total rejection of them (Gyekye 1992: 112).

Gyekye argues that the individual has the capacity of self-assertion, and the individual's capacity for self-assertion that the individual can exercise, "presupposes, and in fact derives from, the autonomous nature of the person.' He clarifies what he meant by autonomous, by saying that "by autonomy, I do not mean self-completeness, but the having of a will, a rational will of one's own, that enables one to determine at least some of his own goals and to pursue them" (Gyekye 1992: 112). This point has brilliantly been explored by Edmund Agyeman who provided a complex intermesh between communalism, belonging and agency. He argued that the idea of communalism did/does not liquidate the agency individuals have as moral beings (Agyeman 2021).

The sociality of the person immediately makes him or her naturally oriented towards persons with whom he must live in relation. Living in relation with others directly involves a person in social and moral roles, duties, obligations, and commitments, which the individual must fulfil. The natural relationality of the person thus immediately plunges him into a moral universe, making morality an essentially social and trans-individual phenomenon focused on the well-being of others (Gyekye 1992: 118).

Gyekye provides some insight into what happens when the interest of the individual clashes with communal values. In this case, I ask the question what happens to the individual when his values conflict with those of the larger society? How would a homosexual be different in his sexual orientation about a dominantly heterosexual society? Gleaning from Gyekye, it is obvious that communitarianism does not proscribe the individual from thinking and living differently from the larger society. Gyekye argues that the individual can express difference if he or she finds the norms of society to be inelegant and irrelevant to him or her. In that case, if the individual's sexual orientation differs markedly from that of the larger heterosexual society, then the individual can express that difference.

It is therefore clear that communitarianism in the Akan society does not compromise the ability of the individual to express difference. Individuals can 'deviate' from mainstream society once they do so rationally, and not an expression of mere rebellion. The individualistic approach to life is rare in indigenous Akan societies. As observed by Brookman-Amissah, "There is then considerable flexibility in the application of proverbs to situations. Proverbs are therefore not intended to be 'frozen' knowledge which could be quoted to clinch every argument and to meet every possible human situation. It is worth noting that the very brevity of proverbial statements do not allow one to draw more conclusions from them than their context would allow" (Brookman-Amissah 1986: 75). Proverbs, as part of folklore, contain cultural resource knowledge. Proverbs as a source of cultural epistemes, are "relevant for the lessons they offer in promoting the goals of collective responsibility, community building, mutual interdependence, and meeting rights and responsibilities of citizenship" (Dei 2010: 81).

As a cultural phenomenon, proverbs are malleable in the reflection of changing social phenomena, as they constitute part of the strategies of dealing with social situations. They are composed by those who are observant, experienced, thoughtful and creative (Kudadjie 1999: 12). Kudadjie further stated that, proverbial wisdom is derived from "observations made about the nature and behaviour of human beings, animals, birds, plants, and other natural as well as supernatural objects and beings" (ibid., 12). Proverbs have literal or primary meaning, and deeper or real meaning. All this implies that proverbs must be interpreted to reflect the experiences and socio-political, cultural life and pragmatic context (Agyekum 2021: 2). The communalistic nature of traditions of knowledge of Africans has been reduced to stupidity by western scholars who parade western epistemic tradition as the canon and standard against which all truth systems must be measured, unfortunately. Robin Horton was among the earliest scholars to have asserted that the communalistic worldview of Africans cannot be considered philosophy (Horton, 1977). But the conclusion that Dzobo arrived on his analysis of proverbs is apt: "Proverbs are a very effective mode communication, and their correct and persuasive use in speech is always taken as a sign of sound education, maturity, cultural sophistication and wisdom" (Dzobo 1992: 95).

Individualistic and communalistic philosophies: A journey into feminist discourse

From the discussion so far, I have highlighted the contestation around proverbs as a source of knowledge about Africa. My basic argument is that profiling proverbs as communally owned, many scholars, including feminist writers conceptualise some proverbs as a canonised source of androcentrism. But in all of this, it is important to consider the role individual freedom and communal freedom play in shaping discourses around feminism and by extension academic freedom in Ghanaian universities. If we are to extrapolate the libertarian ideas of John Stuart Mill to academic freedom in scholarship, it could be stated, though not without the risk of generalisation, to state that individual thinking that tends to be non-conformist to that of society is preferred to any type of knowledge that is dubbed as "communalistic".

Since the reinvention of printing in the west, epistemic production and the processes involved have significantly changed. This is precisely because what appears as a transition from oral sources as the base of society's epistemological traditions to "literacy" has redefined human intellectual freedom, even as it has sustained human rights. Until the reinvention of printing in Europe, episcopal orthodoxies and epistemic control remained a dominant paradigm. Individuals who produced knowledge must relate it to episcopal epistemic standards. Given that religion and politics had seamlessly merged before the Christian Reformation of the 16th Century, it was easy for the episcopal authority to use every means possible, including persecution, to silence dissenting voices. This was particularly the case with individuals, such as Martin Luther and John Calvin, whose ideas were considered revolutionary.

The episcopal group sustained their might through their deliberate suppression of every effort at translating the Bible from Greek and Latin into other European languages. Since these languages, (considered the linguistic base of scholarship), were not accessible to the masses, not everyone could challenge episcopal episteme. In the end, all sorts of social ills were carried out under the banner of Christianity. For example, some of the clergies had to apply politically-induced hermeneutics to the Bible to rationalise the enslavement of non-Europeans, particularly Africans. In summary, episcopal control stifled individual freedom that resulted in wanton human rights abuses.

The Christian Reformation was, therefore, directed at deconstructing the episcopal authority, by decentring biblical knowledge through translation. But all this wouldn't have been possible without the reinvention of printing. This was because, before Martin Luther, some individuals like John Wycliff, had made attempts to translate the Bible, as part of challenging episcopal authority. But they were easily suppressed, as their ideas could not get to see the light of day, in a manner that printing offers. So, with the reinvention of printing in the 16th Century, it was easier for Martin Luther to get his 93 theses easily spread across Germany and Europe. This became the basis of multiple revolutions – scientific, technological, governance, human rights etc.

Dislodging episcopal authority encouraged individuals to openly write and publish their views; it sustained the idea of the modern state; improved on human rights, paved the way for modern science, and more importantly sustained the importance of individual thoughts as critical for epistemological tradition. In all this, the Christian Reformation was not just about religion, but also about every aspect of human life.

This development in Europe was critical in helping Europeans to define their past and their modernity. Religion, which the religious elite had used to suppress dissent, became a target of criticisms. From the 17th Century, a type of secularisation emerged that sought to dislodge religion as the basic source of knowledge production. Pioneers like Immanuel Kant and David Hume were not necessarily atheists, but they sought to argue that humans could apply rationality in formulating moral values, without the God factor, to govern society. We can say that the 17th Century was about the secularisation of knowledge. In the 18th Century, the French and American political revolutions provided yet another level of secularisation. This secularisation was about dispossessing politics of religious influence. The transition from monarchy (which was loosely based on the divine right of kingship) to republican (based on some form of the social contract) contributed to most Europeans choreographing their identity from religion to politics.

Nationalism became very strong, giving rise to multiple conflicts and political tension for control in Europe. As the wars became so intense, Europeans decided to extend their reach beyond Europe to other continents, including Africa and the Asiatic world. The nationalistic feeling was so strong that most Europeans were brutal in looting the human and material resources of the world they came into contact with. Backed by capitalistic inkling, framed around the mercantilist economy, African resources, including graves that had precious metals like gold, were badly looted.[142]

As Europeans launched themselves into the non-European world, they had nurtured the arrogant position of civilising the cultures they came into contact with. This was to the extent that some of the missionaries were brutal in condemning African indigenous cultures, including mundane ones like songs and dance types. But it is important to mention that towards the end of the 19th Century, as Europe drifted further away from God, most of the missionaries encouraged Africans to look unto their cultures for cultural redemption. This was precisely because the industrial revolution had changed the social and cultural climate of Europe, paving way for individualism that threatened family life and the fervour of religion in the public sphere.

The impact of the industrial revolution and technological breakthrough in Europe in the 18th Century, since the Christian Reformation, contributed to reshaping the cultural landscape of Europe. As God was significantly moved away from the public sphere, religious activities declined as church attendance began to suffer. This development led to cultural secularisation where individuals preferred attending art galleries and museums for "awe" as opposed to the "miracles" of the church. As religion showed significant signs of losing its fervour in the public sphere, individuals had to fashion their lives away from a God believed to be the watchdog over people's moral lives. The supposed death of "religion" contributed to the secularisation thesis, fronted by people like Peter Berger and Harvey Cox, that religion would continue to lose its significance in the public sphere. As part of the secularisation thesis, science and technology were tipped to bury and marginalise religion – pushing it to the margins and fringes of life.

---

142 I was shocked when I visited the museums in Oxford and Cambridge only to see the extent to which Europeans were ruthless in looting the resource base of the non-European world.

The supposed demise of religion was premised on the idea that if religion was to survive the onslaught of modernity, at all, it needed to liberalise – giving up all conventional teachings that did not cohere with science. The force of cultural revitalization in Europe led to the 20th Century gaining the profile of the secularization of culture. Christian-embedded cultural practices in Europe began to lose their significance. Europeans revitalised cultural practices in the ancient Greco-Roman Empire, such as homosexuality, which the church had suppressed. For example, since the 16th Century, England passed laws to suppress homosexual practices, by imposing tough punishment, such as trial by ordeal and burning on the stakes for persons considered homosexuals.

With the changing cultural climate in Europe, which involved a further push against religion, religious residues had to be reconsidered. Since the basic challenge that had encumbered freedom is about human beings, new philosophies had to emerge that redefined human ontology. One of such philosophies, which in my perspective form the fulcrum of feminist discourse is Jean-Paul Sartre's existentialism theory. As human essence was pushed to the background, the individual agency became central in virtually every aspect of life, including epistemological production.

As I have said above, religion until the Christian Reformation, serving as a major source of epistemological tradition, became a target of attack. So, as part of Europe's modernity, religion had to be pushed away from the public sphere. Transposing this to Africa, feminist scholars, as I have stated above, tend to see everything tradition as a threat to woman's freedom. Largely, the epistemological source that does not reinforce individualism is rejected as oppressive to women. So, proverbs believed to be communally owned become a threat as an imposition of patriarchal tradition on women.

Journey into feminist discourses

Colonial universities, sponsored by the public, have become spaces for individual theories that in some cases may contradict the views of the public. This is against the background that in pre-industrial societies, knowledge must have both pragmatic and existential value. This implies that knowledge among the Akan, for example, was not just about acquiring cognitive skills, but must lead the individual to answer existential questions such as: "Who am I?", "Where do I come from", "Where do I go from here"? etc. These questions are obviously different from Descartes "I am because I think" – a mark of individualism. They rather led to the deepening of collectivism, known in southern Africa as *ubuntu.* Consequently, the indigenous education system was framed around communalism and condensed in sociogenic activities, such as festivals, marriage, naming ceremonies, funerals, and worship. These sociogenic activities were used to educate the public on communally shared values.

Marriage has been profiled as the critical institution and base of society. It is in a marriage where the virtues of society find expression and are later expressed to the rest of society. Marriage milieu was important in saturating society with shared values and virtues. For this reason, the constitution of marriage and the roles of couples were clearly defined. Indeed, in the Akan society, marriage was practically and socially heterosexual. While it could have hinged on polygyny for various reasons, but hardly romantic reasons, marriage was always heterosexual. This was because heterosexual marriage was/is the only way procreation could take place, not even in the face of advanced science and technology. For human beings to procreate, including supposed gay and lesbian couples, they must incorporate the clearly distinctive biological binary between a biological male and a biological female sperm and egg respectively.

Understanding Akan Proverbs in their social context

Having pointed the failure of several Ghanaian feminist understanding of the logicality of Akan proverbs, I will now dedicate this section, to discussing the critical ways we need to interpret Akan proverbs. My argument here is that, instead of feasting on the "post" theories, e.g., postcolonialism, poststructuralism, and postmodernism that seek to deconstruct structures and impute negativity on the past, we must appreciate Akan proverbs contextually and historically. While I will not attempt to discuss the seeming "androcentric" Akan proverbs, I will provide a tool that academics and students can use to make sense of these proverbs. I must risk saying that the approach I will propose could be similarly used in discussing other indigenous proverbs and cultural structures.

The Akan world, like all pre-industrial worlds, was a world that was oriented more towards order than justice. By this, my point is that the Akan construed the human as social being whose existence is inextricably connected to other human beings and a shared enabling socio-eco system. This creates a symbiotic relationship between the individual and the society, of which priority is given to the society when there is a clash of value. Kwame Gyekye expressed this succinctly as follows:

> [T]he individual is not only is a natural member of human society but needs society and all that it makes available for the realisation of the individual's potential, and for living a life that is most worthwhile. The sort of relation that should exist between the individual and the society is reflected in conceptions of social structure evolved by a community of people. The existence of an outstanding, in fact, a necessary feature of every human society (Gyekye 2004: 53).[143]

The above observation appears trite, but it cannot be treated lightly. This is because the rise of the LGBTQ movement is a direct affront to the Akan social structure of marriage as heterosexual with emphasis on phallic competence in procreation and establishment of heterosexual relationality. This means that until the recent upsurge in the claims of person who claim to queer sexualities, the Akan idea of rights (justice), getting appropriate reward or punishment, for one's action, was circumscribed within the rubric of the social structure of society. This means that any right that any individual claimed that did not resonate with the social structure of the Akan was considered an anomaly for public acceptance. All this was because the Akan world was structured to ensure social and cosmic order. The logicality of the Akan emphasis on social order as opposed individual rights was that the Akan assumed a non-binary world of the spiritual and physical. They assumed that the two worlds interpenetrate each other, with the spiritual world shaping the moral contours of the material world. Individuals with spiritual insights and gifts could transgress the two worlds to contribute to shaping order. As I shall discuss under the section of chiefs, state, religion and ethics in this chapter, the non-binary of Akan cosmogony remains the source of tension in contemporary "secular" governance in Ghana.

The idea of order among the Akan implied keeping both ethical and ontological boundaries. As part of ethical boundaries, it was considered inappropriate and lawless for one to uncover the other's ancestral root (this was part of Komfo Anokye's rule to the Asante, when consolidating Asanteman). Second, it was an ethical infraction for an Akan to insult an elder. Not having sex with another person's wife. It included laws against incest framed around prohibitions of marriage

---

[143] Kwame Gyekye, *The unexamined life Philosophy and the African experience* (Legon: Sankofa Publishing Company Ltd., 2004).

between parallel cousins (especially marriage between children of parents' sisters, since they came from the same matriclan. Cousins born of uterine sisters could not marry, yes because they shared the same forebear. But marriage between children of sisters and brothers was allowed – known as cross cousins' type of marriages). This is because using the matrilineal logic, such cousins belonged to different matrilineages, did not share close uterine connections. It also forbids murder, stealing, and disobeying parental authority. The ethical boundaries also affected food-related taboos, such as not talking while eating; waiting for an elderly person to stop and get up from the table before a child does the same, etc. Akan ethical boundaries ensured social order in inter-personal relationships. Breaking any of such boundaries invited punishment that varied, based on the degree of the crime. I shall return to this soon. In terms of living arrangements for spouses, the Akan post-marital residence could be duolocal, but given the phallic culture of the Akan, a husband is expected to exercise control over his wife and family. A husband must demonstrate phallic competence through childbirth and also provide, protect, and lead his family as a patriarch.

On the other hand, ontological boundaries ensured that the relationship between the Akan people and the pantheon of deities, including the ancestors and Nyame (God) was ordered. There were, therefore, rules serving as guardrails. These rules include not stealing from the shrine, not defying the person of the chief; not having sex in the forest, and not murdering. Infractions of any of these brought different levels of harm to the entire community. Usually, the harm that such infractions brought to the entire community included mysterious death, diseases, drought, famine, flooding, internal political instability, and poor harvesting. To avert all these challenges in the Akan societies, rules were made to ensure cosmic order – that is keeping ontological boundaries.

With such a conception of the world, structures were important – informing how men and women, chiefs and their "subject", and children and parents should relate. For this reason, incest was not just a crime against a person, but against the ancestors, the moral guardians of the material world (Pashington 1996). Murder was not just a criminal issue, but a spiritual one as well. Women being unfaithful was not a matter of her exercising free will, but undermining the sanctity of the family – hence the Akan word " *ɛdwa man*" (to wit, "to split") applied more to the woman than the man. This was precisely because, in the Akan matrilineal conceptual framework, women are the makers and owners of the family – socially. But as I discuss the matriliny puzzle – "a combination of seeming contradictory modes for ordering social structure, involving a hierarchical, differentiated, and stratified society, together with a segmentary lineage type of kinship" (Basehart 1961: 270)[144] – in the section under the concept of marriage later in this chapter, politically, men are expected to exercise power and control over the reproductive and governance of their families. Children must also be obedient to learn the basic rudiments and skills in life. A disobedient child was considered a threat not just to his or her family, but to the entire community.

The above interconnectedness between individuals and the community implies that any individual infractions have communal effects, either at the family level or community level – depending on the nature of the infraction. As I have already mentioned about Busia's observation, if the infraction is minor, it is considered a private délit that affect only the contending parties. But if the infraction is a major one, it is considered a public délit that affect the individuals and the entire community. All this led to the importance of Akan societies attached to structures and order.

To ensure social and cosmic order, therefore, life among the Akan was generally structured in sociogenic terms. Virtually, all social events, such as marriage, child naming, funeral, and installation of chiefs were performed in public and for public knowledge. This ensured that rules around such activities were kept to ensure both social and cosmic order. Given the sociogenic nature of Akan social activities, deviant practices, including homosexuality had to be done in secret (even if it existed at all). I must say that because of the Akan quest for social and cosmic order, rather than justice, individuals had to subject their idiosyncrasies that did not contribute to sustaining order of that of society. So, Nil Ajen is right in stating that, "in the entire region of West Africa and all over Africa the issue of sex is not one that people feel comfortable discussing openly as some in the West do" (Ajen 1998: 130). Other scholars charged anthropologists, including Evans-Pritchard, for "not seriously investing same-sex patterns, failing to report what they do observe, and documenting what they report" (Murray and Roscoe 1998: xi). Why would anthropologists have to "seriously" observe if the practice was obvious – like heterosexual marriages? That anthropologists had to look hard enough for evidence of same-sex

---

[144] Harry W. Basehart, "Ashanti" in David M. Schneider and Kathleen Gough (eds), *Matrilineal kinship*, 270-296 (Los Angeles: University of California Press, 1961).

activities means that homosexuality was not a sanctioned sociogenic activity that was publicly approved and endorsed. Again, it was not only in Africa, but in the Western world, too (Foucault 1986), public discussion of sexuality was hardly encouraged until the 1960s birthed expressive individualism and coming of closet ethos.

To dismantle the African rejection of public acceptance of homosexuality as foreign, Murray and Roscoe suggested, "Requires not only abandoning these myths but also suspending certain deeply held western beliefs and values concerning sexuality, love and personal relationships" (1998: xviii). The supposed imperativeness of deconstructing sex ethics has been made by the Ghanaian pro-LGBTQ+ activist who suggested that "deconstructing sexual deviance in the provisions of social taboos provides an avenue for further unpacking homophobia" (Mohammed 2020: 169). This suggestion falls short of sanity and wisdom -- all completely morphing into lack of appreciation of history. Indeed, such a suggestion is a major reason for the aggression of the LGBTQ+ community to saturate the public with themselves, including criminalising the teaching of Christian values in public schools, including the international organisations attempt at forcing the so-called comprehensive sex education into classrooms.

In all the pro-LGBTQ+ agenda of subverting the values of civilisation is counterproductive because: First, the western values about sex and personal relationships are not western – else how is it that the west has overturned its own "western sex ethics" and become "non-western"? Second, the western values about sex are not western in the sense of human invention, they are part and parcel of the Judeo-Christian heritage that formed western civilisation. Thirdly, the idea of western values about sex and marriage, as decidedly western, is myopic in a sense that western sex ethics are shared values with the rest of the world – having been given by the uncreated Creator God. That in every civilisation heterosexual marriage had been publicly celebrated, endorsed, and sociogenically expressed in practice and proverbs and folklore means simply that: childbirth and population growth is the heartland of every civilisation – since God said, "Let them be fruitful and multiply". Heterosexual marriage is, therefore, a divine-cultural mandate to keep the world afloat. The opposite, homosexuality is a culture of death that can hardly be celebrated in public, but hopefully allowed to subsist in the cultic world. So, instead of subverting life-promoting values, shared by overwhelming Ghanaians and Africans and superimposing the sexual pleasures of a tiny minority on everyone else, it will be wise for pro-LGBTQ+ advocates to tactfully explore ways of protecting and providing help for homosexuals. Fortunately for Ghana, the current Ghanaian Bill in Parliament – which as I understand, it is about: "compassion is stronger than condemnation".

It is important to also say that this is far from conflating skills and moral life. In terms of skills, individual Akans were free to leverage their unique skills in promoting social and cosmic order. For this reason, among the Akan, individuals and families were noted for some particular skills. There were families with expertise in hunting, metalwork, carving, oratory, and song composition. It is, therefore, untrue to argue, from this perspective that the Akan communalistic system was oppressive of individuals.

The next point is the issue of morality. Among the Akan, individuals did not generate their own set of moral values. The moral life of individuals had/has implications for others – either their families or the entire community. As I have said, this is because the moral lives of individuals constitute the bridge between the spiritual and the material worlds. With the ancestors serving as the moral guardians of the Akan world, the moral lives of individuals were not matters of individual preferences and subjectivities.

The Akan communalistic moral values ensured that the moral lives of individuals in public were framed around collectively shared moral values. Individuals must conform to shared norms. And to ensure that individuals conform to the norms and virtues of society, beliefs, taboos, and folklore are used (Ackah 1988). Growing up as an Akan, one of the things we often enjoyed were storytelling, riddles, and dilemma tales. These were so important in the socialisation process that children in the cities in the 1980s enjoyed indigenous folklore.

As a child, one of the dilemma tales I had to deal with was whether I would choose my wife or mother if I could save only one of them from drowning? At the university, in my African Literature Class, one of the dilemma tales we had to deal with was, "Which part of a nude woman at the beach, who saw a prince approach her, would she cover, if she could cover only one of the three parts of the body: the vagina, breast, or face?" The answer to this question also depends on her culture clearly. If going to the beach is accepted, then surely bodily exposure cannot be an issue. In eSwatini, unmarried maidens can show/expose uncovered busts to the king especially during the reed dance. showing one's mouth is not taboo either nor is showing scantily covered thighs and hips. Vaginas are not typically exposed unless one deliberately spreads her legs. In most African settings, spreading the legs is not typical in public. As a result, I do not see the moral dilemma.

Nudity and exposure of body parts clearly depends on socio-cultural contexts.

Some proverbs brought out the criticality of applying ethics to life. For example, concerning the importance of truth ("nokware" [one mouth] – to be consistent in speech), an Ewe proverb says that "If a son had to use his penis to take the truth from his mother's vagina, it is not a taboo". This proverb emphasises the centrality of truth in Ewe culture. I deliberately chose/used these "obscene" and seemingly vulgar expressions to indicate that proverbs are not prescriptions but descriptions of ethical principles that should guide social relations. These folklore genres had didactic values to shape the moral lives of individuals into communal living.

To consolidate all these in practice, the various sociogenic activities were creatively used. For example, marriage was a socially recognised union between a biological man and a biological woman for the prime purpose of procreation. Marriage was/is so important that for a woman not to marry is almost an anomaly, while an unmarried man is called a fool ("kwasea") (Gyekye 1998). Childbirth is considered the ultimate purpose of marriage among the Akan, such that barrenness and infertility are treated as threats to the continuity of human life and existence (Gyekye 1996). When a woman is unable to give birth, she is called *ɔbonini*, which means, "a barren, unfruitful woman or beast" (Christaller 1933: 38). This is because such a woman undermines the ontological function of her womb, which is proverbially stated in Akan as, "birth is what has taken place in your womb" (Agyekum 2010: 118). All this is also because women's reproductive capacity is important for the expansion of matrilineages. Many proverbs indicated the significance of children. For example, a proverb said that "Children are worth more than gold" and "nothing is as painful as the one who dies childless". A man who is also unable to give birth is called *krawa* (a male beast that performs no function ontologically towards procreation) (Ibid. 120) or *saadwe*. His penis was often referred to as *kɔti bɔtɔ* (a penis that has an empty sack – often referring the testicles that supplies the sperm). Both a woman and a man who died without the sex organs fulfilling the role of procreation hardly reincarnated upon their demise (Nkansa-Kyeremanteng 1996). Until my father died, he was always excited that when he died without anything (and indeed he had no car, house or plantation), he had sons who would "throw water on him" (bath him) before burial. Among the Akan of Assin Bosomadwe, it is a deceased father's honour for his son to lead his bathing as he is being prepared for burial.

The importance of childbirth is so central to the Akan mothers who want more children from their own children because becomes an important maternal forebear. This was the case when in 2019 while in Ghana for fieldwork for my doctoral studies at the University of Cambridge, my mother (who had had no western education) could not hold her surprise when I jokingly told her I would have two children. This was during a casual conversation I had with her and my elder brother. Both of them said in auto-response, "You see what western education has done to you!". That childbirth is the base of all civilisations was recently observed in China, when the communist government after repressing childbirth through imposition of one-child policy since 2016, now allows couples to have up to three children.[145] This was, inter alia, because of the depopulation effect of the current coronavirus pandemic. But it is more difficult to force people to give birth than reduce birth rate through abortion and infanticide. I will critique the implications of the overemphasis the Akan place on marriage on women and men in the course of this section.

Naming ceremonies were also important for socialising new members of society into society's cultural moral systems. During naming ceremonies among the Akan, drops of water and alcohol were left on the tongue of the child to signify the need for the child to be discerning in truth and falsehood. Similarly, names were carefully chosen to connect the child to exemplary ancestors. For example, most children have been named "Yaa Asantewaa" to reflect the unique heroism of a female Akan war of Asante root. So, every Akan child may have more than two names, including day-names that had theophoric significance. For example, the day name for a Saturday born, "Kwame or Ama" is used to imply a healer, since God as the biggest healer is called Kwame (Prempeh 2022). Names also reflected the socio-economic and political conditions under which an Akan child is born. A child called "Abayie" (you have come well) is given such a name to show the time of prosperity into which he or she was born. There are also theophoric names to reflect the religious context of the birth of a child. For example, a child may be called "Nyamekye" (God's gift) to indicate that his or her parents struggled to have a child; which is a gift from God. My son is called "Nhyira", because my wife became pregnant a few months after our marriage (on March 5, 2017); I got

---

[145] BBC News (31 May 2021), "China allows three children in major policy shift", https://www.bbc.co.uk/news/world-asia-china-57303592, accessed 15 November 2021.

scholarship offers to Oxford and Cambridge (just two weeks after our marriage) etc.

Funerals were also important in formulating and grounding society's values. The Akan word for a funeral is "ayie" which is a contraction of "ayɛ yi yɛ" (to wit: "to praise"). Among the Akan, therefore, a funeral was an occasion for memorialising and canonising the good deeds of deceased persons, emphasising those that synchronise with the ideals of society. Thus, long before the European introduction of reading of tributes, Akan people had a practice of routinising society's virtues and values in funeral performances. This partly explains why hardly anything bad is said about dead people. In addition to funerals, songs, dance types, and food cultures are all designed to reflect the virtues and values of society.

The sociogenic structure of Akan moral values ensured social and cosmic order that undermined individual brazen expression of deviant characters, including homosexual practices and prostitution.[146] For this reason, if any Akan was suspected of a dubious moral life, he or she was simply told, "Stop hiding, so we will also stop asking who are you". Reasoning from this perspective, it is an inversion of Akan logic to assume that persons called "Kojo Bɛsia" or "Kwasi Bɛsia" were necessarily homosexuals. In fact, these terms are more Fante (one of the Akan languages) in designating a male with feminine characteristics than a gay person. It is also epistemic injustice to the Akan to assume that the name implied homosexuality. The names were hardly known among other Akan groups and other ethnic groups in Ghana. I do not know any local names for homosexuals, transgenders, trans-sexual, pan-sexual and all the "sexuals" in any Ghanaian language.

Indeed, the issues of ethical and ontological boundaries and the sources of Akan moral values have caused philosophers to debate and diverge in opinion. Some have considered Akan values as springing from religion (these include Professor Kofi Asare Opoku); others think it is from the conscience (these include Professor Kwame Gyekye) while others, including Kwasi Wiredu think it is naturally derived. As an Akan and African Studies academic, alongside my evangelical Christianity, I sincerely think it was just for an academic exercise for these scholars to have split hairs over the source of Akan ethics. Having

[146] Professor Emmanuel Akyeampong of Harvard has written about prostitution among the Akan (see: "Sexuality and prostitution among the Akan of the Gold Coast c. 1650-1950" Past and Present, no. 156 (1997), pp. 144-173), but that was not a normative and acceptable practice for free women in Akan society.

treated these sources as discreet and mutually exclusive was the challenge all these authors had.

It is rather puzzling that they never saw these sources as mutually inclusive. Non-recognition of the mutual inclusivity of the various sources of morality by these eminent scholars raises critical issues about morality and individual lives. If someone does not believe in religion, can the person be moral? If morality comes from the conscience and society, can people be excused when they break moral boundaries because they are considered non-rational? Finally, if morality is naturally derived from human observation, then why must society make conscious efforts in socialising its members into its moral culture?

All this implies the need for scholars to consider the mutual inclusivity of the various sources of morality in Akan cultures. For example, because God created human beings (in his image from the Christian perspective), human beings are moral agents with a conscience guiding their moral actions. Also, as creatures of God, human beings are rational beings, capable of observation and analysis to formulate rules to govern their lives. And finally, since the Akan society was not atheistic (away from the simplistic atheistic analysis of Kwasi Wiredu and Okot p'Bitek), God was considered central to the Akan moral life. The centrality of God in the construction of Akan morality was because of the non-binary between the physical and spiritual worlds of Akan cosmogony. More significantly, religion or God as the source of morality renders it imperative for people to obey the rules of society.

While individuals can and must be morally conscious in their social relationships, the issue about why an atheist should do good is not just philosophical, but existentially relevant. Because if one should "do good for the sake of goodness" without any reward or punishment for doing otherwise, why must people be bothered about morality? If there are no externally compelling reasons for people to abide by the moral obligations of society, but rather one's own subjectivities, then it is nearly impossible for cosmic order to be maintained in Akan societies. For the Akan, therefore, the idea that the ancestors, as moral guardians punish and reward the living based on their observation or deviation from moral codes respectively is very key in the formulation of morality.

As we see the sources of Akan moral and ethical values as mutually inclusive, it becomes possible to disentangle moral debate from a rigid binary between individualism and communalism. It also helps in disengaging Akan moral values from the binaries of modernity and tradition where sexual values against homosexual practices are treated as atavism with tradition while sexual liberation of the 1960s is treated as modern. As I have already indicated, homosexuality is a tradition in western histories not just modern. If it is modern, it is because Judeo-Christian values suppressed it and with the pushing of Judeo-Christian values to the background or fringes, the west now feels free to modernise their tradition. But of course, not without cultural wars between religious people and non-religious people over sexual and moral revolution.

More significantly the non-binary between the Akan worlds, morphing into the use of sociogenic activities to mould society defines the idea of individual rights. Individuals have rights and freedom over the kinds of skills and talents they possess. Individuals have the freedom to be creative in the critical ways they put their skills and talents. But an individual hardly has unrestrained freedom to determine their moral values, especially those that affect others. Given that the Akan world incorporates the individual in both the private and public spheres, linked to the spiritual world, the individual's private moral life is as important as his or her public life. For this reason, individuals do not formulate their own moral values. Chiefs, the canonised mediators between the ancestors and the living were/are responsible for ensuring that the ethical codes are efficiently enforced.

It is the difficulty put in the way of an individual to morally self-determining that Ali Mazrui was not entirely correct about when he said indigenous cultures were "tolerant". Indeed, indigenous cultures/religions were tolerant to the extent that emerging cultures and values do threaten social and cosmic order. For example, when some of the practices of the missionaries, especially among the Basel missionaries of the early 19th Century among some Akan groups, in trying to set up separate communities for their converts generated tension. Some Akan chiefs read these separate communities, known as "Salems" that the missionaries created as threatening the unity of chiefly state and the ability of chiefs to enforce ethical codes. Similarly, when the British colonial governor in the 19th Century attempted to "secularise" chieftaincy by determining what Akan Christian converts could do and could not do, was read by the chiefs as an affront to chiefly authority. So, while chiefs and indigenous cultures were tolerant, they tolerate individuals whose moral lives and beliefs do not threaten social and cosmic order. This means that while marriage and naming ceremonies were largely family issues, chiefs as the owners of the land ("hene") were the ultimate source or the arbiter (usually through the ahemaa or queen mother – used to denote the most important woman in the Davidic Kingdom) in family disputes. Before I discuss how colonialism and modern governance have complicated the roles of chiefs, I will discuss the signification of women-related proverbs among the Akan.

Understanding Akan proverbs in their social context

Having pointed out that while the feminist academics provide an insightful perspective on the interface between proverbs and the oppression of women, they did not discuss it contextually 0 bringing out the logicality of Akan proverbs, I will now dedicate this section, to discussing the critical ways we need to interpret Akan proverbs. My argument here is that, instead of feasting on the "post" theories, e.g., postcolonialism, poststructuralism, and postmodernism that seek to deconstruct structures and impute negativity on the past, we must appreciate Akan proverbs contextually and historically. While I will not attempt to discuss the seeming "androcentric" Akan proverbs, I will provide a tool that academics and students can use to make sense of these proverbs. I must risk saying that the approach I will propose could be similarly used in discussing other indigenous proverbs and cultural structures.

The Akan world, like all pre-industrial worlds, was a world that was oriented more towards order than justice as individual rights over society. Definitely, this did mean justice should be overlooked in the world, but it is to say that the understanding of justice in the modern world as legislating individual queer sexualities as publicly and socially acceptable was not part of the Akan's worldview. Similarly, for society to thrive, legislating what is decidedly individual preference, such as same-sex attraction, which, as I have said, do not ontologically fulfil the regeneration of society cannot be accepted. The Akan world was structured to ensure social and cosmic order. The Akan assumed a non-binary world of the spiritual and physical. They assumed that the two worlds interpenetrate each other, with the spiritual world shaping the moral contours of the material world. Individuals with spiritual insights and gifts could transgress the two worlds to contribute to shaping order. As I shall discuss under the section of chiefs, state, religion and ethics in this chapter, the non-binary of Akan cosmogony remains the source of tension in contemporary "secular" governance in Ghana.

The idea of order among the Akan implied keeping both ethical and ontological boundaries. As part of ethical boundaries, it was considered inappropriate and lawless for one to uncover the other's ancestral root (this was part of Komfo Anokye's rule to the Asante, when consolidating Asanteman). Second, it was an ethical infraction for an Akan to insult an elder. Not having sex with another person's wife. It included laws against incest framed around prohibitions of marriage between parallel cousins (especially marriage between children of parents' sisters, since they came from the same matrilineal. But marriage between parents' opposite siblings was allowed – known as cross cousins' type of marriages). It also forbids murder, stealing, and disobeying parental authority. The ethical boundaries also affected food-related taboos, such as not talking while eating; waiting for an elderly person to stop and get up from the table before a child does the same, etc. Akan ethical boundaries ensured social order in inter-personal relationships. Breaking any of such boundaries invited punishment that varied, based on the degree of the crime. I shall return to this soon.

On the other hand, ontological boundaries ensured that the relationship between the Akan people and the pantheon of deities, including the ancestors and Nyame (God) was ordered. There were, therefore, rules serving as guardrails. These rules include not stealing from the shrine, not defying the person of the chief; not having sex in the forest, and not murdering. Infractions of any of these brought different levels of harm to the entire community. Usually, the harm that such infractions brought to the entire community included mysterious death, diseases, drought, famine, flooding, internal political instability, and poor harvesting. To avert all these challenges in the Akan societies, rules were made to ensure cosmic order – that is keeping ontological boundaries.

With such a conception of the world, structures were important – informing how men and women, chiefs and their "subject", and children and parents should relate. For this reason, incest was not just a crime against a person, but against the ancestors, the moral guardians of the material world (Pashington 1996). Murder was not just a criminal issue, but a spiritual one as well. Women being unfaithful was not a matter of her exercising free will, but undermining the sanctity of the family – hence the Akan word " ɛdwa man" (to wit, "to split") applied more to the woman than the man. This was precisely because, in the Akan matrilineal conceptual framework, women are the makers and owners of the family. Children must also be obedient to learn the basic rudiments and skills in life. A disobedient child was considered a threat not just to his or her family, but to the entire community. This gendered role that women are expected to play brings a lot of pressure on them.

At the same time, it legitimises the communal nature of marriage and the sociality of a person. As I have mentioned in the case of Asante traditional authorities forcing women into marriage in the 1930s, when the role society imposes on women is not measured it creates tension in gendered relations. Not only that, the role women play as nurturers of the next generation also creates concerns when people have with the LGBTQ issue. Equally true is that fact that the matrilineal social structure of the Akan implies that, often for the Akan, the emphasis of paternity is on social fathers (*pater*) rather than genitors (biological fathers). But again, the duality of responsibility between men and women and its implication for the Akan cosmogony of children's welfare implies the presence of two different sexes in nurturing a child. For several Ghanaians, as I understand, any attempts at decriminalising same-sex marriage will be read as undermining the gendered role men and women play in the establishment of the family.

The above interconnectedness between individuals and the community implies that any individual infractions have communal effects, either at the family level or community level – depending on the nature of the infraction. As I have already mentioned about Busia's observation, if the infraction is minor, it is considered a private délit that affect only the contending parties. But if the infraction is a major one, it is considered a public délit that affect the individuals and the entire community. All this led to the importance of Akan societies attached to structures and order.

To ensure social and cosmic order, therefore, life among the Akan was generally structured in sociogenic terms. Virtually, all social events, such as marriage, child naming, funeral, and installation of chiefs were performed in public and for public knowledge. This ensured that rules around such activities were kept to ensure both social and cosmic order. Given the sociogenic nature of Akan social activities, deviant practices, including homosexuality had to be done in secret (even if it existed at all). I must say that because of the Akan quest for social and cosmic order, rather than justice, individuals had to subject their idiosyncrasies that did not contribute to sustaining order of that of society. So, Nil Ajen is right in stating that, "in the entire region of West Africa and all over Africa the issue of sex is not one that people feel comfortable discussing openly as some in the West do" (Ajen 1998: 130). Another scholar charged anthropologists, including Evans-Pritchard, for "not seriously investing same-sex patterns, failing to report what they do observe, and documenting what they report" (Murray and Roscoe 1998: xi). That anthropologists had to look hard enough for evidence of same-sex activities means that homosexuality was not a sanctioned sociogenic activity that was publicly approved and endorsed.

To dismantle the African rejection of public acceptance of homosexuality as foreign, Murray and Roscoe suggested, "Requires not only abandoning these myths but also suspending certain deeply held western beliefs and values concerning sexuality, love and personal relationships" (1998: xviii). The supposed imperativeness of deconstructing sex ethics has been made by the Ghanaian pro-LGBTQ+ activist who suggested that "deconstructing sexual deviance in the provisions of social taboos provides an avenue for further unpacking homophobia" (Mohammed 2020: 169). This suggestion falls short of sanity and wisdom -- all completely morphing into lack of appreciation of history. Indeed, such a suggestion is a major reason for the aggression of the LGBTQ+ community to saturate the public with themselves, including criminalising the teaching of Christian values in public schools, including the international organisations attempt at forcing the so-called comprehensive sex education into classrooms.

In all the pro-LGBTQ+ activists are profiled as seeking to subverting the values of civilisation is counterproductive because: First, the western values about sex and personal relationships are not western – else how is it that the west has overturned its own "western sex ethics" and become "non-western"? Second, the western values about sex are not western in the sense of human invention, they are part and parcel of the Judeo-Christian heritage that formed western civilisation. Thirdly, the idea of western values about sex and marriage, as decidedly western, is myopic in a sense that western sex ethics are shared values with the rest of the world – having been given by the uncreated Creator God. That in every civilisation heterosexual marriage had been publicly celebrated, endorsed, and sociogenically expressed in practice and proverbs and folklore means simply that: childbirth and population growth is the heartland of every civilisation – since God said, "Let them be fruitful and multiply". Heterosexual marriage is, therefore, a divine-cultural mandate to keep the world afloat. The opposite, homosexuality is a culture of death that can hardly be celebrated in public, but hopefully allowed to subsist in the cultic world. So, instead of subverting life-promoting values, shared by overwhelming Ghanaians and Africans and superimposing the sexual pleasures of a tiny minority on everyone else, it will be wise for pro-LGBTQ+ advocates to tactfully explore ways of protecting and providing help for homosexuals. Fortunately for Ghana, the current Ghanaian Bill in Parliament – which as I understand, it is about: "compassion is stronger than condemnation".

It is important to also say that this is far from conflating skills and moral life. In terms of skills, individual Akans were free to leverage their unique skills in promoting social and cosmic order. For this reason, among the Akan, individuals and families were noted for some particular skills. There were families with expertise in hunting, metalwork, carving, oratory, and song composition. It is, therefore, untrue to argue, from this perspective that the Akan communalistic system was oppressive of individuals.

The next point is the issue of morality. Among the Akan, individuals did not generate their own set of moral values. The moral life of individuals had/has implications for others – either their families or the entire community. As I have said, this is because the moral lives of individuals constitute the bridge between the spiritual and the material worlds. With the ancestors serving as the moral guardians of the Akan world, the moral lives of individuals were not matters of individual preferences and subjectivities.

The Akan communalistic moral values ensured that the moral lives of individuals in public were framed around collectively shared moral values. Individuals must conform to shared norms. And to ensure that individuals conform to the norms and virtues of society, beliefs, taboos, and folklore are used (Ackah 1988). Growing up as an Akan, one of the things we often enjoyed were storytelling, riddles, and dilemma tales. These were so important in the socialisation process that children in the cities in the 1980s enjoyed indigenous folklore.

Some proverbs brought out the criticality of applying ethics to life. For example, concerning the importance of truth ("nokware" [one mouth] – to be consistent in speech), an Ewe proverb says that "If a son had to use his penis to take the truth from his mother's vagina, it is not a taboo". I deliberately chose/used these "obscene" and seemingly vulgar expressions to indicate that proverbs are not prescriptions but descriptions of ethical principles that should guide social relations. In other words, in Akan cultures, the social structure of the family, as a union between a man and a woman to procreate, is treated as inviolable. These folklore genres had didactic values to shape the moral lives of individuals into communal living.

To consolidate all these in practice, the various sociogenic activities were creatively used. For example, marriage was a socially recognised union between a biological man and a biological woman for the prime purpose of procreation. Marriage was/is so important that for a woman not to marry is almost an anomaly, while an unmarried man is called a fool ("kwasea") (Gyekye 1998). The centrality of marriage and procreation remains very strong among the Akan. While it is the ideal of most Akan men and women to marry and have children, the over-emphasis on the two functions could be oppressive. Nevertheless, childbirth is considered the ultimate purpose of marriage among the Akan, such that barrenness and infertility are treated as threats to the continuity of human life and existence (Gyekye 1996). But this does not rule out the possibility of infertility and bareness. Instead, it demonstrates the extent to which Akan men and women could go to have children of their own. Again, whereas this could be read as oppressive, it forms part of the Akan social reality. When a woman is unable to give birth, she is called *obɔnini,* which means, "a barren, unfruitful woman or beast" (Christaller 1933: 38). This is because such a woman is said to undermine the ontological function of her womb, which is proverbially stated in Akan as, "birth is what has taken place in your womb" (Agyekum 2010: 118). But again, as I have said, if this ideal is enforced without any mitigation, women then find themselves as the oppressed group – because the challenge may be a medical one. Many proverbs indicated the significance of children. For example, a proverb said that "Children are worth more than gold" and "nothing is as painful as the one who dies childless". A man who is also unable to give birth is called *krawa* (a male beast that performs no function ontologically towards procreation) (Ibid. 120) or *saadwe.* Possibly, because men hardly talk consider their impotence as a subject of public discussion, possibly because of androcentric cultures, it is hard to tell the prevalence of male impotence in Ghana. But the penis of an impotent man was often referred to as *kɔti hɔtɔ* (a penis that has an empty sack – often referring the testicles that supplies the sperm). Both a woman and a man who died without the sex organs fulfilling the role of procreation hardly reincarnated upon their demise (Nkansa-Kyeremanteng 1996). Until my father died, he was always excited that when he died without anything (and indeed he had no car, house or plantation), he had sons who would "throw water on him" (bath him) before burial. The symbolic significance of this it marks the penultimate practice of closure before burial. Second, the ritual celebrates his achievement as a responsible father, given the tension in the Akan matrilineal system where tend to pay more attention to their sister's children then their own. Among the Akan of Assin Bosomadwe, it is a deceased father's honour for his son to lead his bathing as he is being prepared for burial.

The importance of childbirth is so central to the Akan mothers who want more children from their own children. This was the case when in 2019 while in Ghana for fieldwork for my doctoral studies at the University of Cambridge, my mother (who had had no western education) could not hold her surprise when I jokingly told her I would have two children. This was during a casual conversation I had with her and my elder brother. Both of them said in auto-response, "You see what western education has done to you!". This was, inter alia, because of the depopulation effect of the current coronavirus pandemic. But it is more difficult to force people to give birth than reduce birth rate through abortion and infanticide.

All said, the emphasis placed on childbirth has brought lots of pressure on women with some of them using every creative means to offset public attention on the childlessness state of their marriage. An example of this is the recent case of a 28-year-old Takoradi woman, Josephine Panyin Mensah who faked pregnancy (even after she had suffered a miscarriage early in her pregnancy) and pretended to have been kidnapped, leading to the loss of her twin children.[147] This situation of high expectation of childbirth after marriage needs to be measured to reduce the undue pressure on married women and their families. As I reflected over the trauma Josephine may have endured following the pressure on her to fake pregnancy, I penned an article to an imagined sister that was published by Ghanaweb.[148]

Nevertheless, the Ghanaian community cherishes childbirth. Children are not only a source of collateral social security; they are considered part of fulfilling God's command for humans 'to fill the earth'. The idea that marriage is a cultural creation is obviously one of the reasons that have been deployed by homosexuals and their academic advocates to push for alternative marriage unions. Consequently, homosexual advocates construe the religious push against the practice in Ghana as backwards and a relic of the religious bigotry of a pre-modern world. In view of this, I will discuss in the next

---

[147] Ghanaweb (24 September 2021), "Detail on why W/R Minister said Takoradi woman was not pregnant", https://www.ghanaweb.com/GhanaHomePage/NewsArchive/Detail-on-why-W-R-Minister-said-Takoradi-woman-was-not-pregnant-1364728, accessed 11 October 2021.

[148] Charles Prempeh (October 7, 2021) 'An open letter to my sisters and future daughters: know your ontological worth in a dangerous world', https://www.ghanaweb.com/GhanaHomePage/features/An-open-letter-to-my-sisters-and-future-daughters-Know-your-ontological-worth-in-a-dangerous-world-1374709 (Accessed: November 12, 2021).

section whether the current Bill in the parliament of Ghana that seeks to ban homosexual practices and advocates is a signifier of relapse to a premodern past.

Naming ceremonies were also important for socialising new members of society into society's cultural moral systems. During naming ceremonies among the Akan, drops of water and alcohol were left on the tongue of the child to signify the need for the child to be discerning in truth and falsehood. Similarly, names were carefully chosen to connect the child to exemplary ancestors. For example, most children have been named "Yaa Asantewaa" to reflect the unique heroism of a female Akan war of Asante root. So, every Akan child may have more than two names, including day-names that had theophoric significance. For example, the day name for a Saturday born, "Kwame or Ama" is used to imply a healer, since God as the biggest healer is called Kwame (Prempeh 2022). Names also reflected the socio-economic and political conditions under which an Akan child is born. A child called "Abayie" (you have come well) is given such a name to show the time of prosperity into which he or she was born. There are also theophoric names to reflect the religious context of the birth of a child. For example, a child may be called "Nyamekye" (God's gift) to indicate that his or her parents struggled to have a child; which is a gift from God. My son is called "Nhyira", (to wit: "Blessings") because my wife became pregnant a few months after our marriage (on March 5, 2017); I got scholarship offers to Oxford and Cambridge (just two weeks after our marriage) etc.

Funerals were also important in formulating and grounding society's values. The Akan word for a funeral is "ayie" which is a contraction of "aye yi ye" (to wit: "to praise"). Among the Akan, therefore, a funeral was an occasion for memorialising and canonising the good deeds of deceased persons, emphasising those that synchronise with the ideals of society. Thus, long before the European introduction of reading of tributes, Akan people had a practice of routinising society's virtues and values in funeral performances. This partly explains why hardly anything bad is said about dead people. In addition to funerals, songs, dance types, and food cultures are all designed to reflect the virtues and values of society.

The sociogenic structure of Akan moral values ensured social and cosmic order that undermined individual brazen expression of deviant characters, including homosexual practices and prostitution.[149] For this

[149] Professor Emmanuel Akyeampong of Harvard has written about prostitution among the Akan (see: "Sexuality and prostitution among the Akan of the Gold Coast

reason, if any Akan was suspected of a dubious moral life, he or she was simply told, "Stop hiding, so we will also stop asking who are you". Reasoning from this perspective, it is an inversion of Akan logic to assume that persons called "Kojo Bɛsia" or "Kwasi Bɛsia" were necessarily homosexuals. In fact, these terms are more Fante (one of the Akan languages) in designating a male with feminine characteristics than a gay person. It is also epistemic injustice to the Akan to assume that the name implied homosexuality. The names were hardly known among other Akan groups and other ethnic groups in Ghana. I do not know any local names for homosexuals, transgenders, trans-sexual, pan-sexual and all the "sexuals" in any Ghanaian language. But as part of the debate, the colloquial names for same-sex is *trumutrumu* (usually indicating anal sex).

Indeed, the issues of ethical and ontological boundaries and the sources of Akan moral values have caused philosophers to debate and diverge in opinion. Some have considered Akan values as springing from religion (these include Professor Kofi Asare Opoku); others think it is from the conscience (these include Professor Kwame Gyekye) while others, including Kwasi Wiredu think it is naturally derived. As an Akan and African Studies academic, alongside my evangelical Christianity, I sincerely think it was just for an academic exercise for these scholars to have split hairs over the source of Akan ethics. Having treated these sources as discreet and mutually exclusive was the challenge all these authors had.

It is rather puzzling that they never saw these sources as mutually inclusive. Non-recognition of the mutual inclusivity of the various sources of morality by these eminent scholars raises critical issues about morality and individual lives. If someone does not believe in religion, can the person be moral? If morality comes from the conscience and society, can people be excused when they break moral boundaries because they are considered non-rational? Finally, if morality is naturally derived from human observation, then why must society make conscious efforts in socialising its members into its moral culture?

All this implies the need for scholars to consider the mutual inclusivity of the various sources of morality in Akan cultures. For example, because God created human beings (in his image from the Christian perspective), human beings are moral agents with a conscience guiding their moral actions. Also, as creatures of God,

---

c. 1650-1950" Past and Present, no. 156 (1997), pp. 144-173), but that was not a normative and acceptable practice for free women in Akan society.

human beings are rational beings, capable of observation and analysis to formulate rules to govern their lives. And finally, since the Akan society was not atheistic (away from the simplistic atheistic analysis of Kwasi Wiredu and Okot p'Bitek), God was considered central to the Akan moral life. The centrality of God in the construction of Akan morality was because of the non-binary between the physical and spiritual worlds of Akan cosmogony. More significantly, religion or God as the source of morality renders it imperative for people to obey the rules of society.

While individuals can and must be morally conscious in their social relationships, the issue about why an atheist should do good is not just philosophical, but existentially relevant. Because if one should "do good for the sake of goodness" without any reward or punishment for doing otherwise, why must people be bothered about morality? If there are no externally compelling reasons for people to abide by the moral obligations of society, but rather one's own subjectivities, then it is nearly impossible for cosmic order to be maintained in Akan societies. For the Akan, therefore, the idea that the ancestors, as moral guardians punish and reward the living based on their observation or deviation from moral codes respectively is very key in the formulation of morality.

As we see the sources of Akan moral and ethical values as mutually inclusive, it becomes possible to disentangle moral debate from a rigid binary between individualism and communalism. It also helps in disengaging Akan moral values from the binaries of modernity and tradition where sexual values against homosexual practices are treated as atavism with tradition while sexual liberation of the 1960s is treated as modern. As I have already indicated, homosexuality is a tradition in western histories not just modern. If it is modern, it is because Judeo-Christian values suppressed it and with the pushing of Judeo-Christian values to the background or fringes, the west now feels free to modernise their tradition. But of course, not without cultural wars between religious people and non-religious people over sexual and moral revolution.

More significantly the non-binary between the Akan worlds, morphing into the use of sociogenic activities to mould society defines the idea of individual rights. Individuals have rights and freedom over the kinds of skills and talents they possess. Individuals have the freedom to be creative in the critical ways they put their skills and talents. But an individual hardly has unrestrained freedom to determine their moral values, especially those that affect others. Given that the

Akan world incorporates the individual in both the private and public spheres, linked to the spiritual world, the individual's private moral life is as important as his or her public life. For this reason, individuals do not formulate their own moral values. Chiefs, the canonised mediators between the ancestors and the living were/are responsible for ensuring that the ethical codes are efficiently enforced.

It is the difficulty put in the way of an individual to morally self-determining that Ali Mazrui was not entirely correct about when he said indigenous cultures were "tolerant". Indeed, indigenous cultures/religions were tolerant to the extent that emerging cultures and values do threaten social and cosmic order. For example, when some of the practices of the missionaries, especially among the Basel missionaries of the early 19th Century among some Akan groups, in trying to set up separate communities for their converts generated tension. Some Akan chiefs read these separate communities, known as "Salems" that the missionaries created as threatening the unity of chiefly state and the ability of chiefs to enforce ethical codes. Similarly, when the British colonial governor in the 19th Century attempted to "secularise" chieftaincy by determining what Akan Christian converts could do and could not do, was read by the chiefs as an affront to chiefly authority. So, while chiefs and indigenous cultures were tolerant, they tolerate individuals whose moral lives and beliefs do not threaten social and cosmic order. This means that while marriage and naming ceremonies were largely family issues, chiefs as the owners of the land *("hene")* were the ultimate source or the arbiter (usually through the *ahemaa* or queen mother – used to denote the most important woman in the Davidic Kingdom (in ancient Israel) in family disputes. Before I discuss how colonialism and modern governance have complicated the roles of chiefs, I will discuss the signification of women-related proverbs among the Akan.

Women in Akan proverbs

I have already indicated that several of the Ghanaian feminist scholars have their versions of interpreting proverbs. As I have mentioned, these feminist scholars hardly discussed the significance of social order as opposed to individual justice and rights in the governance of Akan societies. The idea of order structured gender roles, based on the collective expectations of society. I have stated the importance of marriage as the means of procreation to the Akan. In other words, for the Akan, marriage or heterosexual relations are inbuilt in ethical and ontological boundaries that repudiate the open practice of homosexuality and all the "trans" sexualities. It could be argued that traditional marriages based on bilocal residence where men and women lived in separate spaces seems to create more possibilities for same-sex sexualities than spousal co-residence does. But, as I have said, there is hardly any evidence among the Akan that same-sex sexualities were accepted as sociogenic practice. It is also true that even as part of bilocal practice, men still controlled the sexuality of women (Atobrah and Awedoba 2017).

The significance of procreation to ensure that continuity of society explains the logicality of proverbs such as "A woman's glory is (lit. what causes her to be respected) marriage". This proverb, contrary to feminist interpretation never implied the ontological inferiority of women. It rather fitted the ontological order of the Akan, where women were the only ones responsible for carrying a pregnancy, for expanding the matrilineage and birthing children who would perform labour for their uncles (mothers' brothers).

But as I flagged in the above section, the overemphasis Akan people continue to place on marriage for procreation could be oppressive to women, and, to some extent, men. Women are compelled to use all sorts of means to carry a pregnancy and give birth to please their husbands – both historically and recently – families and society. In simple terms, women are often pressured to prove their "worth" through childbirth. This was/is the case with both matrilineal and patrilineal societies (Amenga-Etego 2013).[150] If women are unable to give birth, mostly for no fault of theirs, husbands use that to divorce them or commit adultery – exposing their wives to all forms of risks, including venereal diseases. Women have been compelled to cow to these pressures by resorting to all charlatans for help – easing of male-centric oppressive regime. Often, Ghana continues to witness charlatans who parade themselves as gynaecologists only to exploit women. Amid the Corona Virus pandemic, one of the worst stories of men abusing desperate women was uncovered by the Fourth Estate media house, led by Ghanaian investigative journalist, Manasseh Azure. Azure uncovered a sex predator who sexually abused several child-searching desperate mothers.[151]

---

150 Rose M. Amenga-Etego, "Categorization of women and human rights," *CrossCurrents* (2013): 138-147.

151 Clement Edward Kumsah (21 September 2021), "'Video Trailer: The licensed sex predator': investigation by the Fourth Estate,"

It is social challenges such as these that feminist scholars have responded to. But, as I have discussed so far, they mostly tend to overreach their response. It is either they encourage women to delay marriage, by practising the current cultural imperative of career before marriage (to take care of themselves as economically independent agents) or not to marry at all. In some instances, women have appealed to legislation, such as the Domestic Violence Act ("DV Act"), passed in 2007 to register their protests against men's dominance and imperialism in marriage. The law sought to criminalise all forms of sexual abuse against women. As expected, the bill, before it became a law, was protested by traditional authorities and religious leaders.

Notwithstanding all the challenges that have burdened women and marriage, it is critical to mention that the gender differential among the Akan never implied any ontological inferiority of women to men. Among the Akan, men and women are ontologically the same – carrying the same worth. Men and women largely differed in terms of function: men performing instrumental roles (providing, protecting, and leading their families) while women performed expressive roles (childbirth, nurturing and homemaking).

The Akan view of the woman's role was reinforced by Christianity in the 19th Century, as the Christian missionaries trained and re-emphasised women's domestic roles (Sill 2010).[152] This was when Queen Victoria's vision of infusing Christian ethics into the British Empire inspired missionaries to establish schools to train women into the performance of expressive roles, under Judeo-Christian family ethics. Schools that the missionaries built trained women for home activities, such as sewing, cooking etc. In short, women were trained to be good wives. But similarly, some women gathered skills that ensured their economic empowerment. The Akan vision of women, reinforced by Christianity, chimes with Islamic gender norms, where women are homemakers and men, providers.

Given the situation of gendered education, at independence, very few women were given administrative offices. It must be stated that while feminist scholars have sought to demonstrate that the Akan women were politically participative, the exercise of power rested in the hands of men. Women largely led women -- issues. On a few occasions, there were instances of women leading men in military adventures like

---

https://thefourthestategh.com/2021/09/21/video-trailer-the-licensed-sex-predator-investigation-by-the-fourth-estate/, accessed: 14 November 2021.

152 Ulrike Sill, *Encounters in quest of Christian womanhood: The Basel mission pre- and early colonial Ghana* (Leiden: Brill, 2010).

the cases of Yaa Asantewaa and Nana Dokuaa of Akropong Akwapim. Otherwise, political power and governance rested with women, against Rattray's observation that the woman's stool was the most important in the retinue of Akan chiefly regalia.

In summing up this section, I want to reiterate the point that Akan proverbs in general and specifically on women are not prescriptive to be taken literally. They are descriptions that reflect deep principles of society. They also teach didactic values to govern all human activities. The proverbs also reflect how the private and public lives of individuals cannot be considered mutually exclusive. Similarly, I must also repeat that Akan societies were more concerned about order than the simplicity of justice as individual freedom and rights. It was this quest for an ordered society that invested a significant amount of power in chiefs and religious or ritual functionaries to ensure that society functioned in support of human flourishing.

The logic of ontological and "social" inequality

In the discussion so far, I have attempted to prove that Akan proverbs are far from being arbitrary and downright androcentric. I have indicated that there was/is purpose in Akan proverbs – including those that are misinterpreted by feminists as promoting patriarchalism. In this section, I want to highlight one lived social reality that several feminist scholars and those who sympathise with their cause often talk about how feminist can negotiate ontological boundary that is biologically determined. The basic argument in this section is that the biological or what I refer to as "ontological" difference between men and women that finds expression in "social" ordering is a necessary "evil" to ensuring cosmic order. To ground in practicality or praxes, I will give some examples, based on my interactions and interviews with women in some areas in Ghana. These women transcend social boundaries: including education, religion, ethnicity, and economic statuses.

Having set the above premise, I want to state that, from the discussion and responses of feminists both radical and liberals – to what they perceive as structural injustice in a "man's world", the issue is more of these women seeking equality. These women want equality that would enable them to do as men do and to act like men act. For this reason, the world is replete with labels such as "What men can do, women can do better". While this terse statement is very confusing, it has partly supported the idea of "gender blindness" (disregarding all visible and psychological differences between men and women) and total disregard for any distinction between a biological male and a biological female. More recently, in the Western world, including England where I studied, when one is filling an official form for an official assignment, as part of the traditional "male" and "female" distinction, one is asked to either remain silent about one's "sex" or choose "other". This implies that one has the right to construct and determine one's sex and must be recognised as such. Beyond that one can transition from one sex to the other – known as transgender. That is not only the issue, one can keep transitioning from one gender to the other at will and appeal to the state for legal support for such culturally-induced biological transitions.

Much as these multiple transitions have their own socio-psychological impact on those who engage in such a practice, the undercurrent issue informing this contemporary fuss is human discontentment. Discontentment is a fact of life. It is a lived experience that virtually every human being experiences. As a result of human discontentment with the imperfection of the world, a world that is in constant crisis, human beings have articulated their creativity, competence, confidence, and skills in the areas of science, philosophy, and economics to advance human flourishing. Discontent, in this sense, is a human race against natural imperfection.

Given the ontological inequality between men and women, which is more about the function that quality of being, both men and women have misconstrued their difference to ferment tension. Historically, while some men have leveraged women's biological characteristics that make them temporarily or permanently withdraw from active public to bracket women from collective and equal access to the resources of the world, women have also reacted, as we have seen, by construing marriage and childbirth as a form of oppression. In the end, both men and women are angry at each other, men seeking to renegade their role as providers, women are also reneging their role as nurturers. These have not borne out well for the world, especially as mimic desire – men wanting to be women and women wanting to be men – continue to deepen gender-based hatred and conflict.

As I have already stated, the anger and hatred from both men and women and against each other are because of the misinterpretation of African proverbs. Men and women were to complement each other with their uniqueness. This brings us back to Francis Nyamnjoh's idea of incompleteness and the need for conviviality. Men are incomplete without women, just as women are incomplete without men – especially in terms of fulfilling procreative and recreative ambitions of life. This reasonably and concurrently implies that instead of men and women seeing their differences as a reason to treat the Other as inferior or superior and to court unnecessary competition, men and women must appreciate ontological differences as an existential reality and work to ensure collaboration to make the world better.

As men and women fail to recognise their ontological differences as a means to forge collaboration to salvage the imperfection they see in the world, women, unfortunately, have tended to suffer more. For example, in my formal and informal interviews with women, I have been pained to see several women, who publicly claim to be feminists go through different layers of self-imposed oppression. Usually, when I broach the conversation about the challenges radical feminism pose to the world, the first impulse of my female academics is to rebut or take the defensive position. But when I carefully choreograph the discussion in a mood of reflexivity, pointing to practical examples, they tend to be quiet and sober in admitting that radical feminism is a threat to the human social order. One of them always complains about the trouble of taking care of her two-year-old daughter and alongside her doctoral research.[153] The other who has recently completed doctoral studies in Astrophysics said she is now concentrating on building her family, as she nurtures her second child. She said, "I am not in competition with any of my male colleagues. I will move at my own pace."[154] Similarly, while I was teaching African Studies at the African University College of Communications, a private-based communications university in Accra-Ghana (2013-2017), I had several of my evening classes made up of young mothers who often complained about hardly seeing their children. Several of them were so distressed about the near-collapse of emotional and social bonding between them and their children that they would often come to me in tears.

The challenge with all this is that the extended family has nearly run into a comatose state in Accra and several cities in the country. As more and more people move into the city of Accra, the extended family continues to break down at a pace that would have been imaginable a few years back. This implies the need to review earlier scholarship on elitism and Akan families. In the 1980s and 1990s, Professor Christine

[153] Personal communication with Lydia Amoah, doctoral candidate Institute of African Studies, University of Ghana, Legon, on January 4, 2022.

[154] Interview with Dr Benedicta Araba Akyeneba Woode on December 12, 2021 in Accra.

Oppong's research indicates that Akan elite families have circumvented the challenges of fathers turning away from their children to take up their sisters' children, based on matrilineal logic. But recent experiences of women, based on my interviews with several of them, indicate that as more elite women join the world of work, they tend to suffer from the performance of dual responsibilities.

As women are pushed deep into the world of work, especially weekend banking which employs more women than men, women tend to provide for their families and also nurture their children. This is largely because the chances of men getting jobs are becoming thinner compared to women. Similarly, while more women are employed in the private sector, as the state encourages more private partnerships in solving the challenge of graduate unemployment, these private enterprises, for profit-oriented and social reasons, tend to give a good image of themselves by engaging more women than men. But these enterprises subtly discourage the young women they employ from marrying early or delaying marriage and childbirth or both. These subtle means include deliberately not employing young and recently married women; asking about the next five years ambitions of young unmarried women; and giving short maternity leave when a young woman gives birth – while this issue of short maternal leave is a national or possibly a global issue, it is very dire in private companies who sometimes do not even pay these young women who go on maternity leave.

Given this situation, several of the young women I interviewed are very frustrated. For example, Tina, a banker who is 35 years and unmarried said to me,

> At my age, remaining unmarried is a huge challenge to me. But the challenge is more than just remaining single, as it is also about the difficulty in marrying any time soon. Because my bosses may hardly give me a long leave of absence to nurture a family."[155]

With all these challenges culminating in several women not marrying early or not having children early enough, older women I engaged in my recent interview alleged that the perceived increased cases in fibroid among Ghanaian women are because of women delaying marriages and not having children early. Agnes Amoah for example said that "Fibroid is a sickness of an idle womb." Others also claim that "bad girls don't get fibroid, but good girls do." Whether these are really true or a socio-

[155] Interview with Tina Obodai on December 5, 2021 in Accra.

biological change in women needs further research attention. But the point in all this is that for men and women to upset the challenges that have burdened them, especially women, there is a need for an amicable solution. A solution built on forgiveness, as several women have taken to illusions and unrealistic ideals of radical feminism because of the deliberate irresponsibility of the men in their lives. I bring in the issue of fibroids to demonstrate the complexity of sexuality in both social and health of women and men.

Forgiveness and Gender: Addressing gender inequality in Akan proverbs

My discussion has clearly shown that gender-related tension, especially in the matrilineal Akan system where women, though considered the source of life, take up a role that is generally perceived as subservient to their male counterparts. The tension then morphs into radical feminism, is largely as a result of anger and mimetic desire in men-women relations. This is because, men have often leveraged women's biological characteristics to push women into a position that is indicative of men's superiority and women's inferiority. Since this constitutes a form of injustice to women, in history, women have also deployed several ways of destabilising what they consider as men's inhumanity to women. One such way is women using their "bodies" to lure men into submission. History is replete with instances where men have been cowed into submissiveness to women because of sex. Some men have been embarrassed as they fell to women's bodily allurement. A recent case is Ghana's current Minister of National Security, whose recorded video with a young woman in a very amorous scene inundated social media, including Facebook. In the video, the young woman, maybe in her early 30s was commanding the Minister to show his underpants and other sexually-suggestive things.

So, as women become highly sensitive about their biological characteristics being used by men to perpetuate injustice against women, I imagine women have increasingly become aware of the world's social imperfection. Given that social imperfection tips the balance against a world where everyone should have an opportunity to thrive, since the beginning of human history, human beings have made every single effort to turn the clock against social imperfection.

The human quest for justice is such that historically, the idea of "forgiveness" was hardly known in human relations. Perhaps, the only point where we read about the word "forgiveness" was when the brothers of Joseph "invented" a story about their father Jacob, asking him (Joseph) to forgive them (Genesis 50:16-18). That forgiveness was virtually unknown in human history has been aptly captured by David Konstan when he said as the thesis of his book, *Before Forgiveness*, that;

> The modern concept of forgiveness, in the full or rich sense of the term, did not exist in classical antiquity, that is, in ancient Greece and Rome, or at all events that it played no role whatever in the ethical thinking of those societies. It is not fully present in the Hebrew Bible, nor again in the New Testament or the early Jewish and Christian commentaries on the Holy Scriptures; it would still be centuries – many centuries – before the idea of interpersonal forgiveness, and the set of values and attitudes that necessarily accompany and help to define it, would emerge (Konstan 2010: ix).

As Konstan observed, instead of forgiveness, human beings were rather accustomed to appeasement, where the guilty person declares that he is not a threat to the offended person. Meanwhile, the idea of appeasement as a conflict management strategy is also known to animals. The lack of forgiveness in the premodern world was also because of the absence of repentance and confession (Ibid. 11). The lack of forgiveness made feud a major practice in some pre-modern societies. For example, the resort to feud was, therefore, a major feature of the pre-Islamic world, such that the Arabs had an idiom that, "Help your brother whether he is an oppressor or he is an oppressed one."[156] In all this, it is critical to mention that the idea of appeasement and vengeance is hardly unique to human beings. This is precisely because, apart from human beings who resort to appeasement to restore social stability, animals also do the same (de Waal 1989: 38).

My emphasis on forgiveness is that there is hardly any disputation that men and women have had to struggle in social spaces that tend to favour men. I surmise, based on what I have said above, men's appropriation of marriage to oppress the supposed human other is part of the reason tension has built over the Bill. As men and women are frustrated by the imperfection in the world, it is important that they see this imperfection as an existential lived reality, so that instead of engaging the underbelly of discontent, they need to see it as an opportunity to reinvent the world – through heterosexual procreation.

---

156 Muhammed Muhsin Khan. *The Translation of the Meanings of Sahih Al-Bukhari* (Arabic-English). The Book of Al-Mazalim (The Oppressions), Riyadh, Saudi Arabia: Darussalam Publishers and Distributors, p. 361.

Nevertheless, the need to recuperate the historic religious means of procreation should be carried out in the spirit of compassion to individuals who identify with other sexualities. This implies that need for societies to destabilise western fawning individualism that rather throws society out of social order by giving people opportunity to blame and ventilate their anger, instead of taking responsibility to change the reality that they see and dislike. To state my point differently, instead of women resorting to blame culture and men seeking solace in superficial penitentiary culture, men and women need to collaborate to restore order to the world. They should recapitulate the divine-cultural mandate for a "man and a woman coming together to fill the earth, as the man tills and keeps the Garden." This also means that the moral outrage that is necessary to change the world should rather focus on responding to a world in need of the redemption of the children of the Lord to redeem it. So, moral outrage used properly and functionally becomes similar to Jesus whipping criminals out of His Temple.

Similarly, the Lord is charging men and women to whip all forms of injustice. As the world looks forward to a perfected world yet to come, men and women should see the asymmetric lived socio-biological world as an opportunity to work together or complement one another to advance human flourishing. In my reading of Akan proverbs, this is what the Akan proverbs that have been misconstrued as oppressive sought to achieve. In other words, the Akan world sought to achieve cosmic and social harmony by ensuring that ontological boundaries were kept clear, especially in terms of what men and women should and could do. This is because men and women are not ontologically the same in terms of ontological function and mission. This ontological difference is the affirming of life, rather than negating it.

My prescription of forgiveness to heal our world of social imperfection is because Christianity is based on forgiveness – forgiveness not to overlook evil. But forgiveness to give room for human beings to repent and re-strategise to work with God to bring about social and cosmic harmony. Forgiveness also helps us to understand that justice will fail men and women, if we resort to legalities as opposed to social covenant to resolve social issues. For this reason, the appeal the LGBTQA+ to the state for legal protection as opposed to social ordering of the world would only exacerbate the social imperfection of the world. As I have said, in all these efforts at canonising the virtues of society, chiefs played an important role.

Chieftaincy, modern state, religion and family issues

As part of the controversies over the LGBTQ debates, chiefs have involved themselves as major stakeholders. As the traditional ruling elites, who have constitutionally mandated to act as custodians of culture, several of the chiefs in Ghana have aligned with the Family Bill. The other point is also that, unlike Tanzania, Julius Nyerere, the country's first president banned the institution, the same is not true of Ghana. In Ghana, chiefs are the custodians of about 80 per cent of land, especially in their constituencies. Currently, since the turn of the millennium, several of these chiefs have identified themselves as Pentecostal Christians, assigning themselves the role of keeping the Pentecostal idea of holiness. Part of this role is that chiefs seek to reconcile the Pentecostalists' discontent with the LGBTQ issue and governance in their traditional areas. Meanwhile, chiefs are expected to be leaders of all, not a section of their constituency whose sexual preferences diverge. But all this means two things: First, while, as we have said, in precolonial times, creative measures such as the invocation of cultic space would have been offered such people, today the story is hardly the same. The second is that as custodians of cultures, discussing the role of chiefs in the Ghanaian society may help in fostering an imagined uniform and inclusive community around dialogue, tact and wisdom.

During the late colonial era of the 19th Century, the British observed that chiefs were the valve around which Akan societies run – leading them to often refer to the Akan groups as "the chief and people of the Gold Coast" (Boateng 1996: 144). But to quell any potential opposition from the chiefs, among other financial and economic reasons, the British strategically introduced the indirect rule system. With the indirect rule system, the authority of chiefs as the mediators between the ancestors and the living, reflecting on the non-binary nature of Akan cosmogony began to suffer. As the British introduced secularisation of chieftaincy politics, chiefs became aware of the erosion of their authority.

The complexities of colonial exploitation made chiefs devise different ways of exploiting their own people. As representatives of their people before the colonial administration, chiefs were nearly reduced to puppets. This was largely because chiefs became the medium through which the colonialists communicate the power of control and dominance over the colonised. Thus, through the idea of indirect rule, which the British introduced as a form of governing their colonies in the late colonial era, chiefs were complexly integrated into the axis of colonial governance (Rathbone 2000). They became more powerful before their people – power they had hardly enjoyed prior to colonial rule; and became very weak before the colonisers – a state of powerless they had hardly anticipated until the colonial era. That chiefs became overly powerful before their people made chiefs what Mamdani referred to as decentralised despotism (Mamdani, 1996: 37-61).[157] While Mamdani is right to some extent, his conclusion was/is rather a hasty generalisation as not every chief cowered to colonial pressures without protests. There are several accounts of chiefs in the Gold Coast and Africa who protested against colonial rule and as result forced into exile by the colonisers (Boahen 1987; Keulder 2010; Aldrich 2018).[158] Also, some chiefs struggled to exercise control over their people in some of the rural areas in sub-Saharan Africa because these chiefs loss the trust of their people (Albrecht 2017; Owusu-Sarpong 2003).[159] So, instead of such blanket conclusions, we could rather argue that the colonial intrusion and the nexus they had with chiefs produced a paradoxical effect on chiefs (Akurang-Parry 2000-2001).[160] Even so, it is important to mention as part of the involvement of chiefs in the sexuality politics and cultural revolution should be read in light of the fact that chiefs have been amenable enough to transform themselves through education and creative innovation to participate in postcolonial governance in Ghana/Africa as part of the ruling elites (Prempeh 2021).[161]

---

[157] Mahmood Mamdani, *Citizen and Subject: Contemporary Africa and the Legacy of Late Colonialism* (New Jersey: Princeton University Press, 1996).

[158] Albert A. Boahen, *African perspectives on colonialism* (Baltimore: Johns Hopkins University Press, 1987); Christiaan Keulder, "Traditional leaders," In Christiaan Keulder (ed), *State, society and democracy: A reader in Namibian politics*, 150 167 (Namibia: Konrad Adenauer Stiftung, 2010); Robert Aldrich, *Banished potentates: Dethroning and exiling indigenous monarchs under British and French colonial rule, 1815-1955* (Manchester: Manchester University Press, 2018).

[159] Peter Albrecht, "The hybrid authority of Sierra Leone's chiefs," *African Studies Review*, 60, 3 (2017): 159-180; Christiane Owusu-Sarpong, "Setting the Ghanaian context of rural government: Traditional authority values," in Donald Ray and P.S. Reddy (eds), *Grassroots chiefs in Africa and the Afro-Caribbean governance?* 31-67 (Calgary, Alberta: University of Calgary Press, 2003).

[160] Kwabena A. Akurang-Parry, "Labour Mobilization and African Response to the Compulsory Labour Ordinance in the Gold Coast (Colonial Ghana), 1875-1899," *Transactions of the Historical Society of Ghana*, New Series, 4/5 (2000-2001): 83-105.

[161] Charles Prempeh, "Religious innovations of chieftaincy in Ghana: Pentecostal Christianity and the complex persistence and transformation of Akan chieftaincy" *Religion Compass*, (2021): 1-13, DOI: 10.1111/rec3.12426

Similarly, as the British interfered with the locales of chiefs, chiefs started losing some control over their "subjects" as the British governor usually shielded Christian converts of Akan societies from undertaking tasks that these British viewed as contradicting Christian beliefs. Among other groups like the Krobo, the British abolished the Dipo rites, which traditional authorities used to initiate and socialise girls into Krobo identity, including womanhood (Quashigah 1999). The Krobo example bring out the extent to which the colonial influence was not limited to the Akan, but had a cascading effect to include other groups in the colony.

As chiefs sought to redefine the role of chiefs, by secularising the institution, the emerging nationalists of the late 19th and early 20th Centuries worked with chiefs to decolonise the colony. But the nationalists of the post-World War II, including Nkrumah, were not comfortable with the role chiefs played in instituting colonialism. At independence, therefore, Nkrumah made several efforts to either demolish the institution like his contemporary Julius Nyerere of Tanzania had done or weaken it. Because he could not weaken it, probably because of the overwhelming opposition from and influence of the Asante Golden Stool, which resented any non-Asante exercising authority over the Stool, Nkrumah failed. This is not to say that he did not succeed in meddling in chieftaincy politics through destooling and enstooling chiefs who either opposed or supported him respectively (Rathbone 2000).[162]

Chiefs regained a few of their glories during the reign of Busia and subsequent heads of state. In 1975, the status of chiefs in Ghana decisively changed. A major shift in cultural policy was announced, one that recognised the relevance of chiefs, sought to incorporate chiefs into the country's new cultural revivalism agenda, and promoted chieftaincy as the cultural bedrock of Ghanaian society.[163] Aside from the official reasons Acheampong's regime gave for incorporating chiefs into his regime, there was his undoubted attempt to ward off criticism against his union government (forming a government through the alliance of the military, police, and civilians) agenda through the incorporation of chiefs in the 1970s (Owusu 1979).

It was, however, during the 1992 Republic Constitution of Ghana that chiefs were freed from partisan political influence. The 1992

---

162 Richard Rathbone, *Nkrumah and the Chiefs: Politics of Chieftaincy in Ghana 1951-1960* (Athens: Ohio University Press, 2000).

163 Ministry of Education and Culture, *Cultural Policy in Ghana* (Paris: UNESCO Press, 1975), 12.

Constitution which restored Ghana's democratic governance insulated chiefs from unnecessary political influence. Chiefs were rightly recognised as custodians of Ghanaian cultures – responsible for determining the cultural values that resonate with national aspirations. The implication of shielding chiefs from political interference for Akan customs and identities has been enablement offered traditional political elites to recuperate some indigenous roles, as such as mediators and guardrails of the ethical and ontological boundaries of heterosexual marriage.

To integrate indigenous culture into Ghana's quest for development in the Fourth Republic,[164] the government, under the leadership of J.A. Kufuor, commissioned a committee of scholars who drafted the Ghana Cultural Policy in 2004. The policy's aim was to ensure the growth of Ghana's cultural institutions and make them relevant to human development, democratic governance, and national integration (Hagan 2004: 10). Because of this, the policy maintained that the institution of chieftaincy was the kingpin of Ghanaian traditional culture, and that its contemporary relevance should be recognised. It also concurred that over the years, the institution of chieftaincy had maintained its vitality, resilience and relevance, and that it remained an important anchor of cultural life in all communities and the nation as a whole. (Hagan 2004: 14). Besides the reasons the government gave for incorporating chiefs, the policy was strategically drafted to seal the political support of the regime in the various traditional jurisdictions in Ghana.

As custodians of culture, chiefs serve as a bulwark against the erosion of Ghanaian family values. Most importantly is the fact that several of the southern chiefs have become evangelical Christians (Prempeh 2021b), while the reformist Muslim clerics, partly the Ahlusunaa, are entering into the domain of chieftaincy as chiefs. Given the family values of Christianity, Islam and indigenous religions tend to converge seamlessly on procreation as important in the family, chiefs have been very vocal in denouncing local and international pressures on the political elites to decriminalise homosexuality. As the custodians of custom and culture, the House have stated concerning the current debate over homosexuality in Ghana that:

> The House wants to state without equivocation that throughout history, nowhere does the Ghanaian culture subscribe to LGBTQ+ which is a taboo, inhuman and alien to our society ... In God's wisdom, man and

[164] The Fourth Republic marks Ghana's fourth recourse to democratic governance after the military had interrupted civilian or democratic administration.

> woman were created to fulfil the procreation of humans on earth to satisfy God's will … The symbolism for sex [and] marriage was between man and woman, as such, the idea of man marrying man and woman marrying woman is an abomination to our tradition and culture as Ghanaians …[165]

The force of chiefs in family matters is such that they still remain the custodians of the land in Ghana, controlling about 90 per cent of lands in the country. This resonates with the Akan origin of the word chief as "he ne". "He" means boundary, while "ne" means "owner". Put together, *hene* or *ohene* is the "owner of the land". This etymological origin of chiefs cannot be taken for granted, as chiefs continue to exert lots of influence over the cultural and political lives of their respective traditional areas or constituencies of authority. Under Ghana's "secular" politics, chiefs could ban political activists or parties from operating in their jurisdiction. An example is when in September 2019, a year before the country's general elections, the Akyem Abuakwa Traditional Council issued a three-day ultimatum to the National leadership of the opposition National Democratic Congress (NDC) to render a direct, clear and unambiguous public apology to the Okyehene, Osagyefo Amoatia Ofori Panin and Okyeman or be "banned from all official functions organised by the Ofori Panin Stool".[166] This ban was after Mr Kwame Zu, the Ashanti Regional Secretary of the NDC, was reported to have made offensive comments about the Okyenhene. To avoid this risk, the NDC disassociated themselves from the comments made by Kwame Zu, as they apologised to Okyenhene.[167]

Similarly, the Asantehene on October 28, 2021, reiterated his ownership over all Asante lands, following reports of some of his sub-chiefs and individuals encroaching on lands of the Kwame Nkrumah University of Science and Technology, Otumfuo Osei II, Asantehene and chancellor of the university, said on the 70th anniversary of the university that:

---

[165] Promotion of Proper Human Sexual Rights and Ghanaian Family Values Bill, 2021 (n.d.), p. 1.

[166] Ghanaweb (24 September 2019) "You have 3 days to apologize to Okyenhene – Okyeman to NDC", https://www.ghanaweb.com/GhanaHomePage/NewsArchive/You-have-3-days-to-apologize-to-Okyenhene-Okyeman-to-NDC-783286, accessed 15 November 2021.

[167] Ghanaweb (26 September 2019), "NDC disassociates from comments against Okyenhene". September 26, 2019. https://www.ghanaweb.com/GhanaHomePage/NewsArchive/NDC-dissociates-from-comments-against-Okyenhene-783817, accessed 15 November 2021.

> Let me warn the communities, the chiefs and whoever, that the lands are mine and you are just caretakers to those lands. There's no family land here in Ashanti. No Abusuapanyin (head of a family) can claim any land belongs to him and therefore has the right to alienate a portion of the university land. You can go to any court. Take it there. I am also sure there will be a judge there who will know that the constitution of Ashanti says that there is no family land in the Ashanti Region … get the lawyers to take you to court but I'll get the court to overturn their decisions to affirm my authority on the lands here.[168]

These are not words to be taken lightly, as they reflect the authority chiefs exert in Ghana. By referring to Ashanti Constitution, the Asantehene was demonstrating his source of authority as traditionally rooted in Asante region and law, not necessarily the "secular" constitution of the land. Similarly, the Asantehene was expressing his authority over any lawyer or judge who may want to use contemporary legal principles to circumvent his authority over the lands in Asanteman.

The importance of chiefs in Ghanaian politics is such that while the 1992 constitution for various reasons, including protecting the dignity of chieftaincy from the banalities of partisan politics, precludes chiefs from politics, chiefs are not without influence. While every society is largely a social construct, traditional societies are of a different kind. This is because while the modern state is established on legalities (social construct), the traditional states in Ghana, predating "modern" politics is based on some form of a covenant (established on religion and shared cultural values). Impliedly, people are usually connected to the "modern" state as legal citizens and their lives in the public sphere are governed by laws. On the contrary, people's connection with their chiefs is rooted in culture, values, and beliefs. So, whereas partisan politics through occasional elections bind politicians and citizens, the relationship between chiefs and their people is socially defined and is rooted in the sociogenic activities I mentioned above. The central role chiefs play in the socio-political structuring of their respective traditional areas is part of the reason they often get involved with sensitive matters, such as the LGBTQ.

---

[168] Ghanaweb (30 October 2021), "All Ashanti lands are mine, you can go to court – Otumfuo warns", https://www.ghanaweb.com/GhanaHomePage/NewsArchive/All-Ashanti-lands-are-mine-you-can-go-to-court-Otumfuo-warns-1391434, 15 November 2021.

Similarly, since the former Asantehene Otumfor Opoku Ware II introduced the idea of Nkosuohene (Development Chiefs) in 1985 (Bob-Milliar 2009), prominent Asante of non-royal origin and other non-Asante have been made non-royal chiefs to contribute to the development of Asanteman. This practice has been replicated in virtually all the traditional areas in Ghana, including areas where Euro-Americans and Asians have been made Development Chiefs. With such a development, Akan chieftaincy has extended their authority to the Akan diaspora in North America, especially the United States of America. Asantehene often travels to the US to participate in Asante festivals or install chiefs to represent him in the diaspora.

The increasing importance of chiefs is also because ethnicity in politics remains quite strong in Ghana. As the two main political parties, the New Patriotic Party (NPP) and the National Democratic Congress (NDC) are identified with the Asante (Akan) and Ewe respectively, people often appeal to their chiefs to compel politicians to extend social services to their traditional areas. Also, since 1992, chiefs have continued to stray from the rule that bans them from participating in active politics (unless they renounce their stool) to support one political party or the other.

As chiefs continue to refer to their traditional root to affirm their authority over "secular" norms and rules, it leads to what Donald Ray (1996) referred to as "divided sovereignty" – where chiefs and the political elites derived their sources of authority from different sources. Chiefs from custom and religion, while politicians get theirs from a "secular" constitution. While this sometimes blurs the lines of demarcation between the authorities of chiefs and the political elites, there is hardly any equivocation that chiefs are in charge of cultural and customary issues. This is to the extent that while European-style courts have jurisdiction over all legal issues, the palaces of the traditional authorities continue to usually serve as an important resort for all family disputes, including marriage, childcare, divorce, and land disputes. The role of traditional authorities in adjudicating family issues is such that Akan people in the diaspora appeal to chiefs and queen mothers to address their marital disputes (Prempeh and Lydia 2021c).

The importance of the courts of traditional authorities is largely based on the fact that chiefs and queen mothers apply the non-binary of the Akan cosmogony in their courts. For example, in the research Lydia Amoah and I conducted on the courts of traditional authorities in Asante, we observed and wrote that, one of the main issues that are taken to the court is imprecation ("duabo"). In Akan cosmogony, imprecations are common in their application to dispute resolution, as they involve the invitation of the deities, ancestors and other spirits to adjudicate highly contentious and sensitive issues. These issues include infidelity in marriage, witchcraft accusation, and land disputes. Because imprecations are not admissible in "secular" courts or are considered as irrational and superstitious to the "modern" mind, issues involving imprecations are taken to traditional authorities. In Asantehemaa's court, for example, Sumankwaahene (the chief ritual functionary) in Asante sits in the court to attend to such matters.

The role of chiefs as custodians of culture is not limited to the Ghanaian context. In almost everywhere in the world where chieftaincy (or monarchy) existed, the institution served as a sign for the continuity of the cherished traditions of the people. For this and many other reasons, when the Asantehene dies, he is said to have rather gone to the village, similar to the British saying "long live the king or queen", even when the king or queen is dead. The King lives on even in death, because whoever takes over must keep the customs and "traditions" of the people in continuity. This explains the horror that some people I spoke with in England felt when Mark Rutte, the Prime Minister of Netherlands, the first country to legalise same-sex marriage in 2001, announced that any king or queen of the country would not have to forfeit their right to the throne if he or she is married to someone of the same sex.[169] In England, I have observed that whenever the Queen is to give a speech, nearly everything comes to a halt. At my church, St Stephen's in Selly Park, Birmingham, we prayed for the Queen every now and then, especially when she is not well or travelling or undertaking national and international assignments. She represents the cultures, religion (as head of the Anglican Church) and family values of the English people. Someone in my church told me, "It would be strange if homosexual practices extend to Buckingham Palace; that would be the end all of us". But it could be argued on the contrary that royals are known to perform duties by finding an ideal marriage partner to allow the birth of a future king and a spare, and only to proceed and find love in not so politically correct partner. With Prince Charles, although not gay, as an example, societal norms are usually considered so flexible that people find ways around them. Thus, it is said that, if

[169] The Guardian (13 October 2021), "Dutch royals can marry a person of same-sex without giving up throne, says PM", https://www.theguardian.com/world/2021/oct/13/dutch-royals-can-marry-person-of-same-gender-without-giving-up-throne-says-pm, accessed: 15 November 2021.

indeed there is a royal who happens to be gay, he can still either have children to sustain the line while also being himself. This flexibility is unthinkable in Ghana, particularly among the Akan, because of the Akan strict categorisation of nature, humanity and roles into a presupposed gender differentiation – male and female. Relating this to chieftaincy, the Akan political symbol of authority – the stool – is categorised into male and female: *mmarimadwa* (male stool) and *mmaadwa* (female stool). The gendered distinction is so clear that a male chief can never sit on a female stool without denigrating his masculinity and role as the protector, defender, and warrior of the Akan society (Owusu and Bosiwah 2015).

The Akan repudiation of gender blindness chimes with my Christian perspective, of which John MacArthur explained as follows:

> Man is also uniquely created to bear the image of God as a ruler, who is given a sphere of sovereignty. In that sense, he was also created to be the **glory of God**. God gave man dominion over all the created world, to care for according to His divine plan. Man was given rulership of the world. Both men and women are created in God's image, but as Paul points out in verse 8, the original creation from the "dust from the ground" was of Adam only (Gen. 2:7). Eve was created later from part of Adam himself (2:21-22). The male was given the dominion and authority over God's created world, and is by that fact the **glory of God**. On the other hand, **woman is the glory of man**. Woman was made to manifest man's authority and will as man was made to manifest God's authority and will. The woman is viceregent, who rules in the stead of man or who carries out man's will, just as man is God's viceregent who rules in His stead or carries out His will. The woman shines not so much with the direct light of God as with the derived light from man. Man is both the **image and glory** of God, while woman is only the image of God (Gen. 1:27) and not the image of man, and the **glory of man**, not the glory of God. The point is that man shows how magnificent a creature God can create from Himself, while woman shows how magnificent a creature God can make from a man (Gen. 2:21-22).[170]

John Piper on his part also distinguished between male and female as different in function, but equal in dignity before God as follows:

---

[170] John MacArthur, *I Corinthians (*Chicago, IL: Moody, 1984), 407, 408; emphasis in original text.

> At the heart of mature masculinity is a sense of benevolent responsibility to lead, provide for and protect women in ways appropriate to a man's differing relationships. At the heart of mature femininity is a freeing disposition to affirm, receive and nurture strength and leadership from worthy men in ways appropriate to a woman's differing relationships (Piper 1990: 22).[171]

In Ghana, chiefs in the Church of Pentecost, as part of registering their protest against the pressure on the government of Ghana to legally allow same-sex unions, said they cannot imagine a royal marrying someone of the same-sex. A lawyer and member of the CoP, who read a memorandum from the chiefs of the church, said the chiefs were distressed about how the duality of Akan chiefly authority (the stool) cannot be conflated in terms of gender. As the CoP representative argued, how, based on a male chief and a female chief would work out if a royal decides to marry someone of the same-sex and pursues legal battle to force himself or herself on the stool? This means, without any equivocation that, if a chief is a male, the co-chief must be female. Speaking for the chiefs, on how dangerous LGBT is to the selection of royals to the stool, he asked: "How will a king and kingmakers deal with a royal who is the next of kin that got involved in gay marriage and member of the Trans-gender community? This question is not about incest, as it is about the gendered roles the dual political leaders play. How is a queen mother who has a lesbian partner as a wife or husband be handled by either the kingmakers or subjects?[172] This depends on the specific feminine role of the spouse. Indeed, it may happen that in some societies, African kings and rulers have been known to have ritual spouses – which means that the king can have a ritual spouse for purposes of his duties if sexuality is that of an issue. But even here, it is important to interrogate whether the ritual spouse was ever the ideal sociogenic practice that the subjects of the kings were allowed to practice. Nevertheless, while other traditional areas may have handled this to ensure inclusivity, Akan chieftaincy has yet to cross that line.

I conclude this section by stating that the cultures of the Akan and the people of Ghana are not fossilised in time and space. They are not unchanging. They are flexible, dynamic, and mutable. The question

---

[171] John Piper, *What's the difference? Manhood and womanhood defined according to the Bible* (Illinois: Crossway Books, 1990).

[172] Pent TV Gh (12 November 2021), Asembi, https://feedback.facebook.com/thecophq/videos/631898051505402/, 15 November 2021.

then is about how Akan chieftaincy would come to terms with a royal with a same-sex partner, especially in the performance of public duties. This explains the changing roles of the qualifications needed for one to become a chief. Since the late colonial era, higher education has become an important qualification for selecting an Akan chief. Equally true is that most Akan chiefs, including the Asantehene, hardly practice polygyny or even inherit wives of previous chiefs for sexual reasons (a practice that was highly cherished in the pre-colonial era). Similarly, postcolonial Ghana has seen Akan marriages take a different dimension, as men and women play important roles in keeping the family. Christine Oppong, a pioneer professor of Family Studies in Ghana, observed in her several researches that modernity, through western education, colonial conquest, urbanisation, wage work, Christianity has indicated have transformed matrilineal marriages (Oppong 1974; 1981; 1987; 1994, 2008). This transformation reinforces my argument that Akan proverbs that are construed by feminist writers are more about principles to keep social and cosmic order than laws to suppress women.

Nevertheless, because the changes revolve around man-made cultures, Akan chiefs have remained unyielding to any attempts to introduce the same-sex marriages in Ghana. This is because also in the various religions in Ghana, same-sex marriages are considered an affront to the ontological boundary of heterosexual marriage as the sole means of procreation. Similarly, since among the Akan, barrenness and sterility are considered a threat to the continuity of human life and existence (Gyekye 1996), then one can only guess the attitude several Akan would have towards same-sex marriages that do not ontologically pro-create.

Anti-homosexual Bill: Backwards or not?

Usually, the pushback from Christians against homosexuality and the anti-homosexual bill is constructed as culturally backward. The anti-homosexual laws are considered a setback to Ghana's democracy. But in a simple response and at the risk of recapitulating my point, the push for homosexuality in the west, arrogantly forming the international standards, is based on pushback against conservative evangelical Christianity, reformed Islam and indigenous religions. (Hunsberger, Owusu and Duck 2009). In Ghana, religion has been identified as the major obstacle to the rights of members of the LGBTQ community. Before I say anything further, the chastising of religion as problematic in the pro-LGBTQ+ attempts at desensitising homosexual debate is a challenge. First, religion, particularly Evangelical Christianity and reformed Islam, are considered relentlessly hostile to homosexual practices. In the petition against the Family Bill, the advocates of the rights of minority group referred to the religious people as demonstrating religious fanaticism. In all this, since religion is generally seen as hardly reformative to accommodate new sexual norms, it is important for us to define what religion is. I take my argument from this stance between quite often the term is used without any particular definition/conceptualisation. Resultantly, people are often polarised between those who challenge the LGBTQ argument on religious grounds and those who do not, because of what I understand as a narrow conceptualisation narrowly defined as strictly about a belief in a deity. Usually, religion is defined in a direction relating to the existence of a supernatural being, such that anyone who claims to define religion must have that nexus established. In the 19th Century, when European scholars embarked on the search for the "sacred". They offered different definitions of religions, but all often focusing on the "sacred" as the epicentre. For example, in his *Elementary forms of religious life*, Emile Durkheim defined religion as a "unified system of beliefs and practices relative to sacred things, that is to say, things set apart and forbidden" (Durkheim 1995: 44).

Surely Durkheim's functionalist views are problematic, as religion cannot only be about the sacred. More so, we still cannot leverage the sacred alone, as presented by Durkheim to explain life's existential imperfection. So, I now turn over to Karl Marx, a 19th Century Jewish thinker whose contributions to knowledge has outlived to shape local and translocal politics. While Marx was not a scholar of religion or write extensively about the subject, his ground theory about class conflict or class struggle has had a metastasised and spill over effect on areas of life, including religion.

In my discussion of Marx and religion, I leverage and summarise my reading of him while pursuing my doctoral studies at the Makerere University (Jan. 2014 – August 2016) to deduce Marxist theory of religion.[173] To begin with, I argue that Marx's understanding of religion formed part of his understanding of reality. Is reality what is seen or it

173 Among the books that have helped me to make sense of Karl Marx include: David McLellan, *Karl Marx: His life and thought* (New York: Harper & Row Publishers, 1973); Karl Marx, *Selected writings* (ed. David McLellan) (Oxford: Oxford University Press, 2000); Karl Marx and Friedrich Engels, *Capital*, 3 Vols (eds. Friedrich Engels) (New York: International Publishers, 1967);

includes the unseen? Is historical event all there is or there is something metaphysically important? Can human beings bracket the world out of the control of the divine and use only rationality to make sense of existential imperfection? How do we understand politics and liberation struggles from the perspective of Marxist' understanding of history and religion? Profiling history as essentially material, Marx argued that the lived realities of socio-economic inequalities are historically human-made. They are not caused by any imaginary god anywhere in the sky. In the Communist Manifesto, which he co-authored with Friedrich Engels, Marx declared:

> The history of all hitherto existing society is the history of class struggles. Freeman and slave, patrician and plebeian, lord and serf, guild-master and journeyman, in a word, oppressor and oppressed, stood in constant opposition to one another, carried on an uninterrupted, now hidden, now open fight, a fight that each time ended, either in a revolutionary re-constitution of society at large, or in the common ruin of the contending class.[174]

Through the deployment of historical materialism, Marx argued that individuals have deployed several chicaneries, since the progression from hunger-gathering to agricultural to industrialisation, to superimpose their economic interest as supreme and an established order over everyone else. Owning the means of production, the capitalist deploys his or her economic power to ensure that labourers are alienated from their labour. Concurrently, relationship between labourers and consumers is reduced from social to transactional to economic transaction – mediated by money. As money mediates human relations, economic fetishism emerges where human value is reduced to the ever-bloating capitalist interest of the bourgeois class. With the ontological value of labourers reduced below money value, the introduction of machines further ditches their productive value. Over time, production is produced in excesses, labourers' service becomes redundant – with idle hands, labourers become aware that they would have nothing to lose, apart from their chains, if they fought violently enough to overturn the exploitative cog in the wheel of capitalism.

Since the capitalists would hardly sit unconcerned for any such sporadic revolution to take place, the capitalist invests in social

[174] Karl Marx and Friedrich Engels, *The communist manifest, in Selected works* (Moscow: Foreign Languages Publishing House, 1935/1955): 1:34.

institutions, such as governance structures, family, law, and religion to cower labourer into submission. These institutions, imbued with imagined ideas, become a form of imprisonments that hold the decidedly strangled labourer from challenging injustice. Laws are passed to criminalise stealing – a necessary part of the revolution to overturn capitalism. Families are coerced by the state to socialise its members to accept their servitude status in the public sphere. Finally, religion becomes the superstructure that knits and concretises the social institutions as social control and guardrails against revolution.

Religion, from the perspective of Karl Marx, is not about supernatural entities or the existence of deities. In his materialistic philosophical predisposition, Karl Marx repudiated the existence of the supernatural world. So, for Marx, religion is the human projection of his or her desires happiness away from the existential reality of economic exploitation. Constituting as an opium, religion gives hope (a sigh) to the labourer and sustains the labourers' illusions of a happy world if labourer becomes non-materialists, but works hard enough to achieve the imagined "pie-in-the-sky" happiness. In sum, religion is the ideal and ultimate happiness of the existential unhappiness of the working class. To dispossess religion of re-creating and legitimising perpetual illusions that sustains injustice, Marx proposed a constant revolution against the forces that hold religion as strongholds against the liberation of the working class.

Marxist understanding history as class struggles, from which a theoretical religion is derived, remains very strong among Marxist and sometimes even Christians, particularly liberation theologians. At the Makerere Institute of Social Research (MISR), Makerere University, where I stayed for three years, as I worked towards my doctoral studies, one of my closest friends was a Tanzanian Marxist, Sabatho Nyamsenda. His first name Sabatho (equivalent would have been "Kwame" or "Ama" of the Akan – indicating a Saturday born) indicates how strong he was as an erstwhile member of the Seventh-day Adventist Church, who spent nearly a year struggle to overcome the guilt around breaking the Sabbath after he left the SDA church in favour of Marxism. He was one of the brilliant young men I had had in all my schooling life. We were not only good friends, we also often shared rooms next to each other. So, reading the overbearing 100s of pages during the day, Sabatho and I would cool off with yet another round of, but non-scored, cognitive exertion over how to rid of the world off its existential imperfection, even if that were possible. Our discussions became more formalised when the Director of MISR became what several of us considered an aporia of Marxism.

During such heated, albeit informed by conviviality, I would often suggest to Sabatho, George Orwell's Animal Farm, which I read in secondary school, to indicate the counterproductivity and inherently incapability of Marxism producing an idea of a utopian classless world. In response, he suggested Ngũgĩ wa Thiong'o's *Devil on the cross*, as a counter-literature. Having had insight into literary critiques of both socialism (Orwell's Animal Farm) and capitalism (Thiong'o's, *Devil on the cross*), I became convinced in my position that the existential reality of inequality cannot be vanquished by both the economic freedom offered by capitalism or the state control of the means of production, offered by socialism. This is precisely because while capitalism would free individual energies to invest in production for prosperity, individuals are hardly given the virtues conviviality to redistribute what they work to amass. In fact, individual's quest for more put them on the path of economic exploitation of consumers. Similarly, the emergence of a socialist state does not end in a classless state, as the lead revolutionaries become oligarchs. Consequently, both capitalism and socialism do not lead human beings in the attainment of freedom and justice – we get locked up in the world of existential imperfection.

Can we overcome existential imperfection if we overthrow religion? There is no doubt that, historically and even now, some individuals have weaponised the interpretation of religious texts on complex subjects such as slavery and remotely racism, to advance both epistemic and socio-economic injustice. In Africa, the myth about Noah cursing Ham, one of his three sons, was one of the bases for European hermeneutics to justify slavery, colonialism, and later racism. That the enslaved Africans in the plantations could compose songs like "Lord, I want to be a Christian in my heart" – a critique of the hypocrisy of the religious sincerity of the slave masters – indicate that it is quite simplistic to draw a direct nexus between Christianity and enslavement. Similarly, that John Newton, a converted captain of a slave ship, could compose "Amazing grace" – a mixture of African rhythm and Christian lyrical motive – implies that when people repent of their sins and stop the pretentious practice of Christianity, we cannot draw any direct connection between religion as opium to give a sigh to an oppressed working class.

That we need to repudiate any Marxist simplistic drawing of a nexus between Christianity and capitalist exploitation explains the Latin American theologians' syncretic deployment of Marxism and Christian teaching to forge liberation theology. Historically, liberation theology has informed armed struggle against oppressive regimes in some countries in Latin America and Southern Africa, particularly South Africa – where Steve Biko played a key role. While I sympathise with liberation theologians in the fight against injustice, I agree with Byang Kato that liberation or black theology water-down the centrality of the Christian dogma about the reason of suffering and injustice; the centrality of salvation by grace in Jesus Christ and denial of hell; and interpreting salvation in terms of political, economic and social liberation (Kato 1985 44).[175] Liberation theologians dislocate the source of injustice from human ontological self-centredness (sin to state it simply) to external person (or demonisation of another human). Secondly, it dislocates liberation from injustice from Jesus Christ, the ultimate answer, to armed struggle – through the shouting of FRELIMO's aluta continua which has never and may never lead to "A luta continua; vitória é certa", meaning "The struggle continues; victory is certain". Finally, while we cannot gloss over the work of visible oppressors, liberation theology privileges blame culture over penitentiary culture. In the face of injustice, it amplifies the question of the victim, "Who did this to us," more than, "What did we do to ourselves?" In the end, identity and victimhood politics take over the fight against injustice. Morphing into the social justice movement, an entire race, the white race, is tagged as evil, while the entire black race is tagged as oppressed. Relating to the LGBTQ issue, black and white spaces are created. It is either one is in the clearly delineated camps of pro-LGBTQ or one is anti-LGBTQ. It is almost as if one cannot exercise compassion without holding unto one's conviction.

Given the complexity of Marxist and socio-cultural contexts, the implementation of Marxist philosophy as a system has also resulted in the perpetuation of violence in human history. It is even surmised that the spilling of blood and mugging of human rights in communist countries surpass the evils of religion in medieval Europe. In Africa, framing colonialism as an overflow of Western capitalism, several of the African elites, including Kwame Nkrumah of Ghana and Julius Nyerere of Tanzania, adopted different variants of socialism. Whether scientific socialism of Nkrumah or ujamaa of Nyerere, African leaders realised that they could not transplant and implement Marxist's anti-religious rhetoric without running into oddities. So, African Marxist leaders, most of whom had had missionary education and having been

[175] Byang H. Kato, *Biblical Christianity in Africa: Theological perspectives in Africa* (Achimota/Accra: Africa Christian Press, 1985).

deeply shaped by Christian virtues, appropriate both Marxism and Christianity as a form of counterhegemonic tool for human flourishing. For example, Nkrumah incorporated religion, through the sacralisation of mundane things like national flags, constitutions, histories that imbued mystical understanding of his birth, to build the postcolonial Ghanaian state. Indeed, having inherited a deeply plural postcolonial state that the colonialists had used different avenues including securitisation of the public sphere to govern, Nkrumah invested in both religion and Marxist oppressive antics. As a Catholic, he inverted Jesus's "Seek ye first the Kingdom of God" as "Seek ye first the political kingdom" to ensure unity against colonialism. When independence was gained, he continued to use religion, but this he also invested in the Marxist non-acceptance of division and polarisation to legislate against freedom of expression and ethno-religious political mobilisation, politicisation of citizens and concurrent deportation of critics and constituting of Ghana as a one-party state in 1964 to ward off all critiques.

Unfortunately, the mixture of Christianity and Marxism did not take Ghanaians to the political kingdom of economic prosperity. In the end, both local and international forces merged to orchestrate his overthrow in February 1966. With all this, on April 24, 2022, at an international online programme, dubbed *The Toyin Falola Interviews*, I was fortunate to have interviewed one of Ghana's neo-Nkrumahist and Marxist citizens – Ernesto Yeboah, founder of Marxist-informed Economic Fighters League. During the interview, he first used the word "ontology". When I asked him whether he meant ontological imperfection, he said yes. And having followed up with: "What is his philosophy about how to end ontological imperfection?" the conversation his zest for revolution became temporarily stale until I had to allow other co-interviewers to come.

My point is not to say that religion has not been weaponised in the hands of mercenaries to perpetuate injustice (Oduro-Frimpong 2021).[176] In Ghana, religious bigotry and fanaticism, as I have already mentioned, have been blamed for the manufacturing and spreading the ideas of homophobia. Similarly, a few individuals have plied the religious enterprise to prey on several unsuspecting Ghanaians. But that religion becomes a tool of oppression is not unique to religion or just beliefs. It is about human ontological selfishness. The religious

---

[176] Joseph Oduro-Frimpong, "'The fake is news': On popular visual media, fakery and legitimacy contestation in Charismatic Christianity in contemporary Ghana," *Journal of African Cultural Studies*, 33, 3 (2021): 325-343;

charlatans and their victims are usually involved in the search for the answers of life's riddles and puzzles. So, whether with religion or not, corruption of different shades, economic and political, remain deeply a moral issue. This explains why Nkrumah's government was accused of corruption – so that, even though Nkrumah may not have been complicit in economic corruption, his own self-centred quest for and monopolisation power corrupted his moral conscience as he either antagonise or imprison some of his trust friends, including Komla Agbeli Gbedemah, who campaigned for Nkrumah while Nkrumah was in prison.

Nkrumah's quest for power also blinded him to the corruption that was sinking the nation, as he allowed himself to be numbed against the canker into slumber amidst loud, sycophantic praise singers. In all this, as I discussed, religion cannot be thrown away, in the manner Karl Marx anticipated. After all, the modern society must necessarily use religion, among nation, ethnicity and nationalism, to establish law and order – fostering good governance.[177] In the end, the end of Nkrumah's regime could be simplistically summarised in the title and content of Ayi Kwei Armah's novel, *The beautyful ones are not yet born.* The question, however, is given the world's existential imperfection, would the *beautyful* one be ever born as a human being?

From the discussion so far, we can clearly see that religion is a complex phenomenon that can hardly be boxed into a single, universally accepted conceptualisation. Even so, I now turn my attention to Max Weber. Max Weber conceptualisation of religion is rather complex and not easily understandable. But having read his major text on the subject, I observe that Weber draws a direct relationship between religion, work and economic prosperity. Weber's intervention was part of responding to both extreme form of ascetism that has created inertia in people's resolve to work and Marx's critique of religion as oppressive. Seeking to answer the economic prosperity of Protestant Christians as opposed to their Catholic counterparts, Weber identified the ethics of industriousness, frugality and investment as key as the spirit of Protestant capitalism. John Calvin's response to Protestant's Christian concerns about the verifiability and assurance of salvation partly influenced Calvin's teaching about hard work frugality as outward expression of the eternal security of the salvation of the elect of God. While Calvinistic ethics may have inspired western capitalism, neo-western capitalism, especially since the 1980s that

[177] Adrian Hastings, *The construction of nationhood: Ethnicity, religion and nationalism* (Cambridge: Cambridge University Press, 1997).

emphasises consumerism, as opposed to production could hardly be associated with Calvinistic work ethic.

Feminist scholars have also been very critical of religion. At any rate, the feminism movement has a root in religion, specifically Christianity. So, it comes as less surprise that feminist scholars have over the centuries considered religion a major male-centric instrument in mainstreaming gender inequality. Institutionalised religion is said to carry the idea of a monotheistic male God that leaves no space for a female deity (Daly 1973).[178] Not only that the construing of God as a decidedly male deity similarly allows men to dominate the interpretation of religious texts (Wadud 2006; Barlas 2002).[179] Religious myths tend to routinise patriarchal control of women and the family, making it easier for men to keep women in the grid of immanent responsibilities. Simone de Beauvoir reflected on the religious endorsement of patriarchy as follows:

> Man enjoys the great advantage of having a God endorse the codes he writes; and since man exercises sovereign authority over woman, it is especially fortunate that this authority has been vested in him by the Supreme Being. the Jews, Mohammedans, and Christians, among others, man is master of the divine right; the fear of God, therefore will repress any impulse towards revolt in the downtrodden female. One can bank on her credulity (de Simone 1983/1949: 632).[180]

Given that above context, I conceptualise religion as a set of worldviews that inform how a group of people live their lives and carry out their daily activities, as well as helping them to make sense of the world. More generally, we could define religion as a set of beliefs that help us to answer the how and why questions of life. In other words, with the "why" answers, religion helps us to satisfy our quest for meaning. With the "how", religion guides us on how to do what we care to do. Put together, religion as a set of beliefs helps us to attend to the adaptive (philosophical) and technical issues of life. Definitely, I do not pretend that my understanding of religion is exhaustive or even

---

178 Mary Daly, *Beyond God the Father: Toward a philosophy of women's liberation* (Boston: Beacon Press, 1973).

179 Amina Wadud, *Insider the gender jihad: Women's reform in Islam* (Oxford: One World Publications, 2006); Asma Barlas, *Believing women in Islam: Unreading patriarchal interpretations of the Qur'an* (Austin: Texas: University of Texas Press, 2002).

180 Simone de Beauvoir, *The second sex* (Trans. And edited by H.M. Parshley) (Harmondsworth: Penguin Books, 1983/1949).

universally shared – far from that. Instead, since everyone has a "why" and "how" for their existence, everyone could be said to be religious. This also means that one may not necessarily be conscious of the set of beliefs informing one's practices. Nonetheless, the same could not be said that one does not have a set of beliefs guiding how one's lives. I take this definition as given for this book, because if we limit the definition of religion to God and the supernatural realm, some groups like Buddhism would hardly qualify as religion. This is because Buddhism does not prioritise the existence of God and gods as sufficient and necessary for one's attainment of enlightenment (or liberation from the pangs of birth and re-birth – *Moksha* (Wan gu 2009). The next issue with defining religion as theocentric (or god-centred) is that, possibly apart from Islam, both Christians and indigenous practitioners did not name themselves. The term "Christians" was given to the followers of Jesus Christ because they exemplified the character of God. Similarly, Africans did not call their religion African Traditional Religion/s, it was a label given to them by one of its earliest scholars Geoffrey Parrinder (1949). Finally, the word "religion" was hardly used as an academic category, delineating the material from the spiritual, until the 19th Century (Stausberg 2008). Much Durkheim argued that religion recognises the existence of the sacred and the material world (profane), the two are hardly separated. The non-binary of the cosmos has part of the tension over whether or not Africans are notoriously religious or not (for those who argue that Africans are deeply religious in all things, please see: Parrinder 1969; Mbiti; 1969; for the counter-argument among those who rather think Africans are pragmatic, please see: Bitek 1971; Wiredu 1998).

Defined as a worldview in responding to life's existential issues, perspicuous understanding religion is largely about people's worldview that inform their response to existential questions such as: Who am I? Why am I here? Where do I go from here? For this reason, everyone has a worldview from which he or she answers life's existential questions. So, yes, the role of religion in the homosexual debate cannot be exaggerated (Siker 2007), everyone is religious in one way or the other – albeit depending on where one places the most emphasis – God or human rationality. But by rationality, no objective consensus can be achieved even about decriminalising LGBTQ+ since one man's rationality is another man's idiocy.

But generally, regarding society's guardrail against sexual revolution as backward is ill-conceived because: it is assumed that time is linear – the past must be discarded completely. The past must not interfere with the present. The past is made up of religious fanatics. The past is primitive. The past is pre-science. It is for this reason that homosexual advocates are pushing against religion, which has always been with humanity and will continue to be with us. Second, if we are to go by the logic of the homosexual advocates, then the homosexual advocates are backwards. This is precisely because the practice was part and parcel of the Greco-Roman civilisation – the historical root of the European world. Alvin I Schmidt has observed that, "Roman literature, written by its own authors such as Juvenal, Ovid, Martial, and Catellus, indicates that sexual activity between men and women had become highly promiscuous and essentially depraved before and during the time that Christianity appeared in Roman society" (Schmidt 2004: 80). He further observed that, "the widespread, licentious sex practices threatened the institution of marriage, so Caesar Augustus in 18 B.C. *enacted lex Julia de adulteriis*, a law that tried to curb the people's addiction to widespread illicit sex" (Ibid. 80).

From the above, it is clear that the west is rather backwards, because they are going for the anti-thesis of their civilisation. They are hacking back to the sexual perversity of their historic past. This connects to the idea of culture as dynamic. This point is usually highlighted by people who are pushing homosexual practices down the throats of Africans. As far as they are concerned, culture is dynamic, malleable and flexible enough to accommodate new trends in society. Unfortunately, these scholars who are strongly in support of *Trumutrumu* – to wit Homosexualism – do not explain which aspect of culture is dynamic and which ones are not. This betrays their trade as African Studies scholars; it shows intellectual bankruptcy. Nevertheless, as feminists, their intellectual position synchronises with their quest to deconstruct all social orders and ontological boundaries. Alongside their western radical feminists, taking inspiration from Simone de Beauvoir, the sexual partner of Jean-Paul Sartre (Johnson 1996), these scholars may have to deal with other forms of "conjugal" unions, including polyamory (Schippers 2016).

Since as academics they did not demonstrate the idea the nuance of culture as dynamic, but that conforms with their deconstruction of religion and social structures, we could conclude that they took the idea of cultural dynamism for granted. About the simplistic view of culture as dynamic – usually a façade to deconstruct social order. The logic here is some non-ontological cultural practices like clothing, food and eating patterns, architecture, sports, human-induced beliefs like *Trokosi*, casteism, murdering of witches etc., may change. These are cultures that change because they are made by human beings. But ontological cultural practices like procreation as an ontological mixture of a man's sperm and a woman's ovum can hardly change. Admittedly, IVF, surrogate motherhood are huge changes, but it does not take way the fact that two ontologically different biological male sperm and female ovum (egg) must offer what is distinctively theirs to procreate. So, IVF as a scientific invention is great, except that it does not fulfil the Christian understanding of marriage as composite unity of heterosexuality and relationality. Given the tension over the definition of marriage in the LGBTQ debate, which is also the core of my book, I dedicate the next section discussing the concept of marriage. My goal is to trace the genealogy of marriage since the 20th Century, highlighting the fact that in several societies, including the Akan, marriage as a sociogenic practice has always been between male and female.

The concept of marriage

Marriage has been profiled as the critical institution and base of society for both procreation and companionship. It is in a marriage where the virtues of society find expression and are later expressed to the rest of society. Marriage milieu was important in saturating society with shared values and virtues. For this reason, the constitution of marriage and the roles of couples were clearly defined. Indeed, in the Akan society, marriage was practically and socially heterosexual. While it could have hinged on polygyny for various reasons, but hardly romantic reasons, marriage was always heterosexual. This was because heterosexual marriage/sexual engagement was/is the only way procreation could take place. For human beings to conceive, including supposed gay and lesbian couples, they must incorporate the clearly distinctive biological binary between a biological male and a biological female sperm and egg respectively, circumscribed by relationality. Indeed, IVF respects neither marriage nor sex as it enables conception in the laboratory away from the fuss about marriage and sex – which is the very reason it creates complications for the biblical understanding of marriage and procreation as both necessary within the context of heterosexual engagement and relationality.

Even so, the definition of marriage and family are not given, especially given the cultural revolution since 1970s. As Berger and Berger as a result of the cultural revolution, "The family now appears an age-old evil. Heterosexuality is rape; motherhood is slavery; all relations between the sexes are a struggle for power" (1983: 25).

Heterosexual marriage that is institutionalised by both the state and religion has become a major hindrance in the way of minority sexual group in Ghana. Constituting part of the sexual revolution agenda, marriage and family have come up for redefinition and reconceptualisation. The family and marriage are hardly about heterosexual parents and their children. As I read the petition against the Bill from a section of Ghanaian academics and activists who are defending minority rights, I found their definition of the family consistent with their ideology. While they were hardly specific about the definition of marriage, I imagine it is possible to glean their position on what marriage constitutes from their understanding of the Ghanaian family:

> What constitutes the Ghanaian family unit is hardly uniform or static. For example, the nuclear family unit or household, comprising two married heterosexual partners and their biological children, though increasingly common among elite or middle-class urban Ghanaian can hardly be said to represent the Ghanaian cultural norm. To many, particularly outside the urban elite enclaves, the family is still reckoned, for example, in "extended" family or polygamous terms, with the nuclear family of the urban elite regarded as foreign. Single parent-headed households are also quite prevalent, as are various other permutations and combinations.[181]

Indeed, from the pro-LGBTQ Coalition's definition of family, one could clearly see that they are not redefining the foundation of the family as ontologically heterosexual. Instead, they try to ply on the rhetoric of changes in the cultural constitution of the family – which is about a shift from over-emphasis on the extended family system to the nuclear family system and single-headed households. Definitely, the pro-LGBTQ Coalition appears to lack the courage to same-sex family to the list. But as I have said above, they have been consistent with their efforts at reconstituting the ontological base of the family, except that they are currently struggling to swim against the cultural tide against LGBTQ practices in the country. Even so, it is important to mention that the cultural shift in the constitution of the family that the pro-LGBTQ Coalition points out is the very reasons families have struggled to nurture and socialise their young ones into socially fit adults.

---

[181] Memorandum to select committee on the constitutional, legal and parliamentary affairs on the: *Promotion of proper human sexual rights and Ghanaians family values bill, 2021*, p. 11.

Broadly, as I shall elicit from the Akan view of marriage, the institution can be conceptualised as a heterosexual sociogenic activity for procreation. Taking an insight of the Twi etymology of marriage, I learn on Owusu Brempong, who said that "Marriage in Twi is designated with the word *awadee*. This lexeme has two morphemes, *awa* from *ware* meaning long and *de* from *dee,* meaning something. In a sense, the word *awadee* literally means something that last a long time, i.e., a legal union of a man with a woman for life" (Brempong 1991: 95). But to arrive at the above definition of marriage, I take a genealogical definition of the concept since the 1930s to demonstrate the consistency with which the idea of marriage as male and female has been retained among different cultures, focusing on the Akan specifically. My aim is to state that while recent definition of marriage since the 1980s has broadened to include same-sex partnership, for the Akan, marriage that publicly accepted as sociogenic and celebrated is heterosexual unions. My point is not to state the same-sex relations may not have existed among the Akan, even in pre-colonial times. Rather, my point is that from extant literature, what was public accepted as marriage among the Akan was a union of a biological man and a biological woman. The reason for this was, as I shall soon discuss, because of the centrality of childbirth – procreation. This means that while different forms of marriages, such as cross-cousin marriages (between children of brothers and sisters – known locally as "ɛfie aware" – to wit, "home marriage" as social construct, the means of procreation in the context of relationality.

Having laid the above foundation, I begin with Ralph Linton's definition of marriage. Ralph Linton who was a respected American anthropologist of the mid-20th Century talked about the sociogenic nature of marriage as follows: "Marriage brings the families on both sides into a series of new relationships, and it is neutral that they should take an active interest in it" (1936: 174). From his perspective, Rynkiewich commented on marriage as:

> Marriage is also a socially sanctioned relationship between families or lineages that involves obligations and duties for the exchange of men and women, goods and produce, or valuables, and thus regulate sexual relations, procreations, and rights over children (2011:93).[182]

---

[182] Michael A. Rynkiewich, *Soul, self and society: A postmodern anthropology for mission in a postcolonial world* (Oregon: Cascade Books, 2011).

Among the Asante, T.E. Kyei who conducted a study of the Ashante in 1945 wrote that, "A marriage in Ashante is not only the concern of the man and the woman contracting it but of their folks also. Its effects on the lineage (*ɛbusua*[183] - to wit family) of each partner are far-reaching and so every marriage, to be lawful, should receive the sanction and approval of the lineage-head (*ɛbusua panyin*) of both the man's and woman's lineages" (1992: 11). Peter Sarpong, one of the leading Akan anthropologists, trained at Oxford and also as a Catholic priest said of the sociogenic nature of marriage as follows: "In Africa as a whole, one may say, without risking the accusation of exaggeration, that marriage is not simply an affair between individuals who have fallen in love. It is a matter in which the lineages of the contracting parties are greatly interested. In a way, every marriage concerns the whole society in which it takes place, for which reason, all societies lay down rules regulating the use of sex in general, and of marriage in particular" (Sarpong 1974: 77). Similarly, as a family affair, marriage among the Akan was beyond the narrowness of romance, as it was about establishing social cohesion and conviviality between two families.[184]

As a sociogenic institution, Sarpong added that, "There may be laws specifying the age below which the citizens may not, under severe penalties, have sex or marry; there may also be laws regulating the degree of relationship that must exist between a man and a woman before they can legally marry, and so forth. This is obviously because the natural outcome of marriage, children, is something that affects the whole society (p. 77). Diedrich Westermann, who was the director of the International Institute of African Languages and Cultures and Professor of African Languages at the University of Berlin observed the sociogenic nature of African marriage as, "An institution of public life, which for the security of both parties is surrounded by definite customs and laws" (Westermann 1934: 122). In a recent work on cultures and customs of Ghana, Steven J. Salm and Toyin Falola observed that, "Marriages serve to establish alliances between families and communities" (Salm and Falola 2002: 130). Even in the face of

---

[183] According to Owusu Brempong, "The word Abusua when etymologised has two morphemes, *ɛbu* literally meaning broken and *sua* meaning to learn. Abusua in a sense therefore means part of the society which is broken or a segment of the society which can be identified. The lexeme *sua* meaning to learn, denotes the learning process within such an institution. This means that individuals within the Abusua learn to identify themselves with the group" 94 See: Owusu Brempong, "Twi etymology: A study of ethno-linguistic," *Research Review*, NS, 7, 1&2 (1991): 93-110.

[184] K.A. Busia, 'The church in town', Address given at a conference in Accra (Gold Coast, May 15th -18th, 1951), pp. 77-92, p. 77.

sporadic modernity, these scholars observed that while men and women are likely to choose their own partners, "marriage continues to revolve around much more than the union of two people. It is still, primarily, a union between two families" (Ibid, 130). These explanations means that marriage in Ghana performs its social and procreative role if it is situated within the context of a union between a biological male and a biological female who nurture their children in a social context.

The sociogenic and public dimensions of marriage *ipso facto* reflect the observed ontological nature (definition) of the institution. So, several anthropological and sociological works, until the end of the 1960s, defined marriage as both sociogenic, public, and heterosexual. For example, as recent as the 1930s, Linton defined marriage as "a socially recognised union between persons of the opposite sex" (Linton 1936: 173). He added that, "[C]onjugal groups cannot exist without marriage, and … in many societies a union is not considered really a marriage until the conjugal group has come into existence, i.e., until a child has been born… In many cases marriages which are not productive of children are *ipso facto* dissolved, while in all societies, even our own (Euro-America), the termination of childless marriages is viewed with less disapproval than is that of marriages with children (Ibid 173).

With this observed definition of marriage, Linton added that "Through the institution of marriage, sexual partners are given social recognition and made still more permanent, thus increasing their utility as a basis for the assignment of activities to individuals" (p. 135). Max Assimeng, a Ghanaian Akan sociologist, defined marriage as, "The coming together of a man and a woman from two different clans to establish a family such that offspring could ensure to replenish and perpetuate the tribe. It is a solemn, social, and happy occasion in all communities" (Assimeng, 1999: 79).

As part of the indigenous marriage system, men often played the instrumental role of providing, protecting and leading their families. This includes matrilineal societies, whereas Linton observed, "We are accustomed to think of marriage as the core of the family that we are likely to jump to the conclusion that, a social system under which a woman rules her husband and dismisses him at will is dominated by women. Actually, in most of these so-called matriarchies, ultimate control is still vested in males" (p. 138). This observation implies the centrality of men in the home as leaders and providers. While this is key, it is also important to mention that in both historical and contemporary times, several men, for various reasons, have abused their leadership in the homes. Whatever these reasons are, men who abuse their wives, from the Christian perspective have violated an important principle of the faith. The Bible equates such a man who abuses his wives and fails to provide for his children as an apostate. Under the inspiration of the Holy Spirit, Paul stated this as follows: Anyone who does not provide for their relatives, especially their own household, has denied the faith and is worse than an unbeliever (I Timothy 5: 8).

The above conceptualisation of family and marriage from the Akan indigenous perspective points to two main things: first, it should be social and oriented towards procreation and second, it should be publicly accepted. If any marriage is not established with the orientation towards procreation, then such a union is not considered marriage and will not be granted social recognition. This implies that marriage from the indigenous perspective is not simply for recreation, which is also new in modern marriage forms. Given the characteristic of Akan marriages, two octogenarians I interviewed for this project said that oral sex hardly existed among the Akan. Admittedly, lack of documentary evidence does not necessarily mean that something was not there. What is rather known is that for over 4000 years, oral sex has had a controversial position, having been banned and often suspected culprits killed. Indeed, in Greco-Romans and Christians have historically considered oral sex as an aberration (Depierre 2016).[185] As part of writing this chapter, I asked an octogenarian woman whether she knew or knows about oral sex, including "blowjob", (fellatio) which is when a man or woman uses her mouth to stimulate a man's genitalia by sucking and licking them. Her response was negative. When I explained to her, she squirmed, and asked "what is that and where from it? It is a taboo that should not be mentioned." But being taboo does not mean it does not happen. It means it should not be talked about in other words, it was not sociogenic. How can you do that?" For these reasons, practices, such as homosexuality, that were considered at odds with indigenous heterosexual marriages in societies before colonialism were either suppressed, conducted in secret or confined to the realm of cultic practices. But, if they took place then possibly it should be dealt with as secrecy. But as to why it may have existed as a secret practice, we could surmise that it did not meet the expectation of procreation

---

[185] David Depierre, *They stoop to conquer: A brief history of oral sex* (OC Publishing, 2016).

and male-centric dominance of the family in both matrilineal and patrilineal families.

It is important to mention at this point that marriage as was traditionally and conventionally defined as a socially heterosexual union for procreation has changed since the 1970s. This change in human-induced definition of marriage chimes with the secularisation of morality – leading to a major cultural shift. The feelings of individuals have become canonised in the definition of marriage to accommodate how individuals, as opposed to society, define marriage. In this, laws, as opposed to morality (though I do not subscribe to any rigid binary between law and morality), is used to rationalise "marriage" types other than heterosexual relations. I will give a brief example of how marriage has recently been redefined by anthropologists. In 1999, William A. Haviland, an anthropologist wrote a textbook on the subject that provided a human-induced definition of marriage as, "a relationship between one or more men (male or female) and one or more women (female or male) who are *recognized by society* as having a continuing claim to the right of sexual access to one another" (Haviland 1999: 277). He clarifies his use of gender terms "man" and "woman" as, "Because gender is culturally defined, the 'man" may be a female or the 'woman' a male" (Ibid., 277). Harvey makes an important observation in explaining the difference between marriage and mating (for animals), "Only marriage, however, is backed by social, legal, and economic forces. Consequently, while mating is biological, marriage is cultural" (Ibid. 227).

In 2017, Haviland and other anthropologists wrote a volume on anthropology and human challenges, wherein they defined marriage as "a culturally sanctioned union between two or more people that establishes certain rights and obligations between the people, between them and their children, and between them and their in-laws. Such marriage rights and obligations most often include, but not limited to, sex, labor, property, childrearing, exchange, and status" (Haviland et al., 2017: 468). They further repeated Haviland's observation in 1999 that, "Notably, our definition of marriage refers to 'people' rather than 'a man and a woman' because in some countries same-sex marriages are socially acceptable and allowed by law, even though opposite-sex marriages are far more common" (Haviland et al.: 468). Similarly, in 2016, Jack David Eller defined marriage as "a socially recognised relationship between *two (or more) people* that establishes a kin-based group and that provides norms and roles for residence, property ownership and inheritance, labor, sexual relations, and *childrearing*" (2016: 148, *emphasis mine*).

From the discursive shift in the human-definition of marriage, it could be discerned that these scholars write to reflect the seismic cultural shift in the western that permits homosexuality. They do not shy away from the fact that the constitution of marriage has changed over the decades to incorporate same-sex marriages. Nevertheless, the authors make important observations that are worth commenting on, as we discuss gender studies and feminism in Ghana. First, the authors admit that marriage is a social institution. It is a practice that must be sanctioned and accepted by society.

This resonates with my point above that in most societies in Africa, including Ghana, marriage is a sociogenic practice that is culturally and publicly accepted and affirmed. This is prior to law and the emergence of the modern state. Heterosexual relations in societies in the pre-colonial era and before the birth of modern Ghana did not see marriage as a legal issue, defined by human-rational laws. Marriages were and are still considered a family affair. Even during the colonial era, the British colonial administrators never disposed families of their rights to determine their marriage practices. They only ensured the Gold Coasters who had become Christians stuck to monogamous, heterosexual unions, non-Christians stuck with their polygynous practice, while Muslims were allowed to engage in polygyny provided they registered the marriage (Anderson, 1955: 5, 249).

So, the state in Ghana does not legislate heterosexual marriages, the state does not determine how families construct a marriage. For the sake of national recognition, the state only requires that couples, after they have gone through the traditional rites of marriage processes, register with the state – through the Registrar General (including its regional offices). Since marriage is anterior to the state, marriage was/is entirely a family affair.

[It] is not a result of social organization in general, but seem rather to antedate both historically and logically the forms of social life? it is not the product of society, but itself produces society (Ellwood 1910: 29).

It is for this reason that there is so much uproar when some individuals decide to appeal to the state to regularise homosexual relations. This is because about 93 per cent of Ghanaian families do not subscribe to homosexual relations. The issue is how the state could negotiate with the minority who prefer a different legal regime for marriage. So, if the state decides to legislate any type of marriage other than heterosexual, most families are most likely going to resist it. It is precisely for this reason that in Ghana's enchanted public sphere, virtually all the religious groups: Christianity, Islam and indigenous religions have joined hands to push back any local (from a minority few, usually elite class working for international civil society groups and feminist scholars) and international attempts at decriminalising homosexuality. concurrently, the promoters of the Family Bill, Sam George and Mr Moses Foh-Amoaning, the principal promoters of the Bill argue that the Bill is to protect the Ghanaian family, which as they admit comes in different shades, must not accommodate same-sex relations. In their argument, the gay community is recruiting young people for the practice, luring them with money. In an interview with a local-based media house, Oyerepa Breakfast Show, Mr Foh-Amoaning alleged that "some senior high schools in Kumasi where some old students with the support of the headmasters are 'sodomizing' their students leading to some health implications of the students".[186]

The appeal both pro-LGBTQ and anti-LGBTQ Coalitions make to the state to regularise homosexual marriage is a usurpation of the rights of families, even though it is part of the activism of homosexuals to appeal to the state for support. This is certainly out of step with the rights of the state. The state governs the public sphere, and as part of the social contract that formed the modern state, the state is to govern and regulate differences. The state, as we have said has no control over how families regulate and organise their marriage, as marriage is essentially a family affair is within the purview of families. Because the state governs more by law than morality (even though state laws reflect society's shared moral values), when the state defines marriage, it transitions the institution from the realm of morality to the realm of law. while this may be read as unimportant or nothing wrong, it creates challenges for families because family relations are governed by love, as opposed to law. It is for this reason that it is said that "Blood is thicker than water" it is better not to use this statement because it is contradictory for what you are discussing. The use of the word "blood" is both biological and sociological. Biologically, it could denote genitor/pater relationship; while sociologically, the "blood" could imply the social/moral relations among individuals, as opposed to

[186] Joseph Marfo (June 11, 2022), "Ayimadu Antwi has become stumbling block for the passage on Anti-LGBTQI Bill – Moses Foh Amoaning says," https://oyerepafmonline.com/ayimadu-antwi-has-become-stumbling-block-for-the-passage-on-anti-lgbtqi-bill-moses-foh-amoaning-says/. (Accessed: September 3, 2022).

legalities. Among the Akan, for example, kinship terminologies are so broad and socially constructed that the word "blood" is both used in biological and sociological sense. For example, as part of the matrilineal social system of the Akan, my mother's sister's children are my brothers; while my sister's brother's children are not yes because their mother and I do not share uterine connections. The logic of this as observed by Fontaine (1972) among the Gisu people is that people cannot be both kinsmen and affines to one another in the same context of social relations.[187] As I have explained above, the issues of Akan marriage rules, post-marital residence, affiliation styles, inheritance and how they were affected by colonialism and Christianity do not did/does not undermine the centrality of Akan phallic culture as male fertility and masculine control of his family – a system that hardly gives any room for gay union. On the other hand, with my mother's sister's children, I share "blood" with them, so I cannot marry any of them – without committing incest. All this is because, among the Akan, "blood" – socially and/or biologically is a symbol of life that is given by mothers, so every Akan belongs to their mother's matrilineage (see: Gyekye 1987).

The relationship between me and my family is a covenant, guided by shared moral values than law. This is precisely because I don't choose my parents, nor my children, so applying state laws to govern consanguineal relationships will run roughshod against families. Similarly, family morals are usually governed by religion. And so, turning the state laws against religion is a violation of the boundary between "church" and state. This boundary is also important because religion preceded the state. That the family operates on love makes it. As part of my own philosophical disposition on the subject, I cite the following, even though it may look dated, the socio-philosophy embedded resonate with my own position.

The chief or almost the sole generator of altruism in human society, and it is upon altruism that society depends for every upward advance in cooperation. It is in the family that children learn to love and obey to be of service, and to respect one another's rights. The amount of altruism in a given group has a very close relation with the quality of its family. If the family fails to teach the spirit of service and self-sacrifice to its members, it is hardly probable that they will get very much of that spirit from society at large. The ideal of a human brotherhood has no meaning unless family affection gives it meaning. If the family is the

[187] Jean La Fontaine, "Gisu marriage and affinal relationships," in Meyer Fortes, *Marriage in tribal societies*, 88-120 (Cambridge: Cambridge University Press, 1972).

chief generator of altruism in human society and if the society depends upon altruism for each forward step in moral progress, then the family is the chief source of social progress (Ellwood 1910: 30).

Given the importance of the family, Adomako and the petitioners (academic in support of LGBTQ minority rights) created their own aporia when they suggested that the state should avert its attention but rather address the moral issues of teenage pregnancy, rape, environmental degradation – which according to them undermine the family. Certainly, they failed to appreciate the fact that without the constitutive heterosexual marriage, raising responsible citizens for society is impossible – since the family is the base of charity. Again, on this, I quote Ellwood who said:

> The rudiments of morality, of government, or religion, and even of industry and knowledge, must be learned by the child in the family. If the child fails, for example, to learn morality, to get moral standards and ideals from his family life, he stands but poor chance of getting them later in society. again, if the child fails to learn what law is and to get proper ideals of the relation of citizen to the state in his family life, there are good prospects of his being numbered among the lawless elements of society later. … The nation, whose family life decays, therefore, rots at the core, dries up the springs of all social and civic virtues (Ibid. 31).

My support for the family as the base for socialising people towards appreciable moral life does not in any sense rule out the fact that perpetrators of corruption, scam, and human trafficking my not come from heterosexual families. My point rather is that it may be safer for a child to have the benefit to biologically different, but mutually reinforcing different roles in nurturing a child. The important of heterosexual families in nurturing a responsible child is also borne out of my own Akan social system, where fathers and mothers play different but mutually reinforcing roles in a child's socialisation. Among the Akan, fathers are responsible for passing on family technical skills to their children, as well as disciplining them. Mothers also nurture children to appreciate family values and histories, as children inherit properties and succeeds from their matrilineage. In Akan mystical causality about health, it is believed that fathers are responsible for securing the health of their children with their spirit, because children get their *sunsum* (difficult to explain but usually referred to loosely as character) from their fathers (Rattray 1923). For example, it is believed among the Akan that a person with a strong *sunsum* can hardly be attacked by witches (See: Onyinah 2012).

So, while the state is not to identify with any particular religion, the state cannot and must not regulate the family rituals and practices of religion. Similarly, the state cannot and must not pass any marital or sexual laws that are at odds with religion and yet seek to impose on religions. In the same vein, because religion is anterior to the state, any state law that unjustifiably seeks to control the church or religion is justifiably resisted. It is for this reason that religious groups, especially conservatives in the west, particularly in America, continue to clash with the state, unfortunately, or possibly reflecting theological liberalism of secular sexual liberalism, some churches have succumbed to pressures from society to redefine sex and marriage to accommodate seismic cultural changes.

The discussion leads to the modern anthropological definition of marriage as cultural. This is quite a big claim, precisely because it assumes that marriage is part of human cultural creations. So, if it is a human cultural creation, then it can be subject to the idioms of culture as dynamic. It must also be shared to the extent that new forms of marriages and sexual relations from the LGBTQ+++ community must be accepted. Nevertheless, it is precisely the modern profiling of marriage as cultural or human-made that creates problems for religious communities. For all the three major religions, Christianity, Islam, and indigenous traditional region, in Ghana, marriage is not just cultural, it is also religious. In Islam, marriage is part of the requirements of faith, usually considered Ibadah. It is believed among Muslims that when Muslims contract heterosexual marriage, they fulfil half of the requirements of their faith. In indigenous traditions in Ghana, the contraction of marriage involves the ancestors and the deities, and the supreme God. This implies that the establishment of indigenous marriage in Ghana, bridges the gap between the spiritual and the material worlds. In Christianity, marriage is simply God's creation, as recorded in Genesis 1. Jesus also repeated the fact that God created marriage as heterosexual and monogamous.[188] For the overwhelming religious constituency in Ghana, marriage is also not just cultural, but religious. As I have said, Christianity sees marriage as a divine-cultural mandate. As a divine-cultural mandate, God allows human beings to determine the processes of establishing heterosexual, monogamous relations according to the ultimate purpose of the institution –

[188] Matthew 19:4; Genesis 1:27.

procreation. In indigenous cultures and Islam, too, procreation is the essential reason for marriage (Mbiti 1969).

The idea of marriage for romance and recreation is a modern development that has been overemphasised by Hollywood and western ethics, since the development of modern contraceptives in the 1970s. Virtually all societies have been keen on marriage as procreation and congeniality than romance (Linton, 1936: 175). Viewed as a divine-cultural mandate, religious communities tend to be more populous than communities that are deeply secular. This is because marriage and childcare involve sacrifices, including sacrificing careers for most people, especially women, who have to devote a significant amount of time to perform expressive duties after marriage and childbirth. Consequently, some women have theorised marriage as oppressive to women (Jeffreys, 2004).

Also, from the human-induced definition of marriage, childrearing takes the place of childbearing. This is quite revolutionary but certainly makes sense within the purview of the sexual revolution movement, which has significantly affected cultural norms around marriage. Whereas in virtually all religious communities in Ghana, childbirth is considered part and parcel of marriage, in most secular-liberal societies, marked by homosexual practices, career pursuit etc., childbirth is not only a sacrifice but a drawback. This runs at odds with Ghana's religious constituency whose quest for children in marriage would send them to every direction, including hospitals and prayer camps, in search of a child/ren. Indeed, sometimes the emphasis placed on childbirth has brought lots of pressure on women with some of them using every creative means to offset public attention on the childlessness state of their marriage. An example of this is the recent case of a 28-year-old Takoradi woman, Josephine Panyin Mensah who faked pregnancy (even after she had suffered a miscarriage early in her pregnancy) and pretended to have been kidnapped, leading to the loss of her twin children.[189] This situation of high expectation of childbirth after marriage needs to be measured to reduce the undue pressure on married women and their families. As I reflected over the trauma Josephine may have endured following the pressure on her to fake

---

[189] Ghanaweb (24 September 2021), "Detail on why W/R Minister said Takoradi woman was not pregnant", https://www.ghanaweb.com/GhanaHomePage/NewsArchive/Detail-on-why-W-R-Minister-said-Takoradi-woman-was-not-pregnant-1364728, accessed 11 October 2021.

pregnancy, I penned an article to an imagined sister that was published by Ghanaweb.[190]

Nevertheless, the Ghanaian community cherishes childbirth. Children are not only a source of collateral social security; they are considered part of fulfilling God's command for humans 'to fill the earth'. The idea that marriage is a cultural creation is obviously one of the reasons that have been deployed by homosexuals and their academic advocates to push for alternative marriage unions. Consequently, homosexual advocates construe the religious push against the practice in Ghana as backwards and a relic of the religious bigotry of a pre-modern world.

The Akan kinship terminology, matriliny puzzle and sexuality

When I had my first child with my wife on January 17 2018, I initially wondered why my wife had to say to me "thank you for making me a woman". This was soon after our son had been born at the City Hospital, Winson Green – Birmingham, England, where I was let in the maternity room to support and later had the boy handed over to me. The act the nurses handing to me, as an Akan, had a symbolic meaning. It was as if the nurses were communicating to me: "We hand over to you and to your paternal care; for your wife has done her part; it is your part to take care of your child." My wife's parents also thanked me profusely.

As I said, initially, I took the expression of gratitude of my wife and her matriclan members for granted, but later I understood the gravity of it within the rubric of the Akan matriliny puzzle, which as I will soon discuss below is circumscribed in and determined by jural and moral tenets and rules relating to the status of persons (Fortes 1972). More to the point, the marriage institution itself is contentious as it involves a transition of a person from affinal status to conjugal status – it is about gaining and losing rights; family negotiations, love and power, and competition of both material and uxorial resources. Since marriage must definitely be between "strangers" or non-kin members, also depended on how it is defined, that two "strangers" seeking to live together would generally generate tension. Do parents desire to lose

---

[190] Charles Prempeh (October 7, 2021) 'An open letter to my sisters and future daughters: know your ontological worth in a dangerous world', https://www.ghanaweb.com/GhanaHomePage/features/An-open-letter-to-my-sisters-and-future-daughters-Know-your-ontological-worth-in-a-dangerous-world-1374709 (Accessed: November 12, 2021).

their daughters to strangers? Would parents freely allow their sons to direct their (son's) attention and resources to taking care of another woman? Did my wife and her matriclan members thanked me for my supposed altruism? What would my matriclan also expect from me, my wife and our (my wife and I) children? The tensions morph into patriarchy, where, whether in matrilineal or patrilineal societies, male-centric control of marriage is always visibly present as a social reality – even if expressed differently.

The Akan matriliny where children belong to their mothers and yet the man has exercises absolute phallic and social control over his nuclear family remains a puzzle to several analysts. Since the middle of the 20th Century, several western anthropologists wrote extensively about the kinship system, including the matrilineal puzzle (Basehart 1961). Postcolonial Africa, since the turn of the millennium has seen increased research about the family structure of the Akan of Ghana. Beginning with Christine Oppong's research on the family in the 1970s at the Institute of African Studies, the Akan family has had extensive research attention. Researchers have often been interested in whether or not the forces of glocalisation have had any seismic transformative impact on the kinship system of the Akan. Merged with the recent rise in the sexual revolution or cultural wars, several feminist/gender scholars have re-studied the Akan matriliny.

The conclusion is that they have been frustrated by the fact that core of the matrilineal system remains that men are in full patriarchal control of the reproductive rights of their wives and absolute social control over their children. Similarly, men's phallic competence continues to be expressed in terms of men's fertility competence to have their own biological children. Consequently, since Rattray wrote about how much Akan men dreaded phallic incompetence in the 1920s, Akan men continue to pray against incompetence – giving rise to several herbalists in recent Ghana mastering their therapeutic skills in producing fertility enhancement medicine, often called "man power". These herbalists, these days more women in the field, ply their business in the *Trɔtrɔ* (local name for commercial mini-bus in Accra).

In one such encounters, a woman herbalist requested permission from the driver's conductor (known locally as mate) to trade her herbal medicine. She was allowed and began with a Christian worship song and a text from the Bible – a usual legitimising entry point to appeal to Ghana's enchanted public sphere. Several people joined in singing. Afterwards, she quoted the Bible Ezekiel 47:12, often focusing on the concluding verse, which read: "Their fruit will serve for food and their leaves for healing." Soon, after she had had nearly the attention of everyone, she began a long unsolicited lecture on the importance of men's fertility, citing the social cost of impotency on marriage. She attributed the increasing of divorce in Ghana to men's impotency, which according to her is a tabooed subject for wives to broach with their husbands. Just then, the passenger seated next to me chuckled in annoyance. So, I thought he was, indeed, not happy with what the herbalist was saying. But incidentally, when the woman gave out her number, again a usual practice among herbalist as part of tapping into modernity, the passenger clandestinely took his phone and saved the herbalist's number. At that point, I just pretended I did not see him writing the herbalist's number, especially after he chuckled so loud in disapproval. When I posted this incident on my Facebook wall, a friend commented as, "ɛkutia nim ne wura" (To wit: "Those insinuations are cast at know themselves").

I definitely may not be able to readily tell the ethnic identity of my co-passenger, but what I definitely know is that the issue of men's phallic competence is the desire of several heterosexual men in Ghana – regardless of their kinship system. The issue is even more complex among the Akan, where emphasis is placed on pater (social father) more than genitor (biological father) and yet, Akan men's masculinity is generally, historically and even now defined along men's phallic competence and patriarchal control over their family. This analogy brings out the Akan matriliny puzzle, which perhaps may never end, since as I have mentioned, the Akan marriage system is both sociogenic that is concurrently oriented towards procreativity – socio-political and biological existential matrix that IVF can hardly resolve fully.

To discuss the matriliny puzzle, therefore, I rely on my own observations and experiences and both old and new literature on the subject – highlighting the fact that the system has not significantly changed. The near lack of cultural dynamisms (or osmotic change) with the puzzle, especially the continuing male-centric control over the family is what remains a source of irritation and frustration to several feminist scholars. But to show that the social system is not just about it, but rather also political, I begin with the Akan political system. This is because, as I discussed in the previous Chapter, the Akan *ɔhemaa* is expected to be powerful and more influential than her male counterpart, but that was certainly not the case and has never been the case. The Akan matriliny, contrary to feminist expectation, never gravitated to matriarchy – female political dominance. Given that the Akan, as I have said, builds on social system that is both informed by biology and social reality, there is hardly any hope that male-centric control, phallic competence among heterosexual men would change as a norm. As a Christian and Akan, this reminds me of the Biblical understanding of masculinity, which I shall discuss soon as part of my concluding reflections.

With all this, I begin with a summary of the heart of the matter – the Akan woman's political authority. The Akan *ɔhemaa* had a stool – symbol of authority – that was rated as senior and higher than her male counterpart, it never translated into matriarchy. The *ɔhemaa* only performed domestic roles that involved largely women. The highest political role she played was to determine who became the next *ɔhene* when the male stool became vacant. Political power, public governance and daily administration of the Akan state was/is invested in the male ruler. The Both during the precolonial and colonial, entering into the postcolonial, the socio-political structure of the Akan has significantly remained the same – in terms of male rulers exercising power.

The dislocation of political power from the *ɔhemaa* to the *ɔhene* though the Akan is matrilineal in social structure, reflected in the family. Just as the Akan *ɔhemaa* had an important political stool that never translated into political power, so is the Akan married woman has the children she gives birth and yet phallic control (or what feminist scholars called masculine hegemony – see) rested with the man. That women are expected to take charge of the Akan family and yet do not in reality have that power has led several scholars to conclude that the Akan family system is oppressive to women. In her study on Ghanaian migrants in Canada and their decisions to return home (*ɛfie*), Takyiwaa Manuh observed that between Akan men and women, men more than women often prefer to return home to Ghana. According to Manuh, Akan men prefer to return home (*ɛfie*) because it gives them the leverage to reinstate their patriarchal control over women and their households; while for the women, they see (*ɛfie*) as a threat to their new-found independence in Canada (Manuh 2003).[191]

Indeed, Manuh is right in her observation about the complexity of the matriliny system of the Akan. My only concern is that her conclusion is a bit of an overstretch, as the lives of Ghanaian women in Canada and elsewhere in the western world is similarly not easy – if not entirely oppressive like the Akan system. For example, in my stay

---

[191] Takyiwaa Manuh "'Efie' or the meanings of 'home' among female and male Ghanaian migrants in Toronto, Canada and returned migrants to Ghana," in Khalid Koser (ed), *New African diasporas*, 140-159 (London: Routledge, 2003).

and ethnographic research on Ghanaian migrants in England (manuscript yet to be sent for review), several Akan women complained about performing dual roles without any kind of kinship support. Thinking they are taking advantage of the benefits women derive with divorce in England, a few of them stage divorce with their husband which, in the long run tends to override the benefit they had anticipated. This is because, often they are put on a welfare scheme that limits the number of hours they could work, which simultaneously translates into their annual household income. Given that several of these Ghanaian migrants in England are wage earners, working either as cleaners or domiciliary caregivers, they tend to rather struggle with the imagined political economy of divorce. The spill over of this social complexity, *inter alia*, is the burden of neglect and deprivation that Ghanaian and several African children suffer when they are taken away from their homes to care homes (Bywaters et al. 2017).[192]

All this issue reflects the multi-layer complexities of the Akan matriliny system. To resolve this debacle of matriliny, Akan families tend to emphasise *pater* (social father) more than genitor (biological father). The logical is to ensure that the Akan man took care of his family. An Akan man who failed to take of his family and home was called *kwasiam pa ni* (a foolish person). As I learned from one of my mentors, Dr John B. Ghartey, the word *kwasiam pani* in Twi is stronger than simply being a fool in English. Situated in the Akan socio-economic matrix, *kwasiam pani* the contraction *ɔko nsa pan ba nsa pan* – to wit: "He goes empty handed and comes empty handed". This reflects the case of an indigenous itinerary merchant who goes on and invests many resources in a long distance, expecting to return home with profit. Btu comes home with an insolvent debt. This sorry state was/is aptly captured in a line in one of Kofi Awoonor's poems, "Song of Sorrow" "Alas! The travellers are back All covered with debt".[193] At least, as far as I can tell, the worst one could tell an Akan man and any egoistic man is that to cast him as an idiot – someone with less brain thana cabbage to hold a family together.

Nevertheless, uncompromising paternal responsibility also produced yet another layer of complexity when gauged against what masculinity meant in this web of social matriliny. Among the Akan, the

---

[192] Paul Bywaters, Josephine Kwhali, Geraldine Brady, Tim Sparks and Elizabeth Bos, "Out of sight, out mind: Ethnic inequalities in child protection and out-of-home care intervention rates," *British Journal of Social Work*, 47 (2017): 1884-1902.

[193] Kofi Awoonor, "Songs of sorrow" in Kofi Anyidoho, *The promise of hope: New and selected poems, 1964-2013* (Lincoln: University of Nabraska Press, 2014).

expected demonstration of masculinity among the Akan man is phallic competency. The Akan man at all costs must prove his masculinity by impregnating and having his own children to perpetuate his wife's matrilineage as well as his ancestral name and legacy. This point produces an antinomy. First, the Akan woman needs the Akan man to perpetuate her family. So, Akan families take interest in the fertility and potency of every potential in-law. Second, the Akan man also expects to biologically reproduce himself by having his own children with his wife (as genitor), as through the power and monopoly over naming his children, he passes on his ancestral legacy to the next generation.

Concurrently, just as the Akan woman biologically and sociologically own her children, the Akan man does same. For example, it is the pride of nearly every Akan man to say that a child is his "*me kɔti anɔ ba*" – (to wit: "A child of my own penis") and to also claim that he has re-membered and memorialised an ancestor through naming (social). Without a child being named by his or her father, a child is socially stigmatised as an illegitimate child of his or her father, even though he or she belongs to her matriclan (Sarpong 1974). The pride of this is expressed as, "*ma to ɛba din*" – (to wit: "I have given a name"). It is for this reason that adoption is not highly priced among the Akan. Also, another layer of Akan masculinity is for a man to exercise control over his wife (biological woman) and children (Rattray 1969). This means that while the Akan woman may be economically richer than her husband, it is a man who is expected to provide for his wife, materially. Men, therefore, take pride when they are praised for the wellbeing of their wives.

Writing on the Akan matriliny, I spoke with several Akan married couple and those in informal conjugal unions that affirmed an observation I made when growing up in Accra in the 1980s. In the 1980s, during the heat of the country's economic morass, I observed that several Akan women would hardly build permanent commercial shops, while still with their husbands in Accra. Indeed, this was against the fact that several of them were in the economic status to be able to expand and concretise their businesses. Instead, these women, including my mother (though not as rich as the other women) preferred to carry things on trays that are well balanced on their heads, supported by a head pad, and hawk in their communities.

Later when I enquired from my father and his generation, they told me that, Akan women often followed the advice of their matriclan that they should make sure that they did not engage in any joint business enterprise with their husbands and that running their business on the small scale ensured that they fulfilled that matriclan obligation. The second was that because the Akan marriage, like several matrilineal system, was highly susceptible to divorce (Gluckman 1950),[194] Akan women often engaged in low-scale business so ensure easy mobility back to their matriclan in case their marriages hit the rock.

Indeed, since the turn of the millennium, the economic itinerary of several Akan women has changed, including several of them working as public servants and running large-scale business. But the fact still remains that Akan women expect their husbands to take care of their (women's) needs, even when the women earn the same or more salaries than their husbands. In fact, in several of my interviews with Akan couples, the men often talked about how their wives would prefer to spend money on their (matriclan), instead of supporting their husbands.

All this also brings to the fore several other issues. Among the Akan, a man is expected and held responsible for taking care of his children. That an Akan man exercise absolute control over the moral upbringing of his children. The mystical belief in *ntorɔ* (sometimes translated as soul or male totemic spirit – Rattray 1969/11911) implies the moral character and personality of a child.[195] The Akan beliefs that this mystical *ntorɔ* is passed on solely from male to their children. The *ntorɔ* representing the moral aptitude of a child, transmissible from fathers to their children, places an obligation on fathers to take absolute control over the moral training of their children (Fortes 1963).[196] Because of the idea of *ntorɔ*, the Akan firmly place the health or otherwise of a child on the child's father. This entwinement between the *ntorɔ* and a child's wellbeing finds an expression in the Akan saying, "Agya de ni sunsum kata nimma so" (to wit: Fathers cover their children with father's soul/spirit. So, a child a child constantly falls sick in the absence of the child's father, a herbalist would potentially ask about the whereabout of the child's father. The idea of *ntorɔ* implies the social and political significance of males in Akan matriclan system. For example, it is the Akan father who finds a wife for his son (Rattray 1969: 9) and also hands over his daughter for marriage.

---

194 Gluckman Max, "Kinship and marriage among the Lozi of Northern Rhodesia and the Zulu of Natal," in A.R. Radcliffe-Brown and Daryll Forde (eds), *African systems of kinship and marriage* (London: Oxford University Press, 1950).

195 R.S. Rattray, *Ashanti law and constitution* (New York: Negro University Press, 1969/1911).

196 Meyer Fortes, "Time and social structure: An Ashanti case study," in Meyer Fortes (ed), *Social structure: Studies presented to A.R. Radcliffe-Brown*, 54-103 (New York: Russell & Russell, Inc., 1963).

From the foregoing, until a man marries a woman, a woman's reproductive rights are controlled by her father and/or the male figure of her matriclan. Once the Akan man marries, the male matriclan head of the Akan man's bride hands over the bride's reproductive rights to the bridegroom, usually after the groom had paid or offered the bridewealth (known as *trinsa*). The *trinsa* is both cheap and also serve as the point of legitimising the *uxorial* rights of the groom. Through this *uxorial* right, a groom becomes the owner of his children and demonstrates that, as I have said, through naming. The Akan woman does not name her children and the Akan groom is not under any obligation to name his children after his wife's matriclan. If the bride wants the groom to consider naming any of their children after her matriclan, she had to plead with the groom.

The relatively low cost of the Akan bridewealth compared to patrilineal societies had several social implications. I will just focus on a few critical ones. First, divorce rate was very high, as the Akan woman never became part of her husband's matriclan even after marriage and it was also easy to return such a low-cost bride wealth. Second, she also returned with her children, if the man was the reason for the divorce. The low-cost of the bridewealth also demonstrated the non-economic motive of Akan marriage, but rather the forging of social affinal alliances.

This affinal alliances are very important, because the Akan man marries into a woman's matriclan where the matriclan head is the authority figure. This undermines the absolute control the Akan man could exercise over his bride in his bride's matriclan. That the matriclan head does not transfer every right to the groom is also grounds for easy divorce. This is because it allows the woman enough freedom, and rightly so, to return easily to her matriclan in the event of marital conflict. This point is reinforced by the fact that the kinship/affinal ties between the bride and her family is strong than the conjugal ties between her and her husband. I have often heard the Akan parents said to their daughters that when getting ready for marriage not to conflate *awareɛ*. (marriage) and *ɛbusua* (matriclan family) the former is more dispensable than the latter. An Akan man who is also suspected by his matriclan to be paying more attention to his wife than his natal family is often reminded not to conflate marriage and family. Resultantly, one my maternal cousins is often berated for paying more attention to his wife than his mother, my maternal uncle. He is often reminded of the statement above. This is usually the case during funerals where the Akan man hands over the remains of his deceased wife to her matriclan for burial rituals. The same is true with the Akan woman handing over the remains of her deceased husband to his matriclan during burial rites.[197]

It must also be said that a woman cannot simply acquired divorce because of low-cost bridewealth and the strong affinal connections she has with her family, even after marriage. For example, while the Akan woman appears to be favoured in areas of divorce, since she returns to her matriclan, it is not also the same as saying that she would be materially resourced. Even as a woman is entitled matriclan resources, it is a male figure who distribute the resources. The male matriclan head may at will choose to refuse a female kin member a share in family's resources. What this means is that, however we look at the matriliny system, the woman's social and political status is precarious. She is not completely different from the woman in a patrilineal society who often suffers double alienation – where she does not belong to the family she is married into until she has a number of children and where she is also hardly accepted into her own family once she first stepped out in marriage.

Clearly, the Akan marriage and, of course, marriage in general is a complex institution that intersect several social relations. It is also a form of social control of the lives and bodies of individuals that is influenced by several structures. These structures include religion, the schooling system, kinship ties, political structures, inheritance and succession systems, mortuary and burial rites, male phallic competence and demonstration of masculine authority over female sexual rights, female fecundity, elaborate public celebration of marriage as a sociogenic effect and allocation of resources.

The above are all incorporated as non-negotiable worldview into the socialisation of individuals and legitimised on the stanchion of a non-binary worldview where the ancestors and God are considered the ultimate moral guidance. Nevertheless, in both the matrilineal and patrilineal society, male phallic competence, demonstrated through the idea of genitor, is the line of demarcation that determines how women

---

[197] Example of how modernity has not significantly affected this practice was in the case of two elitist Kenyans of mixed ethnic backgrounds who thought they could subvert traditional kinship system by living in Nairobi and supposedly cutting kinship ties with their kinsmen and women in their respective home villages. But upon the death of the husband, custom and tradition, as a modern court ruled in favour of the man's family to determine where the man was buried. See: David Cohen and E.S. Atieno Odhiambo, *Burying SM: The politics of knowledge and the sociology of power in Africa* (Portsmouth, NH: Heinemann/London: curry, 1992).

are treated and counts as marriage and what counts as an exceptional case.

To overturn the composite, male-centric-phallic-oriented marriage institution, therefore, would imply a huge assignment of overturning an entire society. As Margaret Archer has said this kind of social change or progressive change of marriage and the family system cannot be overcome with linguistic instrument. In the end, heterosexual marriage that has been traditionally and contemporary institutionalised and legitimised by the postcolonial modern state is treated as the norm rather than the exception. This means that Ghanaians, as I have always mentioned, may accept individuals who are gay on the quiet in their private spheres, but to have the practice similarly institutionalised would be contested. This is because institutionalising same-sex would similarly affect nearly all the institutions of social control.

Consequently, the issue of Ghanaian accommodativeness of difference is always ambiguous and complicated. For example, a Ghanaian professor of mixed raced background is hardly accepted in one of the countries in the West where his maternal ancestry is located – largely for racism reasons. But his same-sex status is accepted and legally institutionalised as public practice, even though in private it is not accepted by several religious constituencies. Yet, his paternal ancestry and family readily accommodate him, even though per the paternal matrilineal system he would hardly assimilated. Incidentally, the same paternal matriclan family rejects him for his openly expression of his same same-sex status, which is considered a taboo (Sarpong 2019: 43).[198]

Indeed, if he were to go quiet about it, he would be accepted by his immediate matriclan members. The moral revulsion against him, legitimised by law that would not allow the public hotels to accept him and his wife in the same room, is so strong that he finds himself unable to stay in both his paternal and maternal social spheres.

Ordinarily, this individual should not suffer dual institutionalised *othering* and yet because every society is institutionally structured, allowing one thing is often thought of as allowing several, if not every other thing to stand. What would it mean if Ghanaians decriminalise homosexual practices? What would it mean if the western world criminalises systemic racism, which Afua Hirsch has brilliantly

---

[198] Peter K. Sarpong, *Aspects of Ghanaian ethos: A compendium of articles, lectures and talks on various socio-cultural and religious topics* (Tema/Ghana: DigiBooks Ghana Ltd, 2019).

discussed in her book, *Bri(ish)*?[199] In view of this, I will discuss in the next section whether the current Bill in the parliament of Ghana that seeks to ban homosexual practices and advocates is a signifier of relapse to a premodern past.

Must the state legislate against people's sexual preferences?

As I have indicated above, marriage and procreation are not part of human-induced creations. These are natural facts of life. God created marriage. God defines the boundaries of marriage. God rules over marriage. Critiques may argue that this is acceptable when stated from the pulpit to people in the pews, but may not be tenable for academic discourse. I accept this criticism, but still stick to my methodological social sciences can hardly produce universally acceptable value judgments. With this, I firmly believe in the multiplicity of ideas and their acceptance in public institution, after all, public institutions are also not neutral. Given my understanding of marriage as a divine-cultural mandate, I find it relatively easy to explains why no human society in recorded history is said to have originated any law on marriage. If there is any law on marriage, it is the state seeking to protect the sanctity of law against the excesses of industrialisation in the 18th century. Otherwise, historically, marriage was a communal, family affair (Linton 1936). Sources please. By implication since the state, a creation of civil society, part of human culture, is not the creator of marriage, the state cannot determine and define marriage. The state must rather protect God's (or Ghana's Triple Heritage – Islam, Christianity, indigenous traditions, and more recently Eastern Religion) ontological vision of marriage as the sole ontological means of procreation. Procreation-induced technologies may appear to provide alternative means to procreation, but the fact remains that it takes the fusion of the sperm and egg of a biological male and a biological female to procreate. Even homosexual families must conform to this ontological boundary of procreation. While what the technologies imply is that the sperm and ovum can meet and need to meet but it does not require: sex and marriage, it requires a union of biological male and female to procreate.

With this said, the state must guard against any practice that subverts, either implicitly or explicitly, the ontological boundaries of marriage. The state has its duty to protect the sanctity of heterosexual

199 Afua Hirsch, *Bri(ish): On race, identity and belonging* (London: Vintage Digital, 2018).

marriage. Since it is not the state that created marriage, the state must rather protect it and not subvert it. If the state violates God's vision for marriage, given to humanity as a divine-cultural mandate to ensure procreation, then the state must legitimately be resisted by Christians and other religious communities who share the vision of creation. As I have often admitted, heterosexual families may not solve all the social and moral challenges of society, but it is the ideal for socialising children into responsible adults.

Individual rights: The Christian root

The idea of the state protecting what God has created, as heterosexual marriage raises questions about human rights. The question is usually about the status of atheists, agnostics, or religious people who hold humanistic liberal theology that supports homosexuality. As part of this debate, I will discuss the question of rights. This is precisely because the homosexual advocates maintain that the current anti-homosexual bill, "Promotion of Proper Human Sexual Rights and Ghanaian Family Values Bill, 2021" under consideration is a violation of human rights. To state my point about human rights, I must say that human rights always have boundaries – ethical and ontological boundaries. Ethical boundaries include the fact that no matter how one lays claim to a particular right one cannot murder another person (merely in the exercise of their human right). There are also human-informed rights that contributes to affirming the dignity of human beings, as accorded by God. Not clear. Here, one has the right to choose the type of house one sleeps in; the right to choose a car; the right to education; the right to health; the right to political participation; the right to social gathering etc., (I will come to this soon in the next set of rights). But all these rights must also be limited by mutually shared ethics. One's right to consume alcohol should not violate the right of others to have the freedom to sleep peacefully without noise from a drunkard. As part of my firm conviction in God's offering of ontological dignity to humanity, a violation of one's rights, regardless of the perpetrators involved should be resisted. One's right to vape and smoke tobacco should not violate one's right to a healthy life.

In terms of ontological rights, one does not have any right over what one has not created. One does not have the right to take one's own life, as part of exercising one's right. This explains the concerns around suicide. Informed by my Christian belief that human beings are stewards of God's creation, one does not have the right to wantonly destroy the environment; the right to violate the sanctity of human life. One does not have the right to take another life, including the life of an unborn baby. There should also be no right to manipulate or sweet talk women into having unprotected sex which leads to an unplanned pregnancy. This is because, as informed by my faith, a baby is a human being, right at conception.[200] At conception a baby is a full human being, until he or she is born, he or she does not add anything to its natural makeup, except progressively develop them. So, a baby's life must be respected. This means indiscriminate abortion is a violation of human rights. That a baby remains a baby even in the womb does not contradict the Akan rituals of socialisation that welcomes the child into the world. The socialisation does not affect the ontological dignity and inviolability of the child; it rather orients the child for social living. This also aligns with the Bible's assertion that, in the heart of every child is foolishness/deviance, socialisation (symbolised by the cane – as discipline/not punishment) should help make the child socially fit.

This view of human rights cannot be given by humanistic philosophies, including evolution and existentialism. This is because, based on these philosophies, human beings do not have any essence to be protected. It is only from Christianity that human inherent rights are protected. From the perspective of Christianity, these ontological human rights are based on God's majestic statement, "So God created man in His own image, in the image of God He created him; male and female He created them".[201] This statement reinforces the relevance of Christian anthropology as revolutionary. This is because, in all non-Christian cultures, human beings were never in the image of God. While those who ruled over others were in the image of a god or representative of a particular god, they alone had the right to rule. They alone had the right to determine the life of others. They alone had access to esoteric knowledge needed for the governance of society. That is why in all pre-Christian and non-Christian societies, leaders were considered gods in the guise of men. This was the case in ancient Egypt, Asante, and pre-Christian Europe. It gave leaders the right to take the lives of the "subjects". This explains why almost all leaders of the pre-modern world were also priests – holding the ontological rights to control natural order, including rain, storm, drought, etc. and must

---

[200] Cf. James V. Hiedinger II (2014). *About abortion: 10 things a new generation of Christians should know.* Kentucky: Seedbed Publishing.

[201] Genesis 1:27.

be worshipped. These leaders demanded worship because they performed dual roles as priests and political leaders.

However, the breakpoint of this unequal relationship, induced by human-religion, was the rise of Judeo-Christian values. With the assertion that human beings are made in the image of God, Christianity has often held the conviction that all human beings have ontological value – self-worth and dignity. All human beings are ontologically equal before God. This influenced Jefferson's declaration that all human beings have inherent rights to happiness, liberty, and life. (until you think of slavery, colonialism, racism etc, then it all falls apart) This is different from the Akan saying that "All human beings are the children of God". This is because such a statement still made the Asantehene more influential and powerful to determine who had access to Nyame in Asante's history in the 18th Century (Akyeampong and Obeng 1995). The implication of this for decolonisation is that it is important for all views to be considered, as well as the dignity of all human beings respected.

Since the last few decades, some professed Christians have violated the ontological values of all human beings and engaged in the enslavement of others. But it is important to mention that such individuals were not Christians in the true sense of the word. This is because, at the time of the so-called trans-Atlantic slave trade, religion and politics were intimately conflated – something that Jesus opposed with his statement, "You are in the world, but not of the world". Similarly, Jesus had severally warned the church to stay away from considering the world as their native home. But until the Christian Reformation of the 16th Century that supported the separation of church and state, everything had to be religiously rationalised, even if remotely from the perspective of religion, specifically Christianity. This was because religion was the dominant paradigm. So, European enslavers had to force interpretations of the Bible to fit their enslavement of non-Europeans, including Africans. This was against the fact that the Old Testament word "slave" did not imply de-socialising or de-personalising a human being. It was not chattel slavery or the slave did not suffer social death – to use the expression of Orlando Patterson (1982). Slavery in the ancient world of the Bible was also similar to pre-modern Asante, as discussed by Ghanaian historian Akosua Perbi (2004). My goal is not to justify slavery as recorded in the Bible – far from that. My goal rather is to say that it is quite simplistic to conflate premodern slavery and modern slavery and summarily dismiss the Bible as oppressive.[202]

The changed attitude of erstwhile individuals who were neck-deep in the enslavement of non-Europeans adduce evidence that they violated Christianity. One such person is John Newton. Born in 1725, John Newton was a captain of a slave ship. But later, through the grace of God, he saw the evil in what he was doing and repented and became an English cleric. His famous hymn, "Amazing Grace" with the words, "I was once lost, but now found, was blind, but now seen", captures the irreconcilability between chattered slavery and the Christian virtue of human ontological nobility. In addition to this, the Negro spiritual, "Lord, I want to be a Christian" was composed in the challenge of slavery. Composed in the 1750s, at the height of European enslavement, by enslaved African-American persons exposed to the teaching of Evangelist Samuel Davies, this song was to challenge the European slave master who claimed to be a Christian. The repeated phrase, "In my heart", according to Eileen Guenther, a professor of church music at Wesley Seminary – Massachusetts, US, was the slave communicating to the European Christian to be a true Christian in their hearts since a true Christian will not enslave a fellow Christian; nor bastardise one. This is because in Christianity we are all priests and free in Christ (Galatians 3: 28). It is for this reason and many more that Christians were at the forefront in the fight against enslavement. This was also made possible as Christians contributed to the industrialisation drive of England in the 18th Century – as part of the reason for enslavement was the need for human labour. Currently, slavery still goes on in different forms in different parts of the world, including England, manifesting in the burgeoning care industry. Admittedly, the above may not count as an "academic" but it gives, at least, it gives a clue to why we cannot simplistically entwine the Bible and modern enslavement.

My point in all this is to say that Christianity is the originator of human rights, based on its unique teaching on the human ontological nobility. Indeed, the reason why Christian Europe continues to suffer accusations for the European enslavement of non-Europeans, other than the Arabs whose enslavement of Africans was prior to Europeans and possibly more pernicious (through their castration of male slaves)

---

[202] Jean Gasho (January 4, 2017), "Why are black people obsessed with the Bible that was used to enslave them," https://www.modernghana.com/news/746917/why-are-black-people-obsessed-with-the-bible-that-was-used-t.html (Accessed: September 3, 2022).

is because, for Christianity the ethical standards are high (Azumah 2001). So, as Christians, when we are sometimes called hypocrites for not upholding our divine ethical principles, we accept it because we know others acknowledge the superiority of our principles.

Relating this to homosexuality, my point is very clear – the practice is a violation of ontological boundaries. For the sake of emphasis, this is because God created marriage as a union between a biological male and a biological female for procreation to fill the earth. Anything other than this is a subversion of divine ontological boundary that the state and all individuals must resist. Any law that supports the breaking of God's laws must be resisted and opposed. This is more, but somehow similar to anyone who attempts to usurp the constitution of Ghana. Marriage is part of God's constitution to humanity. It is for this reason that Christianity is opposed in all countries that have decriminalised homosexuality. It is also for this reason that so-called Christian theologians must water down the clear teaching of the Bible on heterosexual marriage to endorse homosexual practice. Indeed, they usually do this to appease homosexuals and their stomachs, and sometimes their own sexual inclinations.

Homosexuality and the idea of foreignness and nativity to African cultures

I begin this section by making it clear that sin is not foreign to any culture. Sexual perversion is not foreign to any culture. So, homosexuality, as a sinful practice, is not foreign to any culture (Crompton 2003). From the Christian perspective, the debate, therefore, is not so much about whether the homosexual practice is foreign to any culture, as it is about whether a sinful, perverted sexual practice should be decriminalised. It is also about whether in societies prior to the imposition of colonial rule, the people who became the Gold Coasters ever legitimised the public practice of *trumutrumu* – the current local slang for the practice. Indeed, while Christians are to love and to avoid being judgmental, in terms of descending God's ultimate judgment on people, Christians are charged to deploy the Bible as the standard to object to practices, such as homosexuality that is clearly condemned in the Bible. Again, the argument of its exoticness or not should be construed on the linearity of time – constricting static binaries between past and present, tradition and modern, religion and irreligion etc.

I make this argument precisely because, while homosexual practice as a sin wasn't foreign to any culture, including the western world, we must be interested in what it means today. At any rate, a people's sense of their past isn't just about their past that is there, but how they also construe the necessities of their present to peep into the future – unreached time. It should also be measured along with the parameters of what a people consider germane, significant, necessary and central in supporting human flourishing, including the perpetuation of the human race. Impliedly, in my view, anything, including homosexuality that recklessly and needlessly breaks ethical and ontological boundaries should not be debated as a subject of quantitative or historic times frames; such a matter should be discussed around the quality of human life, the vision of humanity and the ultimate goal of the Creator who intended humanity to flourish in population and indignity.[203] It is for this reason that people of every civilised country have always been eager to associate sexual perversions with some other country than their own (Ellis 1906).

Whereas homosexuality, as a perverted sexual practice, wasn't foreign to Africa, it was not pronounced – as there isn't enough evidence in support of its acceptance as a normal lived social reality (Dlamini 2006; Murry and Roscoe 1998). More so, we read from nowhere in literature, including anthropology – colonialism-inspired imposed subject (Wilson 1940) – that Africans were in public adulation of homosexuality. Africans do not praise witchcraft but it exists, or does it not? Similarly, it is not written or recorded in anywhere that homosexuality was celebrated in the public sphere. Neither is rape! In Ghana, for example, there is hardly any evidence of any social institution – festivals, religious rituals, political establishment etc. – that supported, confirmed, and celebrated homosexuality. This is why they are called queer sexualities, they do not need support to exist. Perhaps you should read queer theory literature to fully appreciate how these sexualities exist vis-à-vis the mainstream.

While we have had individual men with feminine physical characteristics, that was hardly any ground for anyone to claim that homosexual practices were commonly accepted in the public sphere. Throughout the history of Ghana, we have not read from any oral or written account that the idea of "Kojo Bɛsia" – a feminine-male – was construed as a patented right for the endorsement of homosexuality. So far, none of the radical feminists in Ghanaian universities have been

[203] Genesis 1: 28.

able to prove that "Kojo Bɛsia" or "Kwesi Bɛsia" was seamlessly construed as homosexual. Of course, it doesn't. Here, the lawyers and scholars blatantly failed to differentiate between homosexuality – as a contorted biological trait – and homosexual practice – actually engaging in homosexuality with open public acceptance.

This similarly implies that random or even regular student deviant practices of *Supi* (lesbianism) and *Azukwaff* (gayism) in our schools cannot be used as a canon to claim that homosexuality was publicly accepted in Ghana.[204] Since the 1960s, the Ghanaian public has rightly rejected students' engagement in *supi* in our schools. I have personally counselled students at the Accra Girls' Senior High School – where I taught briefly in 2010 as part of their long vacation classes – to resist pressures to incorporate homosexuality – more specifically lesbianism – into their lives. The issue of whether my counselling worked in terms of a student reforming her life is not within my power, as counselling means counselling – working with a counselling to take responsibility of their own decisions.

Similarly, as I have said, among the Akan, there is hardly any evidence that queer sexualities were accepted as sociogenic. Elsewhere in ritual practices, queer sexualities could be practised, such as the grotesque popular stories of men sleeping with their mothers for ritual purposes. Indeed, in the world of rituals, the *abnormalities* of the material world are normalised; the destabilisation of the social world is stabilised in the ritual world. We have seen many of such things in Ghana where *Sakawa* (fraudsters) boys and girls are rumoured to be involved in all forms of grotesque rituals – including sleeping at the cemetery at odd hours, consuming female used sanitary pads etc. While these grotesque practices are counter-intuitive to the material world, they make an *imagined* sense in the ritual world.

Currently, South Africa remains one of the countries to have decriminalised homosexuality. This isn't surprising, given the history of the country. Respectable judges and lawyers who were involved in the anti-apartheid struggle also contributed to the constitution making process and sought to include aspirations of activists who were marginalised during apartheid.

---

[204] I stress the "public" because we are not interested in what happens in the private that has no repercussion for the public. Similarly, what happens in the private may not be a subject of public concern except when it is publicly denounced or is of relevance. Equally sexual practices that were allegedly accepted would have found free expression as part of lived social reality in a society.

First, Mandela, based on his own autobiography, was a humanist. He did not believe in a God who directly influences the course of human history – from my reading of him, he was more a deist than a stronger believer in a God who acts in history (Mandela 1994). He also believed in the innate goodness of human beings, including every human being, persons who believe in natural human goodness would hardly consider homosexuality as an aberration to social normativity. So, as part of the processes of re-liberating South Africa, his non-religious stance was strong in pushing for homosexuality – known among the *Sangomas* – but which the white Christians had suppressed to be accepted. Similarly, Desmond Tutu, a venerable "clergy" man of Mandela's generation supported homosexuality for his own personal reasons. He was a liberation theologian, whose ideal was to incorporate Christianity into achieving a political end.[205] In Christianity, feminist theologians who support lesbianism largely derived inspiration from liberation theology, which was popular in Latin America. As Byang Kato has rightly observed the damage to which liberalisation theologians did to the Christian faith as they tend to rate political aspiration over soteriological issues (Kato 1985). The mundane take precedence over the core of the Gospel – the redemption of human beings from sin.

With all this, I must also point out that in the history of the English people, homosexuality was decidedly considered foreign practice – they considered it a foreign importation (Crompton 2003). This was usually the case in the 16th Century. The 16th Century is far back, but it is to show the evolution of sexuality in the European world. It was considered a perverted practice that had sneaked in from France – generally stigmatised in European history as the culturally perverted part of Western Europe. This explains why all elements of homosexuality, framed as "unnatural practices" were regarded as a felony in England, following Henry VIII's 1533 decree that, "offenders being hereof convict by verdict confession or outlawry shall suffer such paynes of death and losses and penalties of their goods, chattels, debts, lands, tenants and hereditaments as felons being accustomed to do androgyne to the order of the Common Lawes of this Realme".[206]

Also, because the homosexual practice was read as foreign to the English and many other European countries, "the Old Testament death penalty for male homosexual behaviour was incorporated into Roman

[205] Needless to say, Desmond Tutu's daughter, Mpho Andrea Tutu van Furth is a lesbian.

[206] The Act 25 Hen. VIII c. first enacted by Parliament in 1533.

Law. Later, this same precedent was cited when death for homosexual behaviour was prescribed by criminal codes in France, Spain, England, the Holy Roman Empire, the Italian states, Scandinavia, and every land settled by European colonists who professed Christianity" (Crompton 2003: 34). That anti-homosexual law is influenced by Judeo-Christian sex ethics is also confirmed by another homosexual advocate and scholar who said it was Judeo-Christianity that criminalised homosexual practices (Gupta 2008). That homosexual advocates admit that the origin of anti-homosexual laws comes from Judeo-Christian ethics implies that it is originally an English culture that was untouched by Christianity. It is important to mention that homosexual advocates maintain that the foreignness of the practice was informed by Christianity – referring to the Old Testament. This reinforces the point I have been making that homosexual practice as sinful isn't foreign to any culture, but as a suppressed practice it is common to all cultures – especially cultures shaped and influenced and rightly so, by Christianity. I will come back to this point in my discussion of why the western world has decriminalised homosexuality and why it is similarly compelling Ghanaians and other Africans to do the same. I will also use this to discuss the reason why anti-homosexual laws, circulated in the British Empire and rightly so, later became part and parcel of the legal code of post-colonial states in Africa, including Ghana.

Where from "homophobic" laws?

The spread of anti-homosexual laws in Africa was part of Victorian England seeking to rightly incriminate European "homosexual men looking for sexual and emotional companionship away from home. It is no surprise that, even in the 'darkest Africa' or 'primitive Oceania', homoerotic writing described a comely local man as Ganymede or Antinous, and harked back to paradigms of 'Socratic love'; some travelers felt that they had discovered a homosexual Eden or equatorial Athens overseas" (Aldrich 2003: 9). Several European men were involved in homosexual practices in Africa. But for the sake of space, I will only refer to Richard Burton. Burton was one of the great imperialist adventurers in the 19th Century with his activities covering South Asia and South America, the Middle East and Africa. He enjoyed a close friendship with men, and considered homosexuality as natural intercourse as he quoted the obscene quatrain to prove it: "The penis, smooth and round was made / with anus best to match. / Had it been made for cunnus' sake, / it had been formed like a hatchet." He preferred male to female beauty, writing in Africa:

> The male figure here, as well the world over, is notably superior, as amongst the lower animals, to that of the female. The latter is a system of soft, curved and round lines, graceful, but meaningless and monotonous. The former far excels it in a variety of forms and in sinew. In these lands, where all figures are semi-nude, the exceeding difference between the sexes strikes the eye at once. There will be a score of fine male figures to one female, there she is, as everywhere else, as inferior as in the Venus de Medici to the Apollo Belvedere (Aldrich 2003: 33).

One of the arguments in support of homosexuality in Africa is that anti-homosexual laws are un-African. This argument flows from whether or not homosexual practices are foreign to Africans. I have mentioned that sin, from the Christian perspective, is not foreign to any culture. Sin is innately human and universal to all cultures – including so-called pre-scientific/pre-industrial and "modern" societies. As I have said, what is rather foreign to most "civilised" cultures is the enforcement of sinful practices, particularly those that suppressed human procreation (Ellis 1906). This explains why "civilised" cultures suppressed infanticide. But sinful cultures do not just go away under the banner of "civilisation", just as civilisation must be predicated on cherished cultural values. After all, civilisation in its simplest understanding is framed as an advancement in the culture of a group of people.

The use of the advancement of culture as an index of civilisation should be read as a culture purging itself of clear, sinful practices that violate human dignity. In other words, civilisation is about restoring boundaries to ontologies and ethics. It is about redeeming the collapse of all forms of natural and moral ontologies. My understanding is that when cultures make progress, they work against environmental degradation, human sacrifices, infanticide, wanton suppression of wanton, and in our case, homosexuality.

This explains why, while homosexuality is not foreign to any culture, it was largely Judeo-Christian values that suppressed the practice in the western world. I have already stated that in England, it was Christianity that rightly discouraged homosexual practices as an indignity to human beings. English civilisation, spreading to the United States of America and other European countries, was primarily driven by Christianity. It was as a result of Christianity that civil society was conceptualised, human rights were clearly demarcated; freedom was guaranteed; and the industrial revolution made possible etc. Indeed, without Christianity western civilisation would have been impossible! It was Christianity that provided the moral foundation for western civilisation (Stark 2005). For this reason, the European missionaries of the 19th Century rightly attributed and identified any form of sexual perversion in Africa as cultural perversion (Gaudio 2009: 184). Modern science wouldn't have been possible without Christian civilisation (Stark 2005). It was Christians who built the best universities around the western world. These include the University of Cambridge (where I studied for my doctorate degree), Oxford (where I recently completed a short programme on research and development), Harvard (built to raise pastors to train the children of Puritans in the fear of God – against all godless practices including homosexual practices. My point in all this is that the Christian view on sexuality, particularly those that object to the practice as sinful, cannot be dismissed as unwelcome in the academia.

Unfortunately, Harvard has become a den of anti-theist secularism, where more recently an atheist is serving as a chaplain – a paradox of the highest order); Yale (built to counteract the liberalism of Harvard); Princeton etc. Even less religious inclined people like Thomas Hobbes, one of the architects of a social contract, quoted severally, at least more than 600 times, from the Bible – not as much as he did with the Greek philosophers (Hobbes 1985/1904). Alexis de Tocqueville, a French political aristocrat who studied American democracy in the mid-19th Century observed that without Christianity, civil society and democracy wouldn't have been possible in the US (Tocqueville 2016/1954).

For Christianity to advance human flourishing, it needed to overcome anti-human practices, one of which is homosexuality. It is for this reason that Christians were instrumental in suppressing homosexual practices, including outlawing the practice. While some of the laws enacted to suppress homosexual practices were sometimes heavy-handed and need not be encouraged, we must appreciate the fact that the practice was considered a total anti-progressive practice that needed to be stamped out.

So, while homosexual practices as sinful practices are universal, the concern of the English was to spread Christian civilisation to the rest of the world. Informed by Christianity, Europeans were quick and, rightly so, to outlaw homosexual practices through laws. As I have mentioned above, European anti-homosexual laws in the colonies were also meant to curtail the extent to which some Europeans were incorporating the practice as part of European adventures in Africa. At the risk of repeating myself: I must state that the law against homosexuality was not *etiologically* English culture, but rather Judeo-Christian sex ethics. The law isn't secular in orientation, but Christian in orientation. It is for this reason that the suppression of homosexual practices in the British Empire took place under the regime of Queen Victoria, whose vision was to reinforce Christian morality in the colonies. So, while homosexuality had been treated as a crime in England since 1533, its resurgence in the nineteenth century compelled the Victorian regime to tighten its law against the practice in 1885 (Hilliard 1982). For this reason, the first colonial state where the British rightly imposed anti-homosexual law was in India. The law was passed in India because as part of the ritual possibilities of the ritual world, Hinduism allowed homosexuality (Vanita 2007). This is precisely because the ritual world of Hindu as the concept of "third sex" – which categorises males and females on the grounds of who they desire does not in Hinduism. In Hinduism, therefore, homosexuals, lesbians, intersex, bisexuals, and impotent were all placed under "the third sex" (Dewan, 2015: 85). Even so, the practice was hardly allowed as a sociogenic practice – it was not allowed to be practised in the open (2015: 85).

The anti-homosexual law was therefore informed by Judeo-Christian sex ethics, which could be easily gleaned from the framing below, as when the final draft of the Indian Penal Code came into force in 1860, the

> "Unnatural Offences" section was modified. The ultimate, historic text—which, in one form or another, influenced or infested much of the British Empire—read:
>
> Section 377: Unnatural offences – Whoever voluntarily has carnal intercourse against the order of nature with any man, woman or animal shall be punished with imprisonment for life, or with imprisonment ... for a term which may extend to 10 years, and shall be liable to fine. Explanation – Penetration is sufficient to constitute the carnal intercourse necessary to the offence described in this Section.[207]

The use of "unnatural" and "carnal" are simply religious words. These are from the Bible, including:

---

[207] Human Rights Watch (2008). *This Alien Legacy: The origins of "Sodomy" Laws in British colonies.* New York: Human Rights Watch, p. 18.

26 For this cause God gave them up unto vile affections: for even their women did change the natural use into that which is against nature:27 And likewise also the men, leaving the natural use of the woman, burned in their lust one toward another; men with men working that which is unseemly, and receiving in themselves that recompense of their error which was meet.[208]

The tension embedded in "unnatural" and "carnal" in the homosexual discourses

"Unnatural" and "carnal" are words that signal the need for humans to respect natural and ontological boundaries. This implies that if a man crosses the natural demarcations to penetrate the anus of a fellow man, it is justly referred to as "carnal" and "unnatural" knowledge in the case of Ghana (Baisley 2015). As it stands, if a man similarly tries to penetrate the anus of a woman, it is criminalised. It is important that whereas science may consider a man having sex with another man through the anus as unnatural, the idea of nature has become contested, following decades of western research work of the post-enlightenment world that seek to deconstruct anything natural. It is for this reason that as part of the call for decriminalising homosexual laws in Ghana, advocates have profiled religion as the major hindrance (Mohammed 2020).

Similarly, the authors in reflecting the seismic cultural shift in the west maintain that marriage is "between two or more people" as opposed to people of opposite-sex. This is clearly a reading of modern liberalised sex ethics into conceptualisation. But I must state that while homosexuality is not new to any culture of the world, including the Greco-Roman world, the supposed progenitors of western civilisation, through the influence of Judeo-Christian sex ethics and marriage norms, the practice of homosexuality was suppressed and, rightly so, until the 1970s. So, it is clear that relative social acceptance of homosexuality in the west, is not a mark of the western being more modern or civilised than countries such as Ghana that continue to oppose the practice. Instead, the practice is part of the western falling back on their "primitive" past to recuperate what they rejected because of Christianity. It is, therefore, unapt to describe Ghanaians who oppose homosexuality as being backwards. If anything at all, the

[208] Romans 1: 26-27.

western world is being more backwards in their acceptance of homosexuality than Ghanaians, who continue to oppose it.

It must also be said that the British colonisers' suppression of homosexuality in the British Empire was part of Queen Victoria's vision of spreading Christian sex ethics in and around Britain.

Decolonisation as a revitalisation of Ghanaian indigenous moral worldview

The debate on marriage and the LGBTQ+ has been part of the academic discourses in the world – making the universities the epicentre for revolutionising public morality on sex. Western scholars are not ashamed to write their sexual orientations into scholarship and theories. Similarly, western scholars who may not be practising members of the LGBTQ+ community write to reflect the domain of the cultural paradigm in their respective countries. This creates a complex paradox where the university theories are the creation of society, while society is the creation of university theories. Nevertheless, through the media of universities and supported by media outlets, liberal sex education is normalised in the public. This reinforces advocacy to reshape legislation to support the current sexual revolution in the west. Concurrently, Ghana/Africa overly gets polarised over the LGBTQ as contesters engage in counter-accusation of who is being influenced the most by western powers. It is critical to mention that for western liberal academics to get away with these sexual revolutionary theories, they push against all religious injunctions against counter-cultural sexual practices as archaic and oppressive to women (Bawa 2019).

As a result of this, the colonial university in Ghana has become a centre of not just epistemic production but an enchanted space animated by conflictual worldviews. Several western trained African scholars, occupying positions in European universities in Ghana, use their spaces to advance their own theories, some of which dovetail into the liberal theories of the west. Like Dr Grace Diabah and Professor Nana Aba Appiah Amfo, whose article I have discussed above, hardcore feminist scholars have been very ruthless in promoting western feminist ideologies. Undoubtedly, these scholars have advocated decolonizing African studies. But their idea of decolonizing African Studies and by extension African universities is of a kind. This is because they continue to use western brewed theories in their study of gender and their advocacy. Currently, these women, apart from Dr

Diabah and Amfo, are pushing for the rights of LGBTQ+ in Ghana. As scholars and public intellectuals, they are at the forefront of advancing alternative sexualities in the country.

The support these feminist scholars give to the LGBTQ+ community in Ghana sits in a history of the rise of Gender Studies in Ghanaian universities, beginning with the University of Ghana, the country's premier university. Since the 1990s, African students, particularly women who studied in western universities, especially the United States of America, returned home to introduce Gender Studies. Before this time, courses such as Family Studies, especially at the Institute of African Studies, University of Ghana, were largely known. Professor Christine Oppong was a British academic trained in Social Anthropology at the University of Cambridge in 1959 and African Studies at the Institute of African Studies (IAS), University of Ghana. At the IAS, she enrolled in 1963 and completed her Masters (M.A.), with a thesis entitled *Sociological aspects of education in Dagbon*. Oppong's thesis "makes an important contribution to our knowledge and understanding of the factors that make for the continuity and discontinuity of cultural transmission in traditional society" (Nketia in Oppong 2013: x). Married to a Ghanaian academic, Professor Oppong settled in Ghana and taught at the Institute of African Studies for twenty-five years. One of the courses she championed was African Family Studies. As an academic, technical and policy advisor, Gender, Population and Development in the Employment and Development of the International Labour Organisation, Geneva, she worked hard to support several of her students to receive funding for their doctoral studies.[209]

By the time I went to the IAS, Professor Oppong had left the institute under what many considered as part of institutional politics at the institute. That IAS, as I observed, had had a tradition of keeping retired professors on contract for them to help in nurturing younger academic. It was, therefore, possible for Christine Oppong who did her did her undergrad in 1959 to still be active in academia beyond her 70s. Rumours had it that she was pushed out to make way for Gender Studies, which was gaining ground in the mid-2000s. Consequently, she retired. We thank her for her contributions to academia. Consequently, in 2010, my colleague (Kofi Atsu Semanu Adzei) and I were the last groups to have been taught by Professor Oppong. Even then, the

[209] Some of her students include Drs Deborah Atobrah, Benjamin K. Kwansah, Bawa Yussif, C. Baataar, Edward Nanbigne, Peter Agbodzah, and Mr Douglas Frimpong-Nnuroh.

course was split among and taught among six professors, including some of her students. So, she travelled to Ghana and taught her part – and that was it. But the first time my colleague and I encountered Professor Oppong, we realised that she was a different breed of a professor. In line with the course, she taught when we first met, the first thing she asked us to do was to tell her about our respective families, after which she asked why we had chosen African Family Studies. This was followed up with a question: How can I help you? At this point, my colleague and I were so mesmerised that we looked into each other's face in disbelief.

The uniqueness of Professor Oppong's approach to African studies was her conscious effort at destabilising western episteme at the epicentre of epistemic production in the institute. This was part of a tradition she had learned from her teacher and mentor, Jack Goody, who taught her Social Anthropology at the University of Cambridge where she first registered as an undergraduate student in 1959. And in line with Nkrumah's vision of the IAS serving as the epicentre of polishing the pearls of traditions of African knowledge, Oppong operated from the Goody's epistemological approach, which "includes his consilient thinking; his courage to address big issues; his attempt to avoid western bias; his rejection of elitism or ethnocentrism; his linking of the micro and the macro and his global/historical vision" (Oppong 2015: 5). Indeed, in his book, *The theft of history*, Jack Goody sought to prove that "Europe didn't invent love, democracy, freedom, or market capitalism" (Goody 2006: 5). These were lies that Europe had gotten away with because "problem of eurocentricity … augmented by the fact that the particular view of the world in European Antiquity, which was reinforced by the authority derived from the extensively used system of Greek alphabetic writing, was appropriated and absorbed into European historiographical discourse, providing an apparently scientific overlay to one variant of the common phenomenon" (Ibid., 5).

I have emphasised Oppong's methodological approach to teaching and research to demonstrate the Afrocentricity that she imbued in scholarship at the IAS. Her approach was part of bridging the gown-town gap which has often been a challenge for universities, often leading to tension between academics and the public.[210]

The departure of Professor Oppong weakened the African Family Studies course in favour of Gender Studies. Gender Studies had

[210] It was partly because of this tension between gown-town that the University of Cambridge was born in 1209.

become part of the Ghanaian academia since the 2000s when women academics of different research backgrounds, later identifying themselves as feminist scholars, began with the Centre for Gender Studies and Advocacy (CEGENSA). With the establishment of feminist-oriented research centres such as the Centre for Gender Studies and Advocacy (CEGENSA) in 2006 by the Council of the University of Ghana, Gender Studies was given a boost. Led by scholars such as Professors Akosua Adomako Ampofo and Takyiwaa Manuh, the Centre had the following as its mission: "To create an interdisciplinary space that positions CEGENSA as a leader in key areas of university policy-making but also curriculum development and service provision". In addition, the Centre aims to: incorporate gender equity into the core values and business of the academy; create a working and learning environment, and culture supportive of social justice for both men and women; be the place of choice for theoretically stimulating and socially relevant programmes and activities; serve as a key driver of advocacy on gender equity in Ghana, but also in the West African sub-region and internationally; serve as a resource base and support centre for countrywide and internationally based gender networks and causes. In terms of vision, "CEGENSA's vision is to be a credible and respected institution for promoting relevant and high-quality research, teaching and learning on gender. Our vision is to be a place of choice for accessing innovative and creative programmes and policies, which are committed to ensuring that gender equity is enshrined in all aspects of the institutional and intellectual culture of the University and in Ghanaian society".[211]

Given the vision and aim of CEGENSA, Gender Studies gradually became part of the university curriculum. This course was introduced as part of mitigating against what was generally framed as the suppression of women's rights in Ghana. Practices such as female genital cutting, widowhood rites? disinheriting women, placing barriers ahead of potential women politicians, *Trokosi*, were also framed as enemies to be conquered by Gender Studies. Over the years, CEGENSA has been involved in drafting policy and directives to stop sexual abuses in the university community. But at the same time, the theoretical foundation of Gender Studies, existentialism, as I have mentioned above is seen as a threat to keeping social, ethical and ontological boundaries. Currently, in Ghana, virtually all the advocates of Gender Studies, all of whom have played key roles at the Institute of

[211] Source of information on CEGENSA: https://cegensa.ug.edu.gh/about-us

African Studies, Legon, are pushing for the rights of LGBTQ+ in Ghana. This, in itself, is not a crime, except that as part of the decolonisation agenda, the sexual worldview of the Ghanaian public should be incorporated into Gender Studies. My observation is that, given the challenges that have burdened women's lives in Ghana, often blamed on patriarchal cultures, some gender academics are less tolerant of indigenous views on sexuality, marriage, and family. For example, in her work on why female Ghanaian migrants in Canada may hardly desire to return home, Takyiwaa Manuh argued that such women often dreaded the patriarchy in Ghanaian cultures. Contrary, she concluded that men loved to return home, because they enjoyed patriarchal rights (Manuh 2003). While such conclusions may be valid, it profiles Ghanaian cultures as patriarchal, fossilised and hardly leaves room engagement and contextual analysis.

This development, involving feminist African Studies scholars, has created concerns about academic freedom in the universities in Ghana alongside decolonizing the universities. These are heavy-weight issues. To what extent do Ghanaian universities enforce academic freedom in institutions funded by public funds, while at the same time decolonizing the institutions. In all of this, the questions are the boundaries that are placed in the way of academic freedom and decolonization. To what extent can an academic have the freedom to write? Can an academic, whose research is funded by the public publish and teach theories that are at variance with what the public consider an affront to their moral sensitivity? There is also the question about the extent are academics so tied up to their funders that they write what the funders want. For example, in Ghana, it can be said that all the three major religions, Christianity, Islam, and indigenous traditions converge uniformly on subjects such as marriage as heterosexual, childbirth as a necessity, and the authority of man in structuring the family. Unfortunately, society's engagement with religious family structures have not always benefitted women and women cannot often take androcentric issues lying down face up. But the question for me is: how could an academic in exercising freedom produce theories or teach such theories that can negotiate the tensions that sometimes generate from religious family structured, as discussed above, to ensure that men and women are justifiably satisfied in family life? Could academics walk the complex terrain between liberal and feminist theories and indigenous worldviews without being profile as pushing for western agenda or being profiled as atavists? Or instead of dialogue, must female academics rebel against the indigenous family system that tends to place the man as the head and divides gendered roles along transcendent and immanence? And how can the universities be decolonized without incorporating the moral worldviews of the religious communities in the universities? My point is that both Islam and Christianity have a long history in Africa since the 1st Century of both religions. Africans played important roles in the intellectual discourse on Christian dogmas (Oden 2007); while Bilal bin Rabah, was the first to call Muslims for prayers. That Christianity and Islam have a long history on the continent implies that we cannot take it as given that the Bible as a colonised instrument of oppression or alien to Africans (Sundkler and Steed 2004). If Christianity is alien to Africans, it is as well alien to every culture, since the moral teachings (especially on sexual purity) of the faith are hardly in alliance with any particular culture, after all, Christ is above all cultures.

In the quagmire of these questions, I have already stated that the Gender theories tend to dismantle religiously-inspired social order that defines men and women relations. As I have said, this is not uncalled, but it should incorporate other worldview, including both Christianity and Islam. Meanwhile, the western world has largely succeeded in pushing through Gender theories to an infinite end including women promoting polyamory, because religion has been pushed away from the universities. But in Ghana, religion has since the 1970s become more visible, more engaging with the public, and does not show any sign of declining. The religious resurgence in Ghana is part of the global resurgence of religion in the 1970s, which led some of the proponents of secularisation thesis to recant or refine their theory.

This includes Peter Berger who reproduced a theory about de-secularisation (Berger 1999). The religious resurgence in Ghana since the 1970s has implied that the Ghanaian public that funds public universities is deeply religious with a moral orientation that supports heterosexual relations. Similarly, the public, while it shows signs of western "modernisation" has not departed from the traditional values of the family which includes marriage and procreation. This is against the fact that institutions of funerary homes and insurance companies are gradually encouraging the role of families. This is because funeral performance which is highly sociogenic in orientation and reinforces gerontocracy and group solidarity and cohesion has significantly been taken over by funerary homes – especially in the case of the middle class and elites. Similarly, insurance companies have consolidated individual financial independence, diverting the attention people repose in the family as a form of social security.

Nevertheless, as I have said, the ontological role of heterosexual relations as the main means of procreation is still very strong in Ghana. This is to the extent that women who rise through the academic ranks or in their pursuit of a professional career live within societal expectation to marry and have children, as well as submitting themselves to the indigenous structure of the family when a man is a head while women perform largely expressive roles. It is this persistence of indigenous family values that angered Diabah and Amfo to conclude that despite women rising in social status, they are expected to imbibe the values of submissiveness, hard work, and respect. As I have stated, it is for this reason that heterosexual marriage has been misconstrued by some radical feminists as an oppressive, sexist institution.[212]

That women should object to submissiveness in marriage is similar to Darkwah and Arthur whose study of three Virgin Clubs in Ghana seeks to "document the extent to which these clubs in their insistence on virginity, provide yet one more avenue for patriarchal control of female bodies" (Darkwah and Arthur 2006: 124). Indeed, the clubs, as the authors admit partly, follow the need for abstinence as suggested by President George Bush when he became the president of the United States of America in 2000. It must be stated that the Republican Party, a centre-right party of Bush, tends to have a political ideology that tends to favour the sex ethics of evangelical Christians. Consequently, the importance of abstinence to control the spread of HIV/AIDS resonates with Ghanaian Christianity, which has become largely evangelical since the 1970s (Asamoah-Gyadu, 2005). In the conclusion of these authors, Christian sex ethics of abstinence to control the spread of HIV/AIDS could turn women into asexual beings (Darkwah and Arthur 2006: 144).

I must also admit the complexities embedded in the abstinence-only policy. Abstinence-only sexuality education could be treated as unethical as it entails misinformation and deliberate withholding of information, it is unsustainable, unscientific because full information and access to reproductive technologies is proven to work (see Kantor et al 2008) One does not deal with vulnerable young people by denying them information. Rather teach them honestly, but tell them that abstinence is ideal but if they cannot abstain, they can protect

---

[212] Sara M. Moniuszko (4 August 2021), "Why marriage is still a sexist institution – and what we can do about it" https://eu.usatoday.com/story/life/health-wellness/2021/08/04/marriage-sexist-institution-experts-say-yes-but-we-can-change-it/5459310001/, accessed: 15 October 2021.

themselves. If abstinence-only strategies were effective, why does Africa have the highest teenage pregnancy rate when every African government chooses this tried and failed strategy? It is a pity most governments choose not to critically engage with their own policies. Are the teenagers falling pregnant from breathing alone? Admittedly, these youngsters are potentially sexually active and empower them to resist the risks. Many fall pregnant because they do not know how pregnancy comes about.

The conclusion of these women authors is rather surprising (though remains consistent with the feminist ideology of deconstruction of social structures of religion as oppressive. This is because among several socio-cultural and economic reasons, biological reasons are key since,

> The ability of HIV to pass through the cells of the vagina lining and the larger surface of the vagina area. … Adolescent girls may further be at increased risk due to the existence of greater proportions of genital mucosa, which are present in an immature cervix. Adolescent girls are also susceptible to relatively high levels of genital inflammation which may also increase their risk of HIV acquisition. Due to the lower uptake of ART (Anti-Retroviral Treatment) among men, in most countries, likely fewer men than women are virally suppressed, which means men are more likely to pass the virus on to others in settings where the main mode of transmission is heterosexual sex, this further increases women's risk of acquiring HIV.[213]

Given that, as I have already mentioned, (for the religious Ghanaian public), marriage is an act of faith, necessary for human continuity. And as a sociogenic activity that enforces society's reinforcement of heterosexual relations, marriage is more than a private affair between two consenting adults – either of the same-sex or opposite-sex. It is a wedding that is shrouded in religious rituals, usually invoking the presence of the Divine – it is, however, a sociogenic event. Also, because marriage is believed to redeem one's loneliness, individuals are called on to marry (I will discuss more of this in the next Chapter). With all this, the Ghanaian religious public finds it an offence for women professors, leading an institution that is expected to promote African family values, promoting the counter-cultural activities of the

[213] Women and Girls, HIV and AIDS. April 23, 2020. Accessed: October 18, 2021. https://www.avert.org/professionals/hiv-social-issues/key-affected-populations/women.

LGBTQ+ community in Ghana under the guise of protecting human rights.[214] In a discussion with one of the research fellows at the IAS, who pleaded anonymity, he said he is ashamed to be identified with these women activists as colleagues.[215]

As these female scholars continue to push for western liberal sex ethics which are frowned upon by the Ghanaian public, issues are raised about the role of the public in university education.[216] It is important to restate that the late Professor J.H. Kwabena Nketia, Ghana's foremost ethnologist and first Ghanaian Director of the IAS, had praised Christine Oppong's work because he expressed concerns that, "Those who go through it (western schools) tend to become alienated from the traditional African way of life … . Hence, we continue to face not only problems of political integration but also those of cultural and social integration" (Nketia in Oppong 2013: ix).

It was for this reason that the IAS was established to incorporate African social values into the academic curriculum. Nevertheless, Nketia observed that, "it seems unlikely, however, that these measures will be effective for achieving maximum cultural integration until the learning situation in the classroom is reinforced by community experience, for it is one thing to learn about a culture and another to live it and make it part of one's way of life" (Ibid.: ix). From Professor Nketia, there is hardly any doubt that the public that funds the university must have a stake in the courses – especially family issues – that are taught in the schools. In 2020 the current government of Ghana of the New Patriotic Party (NPP) introduced a bill, Public University Bill 2020 that sought to "provide for the establishment, governance arrangements and management of public university in the country". As part of the bill, the public university is mandated to undertake functions, *inter alia,* Clause: "prohibits discrimination in a public university. A public university or an officer of the university is prohibited from discriminating against a person on the basis of the race,

---

[214] Ghanaweb (October 8, 2021), "LGBTQI+: We want this abominable practice made illegal in Ghana – Catholic Bishop," https://www.ghanaweb.com/GhanaHomePage/NewsArchive/LGBTQI-We-want-this-abominable-practice-made-illegal-in-Ghana-Catholic-Bishops-1374901 (Accessed: September 2, 2022).

[215] Personal conversation with a senior research fellow at the IAS on October 14, 2021.

[216] Currently, the Bill that seeks to promote proper Ghanaian family values as against homosexuality is the only bill in Ghana's political history since the country re-democratisation in 1992 that the entire nation (93 per cent) is rallying behind. It is also a bill that has seen less political polarisation in the country's parliament.

ethnic origin, political opinion, colour, gender, occupation, religion or creed, disability, social or economic status of that person."[217]

This provision is very important in the discussions that have animated female professors supporting LGBTQ+ activities. It is clear from this provision that the framers carefully use words that are consistent with the general position of Ghanaians. The framers use "gender" (which is a cultural construct based on the cultural and social functions people undertake) as opposed to "sex," which is biological (which if applied to the LGBTQ+ logic transgresses ontological boundaries frowned upon by the general Ghanaian community). Simply put: the bill does not support LGBTQ+ activities in Ghana, not least about women scholars forcing it on Ghanaians.

To protect cultural values, the aim of the university is to create, disseminate and preserve knowledge and understanding through: teaching, skills development and research, scholarly publications, technological transfer and extensions; and community service.[218] This provision may imply the reason the university council is expected to ensure "control of the finances of the public university and determine the allocation and proper use of funds".[219]

All this should read in the context that, the bill was introduced in recognition that while the university is expected to offer higher education and training to support human capital in any society, "university education since independence has remained highly elitist as it is accessible only to a relatively small segment of the relevant population".[220] In all this, the bill was expected to support academic freedom, but certainly not an unlimited freedom.[221] This is definitely reasonable since the university is funded by the public: the public must have a stake in its administration.

While the political elite considered the bill as necessary for ensuring that the public university remains accountable to the public, the "highly elitist" mounted a protest against the bill. One of the elitist establishments that mounted an organised protest against the proposed University Bill was the Ghana Academy of Arts and Sciences (GAAS). The Academy was founded in 1959 through the initiative of Ghana's first President, Osagyefo Dr Kwame Nkrumah, to promote the pursuit,

217 Public University Bill, 2020, p. vii.

218 Ibid., p. 5.

219 Ibid., p. 9.

220 Ibid., p. ii.

221 Ibid., p. ii.

advancement and dissemination of knowledge in all branches of the sciences and humanities.

The Academy raised many concerns, including the government's attempts at regulating the finances of the university. The Academy reads this as part of the government's efforts at curtailing academic freedom and the autonomy of the university. On this, the Academy stated that, "Academic freedom refers to the right that any academic has to research *any relevant issues*, present ideas and facts from research to students and *the general public*, without fear of repression or censorship from their employers or any other person in authority. Such ideas or facts may sometimes be inconvenient for their employers or government, but they need to be protected as much as possible. Most universities around the world provide guidelines on the limitations imposed by *common sense*".[222]

The key expressions used by the GAAS as they protested against the University Bill, call for some analysis, to academic freedom. The GAAS argues that academics and their respectful institutions must be allowed the freedom to research any relevant issues. This is answered in the second sentence when it talks about academics presenting ideas and facts from their research to students and the general public. At this point, it is very clear that the public is brought into the discourse on academic freedom. Nevertheless, it is not clearly stated whether the role the public plays in epistemic production in the university, except that as it stands, it looks as if the public is to remain a passive recipient of any relevant knowledge produced by academics.

It also appears there is a check on academic freedom when common sense is imposed on the university to define the boundaries of their academic freedom. But the challenge is that common sense is not common to all, as one man's common sense is another man's idiocy. So, clearly, the academy moves away from the simplicity of common sense, which is usually nothing but the imposition of presumed learned lawyers and academics on a public that is misconstrued as ignorant.

Indeed, many scholars, including Frantz Fanon and Kofi Tetteh have highlighted the failure of academics to break free from western epistemic enslavement. In many cases, these scholars and elite operate and ply their profession through the prisms of western epistemes, some of whom, especially those related to sexual morality, contradict, the moral sensitivity of the general Ghanaian religious public. Fanon was clear in his observation that the elite are unable, based on their own

---

[222] Ghana Academy of Arts and Sciences: Position Paper, Public University Bill (n.d.), p. 5.

bourgeois interest, to overturn colonialism and all its manifestations. Just as the colonial working class and proletariat were not revolutionary enough to birth the African quest for redemption from western imperialism, can it be said of Ghanaian radical feminists that they have failed to redeem the African family from the epistemic injustice of the west. This is because these Ghanaian radical feminists are part of the colonial establishment that seeks to use the university to retain European totalising epistemic arrogance in post-independent Ghana.

Certainly, my critique is not limited to radical feminist scholars in Ghana, but the general post-colonial system in the country. In the courses in Gender Studies at the Institute of African Studies, University of Ghana and the Philosophy of Social Science Education at the same university, there is not a single Gold Coaster or Ghanaian philosopher on the list. This is simply against the background that both courses include topics such as, structuralism and saturation theory, poststructuralism/postmodernism, postcolonial studies, feminist theory, and existentialism. The reading list is not only an exemplification of self-debasement from Ghanaian academics, but a betrayal of the public that funds these institutions. It also betrays disloyalty and lack of respect to the traditions of knowledge of the people of Ghana – both written and oral forms – that can be incorporated into the university "to contribute actively to the development of Ghana and Africa generally by examining and addressing crucial issues of development" as identified by GAAS in their protest against the state-sponsored University Bill. If indeed, the university is to operate on "common sense", which kind of common sense engages this banal form of epistemic self-debasement?

It should be borne in mind, as part of rearticulating the concerns of Busia and Fanon that, the course is taught by Ghanaian professors, without any single Euro-American or Arab.[223] Obviously, the humanistic value-ridden theories these professors teach Ghanaian students to present themselves as globalised epistemes must set the pace for homogenising modern universities. And yet, the homogenisation, as can be seen in the reading list, is nothing short of western hegemonisation, headed and led by Ghanaian academics professors of international repute, but unknown by the pedestrian in Nima and Maamobi urban slums of Accra whose sweat funds the university. The combination of homogenisation and hegemonisation

[223] Professors Samuel Agyei-Mensah; Joseph Yaro, Joseph Kofi Teye, and Dr Amanda Cofie.

provincialises the west as it peripherises Ghanaians and, by extension, Africans.

Certainly, if this is the "common sense" that is to be used to define the boundaries of academic freedom, then Professor Kofi Asare Opoku, an octogenarian and generational mate of Agnes Amoah was right when he said,

> [M]ore than political and economic independence, is *the independence of the mind*, which is the *sine qua non* of any genuine independence and which provides the only true bedrock upon which any lasting and meaningful effort at national self-assertion and development can be based" (Opoku 1970: 179, emphasis in the original).

The themes of the social science course, including pragmatism and phenomenology, critical realism, post-structuralism/postmodernism, critical social theory, postcolonial studies, and feminist theory, are all anti-structures, anti-order and designed to deconstruct "traditions" and conventional truths as archaic, frozen in time and must be gracelessly consigned to the backwaters of a "primitive" past. With such brazen contempt for the past, Professor Opoku said that "In like manner, the control of the minds of the colonial subjects by their masters renders them powerless and ineffective, and *takes away from them the very substance, which they need for national survival.* This renders them mere puppets or walking shadows, even though their former masters may be said to have relinquished power" (Opoku, 1970: 179, emphasis mine). The idea for me is not to dismiss this theory as unimportant, but rather the African worldviews should also be considered.

That western post-truth, humanistic episteme renders Africans' powers ineffective and takes away from them the very substance which they need for survival and sheds important light on the dangers involved in Ghanaian female feminist scholars campaigning for the decriminalisation of LGBTQ+ - a practice that breaks ontological boundaries of procreation, a necessity for the survival of Ghanaians, Africans and the human race. Strangely, only a little over 30 European countries have decriminalised homosexual practices for political reasons, as opposed to the majority of the country that have kept the law against the LGBTQ,. For this reason, the push against Ghana's Family Bill could stir tension and conflict, especially in a country where the majority of the population prefer heterosexual norms to be as the norm. Nevertheless, as I have said, the issue will then fall on how the country protects the rights of the minority.

From all this, it is important to highlight the complexities in the discourse around academic freedom. It also brings to the visible presence the need for the views of the public to be incorporated into the ideas of academic freedom and what constitutes relevance for human flourishing. This is because, given the nature of the courses taught at the public universities, with the country's premier university, failing to incorporate Ghanaian traditions of knowledge into the philosophies of social science education, I cannot agree less with Fanon's observation that:

> It is within this mass humanity, this people of the shanty towns, at the core of the lumpenproletariat, that the rebellion will find its urban spearhead. For the lumpenproletariat, that the horde of starving men, uprooted from their tribe and from their clan, constitutes one of the most spontaneous and most radically revolutionary forces of a colonised people (Fanon 1963: 129).

The discussion points to the complexity involved in using "common sense" as the guardrail of defining academic freedom. As I have said, common sense is highly relative, as one man's common sense is another's idiocy, and usually, indigenous moral values are considered a drawback on modernity, usually framed from the perspective of the west. In the next section, I will discuss the need to renew the debates over academic freedom in Ghana. This is because the elite uses the idea of a "secular public sphere in academia" to divert the attention of the public from the kinds of contradictory, western humanistic theories that are taught in the universities.

The distinction between ontological truth (truth about how things are – the need for human rights, democratic principles,) and social truths (truths on how things ought to be). There is ontological truth in all cultures that are universally shared, but there are particularistic truths that are particular to different societies, based on their cherished cultural values.

The University as a secular institution?

The de-secularisation thesis assumes that secularism does not have its own values. But this is simplistic in the sense that secularism has values that break all ethical and ontological boundaries. It has values that restrict the imposition of traditions and religious virtues on people. It has values that reinforce individualism *qua* individualism and the autonomy of human reason to discover truth without the aid of God – God is not needed in the production of knowledge, according to the secular thesis since 18th-Century Enlightenment Europe.

This implies that the force of secularisation cannot be wantonly brushed aside. For example, while individuals in Ghana may still throng the church, their views about moral issues may not necessarily be "conventional". This is mostly the case with most university students and graduates. Similarly, the globalisation of western liberal sex values through social media, apart from the universities, continues to challenge the orthodox teachings of religion. So, while religion has indeed surged back, the moral force of religion is in a contest against a public who are intricately connected with a local and global circus of values.

Social media and the universities have become epicentres for rendering it possible for Ghanaians to 'travel' without travelling as they consume (not without criticality) western moral values. Similarly, some western-trained African scholars, who even claim Christian identity and yet teach Gender theories have become critical in their acceptance of Christian sexual ethics. These scholars renounce any absolute moral values imposed by religion. For example, in her epistle to Christians that was publicly circulated, a supporter of LGBTQ+ rights in Ghana, one of the petitioners against the Bill premised her call for Christians to open up to the gay community with the question: "Whose morals become the benchmark, and who becomes the judge? p. 3. As it is with the internal contradictions of relativistic moral philosophy, her own aporia comes out when he said:

> Over the last several years these issues of hypocrisy have loomed large: so-called Christians have been silent when Christian leaders have sexually abused young women (and men) in the church; many are silent as brazen corruption among political, civic and religious leaders takes place; and as for issues such as women dying in childbirth due to poor access to medical services; the murder of women for being alleged witches; the rape of children; the pollution of our water bodies through poor mining whether by galamsey or large mining concessions; the destruction of our forests; unemployment and frustration of the youth— the silences have been loud.[224]

[224] Akosua Adomako Ampofo (2021), "Why Christians Should Extend Grace and so not support the 'Promotion of Proper human sexual rights and Ghanaian family values"' Bill, p. 2.

Certainly, she is consistent with gender theories that seek to deconstruct all social orders and ontological boundaries. Definitely, deconstruction may not be wrong, but certainly when it runs against established, heterosexual sex ethics, it will potentially generate tension in public governance. This consistence is also because in reality, all truths must connect. So, gender worldview must be consistent with its first principle of activism, advocacy, deconstructing culture, gender, and biological boundaries as oppressive So, beginning with the simplistic assumption of gender as a culture and culture as dynamic without explaining what this means, feminist scholars, with genuine concerns, are often seen by the male constituency as embarking on the clitoral battle of deconstructing all pretences of phallic impediments, including differential gender roles. Not only that, the existential challenges that have burdened marriage has rendered biological facts, such as pregnancy are all construed as irrationally oppressive to women that must be rebutted – hence radical feminists turning to lesbianism, abortion, polyamory etc.

With African feminist scholars seek to deploy education in formal institutions to circulate critical ideas as part of restructuring what they read as male-centric oppressive social system. A few of these feminist scholars are convinced that while the majority of Ghanaians detest homosexual acts and argue that sexual love and pleasure could only be fully fulfilled in a heterosexual marriage, and proposing the need for children to be socialised in this regard, they are convinced that their, "findings point to promising directions where education can propel new meanings of sexuality and the production of sexual diversity" (Dery, Fiaveh, Apusigah 2019: 353). Certainly, the hope to use the classroom to subvert the cherished heterosexual values of Ghanaian society may run into tension with the country's enchanted public sphere. In all of this, one of the authors, Isaac Dery concluded his study on African understanding of Africanism that while a few men have benefited from patriarchalism, which feminism seeks to subvert, "feminism was largely perceived by most men and women as a dangerous feminising and Western construct, capable of destabilising the cultural exceptionalism of Ghanaian society" (Dery 2020: 1). As Dery mentioned, several men treat feminism as dangerous because of two reasons: the theoretical tools in feminism to re-centre historically marginalised narratives and the preponderance of women in feminist scholarship. This means that while the impact of neoliberal regime, imposed on Ghana and other African countries by international financial institutions, forced men to do women's work, the public hardly draw fast rule around traditionally defined gender roles, it still profiles such men as misfit for their masculinity (Overa°2007; Dery and Amoah 2022). In his recent article, Dery has moved more towards recuperating traditions of indigenous knowledge, particularly the wisdom embodied in communalism and indigenous court system to negotiate for the rights of women (Akurugu, Dery and Bata 2022). This recent position of Dery is precisely his ethnographic research has revealed to him that Northern women do not necessarily read oppression into cultural institutions, such as the bridewealth that has become a subject of contestation in radical feminist scholarship.[225] Instead, as his study found out, Northern women want the system revitalised through cultural creativity to advance their interest in marriage, including childcare practices.

Away from Dery and in contrast to his call for academics to explore ways of polishing the pearls of indigenous wisdom and institution to advance women's interest, another female scholar, a Northern but domiciled in the US takes a different position. Wunpini Fatimata Mohammed feels that Ghanaian feminists and their associated female-oriented NGOs and movements are not radical enough in advancing the interest of the so-called marginalised (Mohammed 2022). Charging them as southern Christian elites who are largely interested in their own interest and social standing, she conflated radical feminism from the West with the demands of minority groups, including Muslims, women in Northern Ghana and people in the LGBTQ community (Ibid). Long before Mohammed, Ifi Amediume had criticised colonial elitist women for promoting their privileged position as opposed to overturning the wheels of so-named patriarchalism (Amadiume 2000). So, Wupini's critique is not new. However, Kwabena Akurang-Parry has demonstrated that it is simplistic to claim colonial elitist were only interested in their protecting their status. Thus, beyond Amadiume's charge, Akurang-Parry through is appropriation of primary sources argued that the colonial elitist women of the Gold Coast sought not only to better their own conditions but also to make society more livable (Akurang-Parry 2004).

In her article, one could clearly discern how Mohammed is seeking to court the sympathy of Muslims, by confusing the demands of Muslims for public recognition of the veil with the LGBTQ community. Indeed, Muslims and Christians are completely in unity against the demands of the LGBTQ community. Similarly, from the

[225] Ibid.

work of Dery, it is clear that Northern women are not waiting for saviours in the West to engineer radicalism in activism to overturn indigenous institutions. Concurrently, just as Lilla Abu-Lughod concluded in her research on Muslim women that Muslim women do not need saving from the West (Abu-Lughod 2013), so would Northern women, at least from the scholarship of Dery, do not need Mohammed's recommended Eurocentric radical feminism – a major source of anarchy in the contemporary world. This, as I have said, implies the need for contextualisation and centring of indigenous worldviews in the study of Gender, without, of course, displacing completely western theories.

As the debate over moral issues wage on, the question about academic freedom is assuming a new dimension and rigour. Last year, the Parliament of Ghana proposed a Bill that sought to regulate the running of public universities in the country. As part of the regulation of the state – representing the public – was to have a stake in who gets funding for research. This was quickly rebutted from the academic community as an attempt at curtailing their freedom. But because the conversation was couched under a political and supposedly intellectual tone, the unsuspecting public was hardly involved. Similarly, since it was not framed as a moral issue, but defined as simply academic, the public was barricaded from the conversation. As the pushback from the universities intensified, Parliament was compelled to temporarily withdraw the Bill.

Obviously, given the challenges that have encumbered academic freedom and decolonising the university, the Bill needs to be reopened and presented to the public in daily language that would incorporate their views. I say this with the view that since the beginning of Ghana as a "modern" state, the political elites have deliberately choreographed their governance from the prying eyes of the public. English is imposed on everyone since the 1950s. Even Nkrumah, a notable pan-African did not deliberately push for the incorporation of any Ghanaian language in public schools.

Similarly, the Parliament of Ghana hardly encourages the use of local languages in deliberation. With all this, the public is usually fed with politically infested opinions as opposed to "real" information in public. How can academic freedom and decolonisation really take place if the views of the majority of the public who fund the universities are not incorporated? To what extent should the public remain quiet when western trained African scholars continue to saturate the universities with western liberal theories that explicitly contradict public morality?

Why do western trained feminist scholars continue to denigrate traditions of knowledge of the people of Ghana, especially those that border on gender and feminism? I ask this question because anytime moral issues are explained to the public, the public engages in a lively discussion. For example, when as part of Gender Studies, some civil society groups, such as Planned Parenthood Association attempted introducing liberal sex education into the classroom, the public resisted it in Ghana. This was because the curriculum was clearly framed as moral, not just academic freedom.

In the conversation about the running of public universities, several of these feminist scholars have joined other African scholars in the continent and around the globe to advocate the need for a decolonisation of the university. But the decolonisation of the university in Ghana has hardly been conceptualised as a matter of worldview as opposed to merely getting African scholars to publish with western journals or publishing institutions. This, in my opinion, means that indigenous worldviews on family and sexuality have been marginalised in Ghanaian universities. Similarly, the decolonisation of Ghanaian public universities is not about a debate over scientific principles, as such principles are given and left for human beings to discover.

My understanding is that the issue about decolonisation is practically and theoretically about worldviews – two worldviews that collide on the subject of morality and its source. While this is really the cause of the tension over the decolonisation agenda, several African scholars have carefully stayed clear of the moral debate. The pretension is that the university is expected to be value-free; the classroom is expected to be value-free, while academic curricula are not to be valorised. Undoubtedly, this is a nirvana type of vision that has never been achieved since the beginning of pre-modern and modern universities. Pre-modern education in Africa was basically moral in orientation. For this reason, decolonisation should imply the privileging of Ghanaian shared worldviews on the family and sexuality in public universities.

While individuals were taught the practical things of life and how to survive, morality remained its core foundation. Moral education was considered the guardrail that must govern the activities of individuals as a function in society. My point is that the centrality of morality as the foundation of pre-modern education was because of the need to build a society of responsible men and women who were morally alert enough to keep ethical and ontological boundaries in the society. The ideas of rights and responsibilities among husband and wife, parents and children, and neighbours were all located within the rubric of morals that defined ethical and ontological boundaries.

Within this locus is a determination of what constituted violation and sin and the extent to which such violations were handled. For example, minor offences such as insults and stealing petty things were considered private delitescence that were handled by the family heads of the contending parties. On the other hand, offences such as murder, rape, incest, and wanton destruction of water bodies, flora and fauna were considered public delitescence that were severely punished, including socially ostracising the offender. Breaking public delitescence was considered a serious offence because it involved breaking ontological boundaries. The rules were strictly enforced because human beings were considered social beings who must live within the boundaries to sustain group living.

Consequently, the moral rules around ontological boundaries were clear, absolute and unambiguous. As part of enforcing these moral foundations of life, the rules were incorporated in sociogenic activities such as marriage, naming ceremonies, funerals, and festivals. There was also folklore that was carefully and creatively invented – through observation and lived experiences – to enforce these ethical and ontological boundaries. This most likely explains why practices such as homosexuality never received any sociogenic support. It also explains why in societies where individuals like the Sangomas were said to have practiced some form of same-sex conjugal engagement, homosexual practices may have been considered extra-conventional, confined to the cultic world of rituals.

The cultic world is made up of three kinds of spirits: moral, immoral and amoral spirits (Prempeh 2022: 279) Given the constitution of the spirit world, it was largely a democratic sphere where any individual with knowledge about the spirit world could appropriate to his or her advantage. Individuals could tap into the powers of the spirit realms to achieve a purpose (Akyeampong and Obeng 1995: 483). This explains the rumours of grotesque ritual practices associated with *Sakawa* (online fraud) and *Sika duro* (ritual money). The spirit world is fluid and orderly, away from the material and social lived world. The material and social world (where human beings live) has a world of rules to govern human conduct. The fluidity of the spirit world allows for queer sexuality, including same-sex.

So, while there was a crisscrossing of the spirit and the material world in African cosmogony (Asamoah-Gyadu 2013: 42), the manifestation of the spirit world in the social lived world was consigned to the realm of cultic practices. Even among some Papua societies in New Guinea, for example, where, according to a group of anthropologists, certain male-to-male sexual acts are part not only accepted but prescribed, they were sincere in writing that such sexual acts "are part of initiation rituals required of all boys to become respected adult men (Kirkpatrick 2000, cited in Haviland and others 2017: 466). Herdt's study of ritual fellatio among the Sambia in fact demonstrates that for men these rituals of masculinity co-exist with heterosexual marriages. Women and men have separate living spaces. Men's huts in the forest and women's huts elsewhere. After sex, men go to the forest to cleanse and replenish their energies. Women's sexual energies exhaust men leaving them weak. Fellatio replenishes men. In these cultures, all this is symbolic and may not be spiritual. While the authors move on to indicate that, "across the globe, the expression of homosexual ranges from lifelong loving relationships to casual encounters, and from being fully open to being utterly private and secretive" (Haviland, p. 466), They never provided any shred of evidence to indicate any social institution that supported the practice. Among the Sambia, there were clear beliefs and systems of gender that supported this practice as a sociogenic.

To ground these in compliance, religion was incorporated. Thus, myths, taboos, and rituals were integrated into sustaining the base of moral foundation. The appeal to God and ancestors to ground rules around ethical and ontological boundaries were so strong that since independence and the rise of African philosophy, several scholars have debated the sources of African moral values. Some support the idea that the sources of African values are religion; others appeal to society; while few appeal to conscience. Whatever these scholars consider the source of African moral boundaries, it is clear that these moral rules were not left to individuals to decide through their whims and caprices. The rules became canonised as "traditions" and "conventions" of society (I will return to this in my critique of the decolonisation agenda).

Human beings were also considered moral agents capable of living a morally acceptable life. As moral beings, not biologically straitjacket beings made of a concatenation of chemistries, everyone was held accountable for what he or she did, because human beings could and must live a moral life.[226] This explains the logic of the Akan adinkra, "He who does not know can know if he learns". No human being was

[226] Sometimes the overemphasis placed on the ability of the individual to learn may have resulted in killing individuals who were considered to have some deformities – usually considered a curse in some cultures, like the idea of spirit children.

incorrigibly unteachable. To provide an enabling environment for people to fulfil their moral obligation, I have mentioned the incorporation of sociogenic activities and folklore. I must also say that the rules were not imagined, neither were they considered as having emerged from nowhere. The rules were largely based on lived experiences. And so, the rules governing human experiences could not be undermined without consequences. At any rate, the moral values of the Akan society are the outcome of the cumulative wisdom and experiences of the sages (Busia 1962).

It is for this reason that Akan chiefs, considered the vanguards of moral values, could not rule arbitrarily. In fact, Nana Kobina Nketsia, the paramount chief of Esikado Traditional Area, has even argued that the word "rule" does not exist in Akan chieftaincy as a way of indicating the extent to which the chiefs were themselves not above the observation of the rules of society. Busia, one of the earliest scholars of Akan cultures argued that the chief could be destooled if he was dictatorial. In some areas among the Ga and Nzema, songs were composed and used to openly criticise chiefs.

The location of morality into the realm of religion has been a subject of contention among African scholars, such as the Uganda literary critic and anthropologist, Okot p'Bitek and Kwasi Wiredu, the Ghanaian philosopher. These scholars among several others have sought to de-mythologise indigenous traditions of Africa, claiming indigenous traditions have essentially anthropological origins. Whether the views of these individuals, including p'Biek who did not shy away from his atheistic worldview, considered the sources of indigenous traditions of Africa, there is no argument that Judeo-Christian/or the Abrahamic religions, generally, were/are considered highly critical in consolidating these values.

Consequently, the African worldview does not bracket the world away from the control of a from both Supreme God and the tutelary deities (Opoku 1978). The God factor is so strong in the construction of the African world, such that Africans perceive the world from the perspective of both the religious and non-religious. This implies that the humanistic logic of most of the radical feminists and founding fathers of social science cannot square easily with the African worldview without tension. Similarly, the fact that African traditions of knowledge do not necessarily involve a rupture with the "past" makes "modern" African scholars look down on their past with disdain. This is precisely because the African past is an enchanted world that fuses the material and spiritual in the construction of an episteme. The significance of the Akan/African past in the epistemic production process is captured in Ephraim Amu's song, "*Tete wo bi ka, tete wo bi kyere*" (The past has a lot to say"). As Amu's biographer, Rev Prof Philip Laryea has observed that Amu was convinced that the past makes it possible to lay a solid foundation for posterity. He reinforced this idea by making use of a proverb, "It is the crooked stem that bears straight branches". This was rearticulated by Professor Nketia who reflecting on Amu's song said as follows:

> Tradition may appear to one generation like a crooked tree or as something defective or outmoded. But we must remember when the materials we build on appear crooked or defective from our perspective that in cultural development, it is the crooked tree that bears straight or not so crooked branches. Our option is not to abandon our music and culture because the alluring presence of other cultures makes them seem crooked but master them properly, work on them, add to them or modify them in the light of new ideas (Nketia 1998: 28, cited in Laryea 2012: 223).

In reflecting on Amu's "Yen ara asase ni" and its contextual significance in drawing the boundaries of knowledge, Prof. Lawrence Boadi believes that Dr. Amu's words should not be taken literally. He is of the view that, by 'Nimdeɛ ntraso' Tata Amu meant extraordinary claims to knowledge; claims to knowledge that go beyond natural bounds'. 'Such claims', he said, are 'always accompanied by arrogance and petty haughtiness'. In the first line of the second stanza, Dr. Amu uses the phrase, 'Nhoma nimdeɛ huhu gyan'.[227]

The explanation of this phrase underscores Prof. Boadi's belief that 'Nimdeɛ ntraso' is a claim to knowledge not backed by experience, or that is so-called 'empty knowledge'. Such knowledge is derived from studying books just for the sake of it and is commonly referred to as book-knowledge or head-knowledge. His philosophy of education elucidated in the song, 'Tiri ne ne nsa ne koma', Dr. Amu indicates that the use of the head is only one of the means by which knowledge is acquired. He therefore had no difficulty with such knowledge. He was, however, concerned about the kind of nhoma nimdeɛ' (book-knowledge) he described as 'huhu gyan'. 'Nimdeɛ traso' therefore means 'cerebral knowledge acquired only for its sake'. Such knowledge

---

[227] Philip Laryea, "Yen ara asese ni": Revisiting Dr. Ephraim Amu's Ideals on Patriotism and Nation Building", Lecture Delivered b Zoom to mark the 122nd Birthday Anniversary Celebration of Dr. Ephraim Amu and Hosted by the Institute of African Studies, UG, Legon, September 16, 2021, p. 6.

does not translate into industry (the use of the hand), nor does it result in the transformation of character (affect the heart). Rather, it leads to two negative attitudes Dr. Amu calls, 'nkotokranne ne apɛsemenkomenya'.[228] 'Nkotokranne' means 'cunning' or 'clever deception.' The implications of Amu's sagacious observation is that knowledge should not just be about self-serving, but rather the collective good of society.

In concluding his lecture on Amu's philosophy of education, Prof. Philip Laryea said that he had been informed that in the past, students in some mission schools such as Prempeh College, were made to repeat a class, not because they were academically inept, but because they did not have character. It was possible in those days for a student to top a class and yet repeat that class. The sheer pursuit of knowledge for its sake devoid of character formation is a recipe for disaster. He concluded that, "education should be all-inclusive geared towards equipping a person to be spiritually, morally and physically sound". He summed all this as follows:

> Education that is focused mainly on developing the mental faculties is likely to produce shrewd people who are clever at manipulating and exploiting the inherent weaknesses in systems and institutions to their selfish ends. Alternatively, a policy that has sound moral content and appeal is likely to produce persons with honesty and integrity. Sound education, then, becomes a critical index in measuring the growth and development of a nation (Laryea 2017: 24).

As a minister of the Presbyterian Church in Ghana and academic, Professor Laryea added that, "The three arms of government - the Executive, the Legislature and the Judiciary - have a crucial role to play in this moral reawakening; equally important is the role of the media as the fourth estate of the realm, to properly communicate and educate the citizenry on their role, rights and responsibilities. The Christian religious bodies, which were once vanguards of formal education, should reassert themselves and partner the state institutions in giving quality education".[229]

228 Ibid., p. 6.

229 Ibid. p. 15.

Chapter 4

Christocentric Philosophy: An Approach to decolonisation in Ghana

It must be remembered that theology is not philosophy. It does not assume to discover truth, or to reconcile what it teaches as true with all other truths. Its province is simply to state what God has revealed in his Word, and to vindicate those statements as far as possible from misconceptions and objections. This limited and humble office of theology, it is especially necessary to bear in mind, when we come to speak of the acts and purposes of God. "The things of God knoweth no man; but the Spirit of God." (1 Cor. ii. 11 – Hodge 1940: 517).

Restore us, O God; make your face shine on us, that we may be saved.[230]

For the director of music. According to *gittith* A psalm of David.
1 Lord, our Lord,
how majestic is your name in all the earth!
You have set your glory
in the heavens.
2 Through the praise of children and infants
you have established a stronghold against your enemies,
to silence the foe and the avenger.
3 When I consider your heavens,
the work of your fingers,
the moon and the stars,
which you have set in place,
4 what is mankind that you are mindful of them,
human beings that you care for them?
5 You have made them a little lower than the angels
and crowned them with glory and honor.
6 You made them rulers over the works of your hands;
you put everything under their feet:
7 all flocks and herds,
and the animals of the wild,
8 the birds in the sky,
and the fish in the sea,

[230] Psalm 80:3.

all that swim the paths of the seas.
9 Lord, our Lord,
how majestic is your name in all the earth![231]

Introduction

Decolonisation has become dominant in the universities, except to say that the concept involves the process of revealing and dismantling colonialist power in all forms (Ashcroft et al. 2000: 86).[232] While it may hardly have a universally shared definition, the idea is complexly anchored on the thesis that colonialism was not just about dominating physical spaces, but a whole package that involved:

> European territorial conquests, the various institutions of European colonialism, the discursive operations of empire, the subtleties of subject construction in the colonial discourse and the resistance of those subjects, and, most importantly …, the differing responses to such incursions and their contemporary colonial legacies in both pre-and-post-independence nations and communities (Ashcroft et al. 2000: 169).

Colonialism was system, structured and a composite exercise that incorporated a non-binary worldview of politics and religious philosophies and language in reconstituting and reforming the social and psychological state of the colonised world. The effect of western colonialism of the colonised is said to have resulted in a zero-sum control and production of knowledge severing limiting in their onto-existential locations and outcomes (Abdi 2012).[233] Given the totalising effect of colonialism (often referred to as the colonial matrix of power) since African regained its independence in the 1950s, political independence has incorporated a need for epistemic independence (recuperation of Africa's authentic pre-colonial traditions and customs) – both calling for a total overhaul of any legacies and relics of colonialism.

---

[231] NIV of the Bible

[232] Bill Ashcroft, Gareth Griffiths, and Helen Tiffin, *Post-colonial studies: The key concepts* (2nd Ed) (London/New York: Routledge, 2000).

[233] Ali A. Abdi, "Decolonizing philosophies of education: An introduction," in Ali A. Abdi (ed), *Decolonizing philosophies of education*, 1-14 (Rotterdam: Sense Publishers, 2012).

Nevertheless, it appears history can hardly be revised; while the idea of authentic custom could be nothing short of fossilising and essentialising culture – as the product of colonialism whether in the area of political administration or educational establishment, it appears the legacies of colonialism have some degree of independence. In other words, while the colonial social space may have been invented by the colonisers, the systemic and structured formulation of the colonised world is such that the postcolonial reality of Africa is a composite reality. It is a reality that has cascaded into nearly every facet of life – implying that Africans often live in the colonial moment.

Given the systemic nature of colonialism, the issue is not necessarily about totally collapsing and dismantling all colonial structures to recreate and reform the colonised world. Any attempts at completely undoing and reversing the colonial impact would be such a colossal task that would hardly succeed – but rather polarise the African front. Also, as far as my reading and understanding of colonialism is concerned, the issue of whether colonialism had an episodic or epochal impact on Africans is not as important as the reason for the enduring legacies of colonialism.

Needless to say, several academics, intellectuals, politicians and social commentators have come to appreciate the need for the reversal of some pre-colonial practices such as witchcraft accusation, *Trokosi* and extreme forms of widowhood. As I have already stated, the missionaries were very much involved in deconstructing and displacing these practices. This also means that the issue of decolonisation has largely been about Africans re-asserting and re-centring of African indigenous knowledge or as Nyamnjoh prefers to rightly call it traditions of knowledge. But the call for the recentring of African traditions of knowledge is very important but may also come across as problematic.

I argue that recentring African indigenous knowledge is because of the nature of knowledge production and distribution and the reality of Africa's Triple heritage. African episteme (difficult to conceptualise – though), like knowledge production globally is both dynamic, accommodative, and discursive. Impliedly, while the colonisers may have tickled themselves of introducing and imposing "western" knowledge or civilization on Africans, the idea of Western knowledge is similarly problematic. At any rate, what is referred to as western knowledge is a cumulation of several centuries of European interactions with several people, including Africans, Arabs and Asians.

I consider the fact that Western tradition is hybridised because no particular knowledge tradition is a virgin or has ever been a virgin. The major difference, as I understand it, is that as a result of the Christian Reformation of the 16th Century in Europe, specifically beginning in Germany, Europeans entered its "modernity" – complexly separating religion from politics, which allowed for exploration and adventures into the rest of the world. Consequently, European's accumulative or hybridised knowledge that has formed after centuries of interactions with other cultures was framed as western knowledge that formed the basis of western civilization.

The above, for me, is important in discussing how the Christian beliefs and ethos could help shed light on Africa's quest for decolonisation. My point is precisely that, decolonisation should be read as just deconstructing every legacy of colonialism, but reconstructing elements of the colonial logic that resonate with contemporary worldviews of Africa. Reducing this to marriage as heterosexual, the missionary introduction of Christian morality around marriage and sexuality chimed well with the Akan position on the subject – as I have described above. It is for this reason that several pro-LGBTQ academics identify Christianity, more so Evangelical Christianity, as a major obstacle to the legislation of same-sex unions in Africa.

In all this, the decolonisation agenda has rather proven difficult and frustrating to several African scholars and their western Africanists. So, while Africans have touted the lofty ideas of decolonisation institutional reform of African curricula, pedagogical structures, or epistemologies in a systemic and productive manner have hardly been decolonised in African universities (Nyamnjoh 2019).[234] As Mamdani has rightly observed "The important point is that neither the institutional form nor the curriculum of the modern African university derived from their pre-colonial institutions; their inspiration was the colonial modern" (Mamdani 2016: 70).[235] This is also against the background that the search for a decolonised Africa has had major historical shifts. Mamdani has opined that decolonisation has had significant shifts – largely from the political and economic to the epistemological issue of

---

[234] Francis B. Nyamnjoh, "Decolonizing the university in Africa," History and Politics, World Politics, Online Publication, 2019, DOI: 10.1093/acrefore/9780190228637.013.717

[235] Mahmood Mamdani, "Between the public intellectual and the scholar: Decolonization and some post-independence initiatives in African higher education," *Inter-Asia Cultural Studies*, 17, 1 (2016): 68-83.

what it means to be universal and particular that intimately tied to the notions of what is human (2016: 79). The shifts have hardly affected the epistemic shift in African universities. In a recent study, academics, whose work examined new fields of knowledge as they come into existence – not in the global centres, but in countries of the Southern tier: Brazil, South Africa, and Austria, discussed the massive problem of inequality in the knowledge economy. They concluded that knowledge that dominate these areas are still produced a long way from the 'centre', in the distinctive social and economic settings of post-colonial countries (Collyer 2019).[236]

African academics have given several reasons to account for the failure of major epistemic decolonisation of the colonised world. From the perspective of Ndlovu-Gatsheni, the failure of decolonisation, which he referred to as a myth is because of:

> [T]he hegemony of Euro-American-constructed world is its ability to make African intellectuals and academics socially located in Africa and on the oppressed side to think and speak epistemically and linguistically like the Euro-American intellectuals and academics on the dominant side.[237]

The challenge that has impeded the completing breaking down of the colonial structures, as I hinted above is not just because Africans may not want to decolonise, as it is the fact that these structures have become part of Africa's worldview. The colonial structures of governance have become the postcolonial reality of state building; the colonial languages have become the official languages of several African countries; colonial sports, such as boxing and football have become important elements of recreation (Ngũgĩ wa Thiong'o 1986; Botchway 2019);[238] since the 1970s, some communities in Ghana, such as the Akan Kwahu people of the Eastern Region and the Ewe of Anfoega in

---

[236] Fran Collyer, Raewyn Connel, Joao Maia and Robert Morrel, *Knowledge and global power: Making new sciences in the South* (Victoria/Australia: Monash University Publishing, 2019).

[237] Gayatri Chakravorty Spivak, "'Can the subaltern speak: From the 'History' chapter of critique of postcolonial reason" in Rosalind C. Morris (ed), *Reflections of an idea: Can the subaltern speak?* 801-86 (New York: Columbia University Press, 2010); Hamid Dabashi, *Can non-European think?* (London: Zed Books, 2015); Sabelo J. Ndlovu-Gatseni, *Coloniality of power in postcolonial Africa: Myths of decolonization* (Dakar: CODESRIA, 2013).

[238] Ngũgĩ wa Thiong'o, Decolonizing the mind: The politics of language in African literature (Nairobi: Heinemann, 1986); De-Valera NYM Botchway, *Boxing is no cakewalk! Azumah 'Ring Professor' Nelson in the social history of Ghanaian boxing* (Grahamstown: African Humanities Program, 2019).

the Volta Region have adopted Easter as a major festival for social cohesion and reimaging development.

To all intents and purposes, colonialism was not a piecemeal affair, but a major composite structure that was internally entwined to reshape the colonised mind and social space. Impliedly, whether the African mimic the colonial rule (Fanon 1963) or embarks on a revolution dispelling the myth of universality grounded on theo-and-ego politics of knowledge, privileging Africa's epistemic perspective of knowledge or whether the voices and cognitive capacity of the subaltern or non-Europeans are restored (Spivak 2010; Dabashi 2015; Ndlovu-Gatsheni 2013; Mignolo 2011: xiv).[239] the colonial legacy is an existential reality that needs negotiation.

As part of his contribution to the discourse on decolonisation, Mhango argued that instead of a revisit to Africa's past in order to salvage ancestral epistemic sagacity, it is important to negotiate the current epistemological regime. He summed as his conclusion, emphasising the need to destabilise the pervasive Western grand narrative by coming "together in order to dialogue and negotiate our differences, needs, likes, dislikes, prejudices even histories ready to face the future together as equal partners" (Mhango 2018: xiii).[240] He also argued that it is important to underscore the importance of all narratives and their epistemes regardless of they are modern or traditional (Mhango 2018: xiv).

Indeed, the subject of decolonisation is not just complex; it is also about conflicting worldviews. It is about non-neutrality in epistemic production; it is about knowledge production as a political project, which as Nyamnjoh has signalled, often create a zero-sum game for traditions of knowledge that are considered non-western. For this reason, I agree with Nyamnjoh that:

> [A]ny serious attempt at making African universities uncompromisingly inclusive institutions through embracing African traditions of knowing and knowledge production would require looking beyond the academy in its current configuration for inspiration.[241]

---

[239] Walter D. Mignolo, *The darker side of western modernity: Global futures, decolonial options* (Durham: Duke University Press, 2011).

[240] Nkwazi Nkuzi Mhango, *Decolonising colonial education: Doing away with relics and toxicity embedded in the racist dominant narrative* (Bamenda/Cameroon: Langaa Research & Publishing CIG, 2018), 5.

[241] Nyamnjoh, "Decolonizing," 1.

The curricula structure of the public universities in Ghana hardly incorporate the views of the public in epistemological production. Meanwhile, Nkrumah in the 1960s, I have already mentioned in Chapter Two, encouraged the need for the public to be included in university's knowledge production. Specifically related to the purpose of this book, which is to argue for the incorporation of religious ethos in the study of family and Gender in Ghanaian universities, I take inspiration of Tutuola, whom Nyamnjoh said did not dismiss his Christian faith, but rather embraced it as an opportunity to add to layers of his identity.[242] As a Christian and academic, I embrace the various ideas of decolonising by centring my Christian dogmas about the family and sexuality as an important avenue to understand the contemporary sexual and cultural revolutions in the world.

Consequently, instead of the simplistic profiling of Christianity as an imperialistic western religion, I side with Kwame Bediako (1995) and Lamin Sanneh (2003) that Christian is as African as it is a global religion of people who align with the person, teachings and works of Jesus Christ – concretised in the Bible, particularly the New Testament.[243] More so, Christianity has become an existential part of the African worldview that endorses Akan historic positionality on marriage as sociogenic and procreation as a composite part and parcel of the institution. For this reason, in this Chapter, I reflect on what the Christian faith posits as a worldview in making sense of the current cultural and sexual revolutions.

In this chapter, therefore, I will provide my overview of the world since the turn of the millennium, and I engage the conversation from auto-ethnographic prisms. I focus on my personal experiences because, as I have said in the introduction, knowledge is never neutral and, more so, the social sciences are significantly about worldviews. The goal of this chapter is to provide a broad context for my reflections on western cultural wars from my Christian perspective. It is also to demonstrate the world has suffered seismic cultural climatic change. I began with the text in Psalm 8 because it is, as far as my Christian faith allows me from the Biblical perspective that words such as anthropology becomes

---

[242] Ibid., 15.

[243] Kwame Bediako, *Christianity in Africa: The renewal of a non-western religion* (Edinburgh: Edinburgh University Press, 1996); *Theology and identity: The impact of culture upon Christian thought in the second century and in modern Africa* (Oxford: Regnum, 1992); *Jesus in Africa: The Christian Gospel in African history and experience* (Cumbria: Regnum Africa, 2000); Lamin O. Sanneh, *Whose religion is Christianity?: The Gospel beyond the west* (Grand Rapids, MI.: William B. Eerdmans, 2003).

meaningful. In Psalm 8, the Psalmist under the inspiration of the Holy Spirit gives us an important worldview through which human beings could make sense of the world. This is precisely because at the heartland of all human activities is the human being. For this reason, apart from the Bible narrator of the creation account using create in Genesis Chapter 1 verse 1, it is only when it came to the origin of human beings in Genesis 1: 26-27 that the word *create* is used again.

That the word *create* used in reference to human beings is important because it defies the issues of evolution that reduces human beings to nothing short of depraved animals. But the word creation is not enough. The Bible says God created man (generic) in His image. Though a non-theologian, I have read several interpretations of human beings as image-bearers of God. But from all my readings, I have concluded that the term encompasses the totality of the fact that human beings have an ontological value. As I have written elsewhere, human beings have an inherent value that cannot be devalued and violated. The inverse is that human beings do not have acquired dignity.

Against this background, I deduce that the publish or perish mantra is damaging to human ontological dignity. It reduces human dignity to productivity and achievement. It is simply a message of "if you don't publish, you are less a human being" – this is captured in the "perish" as the consequence of not publishing. Without an understanding of human ontological dignity, based on human bearing the image of God, how does the idea of human rights comes in? What is human about a human being? If human beings do not have a fixed identity as creatures of God, how do homosexual activists advocate homosexual rights?

The idea of rights, as I mentioned above, has become a contentious term that anyone whose views of rights do not conform to humanistic logic is discarded as "old school". Over the decades, several scholars have engaged the issue of rights. The question that has often been discussed is whether human beings have limited or unlimited rights. Whether through the narratives of libertarians such as Jeremy Bentham and John Stuart Mill, or communitarians like Kwame Gyekye, the idea of rights has remained a highly contentious subject.

But while academics may split hairs over the extent of human rights, the realities are that our beliefs about human rights matter and must conform to reality. For example, do I have the right to medication? If yes, can that right be independent of the right of a medical doctor to receive an education? Do I have the right to education? If yes, does my right to education entwine with the right of a teacher to receive education and teach me? If I have a right to practice homosexuality, must others also have the right to marry and have children so I can adopt? If my right to be homosexual is pushed beyond all reasonable limits to displace other rights, what happens if everyone becomes homosexual? Do I need a set of laws to protect my rights? If yes, must my identity be fixed, as the laws? Or my identity and the laws must all be fluid? If laws and my identity are fluid, what does it mean for ensuring social and cosmic order? How do we sustain a society where identities are so fluid and osmotic that every now and then, new laws have to be passed to accommodate? Who determines the laws in the human rights laws? Are the laws determined by an individual, groups of persons or authority beyond human beings? If laws are made by human beings, can human beings change the laws as and when they feel like? For example, if my right to be gay or lesbian is offered by a particular political regime, does it mean that the same political regime or another political regime, on hindsight could withdraw my rights? If the state offers me the right to be gay and/or lesbian, can the state decide to pull the same right back? If my identity is based on my feelings and experiences, how is my identity sustainable since feelings and experiences are highly osmotic? How long can the state change laws to accommodate osmotic identities?

Given what I consider as the complexities of the questions above from the humanistic perspective, I sincerely think that the Christian perspective of human beings carrying the image of God is the most critical in the human rights debate. This is precisely because if we use human reason, experience, and feelings, we will end up glorifying needless abortions, sexual perversions, wanton murdering of those we agree with, and also accentuating the crucifixion of those who do not publish. That failure of human reason, feeling, and experiences in making sense of the world cannot be true in the long run and across cultures. This is for the simple reason that "one man's reason is another man's idiocy". In Ghana, we say it as, "One man's meat is another man's poison." It is for the same reason of the fault lines of centring human reason, experience and feelings as the centre of epistemic production that both cultic religions and secular institutions tend to have a zero-sum mindset that leaves no space for alternative views.

The above brings us back to Psalm 8, which scholars refer to as Messianic – pointed and applied Jesus Christ in all of the New Testament.[244] A careful reading of the Psalm shows that human beings have meaning in as far as God existed as the uncreated Creator of

244 Matthew 21:16 (Psalm 8:2); I Corinthians 15: 27; Ephesians 1: 22; Hebrews 2:6-8.

human beings. That God is majestic and sovereign means that everything about human beings must point back to God who is majestic. This explains Jesus's constant reference to the Genesis account of human origin when He discussed issues of marriage and human dignity. For example, when Jesus was asked about divorce, He referred to the creation to reinforce God's ontological intention of marriage as a monogamous and heterosexual union between a biological man and a biological woman, all created in the image of God with different, but complementary responsibilities.[245]

In Jesus's response to divorce, He was clear in overruling the authority, whose laws, allowed by God, permitted divorce. While the Pharisees, the masters and vanguards of the Mosaic law, expected Jesus to reinforce Moses's authority, Jesus right pointed to God as the ultimate authority over all things. This is because God is the creator, while Moses was a creature who only gave laws allowed by the Creator. What this means is that, whereas Moses's law permitted divorce, such permission was to look back to when there was no divorce and to look forward to when all things are restored. In other words, Moses's laws, including the Decalogue, were to point the Israelites back to the world when there was Sabbath – the serenity of social and cosmic order. The law permitting divorce and Decalogue was/is similar to constitutional history. Every single law does not materially restore us to the "Sabbath". Laws give us a sense of a world of social and cosmic order when everyone remained committed to keeping ethical and ontological boundaries.

So, as God asked the Israelites to remember the "Sabbath" and keep it holy, it will be a narrow interpretation to reduce that to the rituals of worship, as some Seventh-day Adventists (SDA) I discussed then tried to enforce. If God were referring to worship and rituals and doing nothing on a particular day, then was there any precedence for the Israelites to follow, before Exodus 20 when the laws were given? What was the purpose of the Sabbath in the Decalogue? Is it not significant that there was salvation before the law? Why was the Decalogue given only after the Exodus – in other words, why were the Israelites enslaved in Egypt? Unfortunately for Adventists, including the prophet E.G. White, there is no precedence of how Adam, Eve, Cain, Abel, Noah, the people of Shinar, and Abraham kept the Sabbath. Similarly, until the Exodus account, there is no mention of the Israelites keeping the Sabbath in Egypt.

---

[245] Matthew 19: 1-11.

What was God then referring to when He asked them to remember the Sabbath? Well, to understand this important question, we need to understand two things: First, we need to understand when the word was first used and its context, and second, we need to take a surgical look at where it appears in the Decalogue. Finally, as Christians, we need to refer to the history of the Church both in Acts and in the case of the early Church Fathers to know whether they kept Saturday as a day of worship.

With the above, it is clear that the Sabbath has a greater signifier than Sabbatarians tend to assume. The first time the word Sabbath/rest is used is in Genesis 2:1-3. And it was used under the condition of God establishing ontological, social and ethic order. We know this when we go back to Genesis 1:1. In Genesis 1:1, the narrator informs us that "In the beginning, God created the heavens and the earth". Let's take note of the word "created". The fact that it is in the past tense is very important for me, a non-reader and speaker of the Biblical languages of Hebrew and Greek. So, reading the word, "created" implied that creation was, indeed, complete. It was not in the making. It was a complete work of God. The way Chapter 1:2 begins, "Now" creates an understanding of an incomplete creation. If we read the item "Now" to mean a world that was not at any point completed in creation, then we run into a real challenge – a challenge that will be highly contradictory to the word "created".

Since I have said that I don't speak nor read Hebrew, and want to depend on my own understanding of the Bible, I want to focus on the word "created" or "create". We notice that the word create is very important because it means to bring into existence what never always existed. So, the earth and everything in it did not exist, until God brought them into existence. Consequently, it is only in Chapter 1:1 that the Bible uses the word "created"/ "create". Apart from this verse, we never read the word again until we come to its use in verse 27 in reference to the creation of human beings.

The times and episodic use of "creation" are important for me. Because we never read the word again in the context of God bringing something new into existence in the entire Bible, unless Revelations (the last book of the Bible), when we read:

> 5 He who was seated on the throne said, "I am making everything new!" Then he said, "Write this down, for these words are trustworthy and true.

The text in the book of Revelation was used in the context of God making all things new after the material world blows up in the fire – total destruction. After everything is destroyed, God the creator will create all things new: A new heaven and a new earth:

> Then I saw "a new heaven and a new earth," for the first heaven and the first earth had passed away, and there was no longer any sea. [2] I saw the Holy City, the New Jerusalem, coming down out of heaven from God, prepared as a bride beautifully dressed for her husband. [3] And I heard a loud voice from the throne saying, "Look! God's dwelling place is now among the people, and he will dwell with them. They will be his people, and God himself will be with them and be their God. [4] 'He will wipe every tear from their eyes. There will be no more death or mourning or crying or pain, for the old order of things has passed away."[246]

The above text is again very crucial in our understanding of the Sabbath. This is because it creates a seamless parallel between the Genesis account of God's creation in Genesis 1:1 and God's creation of the heavens and the earth again in Revelation 21:1-4. Now in both accounts, especially focusing on Genesis 1:1, creation was completed. Then, something happened. A catastrophic event that we are not told in the Genesis account happened. But we are told about the catastrophic event that undermined cosmic and social order in creation later in the Bible. After the catastrophic event, we read God now re-assembling creation by "calling" them into being or making them. At no point do we read the word "create" in God re-ordering the world or restoring the world.

It was after God had restored everything that the Bible said, "God saw all that He had made, and it was very good."[247] This statement could create a challenge of contradiction if we don't read the entire making of the world into account. The question that this statement potentially generates is: If God is good, how could He create anything that is deformed, such that He had to say all that He created is good? This question is necessary when we read in the light of the fact that God is ontologically good, in whom there is no contradiction or doubt.

Nevertheless, when we read the statement in the light of verse 2 of Genesis Chapter 1, we understand that God was affirming the fact that He had "partly" restored order. It also means that God did not need any human being to endorse the quality of His creation. This solves the

---

[246] Revelation 21: 1-4.

[247] Genesis 1:31a.

philosophical question of aesthetics: How do we know something is good? From the Christian perspective, what is beautiful does not lie in the eyes of the beholder, it lies in the eyes of the Beholder God whom the Bible recorded that "all that He made was very good." It also means that back to my point above, our dignity as human beings does not lie in anyone, in ourselves, or institutions and laws. It lies in God the uncreated Creator.

It was after God had declared His creation good that He pronounced the Sabbath. In other words, it was after the restoration of creation that God rested. He rested not from exhaustion as human beings do because God does not get tired nor sleep. But He rested from completing the restoration of the heavens and the earth – Sabbath (order, serenity, restoration, peace, social and ontological order). He restored ethical and ontological boundaries; He restored cosmic order.

All these happened after God had created human beings and commanded them to take charge of His creation with the dictum:

> So God created man in his image, in the image of God he created him; male and female He created them. God blessed them and said to them, "Be fruitful and increase in number; fill the earth and subdue it. Rule over the fish, the sea and the birds of the air and over every living creature that moves on the ground.[248]

God created human beings only after He had re-set the world. Human beings, therefore, inherited the world that was already in the state of Sabbath – a sinless world. Human beings did not only inherit Sabbath, they also had something residing in them.[249] Human beings also inherited a meaningful world – a world that was ontologically ordered. Human beings did not have to abstract Sabbath and meaning from anything – Sabbath and its meaning had already been defined for human beings by God. The duty of human beings was to rule over the creation of God. Human beings were given the authority to control nature, not the inverse. All these were possible because God created human beings and endowed human beings with the capacity to create at the finite level what God does at the infinite level. It is of interest to me that when God created man He called on man to name the animals, He God had created. The Bible concluded that,

---

[248] Genesis 1: 27-28.

[249] Ecclesiastics 3:11.

> Whatever the man called each living creature, that became its name. So, man gave names to all the livestock, the birds of the air and all the beast of the field.[250]

It is again curious to me that God made human beings His co-creator. Human beings with the capacity to create at the finite level partner God to govern the universe. This brings in the idea of human beings as the viceroy of God on earth. Human beings are also caretakers of the world God created. Human beings would be successful in their role as long as He remains in alliance with God; human beings would use his creative gifts well so long as He recognises that God is superior and the ultimate owner of all that is in the world.

Any time human beings acted to the contrary by negating the existence of God, the world goes sour. If human beings, as I have discussed above, decentre God, they centre themselves. And once human beings centre themselves, the world falls to the hubris of human beings with all the destructions we have seen in human history – slavery, fratricide, homicide, genocide, colonialism, sexual perversions, and all the evils we can think of. In the end, once human beings remain in the centre, all ethical and ontological boundaries are broken.

It is also important to note that man had everything made for him before a woman of a biological opposite sex was created. Adam named all the animals, which for me, implies Adam had a close relationship with all the living creatures. And yet, the Bible says that whereas all the living creatures had helpers,

> But for Adam no suitable helper was found.[251]

The above statement is very insightful and highly philosophical. First, God assigned Adam with what appears to be a simple task of naming the living creatures. The word is "living creatures". Then through the process of Adam's mental exertion, Adam realised that all the animals had suitable helpers. But Adam did not have a *suitable* helper. His word is not just a helper, but a *suitable* helper. This means that animals could be helpers to man, as a man since the agricultural revolution has used animals for all manner of activities: as a beast of burden for sacrifices. But none of these functions of animals or living creatures serve the role of a *suitable* helper for Adam.

---

[250] Genesis 2: 19-20.
[251] Genesis 2:20b.

Instead of Adam going to search for his *suitable* helper (not partner), which he would not find any way, the Bible said,

> So the LORD God caused the man to fall into a deep sleep; and while he was sleeping, He took one of the man's ribs and closed up the place with flesh. Then the LORD God made a woman from the rib He had taken out of the man, and brought to the man.[252]

We notice two things in the text above. First, Adam did not go look within or outside for his suitable helper. God had to bring a suitable helper to him. Second, while Adam ontological knew he needs a suitable helper, the choice was not his to decide the helper he needed – even though Adam knew his suitable could not/cannot come from his own feeling, imagination, and creation. It had to come from the God who created him and who alone will provide the suitable helper. When God brought the suitable helper, Adam knew straight away that the helper was not the same as he was. In fact, while Adam had named all the animals, Adam knew also that the creature that had been brought to him was not one of the animals; but a unique being like him with a different ontological function. So, the Bible records that when God brought the woman to Adam, Adam said:

> This is now bone of my bones and flesh of my flesh; she shall be called 'woman' for she was taken out of me.[253]

It was after Adam had seen a creature with a different ontological function (that will be very clear in Chapter 3) that God pronounced marriage as a divine-cultural mandate between a biological man (Adam) and a biological woman (Eve – but yet to be named). The Lord stated as follows, through the voice of the narrator of the chronicler of Genesis:

> For this reason, a man shall leave his father and mother and be united to his wife, and they will become one flesh.[254]

The only reason marriage takes place is when three things happen as fundamental a priori: First, when a man fails to find a suitable helper among all of living creatures; second, when God brings the suitable

---

[252] Genesis 2:21-22.
[253] Genesis 2: 23.
[254] Genesis 2:24.

helper to man, and three, when man recognises the suitable helper as a person with the ontological capacity to perform a contrary function. While marriage practices may differ across cultures, from the Judeo-Christian perspective, anything short of these three conditions is a subversion of God's creation of marriage. Also, the fact that God created marriage implies that marriage as a heterosexual, monogamous relationship is not left to human beings nor human creation of the state to define. Up until this time, we are very much aware that there was no state nor the idea of human beings defining marriage. What we read is that marriage is anterior to the state.

Similarly, until later in the Genesis account we don't read of any organised religion, be it SDA, Jehovah's Witnesses, Calvinism, Pentecostalism, etc. This also means that marriage is anterior to organised religion. From the above, therefore, any attempt by organised religion to define religion away from God's construction of marriage as a heterosexual and monogamous relationship between a biological man and a biological woman is a subversion of God's Sabbath – God's ontological order. Any attempt by any church to interfere with the Sabbath of a couple is in direct violation of God's command that marriage is God's divine-cultural mandate given to human beings.

Finally, we read that marriage should not be interfered with by families. We read this in

> "For this reason, a man will leave his father and mother and be united to his wife, and they will become one flesh."[255]

Whereas men have their own families and get wives from another family, once a marriage is established, families of the new couple must stay away and maintain a distance that allows the new couple to be united. Any interference from the natal families of the new couple is a violation of marriage as God ordained it. In religious cults, it is common for parents in such cults to seek to influence their "children's" marriage lives even when their "children" are expected to move away and be united to their suitable helpers of the opposite sex. Some church priest, like those in the SDA denomination, often preach sermons that could potentially ruin the families of their members who are married to non-Adventists. The challenge of a professor writing to dictate what families do with their children lends an unfortunate credence to accusation some level against the SDA as a cult of Christianity (Hoekema 1963).

---

[255] Genesis 2:24.

We can tease a few things from the discussion so far: First, marriage is God's creation and so only God determines what marriage is. Second, marriage is anterior to the state as a political entity, the church as a post-sin establishment and takes precedence over natal families after marriage is established. Once any of these is subverted by the state, the church and families, the violation is directly against God who clearly said:

> Therefore, what God has joined together, let no one separate.[256]

Before the "therefore", of this statement, Jesus, as God the creator, had/has overruled the laws of Moses that allowed for divorce; appealed to His creation order in the Genesis account and concluded with the "therefore" no one (state, church, families, and friends) should undermine any marriage that God puts together.

At this point, it is clear that while human beings were to procreate as the reason for marriage, marriage was also about taking away ontological loneliness. Men and women can be alone, but they can hardly survive loneliness. In the modern world, people think they can find a company of things other than a person of the ontological opposite sex. So, we find human beings playing with cars, electronic gadgets, dogs, cats, and buildings. Human beings have strayed in different directions in search of happiness. But in the face of advanced technological improvement, loneliness remains a fundamental challenge of humanity (Turkle 2011).

Before the pandemic, I knew of two British friends, a man and a woman who often travelled around the world, seeking pleasure. They would go to Spain, France, and Italy (Rome) as they enjoyed themselves. To really enjoy, they discarded all ideas of childbirth. The woman and the man agreed to sterilise themselves such that childbirth was nearly impossible for the woman. Before then, anytime they had raw sex and the lady became pregnant, they would quickly abort it. All was going well until the novel virus pandemic struck the world.

Needless to say, the pandemic undermined every illusion of "we have figured it all out through science and technology". The pandemic-induced lockdown and the weaponisation/politicisation and monetisation of vaccination further accentuated human frustrations. For this young man and woman, initially, they thought they could make do with their electronic gadgets. They thought they could transpose the

[256] Mark 10: 9.

temporary awe of sight-seeing in the various museums and "wonders of the world" in their electronic gadgets at home. Before long, reality dawned on them. The couple began to struggle; they noticed they were tired of just seeing each other. The constant report of people dying of COVID-19 in their hundreds, even though Boris Johnson had promised the sufficiency of the NHS to help, further exacerbated their frustration and boredom. Before long, they both called me and said, "We wish to just have the sound of a baby disrupting our boredom."

The history of loneliness, wisdom was recorded in the Bible – Genesis, which was Adam had no suitable helper, even though he lived amid abundance. He lived in a world of Sabbath. It was almost as if, Adam fulfilled the Bob Nester Marley's, "In an abundance of water, the fool is thirsty."[257] Unfortunately, in an abundance of material prosperity, almost everyone without any form of conjugal union with someone of the opposite sex is lonely.

The response to this loneliness did not come from Adam, but God himself. God provided Adam with a woman who was totally different in function to Adam. Impliedly, the woman in my life is not expected to be the same as me. Sameness is ontologically impossible to eliminate loneliness. For this reason, marriage is not just about love, which is very vague from a materialistic perspective. Marriage is also not just about procreation, though very much needed. Marriage is not about romantic expression. Marriage is about curing one's loneliness with a person of an ontological order and function.

For the above reason, the Bible refers to all forms of non-heterosexual relations as decidedly against nature. They are all against the natural order of how God created His Sabbath. All sexual perversions are simply perversions. Nothing will translate sinful desire into acceptable legislative sexual perversion. All sexual perversions cannot be rectified by romance through the anus or law.

I have observed that since the 1970s, the western world has significantly abandoned its Judeo-Christian sex ethics that defined the boundaries of marriage. And yet, such redefinition has not taken away the reality that the sex organs must be presented as ontological opposite to function. So, every now and then, lesbians continue to make use of vibrators and dildos. One day on my way from my college in Wolfson, while walking towards the city centre, a lady in front of me accidentally had her dildo falling to the ground. Because I was very close to her, I just pretended not to have seen what fell. Ordinarily, I could have said

---

[257] John Shaap (February 25, 2015), Bob Marley & The wailers – Rat race< https://www.youtube.com/watch?v=fKvB3WsVd60> (Accessed: March 21, 2022).

my usual Ghanaian polite expression of "sorry" without admitting any guilt or bending down to help. But in this instance, I just walked on. After all, if she did not respect what is before a man and rather prefer a superficial of it, I could not lift what is inanimate but simply an imitation and deeply elusive.

In view of this, it comes as inconsistent when Professor Audrey Gadzekpo said she did not know how lesbians have sex.[258] It also demonstrated the complexity of the LGBTQ when she accused unconverted and self-made bisexuals who practice anal sex in their imagined heterosexual unions. Similarly, Prof. Akosua Adomako comes across as a highly controversial figure who now wants to convert God's love into romantic sinful anal sex of *trumutrumu* as it is said in Akan.

Because of the criticality of heterosexual relations as necessary for curing loneliness, in all societies that my readings allow me, homosexual practices were often not part of the sociogenic activities of people. Any society, like the Greco-Romans that openly accepted homosexuality, showed a strong visible sign of morally bankruptcy, for which reason the practice had to be put in check. Similarly, the depravity of homosexual practices was such that any civilised society had to disallow it from becoming part of an accepted public practice. It was for this reason, inter alia, that the western world, as part of the Judeo-Christian influence, had to hold homosexuality as illegal until they felt they had arrived in their civilisation in the 1960s – when they threw their sense of morality to the dogs.

In Africa, while sexual perversions existed prior to colonialism, there is hardly any evidence that homosexuality was a sociogenic activity. By sociogenic activity, I refer specifically to the public acceptance of sexual perversion as part of the social order. While some scholars have admitted the possibility of homosexual practices in precolonial societies (Bediako-Akoto, 2017: 101-102), my point is to show that there was hardly any sociogenic activity that supported homosexual practices.

Audrey Gadzekpo and her allies who support *trutrumumu* (anal-anal) – a highly disdained and tabooed Akan (Twi) word in the Ghanaian context – decided claimed that the Akan word, *Kojo Bɛsia* represented homosexuals. The Akan name *Kojo Bɛsia* is a descriptive name of a man who has a feminine appearance. The word was never used to refer to a practice of *trumutrumu*. In my four decades of life, I have met such men and women who had the appearance of the opposite sex, but they were

[258] Citi TV (October 5, 2021), #FacetoFace with Professor Audrey Gadzekpo, https://m.facebook.com/CitiTVGH/videos/910760986542724/.

hardly regarded as homosexuals. There were two of such young women in my community – Maamobi – when I was growing up. One of them was an albino called Madam – a Muslim. She played football with us and beat us in tennis games. But we never regarded her as lesbian neither did she see herself as a lesbian.

More importantly, until the media and western-type of Gender Studies contributed to the extension of western identity politics and cultural wars in Ghana since the beginning of the millennium, people had to often suppress their counter-cultural feelings. Potential homosexuals and other forms of queer sexualities had to hide their identities. This is not to say that occasionally we did not hear rumours of homosexuals in the community, especially at Accra Girls' Senior High School (which is in Maamobi). But they are, indeed, issues of rumours and highly secretive that could be researched.

But more recently, feminist scholars and other allies of the LGBTQ community, including CDD-Ghana, have transformed discussions on sexualities. Often profiled by the public as persons either trained in the US or perceived to receive funding from the US, these activists are accused of emboldening individuals to even want to openly lay claim to having their queer sexual lifestyle like lesbianism accepted by law. The LGBTQ debate has also been valorised as the public considers advocates of queer sexualities as moral and sexual revolutionaries, who usually perch the vagina and penis in an immortal sin – making the evil deeds of the dark are now the issues that brighten society. As part of the moral panic built around the same-sex debate, advocates are treated by the public as a bunch of confused scholars in a confused beleaguered world.

As the public debates on the LGBTQ takes a moral turn, I return to the creation account, as part of my contribution to the subject of human beings potentially inheriting a world of sinlessness. Again, as part of my major argument for this book, I maintain that there is a need to curate the LGBTQ debate away from simplistic binaries. Thus, I discuss the relationship between morality and law from the perspective of the Bible. I must once, again, say that my position may not be universally shared – albeit it is my own understanding and contribution to the decolonisation agenda.

In the absence of sin, we do not read about God giving any replica of the Ten Commandments; we do not read human beings spending an entire day in church or monastery chanting, giving communion, giving sacrifices, praying in tongues, clapping and dancing, reading religious materials to know God better, laying claim to prophesy, murdering, killing, cheating, enslaving, etc. We do not read anywhere that human beings were breaking ethical and ontological boundaries that needed pacification of a deity through worship and rituals – including devoting a day for worship. What is more, we do not read about human beings wanting to exit this material world to "heaven".

Instead of all above, we read about God "walking in the garden in the cool of day."[259] The absence of rituals and worship and laws are all because human beings as image-bearers of God bear the moral character of God – to ontologically know good and evil. For this reason, we are told anywhere that God gave human beings any set of moral, civil, and/or ceremonial laws. And yet, human beings were without excuse, because as Paul wrote the indictment of human beings who undertook and/or support evil:

> 18 The wrath of God is being revealed from heaven against all the godlessness and wickedness of people, who suppress the truth by their wickedness, 19 since what may be known about God is plain to them, because God has made it plain to them. 20 For since the creation of the world, God's invisible qualities—his eternal power and divine nature—have been clearly seen, being understood from what has been made, so that people are without excuse.

The reason no one is without excuse is very strong in Paul's reflection that, "For since the creation of the world, God's invisible – his eternal power and divine nature – have been clearly seen, being understood from what has been made, so that people are without excuse." Paul was clear "since creation". So, no one needed to wait for the moral laws in the Decalogue to know good and evil. At the same time, what is morally reprehensible and morally good are not left for human beings to decide. If we were to leave the philosophical question of ethics: "How do we know what is right from wrong" to the banalities of human subjectivity and relativity, we end up destroying the human race. This is precisely because one man's goodness is another man's evilness.

Among the Akan, individuals were never left off the hook of personal responsibility on the basis of ignorance. When people fell afoul of the moral laws of society, they were duly punished. In the last six or so decades since independence, Afrocentric scholars have split hairs over the source of African moral values. The Kenyan and

---

[259] Genesis 3:8.

Ghanaian scholars of religion, John S. Mbiti and Kofi Asare Opoku, respectively have mentioned that religion is the main source of African morality. They are right, but that alone raises fundamental questions: what about those who do not hold any belief in any religion? Must one know about God or the deities before one can know when one is wrong and/or right?

The other opposing camp led by the Ghanaian Kwasi Wiredu and Ugandan, Okot p'Bitek mention human pragmatism and rationality (nearly atheism) as the source of morality. Again, this is also important, but what does it mean for persons who may not be rationally capable of thinking and discerning through wrong and/or right because of ontological biological handicap? What do we do with minors who commit crimes?

The last group is represented by nearly a lone voice: the Ghanaian philosopher, Kwame Gyekye, who appeals to the human conscience. He argued that among the Akan, one's conscience is appealed to, instead of God or mere rationality when one sinned. This logic is expressed in statements such as, "Wo tiri bua ti wo sen?" (to wit: "how does the living animal in your head judge what you have done?) and "Wo nyin na wen hu a wo ye bone a won hu?" (to wit: If you are unconscious when you are growing, can't you be conscious when you are sinning?).

The above points are all insightful, but they make a lot of sense when they are treated as mutually inclusive, rather than mutually exclusive. Because all put together, they support the biblical fact that God created human beings in His image with moral agency and that no one is with an excuse in the face of evil. After his own analysis of the above debate, Lord Elorm-Donkor, concluded in his thesis that the Akan held individuals as morally responsible for their actions and that individuals appealing to "the devil made me do it" as an excuse were hardly tolerated (Elorm-Donkor 2017).

The discussion on morality so far betrays two imbecilities of recent scholarship in both law and anthropology. In law, people simply want to assume that morality is determined by "man" – which is to say that human beings determine what is good and bad. For this subversion of thinking, every moral issue, such as the homosexual quagmire, is settled in court through the use of the law. In Ghana, a celebrated lawyer, Ace Ankomah, in his efforts at proving that Ghana is a secular country and the laws are secular, betrayed his own common sense when he concluded that the laws of Ghana are man-made.

Such a simplistic statement may tickle him and his listeners, but for any discerning person, such misleading statement raises a critical issue. If human beings make laws to determine good and evil, does it mean that someone must define the reality of good and evil? Does it mean that human beings have the right to choose and pick what they consider to be good and evil in law? Ace Ankomah's inverted logic is nothing short of the foolishness of man being autonomous – self-law. I will take this up in the course of this book.

From the text of Genesis 1:27-28, we also understand that human ontological dignity is not based on marriage, procreation, acquisition of degrees, acquisition of material things and regular access to power, money, and sex. Human ontological dignity is based on the fact that there is a God who created human beings in His image and said all His creation *was* good.

He only commanded the man he had created:

> You are free to eat from any tree in the garden; but you must not eat from the tree of knowledge of good and evil, for when you eat of it you will surely die.[260]

I will not attempt to provide any systemic exposition of the above statement, except to respond to a popular question that I am often asked by non-Christian and sometimes Adventist friends. Why did God put the tree in the garden when He knew that human beings would eat it, anyway?

This question is valid. But it is valid so long as it does not excuse human beings from their responsibility in the face of moral evil – as I have discussed above. In Ghana, we tend to blame everything on political leaders. I agree that our leaders are expected to lead. I also agree that some of our leaders have failed us. I, therefore, see some sense in our argument that if the fish rots it rots, from the head, to imply that we hold our leaders accountable for our actions. So, in sum, several Ghanaians think that righteous leadership is equivalent to a prosperous nation. A few Christians would quote texts such as the following to justify the need for a righteous leader for Ghana's quest for human flourishing:

> Righteousness exalts a nation,
> but sin condemns any people.[261]

[260] Genesis 2: 16.

[261] Proverbs 14:34.

> When the righteous thrive, the people rejoice;
> when the wicked rule, the people groan.[262]

These statements are great and forthright in understanding the importance of governance. But we need to contextualise our interpretation. We notice that the use of the word "righteous does not directly refer to an individual, instead, it is used generally. On the contrary, the use of "wicked" is used in direct reference to an individual – wicked ruler. The text rather in reference to righteous says that "when the righteous thrives". This means that the righteous need the space to thrive. How can the righteous thrive if they are not allowed to thrive? What if laws are passed to incriminate the righteous? What if the righteous are punished for being righteous? In sum, how can the righteous lead a nation in prosperity when the nation is not in support of righteousness? Righteousness is a collective act, because it takes a group with a common mind to construct.

The opposite features are all through with wickedness. Wickedness is about destruction and lawlessness. It does not take much mental exertion and cerebral consideration to do evil. One person can easily carry the task of destroying a whole building that took the energy of several persons with different expertise to construct. The wicked do not need several companies to do evil. But the righteous do.

For the above reason, while Ghanaians may rightly crave a righteous leader, we have never liked any "righteous" leaders. All "righteous" leaders were righteous only when they were fighting those we all considered an enemy. I have often argued that Nkrumah was a good leader when he was fighting the European coloniser. He turned to Mazrui's Lenin Czar when he turned to fight against his own people. Whether fighting the colonialists with words of inspiration or positive defiance or fighting his own people with laws, incarceration, and deportation, Nkrumah, at least so we have read, was seeking a righteous leader to fulfil his pre-independence promise of a political kingdom of prosperity.

For the above reason, Nkrumah became the wicked ruler of both the erstwhile colonisers and his own people, who joined forces to overthrow him. In the end, Nkrumah's popularity rose and sunk depending on whom he fought at which period in Ghana's history. The same could be said about the leaders who have come after Nkrumah, and other adaptive leaders such as Yitzhak Rabin of Israel, Muhammad

---

[262] Proverbs 29:2.

Anwar el-Sadat of Egypt, John F. Kennedy, Mahatma Gandhi of India, and Martin Luther King, a civil rights advocate of the US, who were all assassinated.

Incidentally, all these leaders are now posthumous national and international heroes. But why are they now being celebrated? And why were they assassinated? They were assassinated for many right and wrong reasons, but basically, they were assassinated because they wanted to change the mindset of their people. They wanted to hold their own people responsible for their actions. Celebrating them posthumously is simply because they are no more a threat, as dead persons do not threaten anyone. We may also praise them because we feel guilty for betraying them, after all, regret is more painful than offences. Impliedly, while the political elites may under pressure cow to the legislate LGBTQ rights, the peace of Ghana will come up for posterity to judge.

Because adaptive leadership is not the same as efficient leadership, Noah, who was decidedly righteous, did not transform his society. His society perished anyways. The Bible said, Lot who was righteous did not transform the sinful society of Sodom and Gomorrah in which he lived. Incidentally, the world is still dealing with the more aggressive homosexual sins of Sodom and Gomorrah. In the case of righteousness not necessarily constituting good leadership, the Bible said of Lot:

> and if he rescued Lot, a righteous man, who was distressed by the depraved conduct of the lawless[263]

As the world is ditched and forced into a moral abyss by the advocates of LGBTQ rights, the church is forced to accept such queer sexualities. The states globally are passing laws to force the church to acquiesce to what the church read as the banality of sexual perversion. Christian pastors and bakers, as well as professionals, are compelled to accept homosexual perversions. As I have already mentioned, journals and publishing houses have become more radically leftist that any piece of work that does not support the sexual revolution agenda is unlikely to be published. The internet revolution world has even made it easier for state and pro-LGBTQ+s surveillance of Christians who want to keep their Christian conscience sane from the madness of the world.

In all this, Christians have resolved to be the light and salt of the world. We have deployed compassion in the face of hostility from the

---

[263] II Peter 2:7.

gay community to shine the light of Christ as part of driving away from the moral darkness of a sexually perverse world. We have historically built schools of higher learning to bring prosperity to society. Several of the world's humanitarian groups were founded and inspired by Christians who followed the Lord's command to "love our neighbours."

We have historically built churches, like my church in Birmingham (St Stephen's) on a hill to point people to the Cross of Christ. We have loved the old, rugged Cross to point to the world that we have a better world in view. We choose to carry the Cross instead of the Castle of power so we can be bearers of Crowns in heaven. This is not to say that as people on a pilgrim, some of us have not hurt and harmed the world. A few of us wrongly used the Bible, against the explicit instructions of the Lord Jesus Christ to love our neighbours to enslave, colonise, kill alleged witches and even condone genocide.

Nevertheless, in all this, we try to be the light and salt of the world. But the world is not allowing us to be the light and the salt that we must be. The world is seeking to dictate to us what we should believe and practice as Christians. Pro-sexual perversion laws are being passed to suppress Christian counselling that supports families. Everything else is accepted except our Christian faith. Jesus has become the whipping boy in schools. Atheists have reconciled the ontological paradox of becoming chaplains in a high-profile institution of higher learning like Harvard, which was built by Christians to train their children. In short, we have become the title of Stephen McAlpine's book, *Being the bad guys.*

But the sub-title of the book, *How to live for Jesus in a world that says you shouldn't* is the very reason for Christianity since its foundation in the 1st Century. Since the birth of the Church of Jesus Christ on the day of Pentecost, shortly after the ascension of the Lord, our saviour, the church has often had to deal with the immoral cultures of the world. Whether in the Jewish culture, the Greco-Roman culture or indigenous cultures around the world, the church has had to be the moral conscience of the world. The church has done this amid being accused of going against society, and consequently amid Christians being persecuted – leading to the Tertullian axiom, "The blood of the martyrs is the seed of the church."

The good news is that the church always wins, because Jesus Christ said the gates of hell shall not prevail against His ecclesia – His group. While with stint and identification with the political power of Rome, the church nearly lost its stint, the church always bounces back to serve as the moral conscience of the world. Indeed, from the church's experiences with directly taking over political power in Rome and the medieval era, Christians have re-learned to "be in the world, but not of the world." In other words, the church must learn to walk the tight rope of influencing the world without being influenced by the world.

The church is a cultural transformer, not a cultural warrior. So, as Christians, we must exercise compassion and cry, like Jesus did, in the face of pervasive evil. I must admit my own sins and plead for the Lord's forgiveness for my role in sinking the world into its current moral abyss. The irony, however, is that while a minority Christian group turned the world upside down, a minority of morally bankrupt individuals with the support of the state seek to turn the light and salt of the church upside down.

But in all of the culture wars and the victimisation of Christians, I want to heed the counsel of McAlpine:

> [T]he victim narrative is a dangerous game for Christians to play – one that may have an initial sugar rush but risks becoming bitter game indeed. While we may occasionally be victimized for being Christians in the West (and I add Africa), we must resist the current temptation to find our worth or standing in actual or perceived victimhood (McAlpine 2021: 64).

The more the world intensifies its crusade against us, the more we know the world needs the love and light of Christ. The darker the light, the more we must pray to the Lord who is the light of the world to shine through us to dispel the darkness of immorality. The greater the intensity of persecution, the more we should pray the words of the Apostles:

> Now, Lord, consider their threats and enable your servants to speak your word with great boldness.[264]

The more the world seeks to oppress us by controlling the gates of publishing, the more Christians should write and set up their own publishing houses. As Christians, our task as cultural transformers will be daunting, muddy, and rough because fighting attitude is more difficult than fighting militarily. Soft power (culture) is more difficult to fight than the most stable fortress. But it is toughest when soft power and the fortress, represent the political, state-sponsored and cultural wars of today. That several of the institutions of higher learning have

---

264 Acts 4:29.

cowed to the cultural wars in support of moral depravity could easily overwhelm early Christian academics, like me. This is because of the systemic cloning of all academics to think from a sexually liberal and morally lousy perspective.

Nevertheless, in all of this, we encourage ourselves with the words of our Lord to Joshua:

> 6 Be strong and courageous, because you will lead these people to inherit the land I swore to their ancestors to give them.
>
> 7 "Be strong and very courageous. Be careful to obey all the laws my servant Moses gave you; do not turn from it to the right or to the left, that you may be successful wherever you go. 8 Keep this Book of the Law always on your lips; meditate on it day and night, so that you may be careful to do everything written in it. Then you will be prosperous and successful. 9 Have I not commanded you? Be strong and courageous. Do not be afraid; do not be discouraged, for the Lord your God will be with you wherever you go."[265]

The Lord's commands to Joshua are apt for our times. First, when Joshua was going on a military expedition to conquer the land, the Lord simply told him to be strong and courageous, because destruction is always easy, as I have said. But when he was to govern the people, to socialise them to think and act, according to the commands of the Lord, the Lord said to Joshua, "Be strong and very courageous." "Be very courageous" because as a Ghanaian, the "wars" Christian academics would wage against the invading moral depravity of the LGBTQ+ would be so tasking that we are likely to be discouraged.

Our writings, based on Judeo-Christian sexual values, may not be high-ranking liberal journals. The journals that may accept our papers have been politically profiled as predatory journals to discredit any publications that go through such channels. Our promotion may be forestalled by those who disagree with our Judeo-Christian worldview; some of our friends may turn against us; while our moral aptitude may be tempted in the face of immorality.

But in all this, we should stay our ground. We should aspire for excellence. We should pay heed to Paul's instruction to the slaves – servants. This is because we are all servants of the Lord, as we serve humanity in faithfulness:

---

[265] Joshua 1:6-9.

[5] Slaves, obey your earthly masters with respect and fear, and with sincerity of heart, just as you would obey Christ. [6] Obey them not only to win their favour when their eye is on you, but as slaves of Christ, doing the will of God from your heart. [7] Serve wholeheartedly, as if you were serving the Lord, not people, [8] because you know that the Lord will reward each one for whatever good they do, whether they are slave or free.[266]

There is every temptation among some commentators to accuse Paul of condoning enslavement, as one Madam Moore, my African-American classmate at the UCC did when she presented a paper on slavery and the Bible. But the next verse tells us that Paul was similarly commanding masters:

[9] And masters, treat your slaves in the same way. Do not threaten them, since you know that he who is both their Master and yours is in heaven, and there is no favouritism with him.[267]

Clearly, Paul in the entire Chapter Six of his letter to the Church in Ephesus wrote in a manner that was consistent with Christianity – respecting authority, without disregarding human ontological dignity. All Christians are servants of the Lord Jesus Christ who are to serve in faith in the Lord and faithfulness in their service to humanity. There is always the temptation for us Christians to become sluggish in our service to humanity because of the way we are treated. But contrary to returning laziness for hatred from our superiors, Paul in his letter, first and immediately addressed to the Church in Romans, also told us to do the opposite even when we are being persecuted:

[17] Do not repay anyone evil for evil. Be careful to do what is right in the eyes of everyone. [18] If it is possible, as far as it depends on you, live at peace with everyone. [19] Do not take revenge, my dear friends, but leave room for God's wrath, for it is written: "It is mine to avenge; I will repay," says the Lord. [20]

On the contrary:

"If your enemy is hungry, feed him;
if he is thirsty, give him something to drink.
In doing this, you will heap burning coals on his head."

[266] Ephesians 6:5-8.
[267] Ephesians 6:9.

21 Do not be overcome by evil, but overcome evil with good.

It could be very exhausting to continue to do good when we are often repaid with evil. We are also often torn between fighting back with fire when we are attacked. The temptation to return evil with evil is very high because we all feel stressed, as we run out of patience when our enemies never renege. But as the Christian cultural apologist, Jim Denison often writes, "We should see the real enemy as the enemy of all of us – Satan." Once we see the real enemy is Satan who has blindfolded those who do not see the light of Jesus Christ,[268] we will weep for ourselves as we relax in engaging in robust evangelism and those who have chosen the path of eternal destruction.

But we cannot also stand aloof in the face of wanton injustice. In fact, the Lord did not call us to a ministry of passive acceptance of injustice. So, we must as active as possible in correcting with the wrongs of society, but

> [K]eeping a clear conscience, so that those who speak maliciously against your good behaviour in Christ may be ashamed of their slander.[269]

We should pray that the Lord would graciously open the eyes of those perverting His world to see the self-destruction they are in. Finally, in a hostile academic environment, Christians should work hard to achieve more without losing sight of the fact that they have a world better in view. Paul was clear in telling His fellow Christians that Christ's resurrection should be the major source of their inspiration in all things, especially as they faced persecution. In the world of culture wars that lead to cancel culture, sometimes we may feel like drowning. But our fears are actually not so much about the absence of fame as it is about death. We can all play politics with death, claiming it is nothing, but the fear of death is at the heart of every human heart.

But Paul told the Christians that they should not worry in doing good and having evil paid in return, but death will bring them glory. He stated:

> **58** Therefore, my dear brothers and sisters, stand firm. Let nothing move you. Always give yourselves fully to the work of the Lord, because you know that your labour in the Lord is not in vain.

---

268 II Corinthians 4:4.

269 I Peter 3:16.

Jim Denison put the Christian victory over death as follows:

> "The worst that can happen to us leads to the best that can happen to us."[270]

In concluding on this section, Christians can either feel needy or needed, but the Bible clearly enjoins us to feel needed. Feeling needed would reignite the purpose of God inviting Adam and all of us to co-create with Him. God create we procreate. Regardless of where we are in terms of our profession, we all shall receive the same salutation before our Lord and saviour Jesus Christ:

> Well done, good and faithful servant! You have been faithful with a few things; I will put you in charge of many things. Come and share your master's happiness![271]

This statement was the conclusion of Jesus's paragraph of the Bags of Gold. It highlights the need for all of us to be diligent with whatever the Lord has entrusted in our care. Regardless of how we think our gifts are small or big, the Lord will say the same salutation to us if we discharge our service as a servant in faithfulness to Him and humanity. We should endeavour to remain faithful even with the few or little gifts we have. The world where we have converted everything into money can make us think until we receive a monetary reward, we cannot even give a cup of water for free. The world is full of strife and agitations. These have morphed into multiple industrial actions in Ghana, with lecturers who suspending teaching for nearly two months.

Unfortunately, the idea of unionism forces all of us to identify with actions we may not identify with. But as a matter of principle and action, based on my Christian faith as a servant of God to serve humanity, I don't believe in industrial action and I don't support it. For me, it creates several illusions. The first is that it makes those striking believe that until they have good working conditions, they cannot function well as a good and faithful servant. Second, it creates an impression that we must be patted on the back for everything good we do. From my own children's walking practices, I have learned that a

---

[270] Dr Jim Denison (January 28, 2022), When sharks attack and storms threaten: what good is biblical faith in perilous times?< https://www.denisonforum.org/daily-article/when-sharks-attack-and-storms-threaten-what-good-is-biblical-faith-in-perilous-times/> (Accessed: March 22, 20220.

[271] Matthew 25:23.

child learning to walk will walk anyways whether my wife and I praised him or not. Thirdly, strikes can undermine perseverance, which is at the core of our Christian mandate "the one who perseveres to the end will be saved."[272]

The end of Sabbath and humankind's search for it

Returning to the Sabbath, I argue that the serenity of the world God created – did not last. Adam and woman sinned. They sinned by wanting to be God, the very sin Satan committed and was thrown away from his abode in heaven. The hubris of Satan was what denied him the glory he was made with. The Bible records the reason for the pride that led to the downfall of Satan as follows:

> How you have fallen from heaven,
> morning star, son of the dawn!
> You have been cast down to the earth,
> you who once laid low the nations!
> 13 You said in your heart,
> "I will ascend to the heavens;
> I will raise my throne
> above the stars of God;
> I will sit enthroned on the mount of assembly,
> on the utmost heights of Mount Zaphon.
> 14 I will ascend above the tops of the clouds;
> I will make myself like the Most High."
> 15 But you are brought down to the realm of the dead,
> to the depths of the pit.

The multiple "I" in Satan's vain and vague decree has not left the human race. At any rate, Satan went to Eve asking Eve desire "I" instead of "Thou" (God). The Bible says that Satan creates a desire for "I" in Eve, by sowing a seed of doubt about God's command in Eve. After that, Satan persuaded Eve to desire the "I" of becoming like God. This desire of "I" was recorded in the Bible as,

> When the woman saw that the fruit of the tree was good for food and pleasing to the eye and also desirable for gaining wisdom, she took some and ate.[273]

---

[272] Matthew 24:13.
[273] Genesis 3:6a.

In the context of Genesis 3, the wisdom (*sophia*) Eve wanted was to be able to decide for herself, the boundaries of good and evil. This was similar to what I have discussed in Chapter One as a man being the measure of all things. The Bible then adds that "She also gave some to her husband, who was with her, and he ate it."[274] I find something strange here, until I wrote this book, I had questioned where Adam was when the Devil was interacting with Eve. But now, it has become clear to me that Adam was there. The Bible said, he "was with her."

This means that Adam was as guilty as Eve. Perhaps, Adam was more in trouble as the head than Eve. We shall see this with the direction of God's judgment. But before then, it is clear that Adam and woman were equally guilty of wanting to centre themselves. In modern social media parlance, the sin of human beings putting themselves in the middle is called "selfie". The religion of I is framed as "I, me, and myself".

Unfortunately, since this episodic event, the history of the world is the history of the human "I" seeking to rule over everything including God. Since the secularisation of culture in the 19th Century, western "thinkers" such as Charles Darwin, Sigmund Freud, James Frazer and Herbert Spencer have all made clearer and sought to justify the human-centredness of a triumphant "I".

Charles Darwin's natural selection theory is not about physical strength, but how best an organism can protect its "I" – selfishness. So, natural selection is about the survival of the fittest I, instead of anything else. The stronger the "selfishness" the better the chances of an organism surviving. A story is told to reflect Darwin's theory better. It goes as follows:

> Two people got lost in the forest and as they were seeking to find their way out, they heard the story of a lion roar of a lion coming towards them. The two friends had to decide on their escape route. One of them started looking for a place where the two of them could hide from the lion. The other one rather started running away. The one who was looking for a place where the two could hide was rather perplexed about his friend's action. So, he asked his friend: Can you run faster than the lion? His friend responded, so long as I can run farther away from you, I will be fine. Because by the time the lion is done with you, I would be gone.

---

[274] Genesis 3:6b.

Charles Darwin became the Apostle of modern positivistic science that bracketed the world out of the control of God. Through his theory of evolution, Darwin succeeded in saturating the world with a world without a god. His lead was followed by Sigmund Freud, who said God is nothing short of a figment of the imagination; James Frazer, God is nothing short of the human desire to mimic nature – magic – and Herbert Spencer who said God is nothing but the deification of human beings (Whaling 1995).

Since the 19th Century, university education, which began in the west has become a space where an inversion of the Biblical creation account is produced, reproduced and served as a menu to all students. It is in the schools, therefore, where human beings want their "I" to be really "I" – a captain of their own lives. Since these pioneers left God out of the dark, groping in search of humanity, the assault of God appears to go ad infinitum.

Indeed, since Adam and the woman sinned, every act of human beings, as I have already discussed became evil. Human beings have become so ontologically evil that the Bible was clear that, "every inclination of the thoughts of the human heart was altogether evil all the time" (cf. Genesis 6:5). In Romans 1, Paul said every human being was under the judgment of God, because every human being deliberately rejected the knowledge of God. For this reason, Paul concluded that:

> 21 For although they knew God, they neither glorified him as God nor
> gave thanks to him, but their thinking became futile and their foolish
> hearts were darkened. 22 Although they claimed to be wise, they became
> fools 23 and exchanged the glory of the immortal God for images made to
> look like a mortal human being and birds and animals and reptiles.
>
> 24 Therefore God gave them over in the sinful desires of their hearts to
> sexual impurity for the degrading of their bodies with one another. 25 They
> exchanged the truth about God for a lie, and worshipped and served
> created things rather than the Creator—who is forever praised. Amen.
>
> 26 Because of this, God gave them over to shameful lusts. Even their
> women exchanged natural sexual relations for unnatural ones. 27 In the
> same way the men also abandoned natural relations with women and were
> inflamed with lust for one another. Men committed shameful acts with
> other men, and received in themselves the due penalty for their error.
>
> 28 Furthermore, just as they did not think it worthwhile to retain the
> knowledge of God, so God gave them over to a depraved mind, so that
> they do what ought not to be done. 29 They have become filled with every

> kind of wickedness, evil, greed and depravity. They are full of envy,
> murder, strife, deceit and malice. They are gossips, 30 slanderers, God-
> haters, insolent, arrogant and boastful; they invent ways of doing evil; they
> disobey their parents; 31 they have no understanding, no fidelity, no
> love, no mercy. 32 Although they know God's righteous decree that those
> who do such things deserve death, they not only continue to do these very
> things but also approve of those who practice them.

Indeed, as part of reducing human beings to only elevated apes, human beings are not responsible for anything. They could be anything and act anyway according to their desire. In his book on *Sapiens*, the gay Oxford-trained historian further downgraded human beings to nothing but a concatenation of biochemistry! (Harari 2014). This is how low human beings have sunk with the "I" sinfulness.

If we are simply biochemistry and we are "I" without a God we could appeal for dignity, we are never responsible. Because we biochemistry and elevated apes cannot respond to stimuli in rational terms. If responsibility is the "ability to respond" why can a person whose brain is made of billions of biochemistries overcome his desire for same-sex relations? Is it not a puzzle, however, that a mixture of biochemistry could write a book about human beings becoming *Deus* in his *Homo Deus*!

Back to Eden to show the origin of the 19th C radical atheists who have given weapons of mass intellectual destruction to radical feminists today, I look at the responses of Adam and woman. When God approached Adam and the woman, they both denied responsibility – othering and blaming the *other*. Their son, Cain after turning down God's warning and killing his brother, told God he was not his brother's keeper. In other words, and at the risk of repeating myself: he was not responsible for murdering his brother. Adam denied personal responsibility; Cain denied moral responsibility. Noah failed the collective responsibility; while the people of Shinar failed the ontological responsibility.

Human beings have since not refused to take responsibility for their actions. Members of the LGBTQ+ communities want to be anything they feel and are inclined to. So, the "+" means until our desires run into nothingness. And members of the LGBTQ+ community who have a conscience for God will want to create God in their image – a gentle, romantic loving God who enjoys the orgasm from the anus. And says, "I love you even if your anus is tearing apart and leaking. Just wear the pampers like a toddler, after all, it is about fulfilling your desire to be wise and be your own god!"

The judgement pronounced on Adam and the woman is indicative enough of the gender and radical feminist war today. When God was pronouncing judgment, part of what He said, for the sake of my book is:

> "I will make your pains in childbearing very severe;
> with painful labour you will give birth to children.
> Your desire will be for your husband,
> and he will rule over you."

The expression is "your desire will be for your husband, and he will rule over you." The expression "desire" and "rule" over you should make every reader take a break. What is the meaning of the desire here? Is it just "desire"? If it is just a desire, why the power-laden statement of the verdict, "he will rule over you"? To understand this statement, as part of my reading of the text contextually, we know that when the word "desire" was first used, it was used in connection with Eve wanting to be her own God, while her husband was with her. Adam stood by while the woman desired to be her own god. So, as the woman would endure pain, she would still desire to be her own god away from the control of her husband. But it looks like this time, Adam will not sit idle for the woman to subvert his authority and further lead him again away from God. So, Adam would this time exercise control over the woman.

God now turned his attention to Adam, and began the pronouncement:

> "Because you listened to your wife and ate the fruit from the tree about which I commanded you, 'You must not eat from it,'
> "Cursed is the ground because of you;
> through painful toil you will eat food from it
> all the days of your life.
> 18 It will produce thorns and thistles for you,
> and you will eat the plants of the field.
> 19 By the sweat of your brow
> you will eat your food
> until you return to the ground,
> since from it you were taken;
> for dust you are

and to dust you will return."

The judgment on Adam are heavy and needs analysis and unpacking. But for this book, I will focus on a few aspects. First, Adam's judgment was first and foremost because he listened to his wife and disobeyed God. Was Adam not expected to listen to his wife? What does this mean? We shall soon understand. Second, the earth was cursed because of Adam, and yet he would work to feed himself and his family. Why didn't God tell the woman that she would eat bread out of the sweat of her brow, but rather told Adam? Does it mean Adam was created as the performer of instrumental responsibilities?

Until this point, we read of Adam taking any action. Possibly, Adam was aware that he was to work anyway, because God made Adam God's co-creator, who "named" the animals. Also, Adam already knew how to handle the rake and till the land. The major difference is that work as a divine-cultural mandate would be harder because of sin. It would be burdensome. It would make the idea of the Sabbath worse. But in all this, Adam would provide for his wife anyway. How would Adam control a woman who had led him into all this trouble? But was it the fault of the woman? And was the woman held responsible for the sin of humanity?

That God rather called and asked Adam whether Adam had eaten the fruit instead of the woman who first ate the fruit is rather telling. It shows the fact that God established Adam as the head of the family. That God is punishing Adam for listening to his wife, instead of Adam taking instruction from God is also telling. But put together, Adam was held squarely responsible for the sin of the woman, because Adam was the leader.

As God kept reading the judgment, Adam may not have noticed the seriousness of what had happened until God reminded Adam of death. God said:

> By the sweat of your brow
> you will eat your food
> until you return to the ground,
> since from it you were taken;
> for dust you are
> and to dust you will return."[275]

[275] Genesis 3:19.

With the words in the simple expression, "you shall die", Adam knew he was in real trouble. At that point, it was just the question of overworked efforts to provide for his family, but all his efforts will end in dust. While Adam was to procreate and fill the earth, he had not yet done any of that. Worst of all, he had not even named the woman in his life. Adam simply called his wife a woman, and she was a woman, indeed.

As if all of us men are learning from Adam, when we marry a woman, we want to "own" her through several means. In western culture, the man gives his name to the woman, giving rise to "Mr and Mrs… and the man's name follows." This simply implies the woman, once she is married, is subsumed by her husband. Elsewhere, the man would give the woman a ring to demonstrate he controls her and/or owns her.

Returning to Adam, when he woke up from his stupor, the first thing he did was to name his wife. So, it was after God told Adam that he (Adam) would die that Adam named his wife. While Adam had named all living creatures, the only time Adam was naming the woman in his life was when he realised that he needed to outlive the dust – the fight against God. Did Adam think the Sabbath of Eden, where he had been driven away from, would be restored through birth as immortality? Would birth bring Adam resurrection from the dust – where sin would keep him?

Adam named his wife Eve with a meaning that is both telling and revealing of Adam's intentions. The Bible writes:

> Adam named his wife Eve, because she would become the mother of all the living.

Would Eve help Adam to resurrect from the dust to restore Sabbath? Would birth be enough for the restoration of the Sabbath? Later in the Bible, I read that the hopes of Adam were dashed when real physical death was recorded. His dream of resurrection from the dust as a restoration of Sabbath was crushed before his very eyes, when his first son, Cain, killed Abel. The sins of Adam and his wife had not been redeemed with childbirth. The children have demonstrated to Adam the meaning of physical death.

At the same time, Adam had to contend with a woman who would seek to "desire" him. Would the woman use her reproductive powers to "rule over Adam"? And what would be the response of Adam? Would Adam wait for the woman to control him?

As I discussed in Chapter Three, the rise in modern radical feminism began with a woman, Simone de Beauvoir, rebelling against Jean-Paul Sartre, a man she could no longer live with (Johnson 1988). She was a rebellion against a man whose popularity had brought more women around him and in consequence frustrated her desire for control. Incidentally, Jean-Paul Sartre's own theory of existentialism was an authority he handed over to de Beauvoir to reinforce her rebellion. Since de Beauvoir, again as I discussed in Chapter Three, women have taken the feminist debate to its conclusive end, resisting marriage and childbirth as oppressive and as tools men use to control them.

Alas! Adam's Sabbath is forever dashed. Not only did Adam see his children shattering his plans of leveraging the womb for his restoration of Sabbath (resurrection from the dust), but Adam's sons in the contemporary world have had to struggle to secure the right of a woman's womb. For this reason and before the radical feminist movement, the names of women have hardly been mentioned in history. History itself was read by some feminists, as part of men's oppression against women. And so, they named "history" "Her-story" to place women in the centre of history. Why didn't women occupy the centre of history and their names usually missing until fairly recently? Was it part of men seeking to resist the "desire" of women?

The millennium

I have said above that all the cultural issues of gender studies in the 1990s were to turn into culture wars of the millennium. On the eve of the millennium (2000), there were several speculations about humanity and the world. From the perspective of religion, there were eschatological interpretations to the effect that the world would come to an end. There was also the issue of Y2K (the Year 2000 computers), which assumed that all pre-millennial computers would crash. In Maamobi and Nima, there was widespread speculation that a huge stone would drop on humanity. With all these, anxieties were high as the world made slow, but sure incursion into the millennium. Alas, the world entered the millennium with none of the speculations happening. But something else happened that appears to be equally eschatological for religious people. The millennium marked the entry of the internet revolution in the case of Ghana and other West African countries. This means that while at the time I was completing secondary school education in 2001 internet connection was still very limited to a few elite families, by the time I was at the university in 2004, the internet revolution had nearly caught up with the country.

By the middle of the millennium, the impact of the internet revolution had crystallised and become more evident in the social media revolution. Social media, which has become the buzz of society, has fundamentally redefined human civilisation globally. The "social" in social media produces several antinomies that morphed into the fact that we have become social with hardly any offline sociogenic activities. With this phenomenon of social media, the current coronavirus pandemic, holding the world hostage since March 2020, has accentuated the "transmogrification" of human beings from social beings to "virtual" beings.

Becoming "virtual" beings have had multiple implications. Scholars may split hairs over the extent to which social media evolution, exemplified in WhatsApp, Facebook, and other such handles have impacted human beings. But what appears less controversial is the façade of freedom that social media appears to have offered human beings. Freedom has been the desire of human beings since the Biblical narrative of Adam and woman exercising their ontological freedom to be like God. Can freedom make us like God, and to what extent is God free? Does freedom mean choosing between material alternatives or choosing between inherent human desires? Do human beings have freedom over the consequences of their freedom? How thorough is the assertion attributed to Idi Amin of Uganda that, "Freedom of speech, I can guarantee, but not freedom after the speech?" Who defines freedoms and does freedom have boundaries, and who determines the boundaries of freedom? Do human beings have the freedom to significantly "transmogrify" themselves such as the trans-genders without any consequences? Whose freedom takes precedence when communal freedom clashes with individual freedom? But what even constitutes the communal and how an individual is an individual?

While not exhausting the complex issues of freedom, my reading of the crossfires of the world is that social media has become a major channel for views and opinions to be ventilated. Controlling social spaces/public sphere appears easier than controlling activities online. Before social media, several Ghanaian men easily formed what is contentiously referred to as vigilante groups to exert pressure on the political elites to cow to their demands. With the onset of social media when the ruling class passed a law to ban vigilante group activities in 2019, social media has become the space for more robust political engagements. The youthful constituency of the country has often resorted to social media mobilisation to affect offline activities. Perhaps, the most recent and major social media mobilisation by the youth is the morphing of youth anger in what is now known as the #FixTheCountry Movement.

The perceived freedom offered by social media has attracted attention from the older "conservative" Ghanaians. On the 12th May, 2020, during the vetting of Professor Henrietta Joy Abena Nyarko Mensa-Bonsu as a Supreme Court judge nominee, she indicated that it is now difficult to regulate the extent of people expressing their views on social media.[276] She further said, the idea of "the book does not lie" – which refers to the reviewing of written text before it is made public – has succumbed to freewriting on social media. While Prof Mensa-Bonsu's may have a point, especially in reflecting on what appears to be limitless freedom on social media, is it true that "book no lie"? Do publishers just publish? And is knowledge neutral? These questions will be considered in this book.

While I take up the above questions in this book, I argue that while social media appears to have offered some freedom and broadened the frontiers of communication, the issue that also needs inquiry is a digital dictatorship. Are people freer in the world today than in the premodern world? Has technology enhanced contemporary dictatorial regime than in the so-called pre-industrial past? To what extent do issues of state technological surveillance affect freedom? What does it mean for the United States of America to advise its citizens who travelled to China to participate and observe the 2022 Olympics games to avoid taking their phones to China?

Notwithstanding, the progressive technological breakthrough which has a spillover effect in the areas of medicine convinced several observers that the world was getting better. The idea of a world getting better was clearly articulated by the Israeli Oxford-trained historian, Yuval Noah Harari, whose trilogy – *Sapiens*, *Homo Deus* and *21 Lessons* – created an impression of a world where human beings would soon conquer death and in the process become immortal. When I read Harari's trilogy, I recalled the fact that human beings have since the Edenic narrative never ceased to be immortal – gods. In the Genesis account of the fall of human beings, the woman and Adam ate the fruit because of the Devil's deception that they would be like God – knowing

---

[276] Univers TV (14 May 2020), "Vetting of Supreme Court Justice Nominee, Prof. Henrietta J.A.N Mensah Bonsu" https://www.youtube.com/watch?v=NBuVWnXPlcY Last accessed 11 July 2020.

good and evil. This was almost the Devil telling human beings that we would become masters of our morality and ethical values.

The optimistic hope of the world that Harari and others like him expressed appeared to have rather suffered a major shipwreck, especially with the outbreak of the coronavirus pandemic. While before the pandemic, the world was a world of antinomies, summed as several people starving in the face of abundance, the pandemic rendered visible all the challenges of human beings. It rendered more visible the social and ontological inequalities that have always docked the human quest for a perfect world. The stress of social distancing, the unemployment that the pandemic generated, the visible inequality that stared everyone in the face exacerbated anger. This means that while human beings have often been angry, the stress of the pandemic, the illusions of sufficiency it took away, were so overwhelming that the least provocation spiralled into national and global violence. Most specifically, daily cases of racism became epochal cases, with examples from the global street demonstration against a Minneapolis American police officer, Derek Chauvin, who grotesquely murdered an African-American man – George Floyd on May 25, 2020.

While the murder of Floyd was troubling enough, the mass reaction that followed signalled in "mob" destruction and defacing of statues and busts was equally troubling to me. With several young men and women, taking to street demonstrations in several countries of the world and collapsed status and busts of men whose actions and inactions were read as having contributed to racism and social inequality left me with several questions. The basic questions that I asked were: do we rewrite history by trying to reconstruct past realities? Were the demonstrators trying to point to an imagined golden age in human history that never existed? Were the demonstrators assuming that human beings are ontologically good? Was the pulling down of statues enough to end social inequality? Wasn't the issue of social inequality more about morality and ethics than just pulling down statues and busts? Appealing to my Christian worldview, I asked the question: isn't the problem of human beings because of the wickedness of the human heart (cf. Matthew 15:19)? What do we do with history – our past? To what extent can we read selectivity, relativity and subjectivity into the human past?

While pondering over these questions, it also became obvious that the impact of the pandemic was rather going to bleed into other areas of life. As the pandemic devastated global economies, America under an extremely leftist president, Joe Biden, is leveraging economic challenges to push through American sexual and moral revolution around the world. Since 2006, the so-named western world has expressed an interest in tying aid conditionalities to developing economies decriminalising homosexuality. But in all this, countries such as Ghana have succeeded in calling the bluff of the western world.

With the totalising impact of the pandemic that has been worsened by the western world's politicisation and weaponisation of vaccines, several African countries, including Ghana have become more vulnerable. The President of Ghana, Nana Addo Dankwa Akufu-Addo, followed his predecessors including J.A. Kufuor and J.EA. Mills who prior to the pandemic spoke tough against decriminalisation homosexuals had to be moderate on the subject. When the President of Ghana was hosted by Kwami Sefa Kayi on Peace FM, a local radio station in Accra, he was very doggy about the homosexual question. When Sefa Kayi asked the president about the "Proper Family" Bill in parliament that seeks to provide social and medical responses to the homosexual questions, the President surprisingly and contrary to his pre-pandemic position rather praised a few academics and civil society groups who decided to promote homosexual practices in the country.[277] Similarly, when the country's soft-spoken Finance Minister, Ken Ofori-Atta, who often publicly demonstrated his Christian faith with his always white-white custom and quotes of the Bible prior to the reading of budget statements in parliament, was asked about the Family Bill, he was also doggy about it. While he admitted to Paul Adom Otchere that he had not read the Bill, he boldly said the Bill was wrong.[278]

The revitalised discussions on homosexuality brought in the churches and the various religious groups. This time, Ghana's religious constituency buried their real and imagined doctrinal differences to push against the minority group and the international community pushing homosexuality down the throats of Ghanaians. The leadership of the Church of Pentecost, led by its the Chairman, Apostle Eric Kwabena Nyamekye, reiterated his predecessor's (Apostle Prof. Opoku Onyinah's) position that if the nation attempts to decriminalise the practice, he would lead his church in a public demonstration against the state.

---

[277] UT Ghana Online, "Kwame Sefa Kayi Interviews Prez. Akufu-Addo on Peace FM 21/10/21" (October 21, 2021) < https://www.youtube.com/watch?v=W14ehgrHvrw> (accessed: March 12, 2022).

[278] Good Evening Ghana, "Exclusive Interview with the Minister of Finance, Hon. Ken Ofori-Atta on Good Evening Ghana" (November 19, 2021) < https://www.youtube.com/watch?v=vcWWi1ONhMI> (accessed: March 12, 2022).

As half of the year was dedicated to debating homosexuality amid the ravaging effect of coronavirus, I asked several questions: What is the role of academics in a country? Why is the western world, led by America's leftist President seeking to disrupt the nation with a private issue such as homosexuality? How free is the university or academics who feed on the public's purse in their activism? What roles have the western liberal institutions awarding a scholarship to Ghanaian students to study abroad had and continue to have on the homosexual discourse in Ghana? Why are some African academics, including Toyin Falola in the west assuming that supposedly liberal African youth would similarly liberalise sexuality in African when they take over the reins of governance on the continent? (Falola 2022: 327) Why on earth can the entire Ghanaian population of 93 per cent have their cultural aspirations of heterosexual marriage be subverted by a tiny minority who have no claims of being openly victimised? To what extent does the homosexual practice break ethical and ontological boundaries that can have a long-term negative impact on Ghana? Beyond the constituency of either American-trained or American-influenced Ghanaian academics pushing for homosexuality to be decriminalised, what roles are the media playing?

The above questions show how western cultural wars and sexual and moral revolutions have become part of the circuits of neo-colonialism. The west continues to see Ghana and other African countries that do not support the sexual revolution as backward or those on the wrong side of history. Western banalities of modernity as linear social progress is used as a canon to measure the civility or otherwise of Ghanaians who largely depend on religious texts such as the Bible, Qur'an and ancestral logics to consolidate and protect the boundaries of heterosexual marriage as the ontological means of procreation.

As the homosexual debate rages, several of the female academics, including Professor Takyiwaa Manuh, who once headed the Institute of African Studies (IAS), legitimised her support for the practice in her claim that she has a track record of defending human rights in Ghana. Others like Professor Akosua Adomako Ampofo, also a former director of the IAS, said she felt embarrassed that Christians could not show love for the LGBTQ+ *imagined* community in Ghana. Very legitimate reasons indeed, but it is rather curious to know whether the rights they fought for Ghanaians attracted the kind of public uproar the LGBTQ rights have generated. Lawyer Akoto Ampaw, also argued that the Bill proscribed advocacy towards decriminalising homosexuality was wrong because social change is brought about by advocacy – citing the case of slavery. Professor Audrey Gadzekpo was asked about how lesbians have sex, she said she did not know and yet was able to question the legality of anal sex among some heterosexuals, if indeed, homosexuality is unnatural. Knowing how sexual minorities have sex the does not disqualify her to defend them. But possibly if she had answered, the rumours that intersect LGBTQ and ill-health.

In all of the discussions and debate, I reflected on how so much has changed since the internet and the social media revolution. I also mused over the coronavirus as an entry point into a world where the United States is seeking to register its sexual and moral revolution on the rest of the world. Since the 1960s, the western world secularised its moral culture, which cascaded into the sexual revolution. This was to the extent that by the middle of the millennium, several western countries had decriminalised homosexual practices. And as part of the centring and provincialising of the west, western leaders have made every effort to push the homosexual agenda to Africa.

Meanwhile, as the western world sinks deep into secularisation, Ghana is increasingly becoming religious – reflecting both evangelical and reform Islam doctrines on heterosexuality as the normative practice for procreation and sustaining the human family. Similarly, chieftaincy has surged along the lines of evangelical lines with several chiefs becoming evangelical Christians and reformed Muslims. Consequently, the Ghanaian democratic experiment cannot be seamlessly related to the western type. Because all the major institutions of state governance, chieftaincy – charged with indigenous customs – and Christianity and Islam are decidedly against homosexual practices. For the above reasons, I have been reflecting on the following questions: why is the west seeking to destabilise Ghana?

As the elite continue to show the counter-cultural idiosyncrasies in seeking to normalise homosexuality, marriage is also under siege. While I do not seek to go personal, several of the women leading the decriminalisation agenda are radical feminists who are either not married or have been divorcees for decades. As I said, I do not seek to go personal, but I mention this to contrast it with the overwhelming constituency of Ghanaian women whose aspiration in life is to marry, have their own families as part of fulfilling their religious duty. For Christians, while marriage is not a must, if one were to marry, one must enter into a heterosexual relationship. For Muslims, marriage is part of faith (*ibadah*), such that whoever marries is said to fulfil half of his or her religious duties.

For this reason of marriage as a divine-cultural mandate, the majority of Ghanaian women have always resisted any government or institutions that undertake policies and projects that undermine the sanctity of the human family. It was largely for this reason of protecting the human family that the Ghanaian constituency resisted the attempt by the west to reorient Ghanaian children towards acceptance of homosexuality. This was particularly when the Western world attempted sneaking in the so-called Comprehensive Sex Education in 2019 into the basic schools. While the CSE may seek to help African children who are victims of misinformation, the morality built around sexuality implies that the state should have dialogues with parents as stakeholders of education.

Nevertheless, since feminists in Ghana, including the three I mentioned above, returned from encounters with the western world and have been promoting what they refer to as women's rights, women appear to have been liberated. This supposed liberation of women has produced several women graduates since the turn of the millennium. Several women have also broken barriers in entering the world of work. But my observation, however, is that as more women receive higher education and enter into formal work, a few of them married early. This is also because women's rights have come with cultural imperative of career before marriage and childbirth.

Indeed, this cultural imperative of career before childbirth has the façade of redemption for women. But since I started teaching at the tertiary institution about ten years ago, I have observed first-hand the challenge young women go through. At the African University College of Communications in Accra I encountered several young women who often came to me crying. They often cry about delayed marriages or struggle to keep their families together.

Those who complained about delayed marriages had their own concerns, as several of them were developing fibroids. While the causes of a fibroid are many, including genetics, the social cause of fibroid for strange reasons are hardly discussed. Among some of the medical professionals I spoke with, virtually all of them said, African women are more prone to developing fibroids particularly if they delay childbirth. In Ghana, therefore, several euphemisms signal the social cause of fibroid. These include the following: "Bad girls don't get fibroids, but good girls do" and "Fibroids are a disease of an idle womb." For these statements, two medical doctors explained as follows: "Every woman can get fibroids. But Afro-Caribbean women who delay pregnancy are more prone to developing fibroids." They also explained that the reason for women being advised to have children is not to necessarily stop them from getting fibroids, but "to ensure that the fibroid-related surgeries do not compromise the capacity of the womb to carry a pregnancy." Also, since fibroids can develop at any time between puberty and the menopause,[279] it may be reasonable for women who desire to have children to do so as soon as possible when they can. Asking women to have children as soon as they could is not an easy route in a world where education is necessary for women, as well as men to receive the necessary skills. For this reason, society needs to think more clearly about affective actions that will support women and families.

But it appears the chance of pregnancy decreasing women's development of uterine fibroids is burdened by radical feminism. Radical feminism sees pregnancy as oppressive and seeks to repress and discourage it through their promotion of lesbianism and polyamory. Similarly, the cultural imperative of work and career before pregnancy prolongs the time women have to either marry before pregnancy or even get pregnancy. The issue is even more complex since pregnancy or even get pregnant would slow down women in their career aspiration – as they nurture their children. And so, as I have said above, women need to be supported as they desire to have children. I must add that the issue is more complex when several women talk about men becoming irresponsible. With such a complexity, the Ghanaian state could possibly set up a similitude of Social Security Fund, where men who impregnate women, whether married or not, would be compelled to contribute a quote of their earnings to support women and their family.

The second category of female students, were young mothers who hardly saw their children. Several of them complain about the difficulty in combining childcare and workplace culture. More recently, possibly as part of affirmative action, more and more women have been pushed into the world of work. While this was read as a fulfilment of the feminist movement since the 1990s in Ghana, it has brought unspoken, but real consequences – several women feel oppressed as majority of them combined dual roles – performing instrumental and expressive responsibilities. I had one young woman literally breaking down in front of me that, "I want to see my children, because I see them briefly

---

279 NICE – National Institute for Health and Care Excellence, What is the national history of fibroids? (December 2018) < https://cks.nice.org.uk/topics/fibroids/background-information/natural-history-of-fibroids/> (March 12, 2022).

on Sundays." This means that the school make it possible for women to go study and go have their children. If she cannot cope ordinarily nothing prevents her from going home, but the "formal" economy that places emphasis on certificates complicates the chances of these women.

This challenge of women not seeing their children is largely because, since the millennium, the liberalisation of the Ghanaian economy has introduced several private banks into the country. These banks as part of corporate social responsibility and to move with the cultural trends tend to employ more women than men. While workers at the banks spend lots of hours at the workplace, the introduction of weekend banking in Ghana, such that women work on Saturdays, has left women with children less time to attend to their families. The issue is even more daring considering the spatial planning of Accra. Accra is highly congested, for several reasons, including poor decentralisation of development. And while several people work in central Accra, these workers live out of Accra and go to work by spending hours in the country's morning and evening road congestions (known as "rush hours"). Given this reason, these female students of mine tend to see their children not as "playing kids" but "sleeping kids" as these children are often asleep while they go in and out of school. A few of the women who could afford boarding schools, send their infants to boarding houses. The question in all this: How do women feel when they don't see their children? And how would all this feed into the socialisation of children? And those who apply the service of maidservants (*abaawa*),[280] how do they also read their relationship with the maidservants – oppressive or freedom to such maidservants?

The complex situation above has resulted in discontentment among some women, especially as several men are said to renege their responsibilities. Raising the complex issue of men's alleged irresponsibility, a young woman wrote to Evelyn Akagbo, host of the Adventist counselling programme, *RealTalk* as follows:

> Dear Real Talk,
>
> Am I being unreasonable? I don't think so, but my husband of two months thinks I am.

---

[280] To appreciate the vagaries of "Abaawa" as representing pre-modern slavery, please see: Kwabena O. Akurang-Parry 'Transformations in the feminization of unfree domestic labour: A study of "Abaawa" of prepubescent female servitude in modern Ghana', *International Labour Working-Class History*, 78 (2010): 28-47.

Here's my issue. We just got married, and figuring out how to manage our finances as a couple. We both work and earn decent salaries. I have my bank account and so does my husband.

My husband thinks it'll be better and makes more financial sense to have a joint account, one account where we put all our monies, so we are aware of how we spend our monies. I don't think having a joint account is necessary.

I think we can each have our independent accounts and still contribute towards our home and bills. I don't see why we should put our monies in one account.

He thinks I don't want to be transparent with my spending and my money that's why I don't want a joint account.

I don't know why he wants to know everything I do with my money. It's my money and I should decide what I do with it. I don't mind paying some bills and contributing when needed but I don't think it's necessary to have a joint account.

This is causing tension in our very young marriage because it is one of the important issues we disagree on.

Please advise me, am I wrong? Is having a joint account necessary?

#hopechannelghana

#realtalk

#changinglives.[281]

When I read the above concern, I was very sad, and asked myself: Did God design the anatomy of the male and female sexual organs by chance or by design? What does the fact that the vagina of the woman receives, but does not give mean to a woman's social life? What does the fact that the man's penis gives, but does not receive mean for a man's social life? How would a woman feel, as expressed in the text above, when she gives to a man rather than receiving from a man? And what does it mean for a man to keep receiving from a woman rather than giving to a woman?

In all of this, social media has reshaped the issue of narratives about women. Before the social media revolution, the 1990s marked the beginning of the feminist movement in Ghana. The return of a few Ghanaian female scholars from studying in the west, especially the United States of America invested in feminist conversation in the country. Given that the idea of feminism was not strong in the public

---

[281] Hope TV Ghana, *RealTalk* (January 26, 2022), <https://www.facebook.com/hopechannelgh/posts/4991910307567785> (accessed: February 10, 2022).

universities, these women channelled their activism through civil society organisations – forming women-oriented groups, such as ABANTU, that sought to challenge what they considered oppressive cultural practices. The groups fought practices such as child marriage, FGC, witchcraft accusations, and issues of rape.

The fight these women's groups launched against these practices were resisted by a section of the Ghanaian population. But largely, these women's groups had support from several Ghanaians, as well. Even one issue these women's groups championed that was quite controlled was their promotion of the domestic violence bill, focusing also on marital rape. But eventually, the bill passed into law.

I have been very sceptical about social evolution, because the term is controversial. I sincerely think while society may progress technologically, we simultaneously continue to sink so low in moral depravity. Technology enhances individualism, which could strain social cohesion and shared values. Incidentally, the problem of the world is not necessarily a technological one, but rather moral - how best we allow morality to creatively engage with technology. Since the secularisation of morality in the 1960s, we have seen a downward trend in the moral aptitude of human beings. Through the instrumentality of modern science, we have significantly acquired technical skills. We have become more skilful in dealing with the technical problems of the world. We have gone to the moon. We have gone deep under the sea etc. We appear to be conquering nature to a significant degree.

Unfortunately, the acquisition of technical skills has not corresponded with social skills. The more we advance technologically, the more we become individual qua individual. As we sink deep into individualism, our capacity for social skills flattens. We lose our civil language. Social capital, a deeply nuanced subject, shrinks. What Ibn Khaldun calls the collapse of *Assabiyya* begins to signal the collapse of human civilisation. In the end, we are faced with individuals being auto-nomos (constituting a law to themselves). An extreme form of libertarianism advocated by Jeremy Bentham and John Stuart Mill intensifies.

Individuals do as they please. They own their bodies - they do with it as they please. They remain unaccountable to anyone. They can walk naked in public, drink to their death, and even kill themselves as they see fit. Social media has accelerated our individuality. We are now more interested in "likes" than the quality of what we write or post. As faceless, virtual beings, we can insult, attack, and malign against ideas that sound Christian. It is in the light of this that l understand the issue of Rosemond Brown (also known as Akwapim Poloo). I had not paid attention to her, since the few times she hit the headlines, it was for controversial and wrong reasons. This is also because I have not been interested in the movie industry since the late 1990s - when the media increasingly liberalised.

In my generation, it is now easy to condemn the church than celebrities who virtually do nothing but demonstrate opulence and sometimes sheer moral depravity. Since the sentencing of Akwapim Poloo, for the publication of nude pictures of herself and her seven-year old son in Instagram as part of marking her son's birthday,[282] I resisted writing about it, because it did not warrant my time and attention.

But I am compelled to wade into the discussion because in my estimation it forms part of the kind of sexual freedom that gender advocates want for women. As part of the intellectual push for a moral revolution in Ghana, a Ghanaian law professor residing and working in the USA has established himself as a counter-cultural revolutionary. He has established himself as a formidable social commentator. He talks about virtually all social and political issues. But many times, I struggle to see any sense in his arguments.

Unfortunately, he has a large following because his liberal views on moral issues sync with the young men and women in our generation. This Professor says he does not see anything wrong with what Akwapim Poloo showed on social media. Obviously, he had a relativistic view of nudity. He is not alone in reducing everything to the banality of relativism. One young Ghanaian doctoral graduate made similar comments, highlighting a no standard on April 16, 2021, on Facebook as follows:

> Another Sad Day for Mother Ghana!
>
> The state has violated Akuapem Poloo and her son much more than she could have ever done in that post.
>
> The State claims she engaged in domestic violence which undermined the integrity of her son. How was that conclusion reached? Was the child thoroughly examined for possible trauma or harm caused by that post? What team of experts were engaged in that examination, and what were their findings?

[282] Myjoyonline.com (April 16, 2021), "Akuapem Poloo sentenced to 90 days imprisonment," https://www.myjoyonline.com/akuapem-poloo-sentenced-to-90-days-imprisonment/ (Accessed: September 4, 2022).

> She published obscene materials? Ridiculous one! What constitutes obscene material? Loads of men in Ghana post pictures of their bare chest, stomach, etc. Without any clothes, many men confidently display their "six pack" and other muscles. Those are not obscene, are they? Yes, what you are thinking is correct. The judgement is partly rooted in a culture where people think it's okay to control the bodies of women, but give men the absolute freedom.
>
> She pleaded guilty? Well, the charge shouldn't have been filed in the first place.
>
> In the same country, a politician recklessly shot a gun in the public and in few months later got rewarded with a ministerial position. What a joke!

Ordinarily, I would not begrudge these commentators, if they were consistent with his relativistic proclivity. But, in the case of the Ghanaian legal scholar, he said that the judge was wrong in sentencing Akwapim Poloo. This is where we see the faltering of a Prof whose sense of judgement is clouded by faltering logic. How come he thinks his subjective view is better and should be treated as objective and yet a judge does not have an equal right - operating within the law - to sentence a crime?

All the same, I understand the moral climate change. Ghana has entered into a sexual revolutionary era where nudists would be hosted live on television to talk about their sexual escapades. It also appears that the youthful constituency of Ghana hardly have any philosophy of life that incorporates conviviality. For example, on Thursday, April 16, 2021, I watched Paul Adom Otchere, a seasoned journalist, host some students from the University of Ghana to discuss social issues.

To my surprise, these university students had such a warped view of life that I was left nearly traumatised about the future of Ghana. One of them said he plans to amass so much wealth that he could travel to England just to eat pizza. Another said, he is not in any form of conjugal relationship because he wants more money to get more women.

With university students speaking the way they did, I reflected on why teenagers are beginning to murder for money-ritual making purposes.[283] However, if we live with young men with such a materialistic view of life, then the public may want to find a way of

---

[283] Jonas Nyabor and Calvis Tetteh (April 4, 2021), Kasoa: How two teenagers allegedly killed, buried friend for money rituals [Photos]< https://citinewsroom.com/2021/04/kasoa-how-two-teenagers-allegedly-killed-buried-friend-for-money-rituals-photos/> (accessed: March 12, 2022).

appraising the judge for seeking to protect public sensitivity and morality – instead of criticising them from an unsustainable relativistic logic. That the judges must be supported to curate the public from needless indecency is precisely because when we enter into the public sphere, we enter into an unwritten social contract with everyone and everything else. That is why we are not allowed by our conscience - even if not dictated by explicit law - to do as we please in public.

Nevertheless, as we seek to privatise the public sphere, we must reflect on the following questions: When did sheer open nudity become a norm in Ghana? When did narcissistic tendencies become the normative part of public culture? When did cheap celebrities become role models? We will always be divided on moral issues, but we will all equally face the consequences of moral depravity.

Based on this, I sincerely sympathised with the son of Akwapim Poloo, because he was a victim of a mother that the majority of Ghanaians considered wayward. But the problem is deeper than just splashing social media with nude pictures. Our generation continues to record high cases of premarital sex and children born out of wedlock. This would have been a good reason why Comprehensive Sexuality Education (CSE) is important, but the state's exclusion of parents in its introduction rather resulted in public rejection of it. In the wisdom of God, a biological male and a biological female are expected to marry and have children. So, two heterosexual parents are expected to nurture the children to be socially responsible. Consequently, the inversion of the God-ordained type of family becomes the lot of the world.

Unfortunately, while single parenting - with all its challenges - is increasing, the extended family, formally a bulwark against deviance, is quickly eroding. Alas! The family is almost gone. Children have become the victim of a world gone insane, a world spiralling out of its moral compass. So, as we pled for Akwapim Poloo, society must invest energy in restoring the dignity of marriage and human family. The need for a reinstitution of the family is important because "Akwapim" attached to her nickname is an aporia of her behaviour. Because Akwapim was the heartland of Basel missionaries who in the late 19th Century, who introduced the Calvinistic work and moral ethic. This contributed to making the Akwapim assume the fame as the most courteous in the country to the extent that, it is jokingly said that Akwapim person prefixes an insult with "Please". If Rosemond Brown is to merit the "Akwapim" nickname, then she must change her behaviour. This is similar to the advice Alexander the Great is said to have received for one of his coward generals, who was also called Alexander, "You either change your name or your attitude." This also means that we should not excuse sin by pointing to another sin that went unpunished. Evil is evil whether it is punished or not. Those of us who hold onto the Christian faith should live an exemplary life for the world to learn from. For, we are the light and salt of the world.

Back to the impact of the pandemic, as I have said above, this overwhelming disaster has unveiled imperfections that several people felt were fatalistic. But more importantly, since the pandemic affected the bourgeoises – though unequally – who may have remained unperturbed, the world was faced with anger that appeared to be universally shared. This again left me wondering about the world we live in. For several decades, the complex reasons for conflicts in Africa have left several Africans starving in a continent that has historically been the breadbasket of the world.

But none appears to care so much about hunger, since it hardly kills the rich. This means that while elsewhere in the western world, food is thrown away while the impoverished in the west and Africa die, the world's resolve to fight hunger appears to run within the logic of capitalism. There was hardly any uniform resolve on the part of the enriched people of the world to fight against hunger. And since a hungry man is an angry man, Africa is always placed in an eternal terrain of endless conflicts.

It is within my own understanding of the pandemic and its (un)equal impact that the youthful constituency of Ghana, led by its international conveyor, Mawuse Oliver Barker-Vormawor, has called on the political elite to fix the country. This call was not a new call, but it appeared more contentious now than it appeared the 1990s when the country re-democratised. This is precisely because it appears the political elite are struggling to contain any possible spillover agitation into political conflict, especially as the western Africa sub-region is engulfed in political instability – characterised by coups and religiously and politically inspired "terrorism".

Amid the debilitating impact of the pandemic, the political elite have struggled to explain the situation "rationally" to the youthful constituency who will take no explanation other than the country being fixed. The youth are still in their anger which has morphed into their label, #FixTheCountry Movement. But while it appears to call on the leaders to fix the country and even suggest a reform and revision of the country's constitution, the basic question that I ask myself is: how do we fix Ghana without fixing ourselves? I ask this question because, oftentimes, when we call for a nation to be fixed, we assume the position of "holier than thou", blaming those in office as overly corrupt, as if corruption applies to only those in authority. But as a young man, I have observed that several of the young men and women who accuse the older generation of corruption have also been accused of being corrupt when they entered politics to assume leadership.

However, we assess the #FixTheCountry Movement and the homosexual discourse, the fact that is starring at all of us is the existential reality of imperfection. We see all forms of imperfection manifesting in social, economic, and political spheres of life. As far as my reading of history allows me, since the French revolution of the 18th Century that led the western world into the secularisation of power, the world has been dealing with imperfections. At the end of the so-named World Wars, two philosophies as systems emerged to attempt to deal with human imperfections. These philosophies are socialism and capitalism. The socialists believe that unchecked individuals are the reason for the imperfection we see around us.

Consequently, socialists, inspired by their god-father Karl Marx, seek to decentre individuals, by centring the state. But after the state is centred, the promise of fairness in distribution thrives for a short while only for individuals who should have been displaced to re-take the centre position – oligarchs. Similarly, capitalists believe that the imperfection the world is faced with is because the state disallows individuals; the freedom to develop their potentials and to solve their own challenges. So, individuals are empowered. But in the end, individuals, after they have also accumulated least, have the ethics to redistribute. If human needs are insatiable, the re-distribution of acquired wealth in the spirit of altruism becomes nothing short of an illusion.

In the end, the promised utopia and nirvana – economic prosperity that both the socialist and the capitalist world promise in overcoming imperfection leaves the world with no answer but more sorrows. The promise of knowledge minimising or ending all wars, so eloquently expressed by the Oxford-trained historian, if this is necessary then include it for all your sources, please Yuval Noah Harari in *Homo Deus*, has proven to be false illusions, as we see what many thought would have been impossible – the ongoing Russian invasion of Ukraine. That the two philosophies as systems have failed to redeem the world or performed, the political kingdom of economic prosperity has been expressed by several scholars, including two novelists: Ngũgĩ wa Thiong'o's, *Devil on the cross*, and George Orwell's, *Animal Farm*.

I have personally reflected on the imperfections in the world. I have struggled to make sense of it. I have always wondered why I never had enough. But somehow, I have come to make sense of the imperfections in the world, after I re-bounced to Christianity after my secondary school education. Since then, I have become very sober and reflective – focusing on what I could do in my small way to help the people immediately around me than imagine that I could be a saviour to everyone else. I have come to understand the wisdom in brightening the corner where I am.

For the above reason, when on January 15, 2022, my colleagues from Cambridge shared on our common WhatsApp platform the poem of injustice[284] that one of our colleagues, Oliver who is also the lead organiser of the #FixTheCountry Movement shared, I responded as follows (slightly edited for grammar):

> Third Universal Theory! Oliver, my counsel, you remind me of my glory days when I was a studious student of Gaddafi's Third Universal Theory - At age 19 years, I devoured the Green Book like Hausa kooko (Hausa porridge) just after secondary school. I love the issues of revolution, especially the French Revolution of the 18th Century. Certainly, it paved the way for the desacralisation of power, and in alliance with that of the US, power indeed was stripped off all mysteries of divine rights of kingship. Democracy, with all the embedded complexities, was celebrated as the new normal. Then the West felt they had arrived. With liberalism, championed by big guys like John Stuart Mill and Jeremy Bentham, by the time we entered the 19th Century, we killed the divine entirely, as museums and cinemas replaced the church. 'Nyame nfa ne ho' to wit, 'Pay no attention to God'. Then we continued until we got to the mid-twentieth century: the world of expressive individualism leading to modern-day "selfie" - a world of indeed self-centredness. Suddenly, we realised that capitalism knows how to create wealth and not how to distribute it. Then we realised that the social and ontological difference we had fought was staring at us in the face. As if Napoleon Bonaparte's successors couldn't see that every revolution needs a counter-revolution. We remembered Uncle Karl Marx, who had also warned us in the 19th Century to be mindful of economic-induced inequality - classism. Instead of just power and freedom, Uncle Marx said it is about one class - the upper bourgeoise class, controlling the working class. The more the upper-

---

[284] JoyNews (January 15, 2022), Oliver Barker Vormawor recites a poem titled 'resilience and a new Ghana<
(https://www.youtube.com/watch?v=zho1xVaHfXo> (accessed: March 20, 2022).

class controls, the more human relations are reduced to money relationship - commodity fetishism. Uncle Marx then said we need constant revolutions until Nirvana's world of utopia was/is achieved. But Uncle Marx himself died without the fulfilment of his prophecy.

Well, Russia attempted to give Uncle Marx some hope. But Russia could not stand it, and eventually gave up. Today, we are back to systemic inequality. But where from both social and ontological inequality? Is it the enclosure? Is it about terra nullius? Is it about the rule of the liberated Animal Farm characters? But why did Rawlings appear to have failed in his revolution? What about all the revolutionaries we have had. By the way, Russia is now more oligarchic than ever with Putin seeking to lead the rebirth of the Father Land - the Tsardom of Russia, as it seeks to devour Ukraine. But will Biden do anything about it, if common soldiers with pawpaw hunting guns could drive away the so-called superpowers of the world? Possibly, the answer to my own illusions in Ecclesiastes 3:11. 'Nyame wo ho' to wit 'God is Alive'. Prempeh Charles

Western Media and Ghana's Family Bill

In this section, I will engage the nuances of Ghana's efforts at promoting proper human sexual rights and Ghanaian values. Contextually, taking into consideration the religious and political climate in Ghana and the West African sub-region, I argue that stance liberalised western media has taken to blackmail Ghana, as part of the colonial policy of "define and rule" policy is potentially dangerous to Ghana's peace. This is not entirely new, since Western media has often been part of Western imperialistic tendencies (Kaul 2006). While Ghana's overwhelming religious community seek to promote proper sexual rights, conditioned on the country's postcolonial existential reality of a mutually inclusive Triple heritage, framed around Judeo-Christian-Muslim heterosexual family values, the West has labelled the Bill as "Anti-homosexual".

Labelling Ghana's quest for its family values as "Anti-homosexual", Western media, including the BBC and CNN, has become pipelines for hegemonising and homogenising western sexual revolution that has been brewing since the 1970s. I conclude that Ghanaians should determine their own cultural fate without being compelled to discriminate against persons who hold themselves as homosexuals or decriminalising homosexual practices.

With the gown now in a confrontation against the overwhelming public over the homosexual issue, western media have negatively profiled Ghana in favour of these academics. The western media, which has more liberal and leftists in cultural values, have deployed propaganda and false reportage to paint the Ghanaian public "dark". They have all converged on their mislabelling of the Bill in Parliament as the "Anti-homosexual" Bill.

Since ideological terms are hardly ambiguous especially on matters of sexuality, the tagging of the Bill as "Anti-homosexual" unmistakably puts Ghana in a bad light as violators of the rights of homosexuals that must be shamed. While there is certainly no doubt that several Ghanaians are uncompromising about the western push for the country's acceptance of homosexual practices, it is very problematic to call the Bill "Anti-homosexual". This is because, all the various religions in Ghana, and chiefs have openly argued against punishing, maiming and discriminating against homosexuals in the country – especially when the act of sex is more secret than public. Essentially, until one openly holds himself or herself as homosexual seeking to impose the practice on the public, several of these religious people do not support any acts of discrimination against homosexuals. As the proponents of the Bill have made clear in the Bill and in public engagements, their goal is to support homosexuals who are willing to embrace Ghanaian family values. The issue of criminalisation in the Bill is rather connected to advocacy and decriminalisation. Also, it must be stated that there are hardly any reports of government institutions marginalising persons because of these persons' visible physical appearance.

So, western media's framing of the Bill as "Anti-homosexual" imperils Ghana's international image in a pandemic era. Currently, the government of Ghana is choreographing itself away from the international financial institutions by pushing through with a controversial E-levy tax – taxing online mobile money transactions – to support development. This is because, historically, Ghana has hardly benefited from the World Bank and the IMF without financial conditionalities that impinge on the socio-cultural and political values of Ghanaians – this has been severally documented by Ghanaian scholars, including Kwame Akonnor.

As Ghana faces its cultural crossroads, the nation must protect all its citizens in accordance with its laws and sovereignty without feeling obliged by western media to undermine the country's historic family-oriented values. This is because the agenda of western media, as amplifiers of western sexual revolution, could imperil the country's fragile peace.

In the above, I have attempted to prove that all the challenges of the world are not lost on anyone. While people may have different resilience in engaging the imperfections of the world, the fact is that the world is faced with imperfections. These imperfections are either humanly induced or naturally induced. Whatever it is, there are imperfections. As a result of the imperfections, everyone appears to be angry. But I discern two things that are trite in all these: First, we are aware of the imperfections and second, we are angry. But these two are trite because they have been known in all of human history. What we have not been able to overcome as human beings are how to deploy our moral outrage in addressing our imperfections.

That we are angry implies that we may be discontented with the imperfections we see around us. It may mean that we are unwilling to be part of the imperfection. But for me, the question is: How do we utilise our moral outrage and anger for constructive purposes?

When I was in primary school, one of the songs we learned as a marching song, which has stuck with me and become more meaningful as I now have a family and more mouths to feed, is:

> Life in this world is a great struggle
> For both the young and old
> And even those who have great riches
> Have troubles of their own
> Rich men envy poor men
> Poor men envy the rich
> So, what is the sense in envying your neighbour?
> Rich men envy poor men
> Poor men envy the rich
> Therefore, what is the sense in envying your neighbour?[285]

More recently, as the world appears to be spiralling out of control, I shared the song with my primary schoolmate and she quickly rebuffed it saying it is un-Christian. I decided not to reply but allow reality to sink in for a while. Later, when I noticed she was sober, we had a good conversation after which we both agreed that while the Lord says we are more than conquerors, it does not take away the fact that the world

[285] Extra Choral (October 27, 2021), Harmonious Chorale Ghana – Life In This World< https://www.youtube.com/watch?v=jwcygC42vd4> (accessed: March 20, 2022).

is a world of imperfection. I reminded her that while Jesus, as the uncreated Creator of the universe, is rich in everything, once He stepped into our beleaguered world, He tasted the imperfection to the point of being betrayed with the excruciating crucifixion as His lot. I reminded my friend of what Jesus said that,

> I have told you these things so you may have peace in Me. In the world you will have much trouble. But take hope! I have power over the world! (John 16:33).

But Jesus did not leave us to feast on fatalism. He demonstrated what we should do by He Himself doing good to all those He met without taking on any political appointment. Jesus, as the Creator, served what was His mantra that:

> Just as the Son of Man did not come to be served, but to serve, and to give his life as a ransom for many (Matthew 20:28).

Following Jesus's example, as a Christian, I am expected to be light and salt of the world, and occupy till Jesus returns. By being the light of the world, the darkness of moral and political corruption must give way where ever I find myself. If Ghanaians agree that corruption is a basic drawback to Ghana's development (realising the aspirations of decolonisation) then I must really be the light of the country and the world. Secondly, in a world of bitter anger, my presence should be the real salt by giving a taste of hope to everyone I meet. Put together, while my ultimate goal is to be living in a restored paradise where the Lord's Sabbath will be restored again, my penultimate goal here on earth is to make the world better than I came to meet it. For this reason, my Calvinistic Christian philosophy is based on the Bible's definition of religion as serving humanity in the name of Jesus Christ my saviour:

> Religion that God our Father accepts as pure and faultless is this: to look after orphans and widows in their distress and to keep oneself from being polluted by the world (James 1:27).

Whenever I am tempted to blame someone else, which is very easy to do, I again, reflect on a poem I learned while in primary school, which goes as follows:

Look To Yourself.
For all things look to yourself first;
You have all things and you'll never thirst
Your land has many things great and good
Rich soils, minerals and other things
Do not go friend cup-in-hand
Honey and milk flow in your hand
Don't say, "Grass is green at their feet"
For grass is greener at your feet
You have got all the richest gift, others have not got half your gifts
Look to yourself then and great
Use all that you have and be great

Concluding reflections on human rights

I have argued that the idea of human rights, at least from basic understanding implies that there is something called human. Rights also imply that when we see what is right, we should be able to tell. But the issue that has often be left out of the discussion on human rights is whether we can know and do right by ourselves without any absolute reference point. In other words, how should we define human rights without any reference to natural rights? Or to state it bluntly, can we have human rights without God – an intelligent being? The succinct response to whether rationalism is enough to provide a formidable basis for human rights is that as Bernard Williams concluded, 'moral philosophy cannot meet them' (Bernard 2006: vii). Since the end of World War II in 1945 and the collapse of the communist bloc, the United States of America and international organisations, such as the United Nations Charter and the Universal Declaration of Human Rights, have tied developing nations to western notions of human rights. The idea of human rights, fashioned as American version of civilisation and arbiter of human rights, has become the standard for all nations to follow (Lal 2002: 61).

The challenge with western notions of human rights is that there is hardly any human in their rights, as the "human" is actually the individual. As I discussed in the Chapter Three, in Ghana and other African countries, the idea of individual *qua* individual is not the basis of human rights, since to be human is to be socially connected. This means that whether Michael Eze's idea of constitutive individual or not, the Ghanaian understanding of the human is largely a social being whose welfare is intricately and intimately entwined with the existence of other human beings.

For this reason, any banal desires of individuals that contradict the common good of society – simply the continuity of society, such as childbirth – is always rejected. For this reason, although prostitution or pre-marital sex might exist in pre-colonial Akan societies, the practice was not celebrated and sociogenically endorsed. Similarly, the utilitarian idea of "do good for the sake of goodness" to accentuate individualism and individual rights is unsustainable in the conclusive and logical sense. This is precisely because we all run out of patience and the material and intellectual resources to do good. So, in the end, it will take Christ's admonition for us to "Give a cup of water in His name" and also consider the interest of others more than ours is the only way to sustain collectively-based human rights. On my Facebook page on Tuesday, June 28, 2022, I wrote as follows: "We are all strategically coping towards "self". It will take a true and sincere faith in Christ to cope towards others."

Chapter 5

Conclusion

The discussion on gender and feminism points to the complexities of identity. Sociologically and in "traditional" societies, identity is presented as self-evidence condensed in sociogenic activities and oral cultures. One's ontological identity as a man and a woman are all inscribed. This is achieved through cultural sociogenic practices such as naming ceremonies, marriage rites, and socialisation practices – all these are public. In traditional societies, such as Nima and Maamobi, therefore, one's sense of worth is intricately linked to what one does in connection to the collective good than one asserting one's individualism. Identity is achieved when one sublimates one's individuality and subjectivity to the community in fulfilment of roles. Indeed, this sense of collectivity, which Ibn Khaldun, the 14th-Century Arab scholar calls *Asabiya* is the base of all society and the fountainhead of the civilisation of human societies. In Ibn Khaldun's analysis, therefore, the collapse of Asabiya marks the collapse of a civilisation.

The western culture, particularly the US that has churned out most of the radical feminist theories is based on an identity that is, in turn, based on individuals looking into themselves. This development is one of the features of post-World War II social reality in the west. Following material prosperity and capitalistic communalism, technological improvement, and modern social media that has created the idea of self-centeredness known as, "selfie". "Selfie" incorporates all the "selfs" (self-assertion, self-inspired, self-motivation, self-worth, self-confidence, self-sufficiency, self-determination, self-control etc.) of the western world. This leads to Charles Taylor's construction of the age of authenticity, marked by, "communities are eroding, families, neighbourhoods, even the polity; they sense that people are less willing to participate, to do their habits; and they are less trusting of others" (Taylor, 2007: 473).

Similarly, extensive individualism leads to what Robert Bellah and other sociologists called expressive individualism where individuals look into themselves for identity as opposed to the community (Bella et al., 1986). Indeed, individualism found expression in the sexual revolution of the 1960s (the American Psychiatric Association's removal of homosexuality from its official roster of mental health illness in 1973 (Eller, 2016: 317) and third wave feminism in the US in the 1990s, making its entry into the classroom (Gillis, Howie, Munford, 2007), and the US supreme court's legislation of same-sex marriage on June 26, 2015, authorising the licensing and legal recognition of gay and lesbian marriages (Ojilere, 2018). The extent of sexual liberalisation is one of the ideological bases of the leftist party, the Democrats who usually tend to be anti-evangelical sex ethics.

The saturation of America with sexual liberalism is a virus that is highly infectious in academia where American funders and some of the liberal academic journals tend to have a favourable disposition towards homosexual acts and the LGBTQ+ movement. In all this, funding in scholarship and aid to development have all been attached to sexual liberalisation. For example, when Joseph Robinette Biden Jr, became the 46th President of the US in 2020, his first foreign speech in February 2021 included an order to all US government agencies active abroad to promote the rights of lesbian, gay, bisexual, transgender, intersex and queer (LGBTQI+) people and come up with plans within 180 days. African feminist scholars, in remaining consistent with their deconstruction agenda, tend to follow the sexual liberation trend in the US academy.

I now reflect on the complex entwined issues of the modern state and corruption in Ghana and globally. My goal, therefore, is to glean some nuggets that could facilitate governance in contemporary Ghana and globally. I will, therefore briefly analysed the issues of the modern state and the necessity of religion – virtue – in supporting human flourishing. I discussed the extent to which the claim of Ghana as secular and Ghanaian laws as simply man-made laws demonstrate a deficit of understanding of both the modern state as a social construct and the human nature as often bent towards corruption. I drew the *sacralisation* of Ghana's emblems and vows of entry into national service to demonstrate the role of religion in the making of Ghana as an imagined community of one people with a common destiny.

As part of the emergence of the modern state was the incorporation of myths to foster an idea of a "country of one people with a common destiny". This means that nationalism, which is very superficial but rather socially constructed has become an important factor in ensuring nation-building and also a basis for destroying those considered outsiders. Similarly, the issue of racism which is also very superficial and a cultural construct has been deployed to perpetually enslave and exploit other so-called races.

There is hardly any contestation that the modern state is a natural construct. In the case of Ghana/Africa, it has often been debated among some Afrocentric scholars that Africa is divided by superficial borders, as a result of the Berlin Conference of the late 19th Century (Zartman 1965). So, given the benefit European colonisers derived from the geographical Balkanisation of the continent and its lingering effects on intra-continental border disputes, several of the postcolonial pan-Africanists, including Nkrumah, argued for the collapse of the boundaries to achieve the vision of Pan-Africanism (Nkrumah 1963).

Nevertheless, since independence, the same Pan-Africanists, including Nkrumah, leveraged the logic of the boundaries being artificial to deport those who disagreed with his political policies. For example, shortly into his government, Nkrumah passed the Deportation Act that led to the deportation of two Hausa leaders, who as pioneers of the Gold Coast Muslim Association Party, founded in 1932, identified with the United Gold Coat Convention in 1948, and later decided to follow the CPP and Nkrumah (Weiss 2008: 338). The group later transformed into the Muslim Association Party (MAP) in 1954 to strengthen its political influence. The MAP later supported the National Liberation Movement of the Asante that opposed Nkrumah (Ibid).

At independence in 1957, Nkrumah passed the Avoidance of Discrimination Act of 1957 that banned all political parties formed along religious lines and the 1957 Deportation Act enabled the deportation of two influential MAP-leaders, Alhaji Baba and Alhaji Uthman Ladan, to Kano in Nigeria (Ibid). He also deported several anti-CPP Syrians and Lebanese in the country (Ibid). According to Weiss, Alhaji Baba returned to Ghana after the 1966 coup (Ibid. 339). Nkrumah's civilian successor, K.A. Busia also deported several West African "aliens" as part of his Aliens Compliance Order (Oppong 2009; Peil 1971). Other influential women leaders, including Madam Goma, a trader in Kumasi as well as the heads of the Gao (Songhay) and Mossi communities in Kumasi, Amadu Gao and Amama Moshie, were deported in addition to several others (Weiss 2008: 339).

The National Chief Imam, Alhaji Muhammed Abass, who was known as a supporter of the MAP, was also removed from office and was replaced by Malam Futa, a Muslim Youth Council (MYC) functionary (Ibid). These deportations happened against the fact that several of the deported West African citizens, particularly the Hausa and Wangara, had lived in pre-colonial societies and played a key role in the decolonisation agenda of the country (Wilks 1963).[286] More recently, several African countries, including Cote D'Ivoire and South Africa have been embroiled in citizenship politics, including the coinage of a new term, Afrophobia to designate Africans turning against fellow Africans (Nyamnjoh 2006; Dumbe 2018).

Certainly, the idea that the boundaries of Africa are superficial brings to the fore two complex issues: First, no boundary is natural and second, citizenship is not natural. Both national boundaries and citizenship are social constructs (Nyamnjoh 2018). Ethnic groups are equally artificial. For example, the largest Akan group and perhaps the most politically influential in the colonial history of Ghana (then the Gold Coast) is the Asante, and yet, the Asante is a social construct based on the myth of a Golden Stool that supposedly descended from the sky (Wilks 1996). The Akan ancestors had a proverb that indicated the socially constructed nature of the ethnic group. They say:

> The clan is like a cluster of trees which, when seen from afar, appears huddled together, but which would be seen to stand *individually* when closely approached (Gyekye 1996: 47 emphasis in the original text).

Two leading European scholars who discussed the superficiality of the state and nationalism are Ernest Gellner and Benedict Anderson. These scholars argued that the modern state emerged out of persons reading newspapers in the same language or building their identity based on some symbols. Through such symbols, the idea of nations tends to be more emotionally oriented, which creates an imagined community of oneness than a natural construct (Gellner 1983; Anderson 1983). Historically, therefore, the question had been how to create an imagined community where people conform to rules and laws to ensure social and cosmic order. This debate was also about whether human beings are ontologically good to be able to govern themselves without any interference or potentially bad that needed to be governed. Hobbes had a positive view of human beings being potentially bad and doomed to self-destruction, while Locke viewed human beings as potentially good (Hobbes 1985/1904; Locke 1956). These debates gave birth to the idea of social construct, where citizens give up some of their rights to receive protection from the state. But it is not enough for citizens to give up some of their rights, as it is also about the extent of

[286] Interview with Alhaji Haruna and Imoro Baba Isa, the chief of the Wangara Muslims in Maamobi and Secretary of the Council of Muslim Chiefs on December 12, 2021.

power the state should possess. Consequently, the German sociologist, Max Weber conceived of the state as necessary because it has the power of coercion (Weber 2019).

The complexities of human nature cannot be simplified in terms of laws and acts in ensuring social order. For this reason, religion, which appeals to a transcendental order, has been an important part of creating national consciousness. Religion has been an important social control mechanism in ensuring that human excesses are checked (Ebaugh 2005). This is also against the fact that religion has equally been used to perpetuate injustice and human suffering historically (Omer, Appleby and Little 2015). Even so, the fact that revealed religions (Islam and Christianity) lays claim to eternal truths, eternal rewards and punishment, and creates a sense of an imagined order during a crisis has made belief in the supernatural very critical in nation-building.

This means that whether the pre-modern European concept of the divine right of kingship and the Akan idea of chiefs deriving their authority from the ancestors, the appeal to religion and the sacred compels the "secular" to fashion in a certain way. Impliedly, the binaries between the "secular and profane", the "rational public and irrational private" and "religion and politics" that shaped the modernist and the secularisation thesis in the 1960s were part of the illusions of the nineteenth-century enlightenment that rationality (science and technology) would sink "irrationality" (religion) (Cox 1966; Berger 1967). I have already mentioned that the bounce-back of religion, as if religion or God went anywhere, therefore, led to several of the theoreticians of the modernisation and secularisation thesis to recant, however grudgingly.

The above, therefore, points to the continuing relevance of religion and spirituality in carving the modern state. This means that instead of splitting hairs over the supposed artificiality of the colonial boundaries, postcolonial African leaders have sacralised the state – similar to the logic of the premodern world. During the struggle against colonialism, Nkrumah fell on religion to spur the Gold Coaster on, at any rate, the Christian teaching of human dignity contributed to sowing the see of decolonisation. It was for this reason that Nkrumah and several African leaders leveraged Christian teaching to advance the struggle against colonialism. In inclusion, Nkrumah inverted the Christian text as "Seek ye first the political kingdom, and all others shall be added to you". With this Nkrumah appealed to Christian conscience. In carving a nation of an imagined oneness, Nkrumah's *consciencism* philosophy identified the criticality of merging all the major religions in Ghana – Christianity, Islam and indigenous religions – to support human flourishing (Nkrumah 1964).

It is against this background that virtually all material things, such as national emblems were sacralised with an appeal to religious idioms of vows. In Ghana, the nation is sacralised through the invocation of religious imageries of vows to bind people to remain loyal, live a virtuous life, and eschew corruption. This means that the state often comes back to the question of human nature – almost admitting all the time that human beings' penchant towards evil is rather overwhelming and needs to be "vowed" into submission. It also means that, contrary to Barack Obama's concern for Ghana to have strong institutions, not strong men, what Ghana and the world needs is men and women with strong virtues (from a stable source – religion).[287] Institutions are created and corrupted by human beings, so we cannot just leave human destiny in the hands of institutions. America has "strong" institutions and a great constitution that upholds the dignity of human beings and yet America is racist in every sense of the word.

In the following, I provide examples of how the founders of Ghana saw the wisdom in incorporating the idea of religion in nation-building. My focus here is on national emblems and institutions as part of a religious vow to bind Ghanaians to a virtuous life.

> God bless our homeland Ghana,
> And make our nation great and strong,
> Bold to defend forever,
> The cause of Freedom and of Rights.
> Fill our hearts with true humility
> Make us cherish fearless honesty,
> And help us to resist oppressor's rule
> With all our will and might forevermore.
>
> Hail to thy name, O Ghana,
> To thee we make our solemn vow:
> Steadfast to build together
> A nation strong in Unity;
> With our gifts of mind and strength of arm,
> Whether night or day, in mist or storm,

---

[287] The White House (11 July 2009), Remarks by the President of to the Ghanaian Parliament,< https://obamawhitehouse.archives.gov/the-press-office/remarks-president-ghanaian-parliament> accessed: 23 February 2022.

In every need what'er, the call may be,
To serve thee, Ghana, now and evermore.

Raise high the flag of Ghana
And one with Africa advance;
Black star of hope and honour,
To all who thirst for liberty;
Where the banner of Ghana freely flies,
May the way of freedom truly lie
Arise, arise, O sons of Ghanaland,
And under God march on forevermore.

Ghanaians pledge to boldly defend the country and to make a solemn vow to build the country together; in the pledge, Ghanaians say:

I promise on my honour
to be faithful and loyal to Ghana my motherland.
I pledge myself to the service of Ghana,
with all my strength and with all my heart.
I promise to hold in high esteem
our heritage won for us
through the blood and toil of our fathers;
And I pledge myself in all things
to uphold and defend the good name of Ghana.
So help me God.

THE PRESIDENTIAL OATH

I, having been elected to the high office of President of the Republic of Ghana, do (in the name of the Almighty God swear) (solemnly affirm) that I will be faithful and true to the Republic of Ghana; that I will at all times preserve, protect and defend the Constitution of the Republic of Ghana; and that I dedicate myself to the service and well-being of the people of the Republic of Ghana and to do right to all manner of persons. I further (solemnly swear) (solemnly affirm) that should I at any time break this oath of office I shall submit myself to the laws of the Republic of Ghana and suffer the penalty for it (So help me God)'

To be administered by the Chief Justice before Parliament. '

THE OATH OF THE VICE-PRESIDENT

I, having been elected to the office of Vice-President of the Republic of Ghana, do (in the name of the Almighty God swear) (solemnly affirm) that I will be faithful and true to the Republic of Ghana; that I will at all times preserve, protect and defend the Constitution of the Republic of Ghana; and I dedicate myself to the service and well-being of the people of the Republic of Ghana and to do right to all manner of persons. I further (solemnly swear) (solemnly affirm) that should I at any time break this oath of office, I shall submit myself to the laws of the Republic of Ghana and suffer the penalty for it (So help me God).

To be administered by the Chief Justice before Parliament.

THE JUDICIAL OATH

I, having been appointed (Chief Justice/a Justice of the Supreme Court/a Justice of the Court of Appeal/a Justice of the High Court of Justice, etc.) do (in the name of the Almighty God swear) (solemnly affirm) that I will bear true faith and allegiance to the Republic of Ghana as by law established; *that I will uphold the sovereignty and integrity of the Republic of Ghana; and that I will truly and faithfully perform the functions of my office without fear or favour, affection or ill-will;* and that I will at all times uphold, preserve, protect and defend the Constitution and laws of the Republic of Ghana. (So help me God.) – Italics mine.

To be sworn before the President, the Chief Justice or such other person as the Chief Justice may designate.

THE SPEAKER'S OATH

I, do (in the name of the Almighty God swear) (solemnly affirm) that I will bear true faith and allegiance to the Republic of Ghana as by law established; that I will uphold the integrity of the Republic of Ghana; that I will faithfully and conscientiously discharge my duties as Speaker of Parliament; and that I will uphold, preserve, protect and defend the Constitution of the Republic of Ghana; and that I will do right to all manner of persons in accordance with the Constitution of Ghana and the laws and conventions of Parliament without fear or favour, affection or ill-will (So help me God).

To be sworn before the Chief Justice.

THE OATH OF A MEMBER OF PARLIAMENT

I, having been elected a member of Parliament do (in the name of the Almighty God swear) (solemnly affirm) that I will bear true faith and allegiance to the Republic of Ghana as by law established; that I will uphold, preserve, protect and defend the Constitution of the Republic of Ghana; and that I will faithfully and conscientiously discharge the duties of a Member of Parliament. (So help me God)

To be sworn before the Speaker

THE OATH OF MINISTER OF STATE

I, having been appointed Minister of State (Deputy Minister) of the Republic of Ghana, do (in the name of the Almighty God swear) (solemnly affirm) that I will at all times well and truly serve the Republic of Ghana in the office of Minister of State (Deputy Minister that I will uphold, preserve, protect and defend the Constitution of the Republic of Ghana as by law established; that I will, to the best of my judgment, at all times when required, freely give my counsel and advice for the good management of the public affairs of the Republic of Ghana; and that I will not directly or indirectly reveal any matters that shall come to my knowledge in the discharge of my duties and committed to my secrecy as Minister of State (Deputy Minister). (So help me God.)

To be sworn before the President.

THE OATH OF THE AUDITOR-GENERAL

I, having been appointed Auditor-General of the Republic of Ghana do (in the name of the Almighty God swear) (solemnly affirm) that I will bear true faith and allegiance to the Republic of Ghana; that I will uphold, preserve, protect and defend the Constitution of the Republic of Ghana; and that I will truly and faithfully perform the functions of my office without fear or favour, affection or ill-will. (So help me God).

To be sworn before the President, or such other person as the President may designate.

THE OATH OF MEMBER OF COUNCIL OF STATE

I, do (solemnly swear in the name of the Almighty God) (solemnly affirm) that I will faithfully and conscientiously perform my duties as a Member of the Council of State and uphold, preserve, protect and defend the Constitution of the Republic of Ghana (So help me God).

To be sworn before the President.

THE CABINET OATH

I, having been appointed a Member of the Cabinet do (in the name of the Almighty God swear) (solemnly affirm) that I will not directly or indirectly reveal such matters as shall be debated in the Cabinet and committed to my secrecy; and that I will uphold, preserve, protect and defend the Constitution of the Republic of Ghana. (So help me God).

To be sworn before the President.

THE OATH OF SECRECY

I, . do (in the name of the Almighty God swear) (solemnly affirm) that I will not directly or indirectly communicate or reveal to any person any matter which shall be brought under my consideration or shall come to my knowledge in the discharge of my official duties except as may be required for the discharge of my official duties or as may be specially permitted by law. (So help me God)

To be sworn before the President, the Chief Justice or such other person as the President may designate

THE OFFICIAL OATH

I, do (in the name of the Almighty God swear) (solemnly affirm) that I will at all times well and truly serve the Republic of Ghana in the office of and that I will uphold, preserve, protect and defend the Constitution of the Republic of Ghana as by law established. (So help me God).

To be sworn before the President or such other person as the President may designate.

THE OATH OF ALLEGIANCE

I, do (in the name of the Almighty God swear) (solemnly affirm) that I will bear true faith and allegiance to the Republic of Ghana as by law established; that I will uphold the sovereignty and integrity of Ghana; and that I will preserve, protect and defend the Constitution of the Republic of Ghana. (So help me God).

To be sworn before the President, the Chief Justice or such other person as the President may designate

In their forthcoming book, Mrs Olivia Tsekpoe and Dr Christian Tsekpoe, Senior Clergy of the Church of Pentecost, Ghana's largest Protestant denomination, commented on the criticality of these national symbols as follows:

> At the political level, we took time to read through the presidential oath, the judicial oath, the cabinet oath, and the oath of allegiance as enshrined in Ghana's constitution. We were amazed about the weight of the words in these vows as well. We were surprised that some Ghanaian politicians take these vows but do otherwise when they are inducted into office. Probably, such people are not aware that they are accountable to God for all these vows they take. Whether you are already a politician or an up-and-coming politician, we want to advise you to pay attention to your vows to receive the blessings that go with it ... I think that if all of us obey this pledge alone, Ghana would have been a better country by now. Beyond Ghana being a better place, we must all be aware that God will hold us responsible for this pledge so the earlier we start working on it the better. Oaths, vows and covenants should therefore not be taken lightly at all since God does not take them for granted (Tsepoe and Tsekpoe 2022).

The pledge, anthem and political vows demonstrate the need for the sacralisation of the state for citizens to be "vowed" into living a "righteous" life. It is almost as if the state of Ghana is telling its citizens that until once is righteous as a citizen and public servant, one cannot see Ghana prospering. For me as a Christian, the discussion so far reminds me of the Biblical truism that righteousness builds a nation, while sin is a reproach to every nation. Righteous is not built out of strong institutions but from a transformed life. Righteousness must come before strong institutions. This is because institutions as laws cannot do much to stop the high levels of corruption in Ghana and the world. The laws will at best tell people about what is acceptable and what is not and the consequences thereof. But as to whether the law, backed by the Weberian notion of the use of coercive force, will be enough to put corruption under minimum is something that Ghanaians are very well informed about that has not been the case.

What the above means is that people must be transformed within to work without. People must be convinced about the existential issues of life (why they are here and where they are going from here) to appreciate the criticality of altruism, kindness, and love for one another, as the basis of human civilisation. It is for this reason that one of the outstanding philosophers Ghana ever produced, Kwame Gyekye in his conclusion said that corruption is not a technical or an institutional issue, but rather a moral issue. He asserted that political corruption is essentially a moral challenge; moral pollution of officialdom as well as of the wider society. Because he read corruption as a moral challenge, he was of the view that "political system or process may be improved, its weakness removed; economic situation may improve and salaries of public officials may be increased; legal institutions may be improved, the powers and activities of law enforcement officers augmented and punishments for convicts of politically corrupt acts increased, yet none of these attempts at dealing with political corruption will eradicate it or considerably minimise it" (Gyekye 1997: 203) Arguing about how difficult it is for the law to deal with a moral issue, Gyekye maintained that, "when it comes to the field of morality, the field of human conduct, when it comes to making a man to 'behave like an upright man,' the law becomes virtually powerless (Ibid. 213). He concluded with a recommendation for the need for a moral revolution that is accompanied by an individual's willpower to resist what is immoral. The moral imperative partly undermines any appeal to a malevolent spirit as a scapegoat from moral failure. As Apostle Elorm-Donkor, argued, the Pentecostal Christian should focus on addressing the weakness of self in developing a sound moral character that reflects that of God (Elorm-Donkor 2017: 193).

Relating all this to the issue of domestic violence against women and the criticality of moral intervention in dealing with contentious issues, I liberally cite the considered view of the Nigerian philosopher:

> Taking domestic violence against women as an example, it is crucial to perceive it as a moral issue and not only a legal matter. Legal provisions alone cannot prevent people from taking morally wrong decisions. In other words, moral theories give us the ability to organise our lives beyond the confines of what we are legally bound to do and beyond the view of law enforcement. It is therefore imperative to project an ethical dimension to some of the domestic problems which confront women every day (Ipadeola 2023: xii).

I end this chapter by commenting briefly on Ace Ankomah, a Ghanaian legal practitioner, who excitedly said that Ghana is a secular state with the law made by human beings. He made this statement as part of the state's quest and reinforcement of laws to govern the public sphere. The conversation has gained traction because the current Inspector General of Police, Dr Dampare, a member of the Church of

Pentecost, has proven more resolute than perhaps any IGP Ghana has ever had since the country's re-democratisation in the 1990s. He has been arresting every single person who violates the laws of Ghana without any fear or favour. He also stirred controversy when he cautioned a group of religious clerics, also known as political prophets, who often take to their end of year December "All Night" Service since the turn of the millennium to give doom prophecies, usually about the death of a high-profile figure. And in an electioneering year, these prophets predict the winners and losers. In the end, some of the prophecies of these prophets turn the nation into a near state of pandemonium, similar to the case of the National Chief Imam that I cited above.

The action and initiative of the IGP have sent the Ghanaian state into discussing the role of religion in Ghana's public sphere – bringing back the issue of secularization and secularism. I have discussed the issue elsewhere, so here, I will only argue that Ghanaian lawyers and academics should be very careful about how they throw words around such as "We live by man-made laws".[288] While this may simply imply that Ghana does appeal specifically to Christian or Islamic scriptures to pass its laws, pandering towards a positivistic school of law, such comments could potentially create tension for the nation. It could derail national unity – even as it seeks to promote unity. For example, if laws are man-made, why should I obey man-made law when I don't think such laws, for example as Marxists argue, are made for a selected few? If the laws are man-made, what can prove the durability of the laws protecting the sanctity of life? Does it mean that human beings can decide as and when they allow some rights to be offered and also pulled back?

I was, therefore, shocked when Ace Ankomah made such a simplistic comment. This is precisely because, from the above, we cannot just have simply "man made laws" or simply "human-made institutions" to render human beings pliable to doing right. Why must I live a morally sound life and why must I love my neighbour who isn't like me? Christ answered it with, His new commandments:

> 'Love the Lord your God with all your heart and with all your soul and with your mind'. This is the first and greatest law. And the second is like

[288] Newsfile on JoyNews (30 October 2021), https://www.youtube.com/watch?v=ru6LpnfLULg, accessed: 23 February 2022.

it: 'Love your neighbour as yourself.' All the Law and Prophets hang on these two.[289]

[289] Matthew 22: 36-40.

References

Abu-Lughod, L. (2013). *Do Muslim Women Need Saving?* Cambridge, Mass.: Harvard University Press.

Acheampong, E. 'African socialism; or the search for an indigenous model of economic development?' *Economic History of Developing Regions*, 33(1): 69-87.

Achebe, C. (1959). *Things fall apart.* New York: Anchor Books.

Achebe, N. (2020). *Female monarchs and merchant queens in Africa.* Athens: Ohio University Press.

Ackah, C.A. (1988). *Akan ethics: A study of the moral ideas and the moral behaviour of the Akan tribes of Ghana.* Accra: Ghana Universities Press.

Aderinto, S. (2016). 'Pleasure for sale: Prostitution in colonial Africa, 1880s-1960s', in Frank

Jacob (ed.), *Prostitution: A companion of mankind.* New York: Peter Lang, pp. 469-480.

Agyekum, K. (2010). *Akan verbal taboos in the context of ethnography of community.* Accra: Ghana University Press.

Agyekum, K. (2021). 'Proverbs in Akan highlife lyrics: A case study of Alex Konadu's lyrics,' *Journal of Pragmatics*, 174, p. 1-13.

Aidoo, A.A. (1977). 'Asante Queen mothers in government and politics in the nineteenth century'. *Journal of the Historical Society of Nigeria*, 9(1): 1-13.

Ajen, N. (1998). "West African homoeroticism: West African men who have sex with men". In Murray, S.O. and Roscoe, W. (eds.), *Boy-wives and female husbands: Studies in African homosexualities*, 91-111. New York: Palgrave.

Akurang-Parry, K. (2016). "Obama's visit as a signifier of Ghanaian's 'colonial mentality'". In Konadu, K. and Campbell C.C (eds). *The Ghana reader: History, culture and politics*, 440-447. Durham/London: Duke University Press.

Akurang-Parry, K.O. (1999). Missy Queen in her palaver says de Gole Cosse slaves is free": The British abolition of slavery/pawnship and colonial labor recruitment in the Gold Coast (Southern Ghana), 1874-ca. 1940. PhD thesis submitted to the York University.

Akurang-Parry, K.O. (2002). 'Rethinking the 'slaves of Salaga': Post-proclamation slavery in the Gold Coat (Colonial southern Ghana), 1874-1899'. *Left History*, 8(1): 33-60.

Akurang-Parry, K.O. (2004). "Aspects of elite women's activism in the Gold Coast, 1874-1890".

The International Journal of African Historical Studies, 37(3): 469-470.

Akurang-Parry, K.O. (2010). "Transformations in the feminization of unfree domestic labour: A study of "Abaawa" of prepubescent female servitude in modern Ghana". *International Labour Working-Class History*, 78: 28-47.

Akurugu, C.A.; Dery, S., and Bata, P.D. (2022). "Marriage, bridewealth and power: Critical reflections on women's autonomy across settings in Africa". *Evolutionary Human Sciences*, 4 (2022): 1-15.

Akyeampong, E. (1997). "Sexuality and prostitution among the Akan of the Gold Coast c. 1650-1950". *Past and Present*, no. 156: 144-173.

Akyeampong, E. & Obeng, P. (1995). 'Spirituality, Gender and Power in Asante History. *The International Journal of African Historical Studies,* 28(3): 481-508.

Aldrich, R. (2003). *Colonialism and homosexuality.* London/New York: Routledge, Taylor and Francis Group.

Alexander, M. (2010). *The new jim crow: Mass incarceration in the age of colorblindness* (New York: The New Press.

Allman, J. (1996). 'Rounding up spinsters: Gender chaos and unmarried women in colonial Asante.' *Journal of African History*, 37: 195-214.

Allyn, D. (2016). *Make love, no war: The sexual revolution: An unfettered history.* New York: Routledge.

Alo, A.G. and Olasode, O.A. (2018). "Origin, types and cultural significance of tribal marks amongst the Yoruba tribe," *Nigerian Journal of Dermatology*, 8(1): 7-19.

Amediume, I. (2000). *Daughters of the goddess, daughters of imperialism: African women's struggle for culture, power and democracy.* London: Zed.

Ampofo, A.A. (2007). ""My cocoa is between my legs": Sex as work among Ghanaian women" In Sharon Harley (ed.). Women's labour in the global economy: Speaking in multiple voices. New Jersey and London: Rutgers University Press, 182-205.

Ampofo, J.A.A., Beoku-Betts, J. & Osirim, M.J. (2004). 'Women's and gender studies in English-speaking sub-Saharan Africa: A review'. *Gender & Society*, 18(6): 685-714.

Anderson, B. (1983). *Imagined communities: Reflections on the origin and spread of nationalism.* London: Verso.

Anderson, J.N.D. (1955). *Islamic law in Africa.* London: Routledge.

Ansah, G.N. & Dzregah, A.E. (2020). 'Exploring Ethos in Contemporary Ghana'. *Humanities*, 9(62): 1-15.

Appiah, K.A. (2005). 'African Studies and the concept of knowledge'. In B. Hamminga (ed.), *Knowledge cultures: comparative western and African epistemology.* Amsterdam/New York: Rodopi, pp. 23-56.

Arhin, K. (1983). 'The political and military role of Akan women'. In C. Oppong (ed.), *Female and male in West Africa*. London: George Allen & Unwen, pp. 91-98.

Armstrong, K. (2005). *A short history of myth*. Edinburgh: Canongate Books Ltd.

Arthur, A.A. (2014). *Class formation and inequality structures in contemporary African migration: Evidence from Ghana*. Lanham, Maryland: Lexington Books.

Asad, T. (2003). *Formation of the Secular: Christianity, Islam, Modernity*. California: Stanford

Asad, T. (2003). *Formation of the Secular: Christianity, Islam, Modernity*. California: Stanford University Press.

Asamoah-Gyadu, J. K. (2013). 'Spirit and Spirits in African Religious Traditions'. In Veli-Matti

Kärkkäinen, Kirsteen Kim, and Amos Yong (eds.), *Interdisciplinary and Religio-Cultural Discourses on a Spirit-Filled World: Loosing the Spirits*. New York: Palgrave Macmillan, 41-53.

Asamoah-Gyadu, J.K. (2005). *African charismatics: Current developments within independent indigenous Pentecostalism in Ghana*. Leiden: Brill.

Ashcroft, B, Griffiths, G. & Tiffin, H. (2007). *Post-colonial studies: The key concepts* (2nd Edition). London: Routledge.

Ayesu, E., Gbormittah, F. & Adum-Kyeremeh, K. (2016). 'British colonialism and women's welfare in the Gold Coast colony'. *Africa Today*, 63(2): 2-30.

Azumah, J.A. (2001). *The legacy of Arab-Islam in Africa: A quest for inter-religious dialogue*. London: Oneworld Publications.

Baisley, E. (2015). 'Framing the Ghanaian LGBT rights debate: Competing decolonisation and human rights frames. *Canadian Journal of African Studies*, 49(2): 383-402.

Bakare-Yusuf, B. (2004). '"Yorubas don't do gender": A critical review of Oyèrónkẹ́ Oyěwùmí's The Invention of woman: *Making an African sense of western gender discourses, African Studies scholarship: Concepts, methodologies and paradigms*', Dakar: Council for the Development of Social Science Research in Africa (CODESRIA): 61-81.

Balakrishnan, S. (2020). 'Imperial policing and the antinomies of power in early colonial Ghana'. *International Journal of African Historical Studies*, 53(2): 173-193.

Banks, A.J. (2014). *Anger and racial politics: The emotional foundation of racial attitudes in America*. Cambridge: Cambridge University Press.

Barnhart, J. (2021). *The consequences of humiliation: Anger and status in world politics* (Ithaca: Cornell University Press.

Bauer, P. (2000). *From subsistence to exchange and other essays.* Princeton, NJ.: Princeton University Press.

Bawa, S. (2018). '"Feminists make too much noise": Generational Differences and Ambivalence in Feminist Development Politics in Ghana'. *Canadian Journal of African Studies*, 52(1):1-17.

Bawa, S. (2019). 'Christianity, Tradition, and Gender Inequality in Postcolonial Ghana'. *African Geographical Review*, 38(1): 54-66.

Bayart, J. (2000). 'Africa in the world: A history of extraversion'. *African Affairs*, 99: 217-267.

Beckman, D. (1975). *Eden Revival: Spiritual Churches in Ghana.* St. Louis: Concordia. Bediako-Akoto, D.O. (2017). *Towards holistic sexual flourishing in Africa: Another look at human sexuality from a Ghanaian Christian standpoint with the Presbyterian Church of Ghana as a case* Utrecht: Boekencentrum Academic.

Bellah, R.N., Madsen, R., Sullivan, W.M., Swidler, A. & Tipton, S.M. (1985). *Habits of the heart: Individualism and commitment in American life.* Berkeley: University of California Press.

Berger, B. & Berger, L.P. (1983). *The war over the family: Capturing the middle ground.* New York: Anchor Press/Doubleday.

Berger, P.L. (1967). *The sacred canopy: Elements of a sociological theory of religion.* New York: Anchor Books.

Berger, P.L. (ed.). (1999). The desecularization of the world: Resurgent religion and world politics (Washington, D.C.: Ethics and Public Policy Center; Grand Rapids, Mich.: William B. Eerdmans.

Betiang, L. (2019). 'Naming and the reconstruction of female identity in Bette-Obudu.' *Sociolinguistic Studies*, 13(2-3): 357-378.

Berman, H.J. (1983). *Law and revolution: The formation of the western legal tradition.* Cambridge, MA.:

Biko, S. (1978). *I write what I like.* Ibadan/Oxford: Heinemann Educational Books Ltd.

Bitek, O.P (1971). *African religions in Western scholarship* (Nairobi: East African Literature Bureau.

Bitek, O.P. (1966). *Song of lawino: A lament.* Nairobi: East African Publishing.

Boafo-Arthur, K. (2003). 'Chieftaincy in Ghana: Challenges and Prospects in the 21st Century'. *African and Asian Studies*, 2 (3):125-153.

Bob-Milliar, M. G. (2009). Chieftaincy, diaspora and development: The Institution of *Nkosuohene* in Ghana. *African Affairs*, *108*(433): 541-588.

Bob-Milliar, M. G. (2022). 'Introduction'. In Figueroa, A.M. (ed.). *The impact of foreign interventions on democracy and human rights*. United Kingdom: Emerald Publishing.

Britwum, A.O., Oduro, G.Y. & Prah, M. (2004). Institutionalizing gender and women's studies at the University of Cape Coast in Ghana, *Rwandan Journal of Education*, 2(1): 4-19.

Bronstein, C. & Strub, W. (eds.) (2016). *Porno chic and the sex wars: American sexual representation in the 1970s*. Amherst & Boston; University of Massachusetts Press.

Brookman-Amissah, J. (1986). 'Akan proverbs about death'. *Anthropo*s, 81(1. /3): 75-85.

Brydon, L. (1996). 'Women chiefs and power in the Volta Region of Ghana'. *Journal of Legal Pluralism*, 37(38): 227-247.

Burke, P. (2009). *Cultural hybridity*. Cambridge: Polity Press.

Burke, P. (2016). *Hybrid renaissance: Culture, language, architecture*. Budapest/New York: Central

Burke, P. J., & Stets, J. E. (2009). *Identity theory*. New York: Oxford University Press.

Busia, K.A. (1961). 'Has the Christian faith been adequately presented?' *International Review of* Busia, K.A. (1962). *The challenge of Africa*. London: Pall Mall Press.

Byrd, A.D. & Tharps, L.L. (2014). *Hair story: Untangling the roots of black hair in America*. New York: St. Martin's Griffin.

Card, C. (2002). *The atrocity paradigm: A theory of evil*. Oxford: Oxford University Press.

Carey, B. & Plank, G. (2014). 'Introduction'. In B. Carey and G. Plank (eds.), *Quakers and abolition*. Chicago: University of Illinois Press, 2014, pp. 1-14.

Cesaire, A. (1955). Discourse on Colonialism, translated by Joan Pinkham. New York: Monthly Review Press.

Christaller, J. G. (1933). *Dictionary of the Asante and fane language called Tshi*. Basel: The Basel Evangelical Missionary Society.

Clifford, J. (1992). "Traveling cultures". In Lawrence Grossberg, Cary Nelson and Paula A. Triechler (eds.,), *Cultural Studies*, 96-116. New York/London: Routledge.

Cox, H. (1966). *The secular city: secularization and urbanization n theological perspective* (First Cheap, ed.: S.C.M. Press.

Cox, H. (2000). 'The Myth of the Twentieth Century: The Rise and Fall of Secularization'. *Japanese Journal of Religious Studies*, 23(1/2): 1-13.

Crompton, L. (2003). *Homosexuality & civilisation*. Cambridge, Mass: The Belknap Press of Harvard University Press.

Danquah, J.B. (1960). The culture of Akan'. *Africa: Journal of the International African Institute*, 22(4): 360-366.

Danquah, J.B. (1944). *The Akan doctrine of God: A fragment of Gold Coast ethics and religion*. London: Lutterworth Press.

Darkwah, A.K. & Arhur, A. (2006). '(A)sexualizing Ghanaian youth? A case study of virgin clubs in Accra and Kumasi," *Ghana Studies*, 9: pp. 123-149.

Davis, D.B. (1999). *The problem of slavery in the age of revolution, 1770-1823*. Oxford: Oxford University Press.

de Beauvoir, S. (1952/53). *The Second Sex* (Trans. H.M. Parshley). London: Jonathan Cape.

de Beauvoir, S. (1948). *The ethics of ambiguity* (trans. Bernard Frechtman). New Jersey: Citadel Press.

Dei, G.J.S. (2010). *Teaching Africa: Towards a transgressive pedagogy*. New York: Springer.

Dery, I.; Fiaveh, D.Y. & Apusigah, A.A. (2019). "'You Cannot Be Like That Here': Discourses of Sexual Identities among Urban Ghanaian Families'. *Gender Issues* 36: 342-356.

Dery, S. and Amoah, S.T. (2022). "Disrupting hegemonic masculinity(ies): Unpicking urban men's livelihood survival strategies in Ghana". *Journal of Men's Studies*, 1-8, https://doi.org/10.1177/10608265221095487.

Dewan, T. (2015). 'Hinduism and LGBT rights in India society.' in Centre for International Human Rights (ed), *Rights for all? Sexual orientation, religious traditions, and the challenge of inclusion*, 80-120. New York: City University of New York.

Diabah, G. & Amfo, N.A.A. (2015). 'Caring supporters or daring usurpers? Representation of women in Akan proverbs'. *Discourse & Society*, 26(1): 3-28.

Dillon, M. (1999). *Catholic Identity: Balancing reason, faith, and power*. New York: Cambridge University Press.

Dipio, D. (2019). 'African motherhood proverbs and worldview: A matriarchal perspective'. *Legon Journal of the Humanities*, 30(1): 3-23.

Dlamini, B. (2006). 'Homosexuality in the African context'. Agenda: Empowering Women for Gender Equity'. *African Feminism*, 2(3): 128-136

Dolphyne, F.A. (1991). *The emancipation of women: An African perspective* (Accra: Ghana Universities Press.

Doyle, S. (2007). 'The Cwezi-kubandwa debate: Gender, hegemony and pre-colonial religion in Bunyoro, western Uganda'. *Africa*, 77(4): 559-581.

Dube, G. (2018). 'Afrophobia in Mzansi? Evidence from the 2013 South African social attitudes," *Journal of Southern African Studies*, 44(6): 1005-1021.

Dumbe, Y. (2019). "Islamic polarisation and the politics of exclusion in Ghana: Tijaninyya and Salafist struggles over Muslim orthodoxy". *Islamic Africa*, 10: 153-180.

Dumbe, Y.; Gedzi, V.S. & Seekey, O.I. (2020). 'Contesting religious authority in Ghana: Perspectives on the literary works of Aminu Baba'. *Journal of the Contemporary Study of Islam*, 1(2): 108-127.

Durkheim, E. (1995). *The elementary forms of religious life* (Trans. Karen E. Fields). New York et al.: The Free Press.

Dzobo, N.K. (1992). "African symbols and proverbs as source of knowledge and truth". In Wiredu, K. and Gyekye, K. (eds.), *Person and community*, 85-98. Washington: The Council of Research in Values and Philosophy.

Dzobo, N.K. (1992). "Knowledge and truth: Ewe and Akan conceptions of knowledge and truth". In Wiredu, K. and Gyekye, K. (eds.), *Person and community*, 73-84. Washington: The Council of Research in Values and Philosophy.

Ebaugh, E.R. (ed.) (2015), *Handbook of religion and social institution*. New York: Springer.

Ebila, F. (2015). "'A proper woman, in the African tradition': The construction of gender and nationalism in Wangari Maathai's autobiography Unbound". *Tydskrif Vir Letterkunde*, 52(1): 144-154.

Ekeocha, O. (2018). *Target Africa: Ideological necolonialism in the twenty-first century*. San Francisco: Ignatius Press.

Eller, J.D. (2016). *Cultural anthropology: Global forces, local lives* (Third Edition). London/New York: Routledge Taylor & Francis Group.

Ellis, H. (1906). *Studies in the psychology of sex* Vol. I. London: William Heinemann Medical Books.

Ellwood, C.A. (1910). *Sociology and modern social problems*. New York: American Books Company.

Elorm-Donkor, L.A. (2017). *Christian morality in Ghanaian Pentecostalism*. Oxford: Regnum Books International.

Epprecht, M. (2013). *Hungochani, The history of dissident sexuality in Southern Africa* (2nd Edition). Montreal & Kingston: McGill Queen's University.

Epprecht, M. (2008). *Heterosexual Africa? The history of an idea from the age of exploration to the age of AIDS*. Athens: Ohio University Press.

Epprecht, M. (2018). 'Gender and Sexuality'. In G. Desai & A. Masquelier (ed), *Critical Terms for the Study of Africa*. Chicago and London: The University of Chicago Press, pp. 127-144.

Falola, T. (2022). *Decolonizing African Studies: Knowledge production, agency, and voice*. Rochester, New York: University of Rochester Press.

Falola, T. & Amponsah, N.A. (2012). *Women's roles in sub-Saharan Africa*. California et al.: Greenwood.

Fanon, F. (1963). *Wretched of the earth* (trans. C. Farrington). New York: Grove Press.

Fanon, F. (1967). *Black skin, white masks* (trans. Charles Lam Markmann). London: Pluto Press.

Fortes, M. (1977). 'The prologue: Family Studies in Ghana 1920-1970'. 1-27.

Foucault, M. (1986). *The history of sexuality* (trans. Robert Hurley). Harmondsworth: Viking.

Freston, P. (2001). *Evangelicals and politics in Africa, Asia and Latin America*. Cambridge: Cambridge University Press.

Frimpong-Nnuroh, N. (2006). 'Marital morality and sexual vulnerability in Ellembelle Nzema society'. In C. Oppong, M.Y P.A. Oppong, & I. Odotei (eds) *Sex and gender in an era of AIDS: Ghana at the turn of the millennium*. Accra: Sub-Saharan Publishers, 2006, pp. 91-111.

Fuller, H. (2014). *Building the Ghanaian nation-state: Kwame Nkrumah's symbolic nationalism*. New York: Palgrave Macmillan.

Gaudio, R.P. (2009). *Allah made us: Sexual outlaws in an Islamic African city*. West Sussex: Wiley-Blackwell.

Geest, S.V.D. (1990). 'Anthropologists and missionaries: Brothers under the skin'. *Man*, 25(4):588-601.

Gellner, E. (1983). *Nations and nationalism* (Oxford: Basil Blackwell Publisher Limited.

Gewald, J. (2004). "Imperial Germany and the Heroro of Southern Africa: Genocide and the quest for recompense". In Adam Jones, *Genocide, war crimes and the West: History and complicity*, 59-77. London: Zed Books.

Gills, S.; Howie, G. & Mumford, R. (2007). *Third Wave Feminism: A Critical Exploration* (Expanded 2nd Edition). Hampshire: Palgrave Macmillan.

Goldstein, V.S. (1960). 'The human situation: A feminine view'. *The Journal of Religion*, 40(2): 100-112.

Goody, J. (2006). *The theft of history*. Cambridge: Cambridge University Press.

Gordon, M. (2020). *Extreme Violence and the 'British Way': Colonial warfare in Perak, Sierra Leone and Sudan*. London: Bloomsbury Academic.

Gosine, K. (2002). "Essentialism Verse Complexity: Conception of Racial Identity Construction in Educational Scholarship,"' Journal of Educatoin, 27(1): 81-100.

Green, E.D. (2000). "Leopold Sedar Senghor and the Dialectics of Negritude." Nature, Society, and Thought, Vol.13, No. 4.

Greenberg, G. (2014). "The moral impact theory law". *The Yale Law Journal*, 123: 1290-1342.

Gupta, A. (2008). *This alien legacy: The origins of 'sodomy' laws in British colonialism*. New York: Human Rights Watch.

Gyasi, O. S. (1998). "Akan Death-Prevention Names: A Pragmatic and Structural Analysis2. *Names Potsdam New York-*, 46(3): 163-188.

Gyekye, K. (1992). 'Person and Community in Akan Thought'. In K. Wiredu & K. Gyekye (eds), *Person and Community: Ghanaian Philosophical Studies, I*. Washington: The Council for Research in Values and Philosophy, pp. 101-122

Gyekye, K. (1996). *African cultural values: An introduction*. Accra: Sankofa Publishing Company.

Gyekye, K. (1997). 'Philosophy, culture, and technology in the postcolonial'. In E.C. Eze (ed.). *Postcolonial African philosophy: A Critical reader*. Massachusetts: Blackwell Publishers, pp. 25-44.

Gyekye, K. (2004). The Unexamined life: Philosophy and the African Experience. Accra: Sankofa Publishing Ltd.

Gyekye, K. (2013). *Philosophy, culture and vision: African perspective*. Accra: Sub-Saharan Publishers.

Gyekye, K. (1987). *An essay on African philosophical thought: The Akan conceptual scheme*. Cambridge: Cambridge University Press.

Haddad, Y.Y. (1994). 'Maintaining the faith of the fathers: Dilemmas of religious identity in the Christian and Muslim Arab-American Communities.' In Macarus, E. (Ed.) *The Development Arab-American Identity*, 61-88. Ann Arbor: The University of Michigan Press.

Hansen, K.T. (1992). 'Introduction: Domesticity in Africa'. In K.T. Hansen (ed.), *African encounters with domesticity*. New Brunswick: Rutgers University Press, pp. 1-36.

Harari, Y.N. (2014). *Sapiens: A brief history of humankind*. London: Harvill Secker.

Hastings, A. (1997). *The construction of nationhood: Ethnicity, religion and nationalism* (Cambridge: Cambridge University Press.
Haviland, W.A. (1999). *Cultural anthropology* (Ninth Edition). New York: Harcourt Brace College
Haviland, W.A. (1999). *Cultural anthropology* (Ninth Edition). New York: Harcourt Brace College Publishers.
Haviland, W.A.; Prins, E.L.H.; Walrath, D. & McBridge B. (2017). *Anthropology: The human challenge.* Massachusetts: Cengage Learning.
Hearn, J. (2007). 'African NGOS: The new compradors?' *Development and Change*, 38(6): 1097-1110.
Hilgers, M. (2012). 'The historicity of the neoliberal state'., *Social Anthropology/Anthropologie Sociale*, 20(1): 80-94.
Hilliard, D. (1982). 'Unenglish and unmanly: Anglo-Catholicism and homosexuality'. *Victorian Studies*, 25(2): 181-210.
Hobbes, T. (1651). *Leviathan: The matter, forme, & power of a common-wealth ecclesiasticall and civill.* London: Andrew Crooke.
Hochschild, A. (2006). *King Leopold's ghost: A story of greed, terror, and heroism in colonial Africa.* London: Pan Books.
Hodge, C. (1945). *Systematic Theology* – Volume I (Grand Rapids, MI.: Christian Classics Ethereal Library.
Hoekema, K.A. (1963). *The major cults* (Michigan: William B. Eerdmans Publishing Company.
Holmes, J. (2001). *An introduction to sociolinguistics.* New York: Longman.
Holsey, B. (2008). *Routes of remembrance: Refashioning the slave trader in Ghana* (Chicago: The University of Chicago Press.
hooks, b. (2015). *Ain't I a woman: Black women and feminism.* London: Pluto Press.
Hull, I.V. (2008). 'The military campaign in German Southwest Africa, 1906-1907 and the genocide of the Heroro and Nama'. *Journal of Namibian Studies*, 4: pp. 7-24.
Hunsberger, B.; Owusu, V. and Duck, R. (2009). "Religion and prejudice in Ghana and Canada: Religious fundamentalism, right-wing". *The International Journal for the Psychology of Religion*, 9(3): 181-194.
Igwe, S.C. (2010). *How Africa underdevelops Africa* (Port Harcourt: An Africa Society for Social Pathology Publishing.
Ipadeola, A.P. (2023). *Feminist African philosophy: Women and the politics of difference* (London: Routledge.
Irele, A. (1965). "Negritude or Black Cultural Nationalism." Journal of Modern Studies, Vol.3, No.3.

Itzin, C. (1993). *Pornography: Women, violence and civil liberties.* Oxford: Oxford University Press.
Jeffreys, S. (2000). 'The need to abolish marriage.' *Feminism & Psychology*, 4(2): 327-331.
Johnson, P. (1996). *Intellectuals.* London: Phoenix Giant.
Kato, B. (1985). *Biblical Christianity in Africa*: No. 2 (Theological perspectives in Africa S.). Accra: African Christian Press.
Kaul, C (ed). *Media and the British empire* (London: Palgrave Macmillan, 2006).
Keown, J. and George, R.P. (eds.) (2013). *Reason, morality, and law.* Oxford: Oxford University Press.
Kevane, M. (2014). *Women & development in Africa: How gender works* (2nd Edition). London: Boulder.
Kimble, D. (1963). *The Political History of Ghana: The Rise of Gold Coast Nationalism, 1850-1928.* Oxford: Clarendon.
Kobo, O.M. (2015). "Shifting trajectories of Salafi/Ahl-Sunna reformism in Ghana" *Islamic Africa*, 6(1-2): 60-81.
Kommers, D.P. (1977). 'Abortion and constitution: United States and West Germany'. *The American Journal of Comparative Law*, 255: 255-285.
Konstan, D. (2010). *Before Forgiveness: The Origin of a Moral Idea.* Cambridge: Cambridge University Press, 2010.
Kudadjie, J.N. (1999). 'Using Ga and Dangme proverbs for preaching and teaching'. WAJIBU, 14(1): 12-18.
Kwansa, B.K. (2013). *Safety in the midst of stigma: Experiencing HIV/AIDS in two Ghanaian communities.* Leiden: African Studies Centre.
Lacey, N. (2008), "Philosophy, political morality, and history: Explaining the enduring resonance of Hart-Fuller debate". *New York University Law Review*, 83(1059): 1059-1087.
Laryea, P. (2017). *Patriotism and nation building: Perspective from the life and utterances of Ephraim Amu.* Accra: Sub-Saharan Publishers.
Lewis, D. (2003). "Editorial". *Feminist Africa* Issue 2(Changing Cultures): 1-5.
Linton, R. (1936). *The study of man: An introduction.* New York: Appleton-Century-Crofts, Inc.
Lloyd, J. and Mitchinson, J. (2010). *The second book of general ignorance: Everything you think you know is still wrong* (London: Faber and Faber Ltd.
Locke, J. (1956). *The second treatise of government* (Oxford: Oxford University Press, 1956).

Locke, J. (1997/1689). *An essay concerning human understanding* (ed., by Roger Woolhouse) (London/New York: Penguin Books.

Lorde, A. (1984). 'Age, race, class and sex: Women redefining difference'. In A. Lorde, *Sister outside: Essays and speeches.* Trumansburg, NY: Crossing Press, 112-117.

Mama, A. (1996). 'Women's studies and studies of women in Africa during the 1990s'. Working Paper Series, 5/96 Dakar: CODESRIA, pp. 2-11.

Mama, A.; Pereira, C. and Manuh, T. (2005). "Editorial Feminist" *Africa* Issue 5(Sexual Cultures): 1-8.

Mandela, M. (1994). *Long walk to freedom: The autobiography of Nelson Mandela.* Lancaster: Abacus.

Manuh, T. (1988). 'The Asantehemaa's court and its jurisdiction over women: A study in legal pluralism'. *Research Review* NS, 4(2): 50-66.

Manuh, T. (1993), 'Women and their organizations during the Convention Peoples' Party period'. In K. Arhin (ed.), *The life and work of Kwame Nkrumah.* Trenton, NJ.: African World Press, Inc., 1993, pp. 101-127.

Manuh, T. (2003). "'Efie' or the meaning of "home" among female and male Ghanaian migrants in Toronto, Canada and returned migrants to Ghana.' In Khalid Koser (ed.,), *New diasporas*, 140-159. New York/London: Routledge.

Mazrui, A.A. (1966). 'Nkrumah: The Leninist Czar'. *Transition*, 26: 8-17.

Mazrui, A.A. (1985). 'Religion and political culture in Africa.' *Journal of the American Academy of Religion*, 53(4): 817-839.

Mazrui, A.A. (2004). *Nkrumah's legacy and Africa's triple heritage between globalization and counter terrorism.* Accra: Ghana Universities Press.

Mbiti, J.S. (1969). *African religions and philosophy.* New York: Anchor Books.

McAlpine, S. (2021). *Being the bad guys: How to live for Jesus in a world that says you shouldn't* (London: The Good books Company.

McHoul, A. & Grace, W. (1993). *A Foucault primer: Discourse, power and subject.* London: Routledge.

McLeod, H. (2000), 'Secularization". In Adrian, H; Mason, A. and Pyper, H. (eds). *The Oxford*

McLeod, H. (2000), 'Secularization". In Adrian, H; Mason, A. and Pyper, H. (eds). *The Oxford Companion to Christian Thought* 653. Oxford: Oxford University Press.

McMullen, M. (2000). *The Baha'i: The Religious Construction of Global Identity.* New Brunswick, NJ: Rutgers University Press.

Mead, M. (1950). *Male and female: A study of the sexes in a changing world.* Harmondsworth, Middlesex: Penguin Books Ltd.

Mensah, E. & Mekamgoum, S. (2017). 'The communicative significance of Ngə̂mbà personal Names.' *African Identities*, 15(4): 398-413.

Meyer, B. (1999). *Translating the devil: Religion and modernity among the Ewe in Ghana.* Edinburgh: Edinburgh University Press for the International African Institute.

Miller, J. (2003). *Missionary zeal and institutional control: Organizational contradictions in the Basel mission on the Gold Coast, 1828-1917.* London: Routledge.

Moham, J. (1967). 'Nkrumah and Nkrumaism' *Socialist Register*, 191-228.

Mohan, G. (2002). 'The disappointments of civil society: The politics of NGO intervention in northern Ghana.' *Political Geography*, 21: 125-154.

Mohan, G. 'Adjustment and decentralization in Ghana: A case of diminished sovereignty.' *Political Geography*, 15(2): 75-94.

Mohammed, W.F. (2020). "Deconstructing homosexuality in Ghana' in S.N. Nyeck, *Routledge handbook of queer African Studies*, 167-182.London: Routledge.

Mohammed, W.F. (2022). "Why we need intersectionality in Ghanaian feminist politics and discourses". Feminist Media Studies (2022): DOI: 1-18 10.1080/14680777.2022.2098798, pp. 1-17.

Morgan, R. (ed.) (1984). *Sisterhood is global: The International women's movement anthology.* New York: The Feminist Press at the City University of New York.

Moyo, D. (2009). *Dead aid: Why aid is not working and how there is a better way for Africa.* New York: Farrar, Straus and Girous.

Mudimbe, V.Y. (1988). The invention of Africa: Gnosis, philosophy, and the order of knowledge. Bloomington and Indianapolis: Indiana University Press.

Murray, S.O. & Roscoe, W. (eds.) (1998). *Boy-wives and female husbands: Studies of African homosexualities.* New York: Palgrave.

Murray, S.O. and Roscoe, W. (eds.), (1998). "Preface: 'All very confusing'". In Murray, S.O. and Roscoe, W. *Boy-wives and female husbands: Studies in African homosexualities*, xi-xxii. New York: Palgrave.

Nagel, J. (1995). 'American Indian Ethnic Renewal: Politics and the Resurgence of identity.' *American Sociological Review*, 60: 947-96.

Ndlovu-Gatsheni, S.J. (2013). *Coloniality of power in postcolonial Africa: Myths of decolonization.* Dakar CODESRIA.

Nkansa-Kyeremanteng, K. (1996). *The Akans of Ghana: Their history and culture.* Kumasi: Sebewie Publishers.

Nkosi, G. (2010). "It takes a village to raise a child': Accessibility of social assistance benefits in indigenous African communities". Sa Mercantile Law Journal 22(3), 346-359.

Nkrumah, K. (1963). *Africa must unite.* New York: Frederick A. Praeger.

Nkrumah, K. (1964). *Consciencism: Philosophy and Ideology for Decolonization.* New York: Monthly Review Press.

Nock, S. (1998). *Marriage in men's lives.* Oxford: Oxford University Press.

Nugent, P (1996). 'An Abandoned Project: The Nuances of Chieftaincy, Development and History in Ghana's Volta Region'. *Journal of Legal Pluralism and Unofficial L.* 203: 203-225.

Nyamnjoh F.B. (2020). Decolonising the academy: A case for convivial scholarship, Basel: Carl Schlettwein Lecture 14.

Nyamnjoh, F.B. (2018). 'Citizenship'. In G. Desai & A. Masquelier (eds.), *Critical terms for the study of Africa.* Chicago/London: The University of Chicago Press, pp. 56-68.

Nyamnjoh, F.B. (2018). *Insiders and outsiders: Citizenship and xenophobia in contemporary Southern Africa.* Dakar: CODESRIA.

Nyamnjoh, F.B. (2019) Decolonizing the University in Africa. History and politics, World politics. Online Publication Date: July 2019 DOI: 10.1093/acrefore/9780190228637.013.717, pp. 1-36)

Obeng, P. (1996). *Asante Catholicism: Religious and cultural reproduction among the Akan of Ghana.* New York: E.J. Brill.

Oden, C.T. (2007). *How Africa shaped the Christina mind: Rediscovering the African seedbed of Wester Christianity.* Illinois: IVP Books.

Odotei, I.K. (2006). 'Women in Male Corridors of Power". In I.K. Odotei & A.K. Awedoba *(eds) Chieftaincy in Ghana: Culture, Governance and Development.* Accra: Institute of African Studies, pp. 81-100.

Odotei, I.K. & Awedoba, A.K. (eds) (2006). *Chieftaincy in Ghana: Culture, Governance and Development.* Accra: Sub-Saharan Publishers.

Oduro, T. (2007). *Christ Holy Church International: The story of an African Independent Church.* Minnesota: Lutheran University Press.

Oduyoye, M.A. (2004/2002). *Beads and strands: Reflections of an African woman on Christianity in Africa.* New York: Maryknoll.

Ogot. G.A. (1968). 'The African Writer'. *East African Journal,* 5(11): 35-37.

Ojeda, A. (ed.). (2004). *Homosexuality: Opposing viewpoints.* New York: Greenhaven Press.

Ojilere, A. (2018). 'Diplomacy of Homocapitalism Against Africa: Same-sex Marriage and the West's of Homosexuality'. *World Affairs: The Journal of International* Issues 22: pp. 152-163.

Omenyo, C.N. (2002). *Pentecost Outside Pentecostalism: A Study of the Development of Charismatic Renewal in the Mainline Churches in Ghana.* Zoetermeer: Boekencentrum.

Omer, A.; Appleby, R.S. & Little, D. (eds.) (2015). *The Oxford handbook of religion, conflict, and peacebuilding.* Oxford: Oxford University Press.

Onyinah, O. (2012). *Pentecostal exorcism: Witchcraft and demonology in Ghana.* Dorset/UK: Deo Publishing.

Oomen, B. (2005). *Chiefs in South Africa: Law, Power & Culture in the Post-apartheid Era.* Oxford: Oxford: James Curry.

Opoku, K.A. (1978). *West African Traditional Religion.* Accra: FEP International.

Oppong, A. (2009). 'The origins, implementation and effects of Ghana's 1969 aliens compliance order'. MPhil thesis submitted to the University of Cape Coast, Ghana

Oppong, C. (1974). *Marriage among Matrilineal Elite: A Family Study of Ghanaian Senior Civil Servants.* London: Cambridge University Press.

Oppong, C. (2013). *Growing up in Dagbon.* CreateSpace Independent Publishing Platform, an Amazon Company.

Oppong, C. (2015). 'Theorizing love: A memoir from Ghana (Goody library seminar paper, Valletta, 2015)'. Revised senior seminar paper by Christine Oppong, presented October 16, 2015 at the invitation of the Head of the Dept. of Anthropology, University of Malta, Professor P. Sant Cassia, in the Goody Library, Valletta.

Oppong, C.; Oppong, M.Y.P.A. & Odotei, I.K. (eds.). 2006). *Sex and gender in an era of AIDS: Ghana at the turn of the millennium.* Accra: Sub-Saharan Publishers.

Oppong, J.R. (1998). 'A vulnerability interpretation of the geography of HIV/AIDS in Ghana, 1986-1995'. *The Professional Geographer,* 50(4): 437-448.

Opuni-Frimpong, K. (2012). *Indigenous knowledge and Christian mission: Perspectives of Akan leadership formation on Christian leadership develop*ment. Accra: SonLife Press.

Overa ˚, R. (2007). "When men do women's work: Structural adjustment, unemployment and changing gender relations in the informal economy of Accra, Ghana". *Journal of Modern Africa,* 45(4): 539-563.

Owusu-Ansah, D. and Akyeampong, E. (2019). "Religious pluralism and interfaith coexistence: Ecumenicalism in the context of traditional modes of tolerance". *Legon Journal of the Humanities*, 30(2): 1-18.

Owusu-Ansah, F.E.; Addae, A.A.; Peasah, B.O.; Asante, K.O. & Osafo, J. (2020). 'Suicide among university students: Prevalence, risks and protective factors'. *Health Psychology and Behavioral Medicine*, 8(1): 220-233.

Oyěwùmí, O. (2016). *What gender is motherhood? Changing Yoruba ideals of power, procreation and identity in the age of modernity.* Hampsphire: Palgrave Macmillan.

Oyěwùmí, O. (1997). *The invention of women: Making an African sense of western gender discourses.* Minneapolis: University of Minnesota Press.

Parrinder, G. (1980). *Sexual morality in the world's religions.* Oxford: One World.

Parrinder, G. (1969). *Religion in Africa.* Harmondsworth: Penguin Books.

Parrinder, G. (1949). *West African religion: Illustrated from the beliefs and practices of the Yoruba, Ewe, Akan and kindred peoples.* London: Epworth Press.

Patterson, O. (1982). *Slavery and social death: A comparative study.* Cambridge, Mass: Harvard

Peil, M. (1971). 'The expulsion of West African aliens'. *The Journal of Modern African Studies*, 9(2): 205-229.

Perbi, A.A. (2004). *A history of indigenous slavery in Ghana: From the 15th century.* Accra: Sub-Saharan Publishers.

Pobee, J.S. (1991). *Religion and Politics in Ghana.* Accra: Asempa Publishers.

Poe, D. (2003). *Kwame Nkrumah's contribution to Pan-Africanism: An Afrocentric analysis.* New York/London: Routledge.

Prempeh, C. (2022). 'Decolonising African divine episteme: A critical analysis of the Akan divine name of God (Twereduampon Kwame). *Journal of Religion in Africa*, 52: 269-291.

Prempeh, C. (2020). 'Secularism, interfaith marriages and reengagement with the study of Islam-Christian relations in Ghana'. *Journal of Liberal Arts and Humanities* (JLAH), 1(2), pp. 39-54.

Prempeh, C. (2021a). 'African agency, human rights and issues of homosexuality: Biden and Africa'. In B. Wekesa (ed), *Africa's Policy Towards the US: The Biden Era.* Johannesburg:

African Centre for the Study of the United States/University of the Witwatersrand, pp. 137-157.

Prempeh, C. (2021b). 'Christianity, Culture, and Pentecostalism in Ghana: An Ethnographic Study of Pentecostal Traditional Authorities in Contemporary Akan Society (1990s – Present)'. PhD Thesis submitted to the University of Cambridge, UK.

Prempeh, C. & Amoah, C. (2021d). 'Secular governmentality and the court of the Asante Ahemaa in 21st century: An ethnographic account of Ejisu and Juaben traditional areas'. In E. Abaka & K. O. Kwarteng (eds), *The Asante World.* London/New York: Routledge, pp. 281-300.

Prempeh, C. (2021). "Religious innovations of chieftaincy in Ghana: Pentecostal Christianity and the complex persistence and transformation of Akan chieftaincy". *Religion Compass*, 1-13, DOI: 10.1111/rec3.12426.

Prempeh, C. (2021). "Social media and peace in Ghana". *The Peace Journalist*, 10(2): 18-19.

Prempeh, C. (2021). "Religion and the state in an episodic moment of Covid-19 in Ghana". *Social Science & Humanities Open*, 4(1): 1-8.

Prempeh, C. (2022). "Decolonising African divine episteme: A critical analysis of the Akan divine name of God (Twereduampon Kwame)" Journal of Religion in Africa 52, 269-291.

Prempeh, C. & Amoah, C. (2021d). 'Secular governmentality and the court of the Asante

Quashigah, E.K. (1999). 'Legislating religious liberty: The Ghanaian experience.' *Brigham Young University Law Review*, 2: 589-606.

Rabinow, P. (ed.) (1984). *Foucault reader.* New York: Pantheon Books.

Rathbone, R. (2000). *Nkrumah and the chiefs: The politics of chieftaincy in Ghana, 1951-60* (Oxford: James Currey.

Rattray, R.S. (1932). *Tribes of the Ashanti hinterland.* Oxford: Clarendon Press.

Rattray, R.S. (1923). *Ashanti* (Oxford: The Clarendon Press.

Ray, D.I. (1996). 'Divided sovereignty: Traditional authority and state in Ghana', *Journal of Legal Pluralism and Unofficial Law*, 1(28): 181-202.

Reddy, V. (2009). 'Perverts and sodomites: Homophobia as hate speech in Africa. *Southern African Linguistics and Applied Language Studies*, 20(3): 163-175.

Rich, A. (1971). *Of woman born: Motherhood as experience and institution* (London: Virago).

Sackey, B. (2003). Apuskeleke: Youth fashion craze, immorality or female harassment? *Etnofoor*, 16(2): 57-69.

Sackey, B.M. (2006). *The changing status of women in African Independent Churches.* Lanham/New York: Lexington Books.

Salaymeh, L. (2021). 'Women and Islamic Law: Decolonizing Colonialist Feminism'. In J. Howe (ed). *The Routledge Handbook on Islam and Gender.* London/New York, pp. 310-317.

Sanneh, L. (2009). *Translating the message: The missionary impact on culture.* Maryknoll, NY: Orbis Books.

Sarpong, P. (1974). *Ghana in retrospect: Some aspects of Ghanaian culture* (Tema: Ghana Publishing Company.

Sartre, J. (2007). *Existentialism is a humanism* (trans. Carol Macomber) (New Haven: Yale University Press.

Schippers, M. (2016). *Beyond monogamy: Polyamory and the future of polyqueer sexualities.* New York: New York University Press.

Schmidt, A.J. (2004). *How Christianity changed the world.* Michigan: Zondervan.

Schwarzer, A. (1984). *After the Second sex: Conversations with Simone de Beauvoir* (trans. Marianne Howarth). New York: Pantheon Books.

Schweitzer, A. (1998). *Out of my life and thought: An autobiography.* Maryland: The Johns Hopkins University Press.

Sears, Jr, W.P. (1957). 'Indentured servants in colonial Africa'. *The Dalhousie Review*, 37(2): 121-140.

Sekyi, K. (1997). *The blinkards, a comedy: and, the Anglo-Fanti, a short story* (introduction by J. Ayo Langley). Accra: Readwide Publishers/Heinemann Educational.

Shakespeare, W. (2003). *Romeo and Juliet* (adapted by Tom Gorman) (California: Saddleback Educational Publishing.

Shostak, M. (1990). *Nisa: The life and words of a !Kung woman.* London: Earthscan.

Siker, J.S. (ed.). (2007). *Homosexuality and religion: An encyclopedia.* Connecticut: Greenwood Press.

Squiers, A. (2018). *The politics of the sacred in America: The role of civil religion in political practice.* Cham: Springer.

Stark, R. (2005). *The victory of reason: How Christianity led to freedom, capitalism, and western success.* New York: Random House Trade Paperbacks.

Stausberg, M. (2008). 'Western Europe.' In Gregory D. Alles (ed.), *Religious studies: A global view*, 14-49. London: Routledge.

Stavans, I. (2001). *Art and anger: Essays on politics and the imagination.* New York: Basingstoke.

Steegstra, M. (2008). 'Development Encounters: Westerners and Chieftaincy in Southern Ghana'. In J. Abbink & A. Dokkum (eds),

Dilemmas of Development: Conflicts of Interest and their Resolutions in Modernizing Africa. Leiden: African Studies Centre, pp. 228-241.
Stoeltje, B.J. (1997). Asante queen mothers: A study in female authority'. *Annals of the New York Academy of Sciences*, 810: 41-71.
Sudarkasa, N. (1986a). 'The status of women' in indigenous African societies'. *Feminist Studies*, 12 (1): 91-103.
Sundkler B. & Steed, C. (2004). *A history of the church in Africa.* Cambridge: Cambridge University Press.
Táíwò O. (2010). *How colonialism preempted modernity in Africa.* Bloomington and Indianapolis: Indiana University Press.
Tamale, S. (2016). "Nudity, protest and the law in Uganda," Inaugural professorial lecture, October 28, 2016. Makerere University, Uganda.
Tandon, Y. (2015). 'Development is resistance'. *African Development*, XL (3): 139-159.
Taylor, C. (2007). *A secular age.* Cambridge, MA.: The Belknap Press of Harvard University Press.
Thane, P. (2008). 'Age'. In B.G. Smith (ed). *The Oxford Encyclopedia of Women in World History*, Vol. I. Oxford: Oxford University Press, pp. 62-71.
Tocqueville, A.D. (2016/1954). *Democracy in America: A new abridgement for students.* Bellingham, Washington: Lexham Press.
Tomich, D. (1979). "The Dialectic of Colonialism and Culture: The Origins of Negritude of
Aime Cesaire." Review (Fernand Braudel Center), Vol.2, No.3.
Tsekpoe, O. & Tsekpoe, C. *The Power of Vows* (Forthcoming, p.p. 25-26).
Tucker, H. (2018). The courageous sisters, erotic subjectivity, and the manoeuvring NGO frictions in Accra, Ghana'. PhD thesis submitted to the Central European University, Budapest Hungary.
Turkle, S. (2011). *Alone together: Why we expect more from technology and less from each other.* New York: Basic Books.
Tweneboah, S. (2020). *Religion, law, politics and the state in Africa: Applying legal pluralism in Ghana.* London/New York: Routledge, 2020.
Tylor, E.B. (1871). *Primitive Culture: Research into mythology, philosophy, religion, art, and custom. London*: John Murray, Albemarle Street.
Vanita, R. (2007). 'Hinduism'. In J.S. Siker (ed), *Homosexuality and Religion: An Encyclopedia.* London: Greenwood Press, pp. 125-127.
Verma, V. (2008). 'Caste and caste systems'. B.G. Smith (ed.). *The Oxford Encyclopedia of Women in World History*, Vol. I. Oxford: Oxford University Press, pp. 289-290.

Waal, F.D. (1989). *Peacemaking Among Primates.* Cambridge, Massachusetts: Harvard University Press, 1989.

Walter, D. (2016). *Colonial violence: European empires and the use of force* (Translated by Peter Lewis). Oxford: Oxford University Press.

Wan gu, M.B. (2009). *World Religions: Buddhism* (Fourth Ed). New York: Chelsea House.

Wasserman, H. (ed.,) (2011). *Popular media, democracy and development in Africa.* London/New York: Routledge.

Weber, M. (2019). *Economy and society* (ed. & trans., by Keith Tribe) (Cambridge, Mass.: Harvard University Press, 2019).

Weichs, V.R. (2018). '"What is your *empaako*?" Naming and becoming a Munyoro in Western Uganda.' In Jos D. M. Platenkamp & Almut Schneider (eds.), *Integrating strangers in society: Perspective from elsewhere,* 165-184. Cham: Palgrave Macmillan.

Weiss, H. (2008). *Between accommodation and revivalism: Muslims, the state and society in Ghana from the precolonial to the postcolonial era.* Helsinki: Finnish Oriental Society.

Wiredu, W. (1998). 'Toward decolonizing African philosophy and religion.' *African Studies Quarterly*, 1, 4 (1998): 17-46.

Whaling, F. (ed). (1995). *Theory and method in religious studies: Contemporary approaches to the study of religion.* Berlin/New York: Mouton de Gruyter.

White, E.G. (1884/2002). Letter 5, 1884 cited in Ellen White, *Child guidance.* Maryland: Review and Herald Publishing Association.

Wilks, I. (1967). 'Ashanti Government', in Daryll Forde and P.M. Kaberry (eds.), *West African Kingdoms in the Nineteenth Century, 206-238.* London: Oxford University Press.

Wilks, I. (1996). *One nation, many histories: Ghana past and present.* Accra: Ghana Universities Press.

Williams, E. (2014). *The economic aspect of the abolition of the West Indian slave trade and slavery.* Lanham et al.: Rowman & Littlefield.

Williams, E.E. (1994/1944). *Capitalism & slavery* (Chapel Hill: University of North Carolina Press.

Wilson, G. (1940). 'Anthropology as a public service'. *Africa* 13(1): 43-61.

Wittig, M. (1992). *The straight mind and other essays.* Boston: Beacon Press.

Yankah, K. (1995). *Speaking for the chief: Okyeame and the politics of Akan royal oratory.* Indianapolis: Indiana University Press.

Yeboah, A.A., Ampofo, A.A. & Brobbey, M.K. (2014). 'Women's and gender studies in Ghana'. In S. Agyei-Mensah, J.A. Aryee & A.D. Oduro (eds.), *Changing perspectives on the social sciences in Ghana.* New York/London: Springer, 2014, pp. 285-312.

Zartman, I.W. (1965). 'The politics of boundaries in North and West Africa'. *The Journal of Modern African Studies*, 3(2): 155-173.

Zeleza, P.T. (2005). 'Gender biases in African historiography'. In O. Oyeˇwùmí (ed.), *African gender studies: A reader*. New York: Palgrave Macmillan, pp. 207-232.

Lightning Source UK Ltd.
Milton Keynes UK
UKHW020807060223
416538UK00007B/414

9 789956 552955